C
Compositic
Essay prompts writter
Readings by original authors and edited by John Pfannkuchen.

r.

Elwood Learning
47 Vine St
Binghamton, NY 13903
www.elwoodlearning.com

Ordering Information:
Quantity sales. Special discounts are available on quantity purchases by corporations, associations, and others. For details, contact the publisher at the address above.
Orders by U.S. trade bookstores and wholesalers. Please contact Ingram Distribution at One Ingram Blvd., La Vergne, TN 37086 • 615.793.5000

Printed in the United States of America
Published by Elwood Learning, an imprint of Elwood Publishing.

Special thanks to Karyn Lyn Moyer,
without whom this would have been a complete mess.

For my students at SUNY Broome Community College.

Divergence in Thinking and in Writing

> I shall be telling this with a sigh
> Somewhere ages and ages hence:
> Two roads diverged in a wood, and I—
> I took the one less traveled by,
> And that has made all the difference.
>
> Robert Frost

What is divergence? What does it mean to diverge? It means, in essence, to break off from the crowd, to depart, to go somewhere, or do something, different, or in a different manner. Half of this book is dedicated to the concept of divergence.

The general pattern of creation is to gather materials, and then to remove from those materials, shaping, cutting, gluing, hammering, carving…until you have something.

» Think of carpentry—of all those wood chips and sawdust on the ground when the trees have been turned into a house; not even log cabins use all of the trees that they are built with.

» Think of sculpting—we gather up clay and shape it into a general form, and then take various cutting tools to it to develop fine details.

» Think of sewing—how in one end of the seamstresses work flow goes the rolls of fabric, the thread, the ribbons and lining and all that—you don't think that those scissors are for nothing, do you? What a strange outfit you would have if the seamstress or seamster never actually cut the fabric before sewing the pieces together!

» Think of film making—have you ever heard the phrase "What gets left on cutting room floor"? Or watched a "director's cut"? That's because there's no such thing as a film that uses 100% of what was actually filmed. A film is edited by removing or cutting parts of the film (actual physical film reel—actually cut with a blade—back before the days of digital) to form the final cut. When a director shouts "Cut!" on the set of a movie, what do you think he or she means?

So—there is a pattern that can be generalized from all creative processes—that of collection of raw material; gathering wood, cloth, film, clay—and then removing some, but not all, of that material to form the final product. Addition, then subtraction. In each of these crafts the craftsmen must gather more raw material than they need.

This is where divergence comes into play. Writing is unique in the world of craftsmanship in that it is the one craft in which written words are the raw material. All crafts have behind them ideas, or concepts—paintings, bridges, buildings, they all have a "concept" beyond their basic "function." They are works of art in their own right, the difference between an old cape cod and a modern glass villa, or the new science wing at the local university, or the covered bridge nestled among the woods—these constructions all serve their basic functions, or purpose, but the design choices could have been made in a million different other ways. The covered bridge could have been made merely a concrete slab, or a suspension bridge. The skyscraper could instead be laid on its side like an office suite—and on and on.

So in writing, while there are certain ideas conveyed, or functions served, "an essay about Benjamin Franklin," or "a reflection about my family," or a "literary review"—the possibilities are so open to us, the number of choices we must make seems so numerous, that the very prospect of deciding what kind of "essay about Benjamin Franklin" we should write can be quite overwhelming.

Reading

READING LEVEL: GRADE 8.7

What's true for other creative acts is true for writing. Writers gather more raw material than they need, then cut what is not needed to form a draft. The words divergence and convergence are acts of addition and subtraction. They describe the way in which writers add and subtract material from their work.

Look at the quote from Robert Frost's poem—"Two roads diverged in a wood, and I—/I took the one less traveled by." In the classical sense divergence means to leave or break off from a group. It comes from the Greek di which means "two," and verge which means, "to move."

So that di + verge gives us the sense of "to move into two, to move apart." Writers "diverge from" what they know to create new ideas.

Conversely, we have the word converge. It's the combination of con, which means "with/together" and verge, giving us the opposite sense of diverge. Converge means to come together, or to join. Convergence combines all of the tools. It combines the raw materials: your ideas, and the reader's needs. It combines old ideas, words, images, and processes into something that make sense. Something whole.

Convergence fuses these things into something that didn't exist before. It is the subtraction part of writing. The bringing-together of scenes in the cutting room. Convergence is the sewing of panels and the fusing of metal and concrete.

Record Your First Impressions

READING LEVEL: GRADE 8.1

Look at the title, and write down what you think it's going to be about. Try to predict the outcome of the story, essay, or play—without looking ahead. What's the topic? What's the author's stance on the topic? As you read the story, make notes about how right you were—and about how wrong you were. Perhaps the text will surprise you. Maybe it will be exactly as you thought.

Begin reading the work. How does the text make you feel? Do you agree with all of what the author is putting forth, or merely part of it? Why don't you agree? Did the writing convince you to see something a new way—even if it's only a slight change? Did you learn anything from the text?

Record something you find fascinating, or odd, or mysterious about the text. Something noteworthy. This may be something unexpected, or an idea that you have never heard of before.

Consider the Language

While you are reading the text get a feel for the language, the words. Does the voice sound masculine, or feminine? Modern, or out of date? Are sentences long and rambling, or short and to the point? Do the choices seem deliberate, made on purpose? What purpose, if any, would the author have in using long or short sentences, big or small words? Are the ideas simple or complex? Record your first impressions.

Turn Your First Impressions Into a List

READING LEVEL: GRADE 9.1

One of the most powerful kinds of writing is the humble list.

Lists are easy to write. Lists are good for brainstorming and remembering. It takes less time to make changes to a list than to a finished draft. Paper lists become extensions of our thoughts and memories. The more we use lists to remember and brainstorm, the longer our lists become, and the better we get at using them.

Compose your list by reading and gathering first impressions of the text. List a few "take away" details, points, or questions. List all of the major points, topics, or issues covered in your first impressions. This list need not imply an order or priority of any kind. The list can be jumbled around and reordered without consequence.

DEVELOP YOUR LISTS

Embellish your lists as much as possible—don't remove anything! Add as much as you can. If you notice new things, or make new connections, add them to the list! Writing is really the art of recording observations and ideas.

Experiment with your lists. You should change your list whenever the mood strikes you. Move items around, add and subtract, combine items. Flesh out your thoughts and take down as much material as you can.

With these lists you can plan more research and see your own thoughts from a bird's eye view.

Try this: Make a list of things that confuse you, or that you've never heard of before. For example, in "Story of an Hour," what do the words "bespoke," and "elixir" mean?

Try this: List the comparisons in the story. For example, in "Story of an Hour" Chopin writes: "There was a feverish triumph in her eyes, and she carried herself unwittingly like a goddess of Victory. " Chopin compares Louis to "a goddess of Victory." Write that down.

Try this: List a plot point in the text. For example in "Story of an Hour" a woman dies of a heart attack when her husband is discovered to be alive! Is that even possible? Write that down!

List Subjects & Objects

READING LEVEL: GRADE 7.7

Generally, what is the text about? Break down your observation into smaller parts that you can focus on, apply a lens to, and research.

THE SUBJECTS

Who and what are the subjects of the text? What is the text "about": a yellow wallpaper, a hanging, a bonfire, a huge machine, a blue hotel? What, or who, is acting in the text? How many characters are there? What are their relationships?

THE OBJECTS

What are they holding, wielding, wearing, or using? What are they interacting with, or reacting to? What's reacting to them?

» **THE ENVIRONMENT**

　» Environmental Objects

　» Lighting

　» Colors

　» Walls

　» Ceiling or Sky

8

» Floor or Ground

» PERSPECTIVE

» From what perspective is it written? As you read, in your mind's eye, are you standing above, or below the action? Are you in the middle of things—looking out from within a character? Or do you have a bird's eye view? Does the perspective move between multiple different characters, giving each equal share? Or does the text focus on a particular character, and that character's point of view, or perspective?

IMAGERY WITHIN THE TEXT
READING LEVEL: GRADE 7.6

Focus on the aspect of sight; shapes and color, light and dark, big and small. List anything that a character sees. Include any image that occurs to you while reading, any image implied, anything moving.

SOUND OF THE TEXT

Consider the dialogue between characters. Is it a rapid back and forth? Like Lois and Julie in "Porcelain in Pink"? Or one character delivering long speeches? Like the stranger in "The War Prayer"?

Are there songs sung, or sounds of gunfire? Or words like "bang!" or "plop!" Focus on the sound of the text as you read it aloud or in your head. Add these things to a list.

Observe Through a Lens

READING LEVEL: GRADE 8.7

Imagine having a pair of glasses with dozens of different colored lenses. Each pair of lenses, when popped into the frame, "filter out" objects, people, or actions. Imagine you can only see certain types of things in the world.

Pop on a pair of "historical lenses," and look at the buildings around you. Remove everything newer than 1835. What would be left to see? Perhaps some old rail road tracks. Perhaps main street and front street and River Row. Perhaps a few buildings that today are crumbling but were brand new almost 200 years ago. With everything else filtered out it would be easy to see what you're writing about.

Although you should try to develop, or even research, your own lens, here are a few examples to get you started:

AESTHETIC LENS

What are the main colors? Are they shades of one color, or is it a kaleidoscope? How are objects in the text described? Are things sharp, dull, liquid, flowing, or harsh? Are things geometric, or patterned? What are the comparisons? What's the atmosphere? What's the mood? Why? Make a list.

NATURAL LENS

What's the weather? The season? The geography—is it indoors, or outside atop a mountain, or the bottom of an ocean? Where is it located—and in what time period?

ECONOMIC LENS

Economics deals with currency and consumers, means of production and the like. Buying and selling. When you strip away everything else, human interaction is a series of transactions. An economic lens is interested in the transfer of wealth and power within the text.

HISTORICAL LENS

When does it take place? Consider the time line—and your observation of it. The style of the writing. Read into the attitude of the narrator, and what that may say about the era. Consider the technology and ideas about the future within the text.

SOCIOLOGICAL LENS

How do the characters relate to each other? Are some rich, or some poor? Are they slaves, or masters? Husband or wife? How do you think they feel about their community? Are they outcasts? Why do you think this? What's the social aspect?

Symbolic Lens

Symbols are a system of meaning, of metaphor and analogy—of parallels and comparisons. Symbols "stand in" for other things. They are like place-holders. When you find an image, character, or place you should wonder: what else could this mean? List the symbols.

CHOOSE A LENS

Decide on an essay topic by figuring out what interests you. In the last task, what lens did you write the most about? This may be an indicator of what will be the most enjoyable to write about.

It's always best to follow one's interests and curiosity, instead of what may seem the easiest topic. Interested writers and interesting topics are like peanut butter and jelly. In other words, if you are truly interested the essay will practically write itself, and the writing will shine.

But writing about something you don't care about? Something that may be easier? Easier, boring topics will result in writing that strikes the reader as dull, ill-researched, and uninteresting. The writer's enthusiasm will infect the reader.

Choose a Topic

READING LEVEL: GRADE 9.9

Topic

Start thinking about your topic. Mention of this topic will likely end up in the final essay. Your topic will also help you find sources. With a great topic in hand, the rest of your writing will be much easier.

What's your topic? Your topic is a unique combination of your lens and your observation. Some examples of broad topics, having read Akutagawa's "Rashōmon":

» History: There are no cars, or telephone polls. There are still samurai. And Osaka is the capital.

» Sociology: The main character is an ex samurai's servant. There seems to be no social welfare for people in his class. The samurai he refers to seems to have power over him. But he seems to have power over the wigmaker.

» Economics: The samurai's servant immediately became a homeless thief when his master let him go. People make money by selling snake skin as fish, and plucking hair from corpses to sell wigs.

A subject is a broad area of study. It is smaller than a field of study, such as: "History". A subject might be as broad as "The History of American Marriage." Or "19th Century American Medicine."

A topic is smaller than a subject. For example: "The Role of the Husband as Caretaker in 19th Century America".

A Narrow Topic could be, Gilman's "The Role of Husband as Caretaker in "The Yellow Wallpaper"

Field of Study > Subject > Topic > Narrow Topic

Typically the more narrow a topic, the longer its title becomes. That is because each word added to the title of that topic narrows, or reduces, the size of that topic further.

Balance Your Scope

READING LEVEL: GRADE 9.5

A good essay can be judged by the nature of its thesis. A good thesis is debatable, unknown, and important. The scope of the thesis should also be "significant" to the reader.

WHAT IS SIGNIFICANCE?

The word "significance" sort of means "importance," but not really. What it actually refers to is the impact of your research. For example, a statement about all of the people on Earth (Pop. 7,000,000,000), is more significant than the same statement about all the people in Tuscaloosa, Alabama (Pop. 90,000). Significance is achieved through having a large impact, and a wider scope. The more knowledge your topic creates, and the more useful that knowledge is, the more significant your topic is said to be.

THEN WHY NARROW MY SCOPE?

We all want to write the one essay that changes everything. We want to write something that makes people think differently. But the more wide a topic the less precise and useful it is. The more narrow a topic the more precise, accurate, and useful it will be.

Writing about a narrow topic is like doing surgery with a laser scalpel. Writing about a broad topic would be like performing the same surgery with a hammer.

So our ultimate goal will be to operate within a narrow topic. We should choose a broader subject to begin, then narrow it down.

BALANCE A NARROW SCOPE WITH SOME KIND OF SIGNIFICANCE

Most successful, or good, essay topics find some happy medium between scope and significance. So should your topic. You want to narrow your scope enough to be accurate. But you also want your essay to be significant (important).

WIDE SCOPE

"Where does anti-Hispanic sentiment come from?"

+ Most Significant

- Impossible to Answer

NARROW SCOPE

"Why does my Aunt Ruth hate Hispanics?"

- Little to No Significance

+ Easiest to Answer

BALANCED SCOPE

"Why has the reported incidences of anti-Hispanic sentiment fallen in recent decades?"

Answerable with research

Somewhat significant

Your question should fall in the middle somewhere, balancing significance with answerability.

Ask a Question

READING LEVEL: GRADE 7.7

If you have a topic, observations, and a lens—it's time to ask a question! Asking a question is an important part of writing an essay. A question will make your writing a lot easier for you to write and for the reader to understand.

Asking a question shows the reader you can be trusted. Asking a question will strengthen your arguments and appeal to your reader's sense of ethics and logic. This is because asking a question is the first step in any research project, after observation. Therefor asking a question shows you took the first steps in doing research—and readers want to see that you did research!

All stories pose a series of questions, from "What will happen?" to "Why does it matter?" You may even go so far as to ask: "Why should I care?" The best questions are the ones we do not know the answers to. Your question should be answerable—even if your answer is only a logical conclusion based on research. Your answer should, however, always be more than mere opinion.

The best questions are unanswered. Here are three different types of questions:

PRACTICAL (HOW) QUESTIONS

How to love someone who has wronged you? How to make others love us? How to control others? How to control the self? How to maintain control? How to give up control? How can we explore space?

SCIENTIFIC (IS/WHAT/WHY) QUESTIONS

Why do people love? What is love? What is the benefit of loving? What are the dangers of love? Is there free will? What is free will? Do we have free will? Is free will an illusion? What is beyond our universe? What can we do with this knowledge?

PHILOSOPHIC (OUGHT) QUESTIONS

Should we love? Should we hate? Should we value love? Should we seek it out? Should there be free will? Is the existence, or absence, of free will just, or good? Should we explore space? Are we meant to explore space?

Remove Bias

READING LEVEL: GRADE 10.1

You should avoid biased questions for many reasons. The first is that you'll lose your reader's trust. The second is that bias doesn't find the truth—it is inherently dishonest. People use biased questions to get the answers they want. But a good writer accepts whatever answer is the truth, even if they don't like it.

Bias is often a question of perspective and frame. Biased questions answer themselves—because of the way they are worded.

A biased question:

Why are all men evil?

What do you notice about the above question's structure? It's a "why" question. It uses the qualifier (evil) to characterize the subject (all men). In addition the qualifier evil is a value judgment. Value judgments are a matter of opinion, not truth. Not everyone agrees with them. They are debatable.

The qualifier in this example (evil) makes the overall question more qualitative than quantitative. The difference being that the concept of evil

15

is one of character, or quality, but not of quantity. Evil is not really provable, much less countable or measurable. Take a look at the following quantitative question (a question based on quantity):

How many men are evil?

You see how this question is quantitative? The answer to this question is what's called quantifiable, or in other words, countable or measurable. Not all qualitative questions are bad for great research questions. In fact some of the most interesting and important questions are qualitative. That also doesn't mean that changing a bad question into a quantitative one will clear up all that's wrong with it:

How many men are evil?

Even though the question is quantitative in nature, it's still qualitative as well. The problem is that the author has not defined what they mean by evil. Characterizations used in a sort of lazy way seem to be part of the problem. Consider the following questions:

What is the nature of evil?

Does pure evil exist?

These questions are very qualitative in nature. They also seem unanswerable. There is no physical component of evil. It is only a quality that humans give to certain things, people, and events. It's what one might call abstract. But does this alone make them bad questions? I think they are very good questions, deserving of answers, conversation, research or thought. So what's the difference between these qualitative questions that may have no answer, and biased questions? Let us compare:

What is the nature of evil?

Why are all men evil?

We could say that a writer should "Make sure all of your terms are defined." But that does not fix the biased question "Why are all men evil." Both questions use an undefinable term "evil," yet one is not biased.

Consider our original definition of bias: Bias is the implication of some truth within a question. You'll notice that the first question does not imply anything; it merely asks "What is the nature of evil?" The only implication here is that the reader understands what the author means when she writes the word evil. However, the second question, "Why are all men evil," goes a step too far. It implies something about reality that not everyone agrees with. If this is the case, one way to improve the biased question would be to remove this element:

Why are all men evil—>Are all men evil?

Research Outside the Text

READING LEVEL: GRADE 9.1

Research requires a plan, broken down into a few smaller steps—like a to-do list. Ask yourself "Where can I go, what can I read, who can I talk to, to learn more about this topic?" Try to be as exhaustive as possible: hit up Google, check out a politician's Twitter feed. Look at the op-ed of the New York Times. Fill out your lists with additional points and sub-points, questions and connections. Park yourself on a bench in Walmart for twenty minutes and do some people watching. This list will become a road map for research. It will eventually blossom into an idea (thesis).

Make an outline of everything you've researched, considered, observed and questioned. Be generous with this list and any additional thoughts you might have in the moment. Never assume you'll remember a thought later on—write everything down as soon as you think it!

Make a list of topics you want to research at the library based on all of your other lists. Now—it's time to go to the library! Let's go!

Working with Sources

WHAT'S A SOURCE?

A source is a text that we reference, that we draw on, that we read and respond to, that we criticize or that informs us about something. In short, sources are texts that help us write. They are our inspiration, and our information—they are everything we think we know (assumptions), they are our subject matter. When you reference a text it becomes a source.

DEFINITION

A source is a text that you reference. It's also called a reference text.

» So—what's the difference between a source and a text?

» What's a source text?

» What's the difference between a reference text and a source text?

A reference is a "connection" in your writing to a source or source text. This connection is what's called reference. People will often call sources references—though this is a bit of a misnomer. What they mean are reference texts. For example: "Your essay will require 3 references." If your instructor says this you should clarify whether they mean you should use 3 reference texts or merely that you should make 3 references to a single source text.

There are several kinds of references—but the most common ones in essays are direct quotation and paraphrase.

Go to the Library

READING LEVEL: GRADE 9.7

Drive, take the bus, or walk—once you're there the library is free.

Librarians have advanced degrees, and are intimately familiar with the libraries in which they work. At your local library the librarian in the reference section likely has a Master's degree. They may know your topic and the best authors to read. This is better than endlessly scanning Google search results without a clue. Your librarian will likely know the big names to read and why. They may even show interest in your work and inspire you to keep writing.

AVOID THE INTERNET FOR FORMAL RESEARCH

There are several reasons you should avoid the Internet. Everyone else is using the Internet. Your work may not stand out among your peers. Most Internet content is incomplete, biased or outdated. Plus the amount of scholarly, professional work is limited or very expensive. Additionally using the Internet encourages poor note taking practices. How often do you retype, or physically write down, what you find on the Internet? Never. Most people copy and paste. They don't even read the whole articles, much less read them carefully. Because of all these reasons writing based on Internet research will be just plain bad. Take the easy way out: use the library instead!

PHYSICAL BOOKS FIRST, JOURNALS ARTICLES SECOND

Library journal databases contain mostly academic journal articles. These are published by research universities and independent researchers. Academic journals are important for modern academics, and using them first may seem appealing. But your writing may suffer from relying too early on journal articles. Using scholarly journal articles first may force you to combine unrelated topics.

It's better to begin with a few books. In most nonfiction books there are references to scholarly articles in the back of the book. Read the book to get a broad overview of the subject. Then use the references in the back of the book to understand the book better. You can search for the articles by author name on your college's Online research database.

COME PREPARED

First, come prepared. Bring a bag to carry your sources (books). Bring a notebook. Bring some change or a credit card for the photocopier. Bring your lists and notes.

Search the (Library) Stacks with the Dewey Decimal System

With this handy system you can browse to your heart's content!

» 000 – Computer science, information & general works

» 100 – Philosophy & psychology

» 200 – Religion

» 300 – Social sciences

» 400 – Language

» 500 – Science

» 600 – Technology

» 700 – Arts & recreation

» 800 – Literature

» 900 – History & geography

SCAN THE BOOK FOR RELEVANCE

Look at each book before checking it out. When you pull each book off the shelf begin with the cover and back. Does it seem relevant to your topic?

Now look at the table of contents—that part in the front of the book that tells you all chapters and their page numbers. Look at the Part, Book, Section and Chapter headings. Do any of them jump out to you as especially interesting or relevant to your topic? If so, turn to that place and scan the first page. If it looks useful, take that book. If a book does not seem like it will be useful to you, put it back on the shelf.

Now the next part is key: scan the nearby titles on the surrounding shelves. What do you see? Grab any other titles that may be of interest to you. If you find anything interesting, repeat the steps above. Check the Table of Contents and Chapter headings as usual. If there is nothing relevant, then move on. Repeat this process until you think you have what you need or cannot carry any more.

DOCUMENT YOUR SOURCES

In essay writing you must give credit where credit is due. This is so that your reader can follow up on your research. Every idea that you reference must be cited—that means tell the reader where you got it from. Don't make the mistake of thinking that no quotation marks means no citation! All ideas that aren't your own get a citation, whether they are paraphrased, summarized, or quoted directly.

WORKS CITED/REFERENCES PAGE

Begin a Works Cited (if you are working with MLA), or a References (if you are working with APA) page. This can either be a separate file or piece of paper, or the final page in digital document.

This page will act as a repository for all of your research. The point of this page is to "document" your sources according to the style guide that you are using.

EVALUATE YOUR SOURCES

Look at the title, look at the headings and subheadings. Read the first sentence of each paragraph. Now write down what you think the source is about. Consider the questions below and write out your responses to each of them for every source.

» WHO IS THE AUTHOR?

» What are the author's credentials?

» What else has the author written?

» Who's the publisher?

» What is their stance on, or interest in, the topic?

» What is the publisher's editorial policy?

» Is the publisher an imprint owned by another company, a website run by a government agency, or a private blog?

» What is the purpose, or mission, of the publisher?

» CONTEXT

» Is the research current, and if not, what is the historical context in which it was produced?

» What is the general history of this document?

» Who are the original contributers and authors?

» What other forces have shaped it—political, economic, or others?

Summarize Your Sources

READING LEVEL: GRADE 9

Summarize your sources. You can use some of your summary in your essay. Also summarizing every source will help you connect sources to your topic and other sources later.

In math summary is an act of addition, not subtraction. The ancient Romans counted upward, and likened it to climbing as one does a mountain. So in our minds, let us imagine climbing up a mountain. When we reach the summit—the top of the mountain—we can look at the valley below. Imagine doing this; what do you see? Can you see every individual blade of grass? Or every insect hiding among the trees? Probably not. You can see clouds, but can you count the droplets of water that make them up? The smallest details are so small they cannot be seen, but you know they're there. What stands out? The largest parts of the landscape. Up here you have a sense of the whole.

Summary is not the act of putting things in your own words. Summary is a bird's eye view of the largest features and an honest attempt at including the smaller ones. However, summary is not a method of relating only part of something. You must try to give a sense of the entire text as best as you can.

EMPHASIZE IMPORTANT OR INTERESTING POINTS

You will feel the urge to write more about certain things. This is called emphasis. Feel free to emphasize as much as you like. But you should resist the urge to completely remove small or less important parts. A small amount of emphasis may be useful for you, especially if the topic is slightly out of scope.

Whenever you find a passage that describes your problem or solution, take a direct quote. Write down the author and page number in your notes along with the quote. Make a note about what new perspective, data, or knowledge this source provides, and how it connects to your argument. Note where the work disagrees with your writing. Avoid characterizing any aspect of the source in any way. Do not characterize the argument, the logic, nor the narrator/author of the work. Focus solely on relating the content. In other words don't be biased. This will prove to the reader your integrity as a researcher and thinker.

Compare Your Sources

READING LEVEL: GRADE 9.6

Compare your sources. Some of your comparisons can be used in your essay. Also the comparisons will give you ideas and help build connections between your ideas.

HOW TO COMPARE SOURCES

Comparison is answering the questions: how are they different and why does it matter? Most bad comparisons are not specific enough: Woolf's "The New Dress" is better than Fitzgerald's "Porcelain and Pink." But how is one better than the other? What aspect of each story are you comparing? Why does it matter for your essay? How does it relate to your question? Every comparison should seek to answer these questions:

» What aspect is being compared?

» How are they different?

» How are they similar?

» Why does it matter?

» How does this source's topic connect to the topics of other sources you have read so far? Does it—

» Overlap?—what does it have in common?

» Diverge?—what's different about their subject matter?

» Put two sources into conversation—

» Are their perspectives competing, or complementary?

» Compare their conclusions.

» Compare their assumptions.

» Compare their audiences or genres.

A BAD COMPARISON

The ending of the Dark Tower film is terrible compared to the ending of The Gunslinger.

The end of (director) Nikolaj Arcel's "The Dark Tower" promises Jake not only a happy ending, but one as a gunslinger himself. This ending abandons the harsh and delicately nuanced themes of the series (Jake's death and rebirth, for instance, and Roland's responsibility for it) with a Disney-like ending wherein the bad guy loses, and the good guys live happily ever after. The meaning of the fiction, and our experience of it, is cheapened as a result. The film replaces a feeling of connection and hardship with the same ending as every other Hollywood Blockbuster this year, failing to differentiate it in the ways that made the original novels so successful.

Find More Sources

Try following the "academic paper trail" by looking at the references page of every source. In this way every scholarly source you find is a potential treasure trove of leads to better sources.

Wash, Rinse, Repeat.

Adopt a Style Guide

READING LEVEL: GRADE 8.2

A style guide will tell you how to format your essay. It will include everything from capitalization to in-text citations. Does your genre or instructor require you to format your writing according to a style guide? Answer these questions below:

- » MLA (Modern Language Association)
- » APA (American Psychological Association)
- » or CMS (Chicago Manual of Style)
- » Something else?
- » If no style guide is assigned, how will you format the final draft?
- » Font (Times New Roman? Courier New?)
- » Margin (1"?)
- » Spacing (double?)
- » Running header?
- » Page number?
- » My name?
- » Essay title?
- » Contact information?
- » Essay Heading or Cover Page?
- » Contact information?
- » Record Your Requirements

With your notebook in hand, the first thing you should do, once given an assignment, is to answer some basic questions. Make sure to write these, and everything else, in your notes.

You'll want the answers to these questions before you start writing, as they will help you understand what you have to accomplish, and what your overall writing process will be. In terms of using this book, these questions will allow you to skip certain chapters, and concentrate on others.

- » What genre am I working in?
- » What requirements do I have?
- » Minimum or maximum number of sources?
- » Primary Sources?
- » Are they assigned, or must I find my own?
- » Secondary Sources?
- » Are they assigned, or must I find my own?
- » Should they be peer reviewed sources?
- » Tertiary Sources?
- » Textbooks/Course Handouts/Lectures
- » Assigned sources, such as a textbook or film?
- » Minimum or maximum length?
- » Is it in pages, or words?
- » Are there additional materials required outside of those marked already in these specifications?

Earn Your Reader's Trust, Understanding, and Interest

READING LEVEL: GRADE 8.8

Let's think about some things you must do to earn the reader's trust, understanding, and interest (in no particular order).

Without the reader's trust nothing you've written will be believed, and you've lost the reader's trust and failed the task. Everything hinges on your trustworthiness and authority as a writer. So how can I prove that I am trustworthy (ethos)? By not lying or stretching the truth, first off. The second thing it means is being completely transparent in your argumentation (logos). What does that mean? It means, just like in math class, to "show your work." Walk the reader through all of your research and conclusions—even the ones you scrapped, especially the ones you scrapped. If the reader sees that you struggled with the truth? And if you discuss how you went wrong? The reader will see that you are trustworthy. The reader will get the impression that you are truly after the truth—not just an easy answer.

Walk us through how you proved your guess to be either right or wrong. This is a place to briefly mention some of the reading, thinking, or experimentation you've done along the way. Your summary and comparisons from earlier chapters will be helpful here.

You must also make the reader understand your argument (logos). If the reader doesn't understand your logic you will lose them and fail your task. Ask yourself: what's the best way to organize and introduce this material so that it makes sense to the reader? Outline your argument in a clear manner. This can be cause and effect. It can be chronological. But the order in which you present your argument is key to logos.

Lastly, to earn the reader's trust appeal to their emotions, and why they should care (pathos). What happens if the reader trusts you, understands your argument, but you don't move them? What if your essay doesn't have anything to do with them? If it doesn't concern them, or touch their life in some way? In this case you've lost them and failed your task. Remember to connect your topic to your reader in some way.

Keep going. You're trying to be empathetic to the reader. Predict whether they'll agree with you. Find a way to convince them to trust you, see your logic, and believe in your purpose.

Use list making, outlining, free writing, or any other method you would use when creating content.

Consider Your Reader

READING LEVEL: GRADE 9.1

All writing must balance the needs of two people: the writer and the reader. Sometimes people write solely for themselves. That's okay for some kinds of writing, but not essays. Your job as an essayist is to move the reader—to give them something to think about. Something to do. But it's very hard to know what a reader expects, likes, or wants.

So use our imagination! Who is your reader? Is it your instructor? An editor at a trade journal? A web master? Is it a friend? What is their goal in reading your work? To be entertained, informed, both?

Nobody has ever read anything for no reason—this includes your college and high school instructors. Knowing what your reader wants will make your life a whole lot easier. It will allow you to meet, or even surpass, their expectations—but only if you know what they expect! Consider these questions:

» Who is your reader?

» Why are they reading this?

» What do they want from your writing?

Once you've determined what your reader's expectations are, you will begin to wonder how exactly you can meet them. There are many different expectations and goals readers bring to any written work—whether they know it or not.

Consider What Your Reader Knows

Readers can be generally categorized as professional, well informed, or ill informed. Consider which of these broad categories your ideal reader falls into. You may need to inform your reader of some basic information before going too far. Work this background information into your outline in the most strategic place. Maybe include reminders of it here and there.

But if your reader is a professional, don't insult or bore them. Don't waste their time by including background information they are likely to already know.

In the example of an essay prompt: the course instructor has given minimal instructions to the class. The instructor wants the students to "figure things out for themselves." Let's walk through a round of question-asking to break down a potentially confusing task. Prompt:

Write a short essay. Choose a common problem. Compare two solutions to this common problem. Then choose which solution would be best. You must consider the context of the problem. You must justify your choice.

At first glance this seems like a complex assignment. But let's break it down by asking some questions to get into the instructor's head. What do you know about her, and what do you think she might be looking for in your essay? What's her agenda? Does she want to be entertained, informed, educated, or something else?

» Who's my reader? The instructor.

» Why is she reading this? To assess and grade it. But how is she grading it? Following the instructions. What else? Maybe grammar, spelling, and other things.

» Where can I find the "other things?" The syllabus, or other course handouts. My notes.

» Am I supposed to be learning from this assignment—or is it merely a test of my abilities? It's impossible to say without asking the instructor. Perhaps I should assume that it's both, just to cover my bases.

» What am I supposed to be learning from this assignment. That's a good question. It's both general and specific at the same time. Maybe the assignment is purposefully vague, because she wants me to make some decisions. Why would she want me to make decisions? Maybe this is a project about learning to choose—to narrow down my options. It could also be that she wants to give us the chance to write about something we're interested in.

» What two things should I compare? Clearly something I'm interested in—but also something that I can write about.

» So what am I interested in? Travel, Boardgames, Soccer, Food, and

Music.

» What does she mean by, "in a particular context?" Using the dictionary, it seems context means "woven together," or "connected." So perhaps she means in a particular situation? For example, maybe I can compare two boardgames in the context of travel? Like say, which board game is best to play while camping?

Ultimately you should focus on what your readers want and leave out everything else. So what is the main focus of your writing, according to your reader? The more you add on the more difficult and unwieldy your writing may become. Based on your reader's interests choose up to two of these:

» Entertain the reader

» Educate the reader

» Solve a research problem

» Solve a practical problem

WHAT DOES YOUR READER THINK IS THE PROBLEM?

Does your topic represent a problem that your reader thinks is a problem? Does the topic represent a new problem? If your reader doesn't see the same problem that you do they will need to be convinced.

WHAT IS YOUR READER'S LIKELY OPINION?

Ask yourself if your ideas contradict what the reader believes, and if so, how? Can you anticipate their response? Will showing the reader the steps that led you to the solution change their mind?

Synthesize Values and Ideas

READING LEVEL: GRADE 9.5

What is synthesis? From the Greek, it means to place multiple things together, to compose them into a collection of sorts.

It also means to combine old things to create something new. In writing synthesis is creating new ideas by combining texts.

Perhaps the first stage in this should be finding what's common between two texts—or drawing connections.

DRAW CONNECTIONS—ASKING QUESTIONS

What does one reading have to do with another? What can the combination of two texts tell us about life, about what it means to be human? What do they have in common—and how are they different?

One way to connect texts is to find common themes, aspects, or topics among them. For example, both Mark Twain's "War Prayer," and Bierce's "Occurrence at Owl Creek Bridge," have something to do with war. But they are not the same exact story—in fact they are very different. They are both about war but in two very different ways. So we can learn twice as much about war in literature from comparing how two different stories show it. These are called "aspects." By connecting these texts via the theme of war we are uncovering two different aspects of war.

Identify a common topic, or a common aspect or theme between two texts. Then create a list of questions about the topic that the texts might tell you about. For example—what are the common questions we often ask about war?

 » Is war necessary?

 » Is war glorious?

 » Is war a good thing?

You can read the texts and ask specific questions that seem to be brought up by that text:

"The War Prayer," begs the questions: Should we celebrate the defeat of our enemies? Should we ask God for aid in waging war?

While, "Occurrence at Owl Creek Bridge," begs the question of whether war is truly glorious? What is the experience, or nature of war?

Then you can combine certain questions. For example, the question of whether war is good, and whether war is necessary. You can ask:

If war is not good, then is war necessary?

or

If war is not necessary, then is war good?

Develop a Thesis

READING LEVEL: GRADE 8

What if I told you that it doesn't matter whether the hero wins or loses. The only thing that matters is what it means that she won or lost? The hero lost. What does it mean? The hero won! What does that mean? The conclusion of a tale tells the audience what it means that the hero won or lost. Without meaning we don't care. And if we don't care there is no meaning.

What does it all mean? That is the question every essay must answer in the end. But how does one create meaning? Let's forget what we know about thesis statements, introductions and conclusions. All your reader needs is meaning.

Think of the Reader

If the hero saves the day, does it mean that good triumphs over evil? If the hero loses, does it mean that there are no simple answers? In a film or novel meaning is never spelled out directly. But a successful piece of fiction invites the viewer or reader to put themselves in the story. Essays do the same thing. This meaning comes from your reader relating to the essay. You must invite the reader into your essay. Ask yourself: "How does my essay relate to the reader? What new thing has the reader learned about their world, or the world of others? What does it have to do with them?"

Experimentation in Essay Writing

In a scientific essay you must prove or disprove an educated guess (a hypothesis). Your thesis is something like: "There is no evidence to support the hypothesis that…".

But there are different ways to experiment. Our experimentation must happen in the writing itself. The essayist's experiment is life itself. Our tools are sense and sensibility; our cause is the love of the human experience—and the search for higher truths. Not so much, "How can I create a holographic dating platform and monetize it?" so much as "What is the nature of love?"

To get a grip on what your essay means look back at your notes, what was the significance of your topic? In other words—what does your topic matter to the reader? Look at some of the questions you raised regarding the theme—and choose one you are most interested in: "Is war glorious?"

Now what does this question have to do with your reader? Is there a point to asking? If you have stumbled across an idea, or a truth, how does it change things for your reader?

Start here, and break down the question of meaning into parts:

» What should the reader believe (what is true)?

"Should the reader believe that war is glorious?"

» What should be done (now that the reader knows the truth)?

"If war is not glorious, as it seems in "Occurrence at Owl Creek Bridge," and "The War Prayer," what should be done?

» Why is it significant (who or what does this truth affect, what does it change)?

"How does the lie of glory in war affect the world? How should one live knowing that war is not glorious?"

» What would happen if no action is taken (now that this truth is known)?

"What would happen if people ignored the fact that glory is a lie?"

Conclude with Meaning

When writing your conclusion make sure to end on these points—
answering these questions for your readership. It may be helpful to drudge
up a few prior points to connect the dots. Just don't just rewrite your
introduction and call it a conclusion. Remember: a conclusion focuses on
meaning! Not summary!

Write Your Thesis

The word thesis is from Greek, meaning: "a proposition."

Have you uncovered an answer to a question? If so you should have
all the necessary ingredients for an excellent thesis statement.
QUESTION(S)

Is war glorious? What is the nature of glory and war in Twain's "The
War Prayer"?
ANSWER (THESIS)

In Twain's "The War Prayer" war is defined by the crowd. There is a
battle over the nature of war and God. The priest asks that God bless their
soldiers and grant them victory. The stranger suggests that God cannot do
such a thing without bringing ruin and death upon the other country. It
would seem that war is glorious, but only for those who haven't fought in
it. Glory is the lie people tell themselves to go to war.

Get Organized

READING LEVEL: GRADE 8.8

Reorganize your writing into discrete paragraphs for the purposes of planning a second draft. Hit the enter button a few times between one part of your draft and another-to move things around. Label the paragraphs so you can see what they're about at a glance. Order them so that the ideas progress naturally. Note questions you have in the margins and rethink your content.

If working on paper use a slash / to divide these walls of text into paragraphs. Explain your rationale between the lines so that you may remember later when rewriting.

CREATE A NEW OUTLINE/SECOND DRAFT

Your original draft may be messy or confusing. In a new document begin an unordered list of the things that work. This list can form the basis for streamlining or reshaping your draft. Find a new logic, and a new order, for your ideas. Write a new list.

Go ahead and start writing a new list using the old draft. Go back and forth between your first draft and this new list. Revise the new list as you go. If one idea in the old draft complicated, break it up into multiple new items in the new list.

Make special note in the new list where research or argument is lacking or weak in the old draft. This may be a good time to delve back into the text to discover what your old draft is missing—and add it to your new list.

MOVE THINGS OVER

Treat headings and points in your new list, as "bins" that you can put parts of your old essay into.

Comb and scan your first draft for related materials and group them together in the new list. You're basically shopping for material. Now, compare your old draft to your new list. Does the list follow the same flow, or logic, as your old draft? Chances are it does not.

Cut and paste for as long as possible, until you've pulled as much material from your first draft as you can use.

FILL IN THE GAPS

Add points to your new list to fill in the blanks or gaps of your newly remapped argument. This will provide a kind of to-do list. Generate additional content by asking questions in the new list. Do research and write the answer into the list. Your new list will soon become a new draft!

Revise Your Draft

READING LEVEL: GRADE 9.6

Writing is rewriting. The techniques in this book are designed to create a first draft quickly so the "true" writing may begin. Writing in this case comes by other names as well: rewriting, revision, composition.

So you have a draft, and it's ugly. It's a big, lumpy, hairy, genetic mutant of a draft. You should show this thing to no one, because there is nothing yet to show. Your "first draft" is the raw materials out of which you craft your masterpiece. Like a samurai's katakana is forged by folding a single piece of steel over and over again, so too will this draft of yours be heated, hammered, folded and so on.

Refine Your Argument

An argument is about truth and logic, sense and sensibility. Revising your argument is a process of not only making sure that your work is convincing to your audience, but to yourself as well.

Think about your research. What do you believe? Take a step back and try to look at the argument from a distance. Then step forward, picking the argument apart and putting it back together again. We will pull on all the loose threads to see if it unravels.

Change how you look at your draft, to catch its flaws and imperfections. This is similar to joining a writing workshop or asking a friend to read your work. Your friends and fellow work shoppers will hopefully see something you can't.

WAIT

Some people call this, "gaining distance." But by distance they really mean "time." The technique is simple: if you wait a really long time before seeing your work again, you'll see it with "new eyes". What's really happening when you hide a draft in a drawer somewhere and wait to look at it again? You change, not the draft. You're waiting to forget, to gain "distance," in time, from the last day you sat down and really looked at the work. To really accelerate this process work on an assignment for another class. Come back to this draft later.

CHANGE FORMAT

This is the easiest one to do quickly, but only if you have a digitally typed draft. Basically change the format; the most common way of doing this is printing the draft. Sometimes just going from screen to paper can show you mistakes you couldn't see before. It also slows you down. You'll come up with more ideas and solutions by thinking more and writing less.

Another way of fooling your eyes is to upload the draft to your E-book or smart phone. The smaller screen, different font and form factor will definitely make your draft seem new.

Bonus tip: don't revise essays on your smart phone. Take revision notes on a print out or in your notebook.

Ask for Help: Decide what stage of revision you are in. Never ask for feedback on "whatever," "anything," or "everything." Ask for the feedback to be limited to just one or two things. For example, ask if the topic is clear. Ask if the logic is convincing. Ask if the language is compelling. Find someone to look over your work, perhaps someone with experience or interest in your field of study.

FOLLOW THE STAGES OF EDITING

Start with developmental editing. Editing on this level is fundamental. It's revisiting the basics of the essay, like the topic and question. Do this earlier in the writing process, before the draft is complete.

Edit the content. The substantiative stage of editing can be thought of content editing. It covers everything from what is said, to how it is said, to when it is said. It covers such sweeping issues as presentation and purpose. If your argument doesn't appeal to the reader's sense of logos, pathos or ethos, this is the stage to fix those problems.

Last but not least, copy edit. Here you're finding mainly typos, and small grammatical issues, like missing or misplaced commas and apostrophes and misspellings.

Format and Submit Your Writing

READING LEVEL: GRADE DDDD

You're almost there. The last thing you should do before turning in your final draft is to make sure it's formatted correctly. It'd be a shame to have your essay be rejected because of a silly mistake.

This is where your Style Guide and essay requirements come in handy. Answer these questions:

» **How will you turn in the draft(s)—**

Digital

Hard copy (print)?

If you are turning in a digital file, how should you submit it? Will I turn it in—

Email

Upload

Share a link/giving access to a cloud application/file

» **Do you need to use a particular file format, such as—**

Microsoft Word (.doc, .docx),

Open Document Format (.odt),

Post Document Format (PDF),

Rich Text Format (rtf),

Text Format (.txt), or

Power Point Presentation (.ppt)?

If you are turning in a hard copy of your writing, how should you submit it?

» **Will you turn it in—**

» during class

» during conference

» to an instructor's mailbox

» by post or mail?

» **ARE THERE ANY SPECIAL CONSIDERATIONS FOR THIS HARD COPY? SHOULD IT BE—**

- » Stapled
- » Double Sided
- » Typed
- » Handwritten
- » Sealed (in an envelope)?

READINGS

The Story of An Hour

By Kate Chopin

1,017 WORDS. 6 MINUTES.
READING LEVEL: GRADE 9

Knowing that Mrs. Mallard was afflicted with a heart trouble, great care was taken to break to her as gently as possible the news of her husband's death. It was her sister Josephine who told her, in broken sentences; veiled hints that revealed in half concealing. Her husband's friend Richards was there, too, near her. It was he who had been in the newspaper office when intelligence of the railroad disaster was received, with Brently Mallard's name leading the list of "killed." He had only taken the time to assure himself of its truth by a second telegram, and had hastened to forestall any less careful, less tender friend in bearing the sad message.

She did not hear the story as many women have heard the same, with a paralyzed inability to accept its significance. She wept at once, with sudden, wild abandonment, in her sister's arms. When the storm of grief had spent itself she went away to her room alone. She would have no one follow her.

There stood, facing the open window, a comfortable, roomy armchair. Into this she sank, pressed down by a physical exhaustion that haunted her body and seemed to reach into her soul.

She could see in the open square before her house the tops of trees that were all aquiver with the new spring life. The delicious breath of rain was in the air. In the street below a peddler was crying his wares. The notes of a distant song which some one was singing reached her faintly, and countless sparrows were twittering in the eaves.

There were patches of blue sky showing here and there through the clouds that had met and piled one above the other in the west facing her window.

She sat with her head thrown back upon the cushion of the chair, quite motionless, except when a sob came up into her throat and shook her, as a child who has cried itself to sleep continues to sob in its dreams.

She was young, with a fair, calm face, whose lines bespoke repression and even a certain strength. But now there was a dull stare in her eyes, whose gaze was fixed away off yonder on one of those patches of blue sky. It was not a glance of reflection, but rather indicated a suspension of intelligent thought.

There was something coming to her and she was waiting for it, fearfully. What was it? She did not know; it was too subtle and elusive to name. But she felt it, creeping out of the sky, reaching toward her through the sounds, the scents, the color that filled the air.

Now her bosom rose and fell tumultuously. She was beginning to recognize this thing that was approaching to possess her, and she was striving to beat it back with her will—as powerless as her two white slender hands would have been. When she abandoned herself a little whispered word escaped her slightly parted lips. She said it over and over under her breath: "free, free, free!" The vacant stare and the look of terror that had followed it went from her eyes. They stayed keen and bright. Her pulses beat fast, and the coursing blood warmed and relaxed every inch of her body.

She did not stop to ask if it were or were not a monstrous joy that held her. A clear and exalted perception enabled her to dismiss the suggestion as trivial. She knew that she would weep again when she saw the kind, tender hands folded in death; the face that had never looked save with love upon her, fixed and gray and dead. But she saw beyond that bitter moment a long procession of years to come that would belong to her absolutely. And she opened and spread her arms out to them in welcome.

There would be no one to live for during those coming years; she would live for herself. There would be no powerful will bending hers in that blind persistence with which men and women believe they have a right to impose a private will upon a fellow-creature. A kind intention or a cruel intention made the act seem no less a crime as she looked upon it in that brief moment of illumination.

And yet she had loved him—sometimes. Often she had not. What did it matter! What could love, the unsolved mystery, count for in the face of this possession of self-assertion which she suddenly recognized as the strongest impulse of her being!

"Free! Body and soul free!" she kept whispering.

Josephine was kneeling before the closed door with her lips to the keyhole, imploring for admission. "Louise, open the door! I beg; open the door—you will make yourself ill. What are you doing, Louise? For heaven's sake open the door."

"Go away. I am not making myself ill." No; she was drinking in a very elixir of life through that open window.

Her fancy was running riot along those days ahead of her. Spring days, and summer days, and all sorts of days that would be her own. She breathed a quick prayer that life might be long. It was only yesterday she had thought with a shudder that life might be long.

She arose at length and opened the door to her sister's importunities. There was a feverish triumph in her eyes, and she carried herself unwittingly like a goddess of Victory. She clasped her sister's waist, and together they descended the stairs. Richards stood waiting for them at the bottom.

Some one was opening the front door with a latchkey. It was Brently Mallard who entered, a little travel-stained, composedly carrying his gripsack and umbrella. He had been far from the scene of the accident, and did not even know there had been one. He stood amazed at Josephine's piercing cry; at Richards' quick motion to screen him from the view of his wife.

When the doctors came they said she had died of heart disease—of the joy that kills.

COLLEGE WRITING 1: REFLECTION WITHIN THE TEXT

essay topic

Conduct two interviews with Brently Mallard. Interview him before the story takes place—investigate what his life is like and how he feels about it. Interview him again after the events of the story—what is his perspective on everything that occurred?

COLLEGE WRITING 2: RESEARCH OUTSIDE THE TEXT

Research the institution of marriage in the 1890s. What options did women have during this time? Is it reasonable to assume that other women of the time would feel and react the way that Louise Mallard does, and why?

IDEAS AND VALUES: CONNECT THE TEXT

In Chopin's "Story of an Hour" Louise Mallard's marriage seems to have ended abruptly with a sudden "railroad accident," and we find her in her room, celebrating her newfound freedom, while in "The Yellow Wallpaper," the narrator's husband uses his role as patriarch and physician to prescribe his wife's country home into a prison. Lastly, in E.M. Forester's "The Machine Stops," Kuno's mother, Vashti becomes increasingly alarmed at her son's rejection of their underground culture, as he derides her unquestioning fealty to the machine as mere worship—and eventually he reveals to her his will to live on the surface. In these three texts there is a force that holds captive one or more person; consider these forces individually, and explore how they operate, their functions, how they came into being, and what good or evil they do. What is the essence of captivity? Why does it exist? Is it pure cruelty—or is there something else?

The War Prayer

by Mark Twain

1,304 WORDS. 7 MINUTES.
READING LEVEL: GRADE 11.1

It was a time of great and exalting excitement. The country was up in arms, the war was on, in every breast burned the holy fire of patriotism; the drums were beating, the bands playing, the toy pistols popping, the bunched firecrackers hissing and spluttering; on every hand and far down the receding and fading spread of roofs and balconies a fluttering wilderness of flags flashed in the sun; daily the young volunteers marched down the wide avenue gay and fine in their new uniforms, the proud fathers and mothers and sisters and sweethearts cheering them with voices choked with happy emotion as they swung by; nightly the packed mass meetings listened, panting, to patriot oratory which stirred the deepest deeps of their hearts, and which they interrupted at briefest intervals with cyclones of applause, the tears running down their cheeks the while; in the churches the pastors preached devotion to flag and country, and invoked the God of Battles, beseeching His aid in our good cause in outpouring of fervid eloquence which moved every listener. It was indeed a glad and gracious time, and the half dozen rash spirits that ventured to disapprove of the war and cast a doubt upon its righteousness straightway got such a stern and angry warning that for their personal safety's sake they quickly shrank out of sight and offended no more in that way. Sunday morning came — next day the battalions would leave for the front; the church was filled; the volunteers were there, their young faces alight with martial dreams — visions of the stern advance, the gathering momentum, the rushing charge, the flashing sabers, the flight of the foe, the tumult, the enveloping smoke, the fierce pursuit, the surrender — them home from the war, bronzed heroes, welcomed, adored, submerged in golden seas of glory! With the volunteers sat their dear ones, proud, happy, and envied by the neighbors and friends who had no sons and brothers to send forth to the field of honor, there to win for the flag, or, failing, die the noblest of noble deaths. The service proceeded; a war chapter from the Old Testament was read; the first prayer was said; it was followed by an organ burst that shook the building, and with one impulse the house rose, with glowing eyes and beating hearts, and poured out that tremendous invocation —

"God the all-terrible! Thou who ordainest! Thunder thy clarion and lightning thy sword!"

Then came the "long" prayer. None could remember the like of it for passionate pleading and moving and beautiful language. The burden of its supplication was, that an ever-merciful and benignant Father of us all would watch over our noble young soldiers, and aid, comfort, and encourage them in their patriotic work; bless them, shield them in the day of battle and the hour of peril, bear them in His mighty hand, make them strong and confident, invincible in the bloody onset; help them to crush the foe, grant to them and to their flag and country imperishable honor and glory — An aged stranger entered and moved with slow and noiseless step up the main aisle, his eyes fixed upon the minister, his long body clothed in a robe that reached to his feet, his head bare, his white hair descending in a frothy cataract to his shoulders, his seamy face unnaturally pale, pale even to ghastliness. With all eyes following him and wondering, he made his silent way; without pausing, he ascended to the preacher's side and stood there waiting. With shut lids the preacher, unconscious of his presence, continued with his moving prayer, and at last finished it with the words, uttered in fervent appeal, "Bless our arms, grant us the victory, O Lord our God, Father and Protector of our land and flag!"

The stranger touched his arm, motioned him to step aside — which the startled minister did — and took his place. During some moments he surveyed the spellbound audience with solemn eyes, in which burned an uncanny light; then in a deep voice he said:

"I come from the Throne — bearing a message from Almighty God!" The words smote the house with a shock; if the stranger perceived it he gave no attention. "He has heard the prayer of His servant your shepherd, and will grant it if such shall be your desire after I, His messenger, shall have explained to you its import — that is to say, its full import. For it is like unto many of the prayers of men, in that it asks for more than he who utters it is aware of — except he pause and think.

"God's servant and yours has prayed his prayer. Has he paused and taken thought? Is it one prayer? No, it is two — one uttered, the other not. Both have reached the ear of Him Who heareth all supplications, the spoken and the unspoken. Ponder this — keep it in mind. If you would beseech a blessing upon yourself, beware! lest without intent you invoke a curse upon a neighbor at the same time. If you pray for the blessing of rain upon your crop which needs it, by that act you are possibly praying for a curse upon some neighbor's crop which may not need rain and can be injured by it. "You have heard your servant's prayer — the uttered part of it. I am commissioned of God to put into words the other part of it — that part which the pastor — and also you in your hearts — fervently prayed silently. And ignorantly and unthinkingly? God grant that it was so! You heard these words: 'Grant us the victory, O Lord our God!' That is sufficient. The whole of the uttered prayer is compact into those pregnant words. Elaborations were not necessary. When you have prayed for victory you have prayed for many unmentioned results which follow victory — must follow it, cannot help but follow it. Upon the listening spirit of God the Father fell also the unspoken part of the prayer. He commandeth me to put it into words. Listen!

"O Lord our Father, our young patriots, idols of our hearts, go forth to battle — be Thou near them! With them — in spirit — we also go forth from the sweet peace of our beloved firesides to smite the foe. O Lord our God, help us to tear their soldiers to bloody shreds with our shells; help us to cover their smiling fields with the pale forms of their patriot dead; help us to drown the thunder of the guns with the shrieks of their wounded, writhing in pain; help us to lay waste their humble homes with a hurricane of fire; help us to wring the hearts of their unoffending widows with unavailing grief; help us to turn them out roofless with their little children to wander unfriended the wastes of their desolated land in rags and hunger and thirst, sports of the sun flames of summer and the icy winds of winter, broken in spirit, worn with travail, imploring Thee for the refuge of the grave and denied it — for our sakes who adore Thee, Lord, blast their hopes, blight their lives, protract their bitter pilgrimage, make heavy their steps, water their way with their tears, stain the white snow with the blood of their wounded feet! We ask it, in the spirit of love, of Him Who is the Source of Love, and Who is the ever-faithful refuge and friend of all that are sore beset and seek His aid with humble and contrite hearts. Amen."

(After a pause.) "Ye have prayed it; if ye still desire it, speak! The messenger of the Most High waits!"

It was believed afterward that the man was a lunatic, because there was no sense in what he said.

COLLEGE WRITING 1: REFLECTION WITHIN THE TEXT

Report on the events of "The War Prayer" from two different news stations—one liberal, and the other conservative.

COLLEGE WRITING 2: RESEARCH OUTSIDE THE TEXT

Research the relationship between war and religion; look at the history. Look specifically at the Abrahamic religion referenced in "The War Prayer," namely Christianity, Judaism, or Islam—choose one. How compatible is the practice of war with the teachings of this religion? Is it truly a problem, as Twain implies in "The War Prayer"?

IDEAS AND VALUES: CONNECT THE TEXT

» In Twain's "The War Prayer" he writes that "The country was up in arms, the war was on, in every breast burned the holy fire of patriotism," when a stranger mounts the stage, declares himself the messenger of God, and explains what the people's "War Prayer" truly means for the enemy. In "Occurrence at Owl Creek Bridge," Peyton Farquhar seems to be the "enemy," the one that doesn't belong—and finally in "The Machine Stops," E.M. Forester writes about a different kind of belonging—not to a nation, but to a way of life; to a machine not unlike today's Internet. These are three different views of belonging; what does it mean to belong? What is it for? What is the "other side" of belonging? In order for one to belong, must there be others who do not belong? What effect does it have, and why do humans do it? Is belonging ultimately a good, or a bad thing?

» How does the thought of glory motivate the characters in Mark Twain's "The War Prayer," Ambrose Bierce's "Occurrence at Owl Creek Bridge," and Twain's "The Stolen White Elephant"? Does glory motivate people to do good? Is one man's glory another man's glory as well? What is glory, after all?

» In Chesnutt's "The Sheriff's Children," Twain's "The Stolen White Elephant," and Twain's "The War Prayer" there exists forms of conformity and nonconformity. What is conformity—is it one's actions, one's thoughts, more, less? And how is it determined what conforming is and what isn't? Why does one conform in the first place? Why would one choose to not conform? Look at the challenges faced by the nonconformists in these stories: are the nonconformists successful? What challenges do they face?

Rashōmon (羅生門)

By Ryunosuke Akutagawa

2,272 WORDS. 13 MINUTES.
READING LEVEL: GRADE 8.4

The "Rashōmon" was the largest gate in Kyoto, the ancient capital of Japan. It was 106 feet wide and 26 feet deep, and was topped with a ridge-pole; its stone-wall rose 75 feet high. This gate was constructed in 789 when the then capital of Japan was transferred to Kyoto. With the decline of West Kyoto, the gate fell into bad repair, cracking and crumbling in many places, and became a hide-out for thieves and robbers and a place for abandoning unclaimed corpses.

It was a chilly evening. A servant of a samurai stood under the Rashōmon, waiting for a break in the rain.

No one else was under the wide gate. On the thick column, its crimson lacquer rubbed off here and there, perched a cricket. Since the Rashōmon stands on Sujaku Avenue, a few other people at least, in sedge hat or nobleman's headgear, might have been expected to be waiting there for a break in the rain storm. But no one was near except this man.

For the past few years the city of Kyōto had been visited by a series of calamities, earthquakes, whirlwinds, and fires, and Kyōto had been greatly devastated. Old chronicles say that broken pieces of Buddhist images and other Buddhist objects, with their lacquer, gold, or silver leaf worn off, were heaped up on roadsides to be sold as firewood. Such being the state of affairs in Kyōto, the repair of the Rashōmon was out of the question. Taking advantage of the devastation, foxes and other wild animals made their dens in the ruins of the gate, and thieves and robbers found a home there too. Eventually it became customary to bring unclaimed corpses to this gate and abandon them. After dark it was so ghostly that no one dared approach.

Flocks of crows flew in from somewhere. During the daytime these cawing birds circled round the ridgepole of the gate. When the sky overhead turned red in the afterlight of the departed sun, they looked like so many grains of sesame flung across the gate. But on that day not a crow was to be seen, perhaps because of the lateness of the hour. Here and there the stone steps, beginning to crumble, and with rank grass growing in their crevices, were dotted with the white droppings of crows. The servant, in a worn blue kimono, sat on the seventh and highest step, vacantly watching the rain. His attention was drawn to a large pimple irritating his right cheek.

As has been said, the servant was waiting for a break in the rain. But he had no particular idea of what to do after the rain stopped. Ordinarily, of course, he would have returned to his master's house, but he had been discharged just before. The prosperity of the city of Kyōto had been rapidly declining, and he had been dismissed by his master, whom he had served many years, because of the effects of this decline. Thus, confined by the rain, he was at a loss to know where to go. And the weather had not a little to do with his depressed mood. The rain seemed unlikely to stop. He was lost in thoughts of how to make his living tomorrow, helpless incoherent thoughts protesting an inexorable fate. Aimlessly he had been listening to the pattering of the rain on the Sujaku Avenue.

The rain, enveloping the Rashōmon, gathered strength and came down with a pelting sound that could be heard far away. Looking up, he saw a fat black cloud impale itself on the tips of the tiles jutting out from the roof of the gate.

He had little choice of means, whether fair or foul, because of his helpless circumstances. If he chose honest means, he would undoubtedly starve to death beside the wall or in the Sujaku gutter. He would be brought to this gate and thrown away like a stray dog. If he decided to steal... His mind, after making the same detour time and again, came finally to the conclusion that he would be a thief.

But doubts returned many times. Though determined that he had no choice, he was still unable to muster enough courage to justify the conclusion that he must become a thief.

After a loud fit of sneezing he got up slowly. The evening chill of Kyōto made him long for the warmth of a brazier. The wind in the evening dusk howled through the columns of the gate. The cricket which had been perched on the crimsonlacquered column was already gone.

Ducking his neck, he looked around the gate, and drew up the shoulders of the blue kimono which he wore over his thin underwear. He decided to spend the night there, if he could find a secluded corner sheltered from wind and rain. He found a broad lacquered stairway leading to the tower over the gate. No one would be there, except the dead, if there were any. So, taking care that the sword at his side did not slip out of the scabbard, he set foot on the lowest step of the stairs.

A few seconds later, halfway up the stairs, he saw a movement above. Holding his breath and huddling cat-like in the middle of the broad stairs leading to the tower, he watched and waited. A light coming from the upper part of the tower shone faintly upon his right cheek. It was the cheek with the red, festering pimple visible under his stubbly whiskers. He had expected only dead people inside the tower, but he had only gone up a few steps before he noticed a fire above, about which someone was moving. He saw a dull, yellow, flickering light which made the cobwebs hanging from the ceiling glow in a ghostly way. What sort of person would be making a light in the Rashōmon... and in a storm? The unknown, the evil terrified him.

As quietly as a lizard, the servant crept up to the top of the steep stairs. Crouching on all fours, and stretching his neck as far as possible, he timidly peeped into the tower.

As rumor had said, he found several corpses strewn carelessly about the floor. Since the glow of the light was feeble, he could not count the number. He could only see that some were naked and others clothed. Some of them were women, and all were lolling on the floor with their mouths open or their arms outstretched showing no more signs of life than so many clay dolls. One would doubt that they had ever been alive, so eternally silent they were. Their shoulders, breasts, and torsos stood out in the dim light; other parts vanished in shadow. The offensive smell of these decomposed corpses brought his hand to his nose.

The next moment his hand dropped and he stared. He caught sight of a ghoulish form bent over a corpse. It seemed to be an old woman, gaunt, gray-haired, and nunnish in appearance. With a pine torch in her right hand, she was peeping into the face of a corpse which had long black hair.

Seized more with horror than curiosity, he even forgot to breathe for a time. He felt the hair of his head and body stand on end. As he watched, terrified, she wedged the torch between two floor boards and, laying hands on the head of the corpse, began to pull out the long hairs one by one, as a monkey kills the lice of her young. The hair came out smoothly with the movement of her hands.

As the hair came out, fear faded from his heart, and his hatred toward the old woman mounted. It grew beyond hatred, becoming a consuming antipathy against all evil. At this instant if anyone had brought up the question of whether he would starve to death or become a thief-the question which had occurred to him a little while ago-he would not have hesitated to choose death. His hatred toward evil flared up like the piece of pine wood which the old woman had stuck in the floor.

He did not know why she pulled out the hair of the dead. Accordingly, he did not know whether her case was to be put down as good or bad. But in his eyes, pulling out the hair of the dead in the Rashōmon on this stormy night was an unpardonable crime. Of course it never entered his mind that a little while ago he had thought of becoming a thief.

Then, summoning strength into his legs, he rose from the stairs and strode, hand on sword, right in front of the old creature. The hag turned, terror in her eyes, and sprang up from the floor, trembling. For a small moment she paused, poised there, then lunged for the stairs with a shriek.

"Wretch! Where are you going?" he shouted, barring the way of the trembling hag who tried to scurry past him. Still she attempted to claw her way by. He pushed her back to prevent her... they struggled, fell among the corpses, and grappled there. The issue was never in doubt. In a moment he had her by the arm, twisted it, and forced her down to the floor. Her arms were all skin and bones, and there was no more flesh on them than on the shanks of a chicken. No sooner was she on the floor than he drew his sword and thrust the silver-white blade before her very nose. She was silent. She trembled as if in a fit, and her eyes were open so wide that they were almost out of their sockets, and her breath come in hoarse gasps. The life of this wretch was his now. This thought cooled his boiling anger and brought a calm pride and satisfaction. He looked down at her, and said in a somewhat calmer voice:

"Look here, I'm not an officer of the High Police Commissioner. I'm a stranger who happened to pass by this gate. I won't bind you or do anything against you, but you must tell me what you're doing up here."

Then the old woman opened her eyes still wider, and gazed at his face intently with the sharp red eyes of a bird of prey. She moved her lips, which were wrinkled into her nose, as though she were chewing something. Her pointed Adam's apple moved in her thin throat. Then a panting sound like the cawing of a crow came from her throat:

"I pull the hair... I pull out the hair... to make a wig."

Her answer banished all unknown from their encounter and brought disappointment. Suddenly she was only a trembling old woman there at his feet. A ghoul no longer: only a hag who makes wigs from the hair of the dead to sell, for scraps of food. A cold contempt seized him. Fear left his heart, and his former hatred entered. These feelings must have been sensed by the other. The old creature, still clutching the hair she had pulled off the corpse, mumbled out these words in her harsh broken voice:

"Indeed, making wigs out of the hair of the dead may seem a great evil to you, but these that are here deserve no better. This woman, whose beautiful black hair I was pulling, used to sell cut and dried snake flesh at the guard barracks, saying that it was dried fish. If she hadn't died of the plague, she'd be selling it now. The guards liked to buy from her, and used to say her fish was tasty. What she did couldn't be wrong, because if she hadn't, she would have starved to death. There was no other choice. If she knew I had to do this in order to live, she probably wouldn't care. "

He sheathed his sword, and, with his left hand on its hilt, he listened to her meditatively. His right hand touched the big pimple on his cheek. As he listened, a certain courage was born in his heart-the courage which he had not had when he sat under the gate a little while ago. A strange power was driving him in the opposite direction of the courage which he had had when he seized the old woman. No longer did he wonder whether he should starve to death or become a thief. Starvation was so far from his mind that it was the last thing that would have entered it.

'Are you sure?" he asked in a mocking tone, when she finished talking. He took his right hand from his pimple, and, bending forward, seized her by the neck and said sharply:

"Then it's right if I rob you. I'd starve if I didn't."

He tore her clothes from her body and kicked her roughly down on the corpses as she struggled and tried to clutch his leg. Five steps, and he was at the top of the stairs. The yellow clothes he had wrested off were under his arm, and in a twinkling he had rushed down the steep stairs into the abyss of night. The thunder of his descending steps pounded in the hollow tower, and then it was quiet.

Shortly after that the hag raised up her body from the corpses. Grumbling and groaning, she crawled to the top stair by the still flickering torchlight, and through the gray hair which hung over her face, she peered down to the last stair in the torch light.

Beyond this was only darkness... unknowing and unknown.

COLLEGE WRITING 1: REFLECTION WITHIN THE TEXT

Put yourself in the position of the samurai's servant—now homeless, in the rain, and hungry. How would you treat the old wigmaker? What would you do to survive? And why? What is your philosophy regarding what is and is not okay to do to survive?

COLLEGE WRITING 2: RESEARCH OUTSIDE THE TEXT

Look at the history of the "gates" like the Rashōmon. Now consider the meaning of the gates in the context of the events of the story—look at the general economic and cultural conditions and beliefs of Osaka at the time of the story's publication—1915. Research the Rashōmon—what significance does it hold to the events of the text? What were they for? What did they mean to their society?

IDEAS AND VALUES: CONNECT THE TEXT

»   In Jack London's "To Build A Fire" the main character is faced with the necessity of building a fire to ensure his survival. Yet his need for fire is determined by earlier choices he made. In Ambrose Bierce's "Occurrence at Owl Creek Bridge" Peyton Farquar is fighting to escape his situation in order to survive—but again, his earlier choices are what led to his hanging. In Rynokuke Akutagawa's "Rashōmon" Rashōmon must make a choice that will determine his ability to survive after he is let go a servant due only to the economic situation of his master. His conversation with the wig-maker leads him to his decision. How do each of these characters survive? What specific elements affects each of their ability to survive? What choices do the characters face that affect their ability to survive? What sacrifices are worth making in order to survive? Why are the characters willing and able, or not, to make these choices?

»   In Akutagawa's short story "Rashōmon" the ex-servant of a samurai struggles with whether or not to become a thief, and in Virginia Woolf's "The New Dress," Mabel is absolutely consumed with the question of her appearance in her new dress, and the judgments of those who surround her, and in W.E.B. Du Bois's "Of Our Spiritual Strivings" he writes, "It dawned upon me with a certain suddenness that I was different from the others; or like, mayhap, in heart and life and longing, but shut out from their world by a vast veil." In these three texts there are three extremely different accounts of a struggle for identity—of that question of sameness and of quality of a person. What can be said for all of them? What makes them different? What can be made of this struggle for identity—why is it important—is it?

»   In Chesnutt's "The Sheriff's Children" the townspeople want to lynch Tom in order to achieve justice for the death of Captain Walker. In Akutagawa's "Rashōmon" the wig-maker weighs her own survival against justice for the dead. In Bierce's "Occurrence at Owl Creek Bridge" Peyton Farquhar is facing justice for attempting to sabotage the enemy's supply line. What forms of justice occur in each of the stories and how do they differ? Who has determined the laws in each story and how do the punishments, or lack of punishment, fit the crime? What, ultimately is justice? Is justice itself always just?

Impressions of America

By Oscar Wilde

2,487 WORDS. 14 MINUTES.
READING LEVEL: GRADE 11.3

LE JARDIN.

The lily's withered chalice falls
  Around its rod of dusty gold,
  And from the beech trees on the wold
The last wood-pigeon coos and calls.

The gaudy leonine sunflower
  Hangs black and barren on its stalk,
  And down the windy garden walk
The dead leaves scatter,—hour by hour.

Pale privet-petals white as milk
  Are blown into a snowy mass;
  The roses lie upon the grass,
Like little shreds of crimson silk.

LA MER.

A white mist drifts across the shrouds,
  A wild moon in this wintry sky
  Gleams like an angry lion's eye
Out of a mane of tawny clouds.

The muffled steersman at the wheel
  Is but a shadow in the gloom;—
  And in the throbbing engine room
Leap the long rods of polished steel.

The shattered storm has left its trace
  Upon this huge and heaving dome,
  For the thin threads of yellow foam
Float on the waves like ravelled lace.

I fear I cannot picture America as altogether an Elysium—perhaps, from the ordinary standpoint I know but little about the country. I cannot give its latitude or longitude; I cannot compute the value of its dry goods, and I have no very close acquaintance with its politics. These are matters which may not interest you, and they certainly are not interesting to me.

The first thing that struck me on landing in America was that if the Americans are not the most well-dressed people in the world, they are the most comfortably dressed. Men are seen there with the dreadful chimney-pot hat, but there are very few hatless men; men wear the shocking swallow-tail coat, but few are to be seen with no coat at all. There is an air of comfort in the appearance of the people which is a marked contrast to that seen in this country, where, too often, people are seen in close contact with rags.

The next thing particularly noticeable is that everybody seems in a hurry to catch a train. This is a state of things which is not favourable to poetry or romance. Had Romeo or Juliet been in a constant state of anxiety about trains, or had their minds been agitated by the question of return-tickets, Shakespeare could not have given us those lovely balcony scenes which are so full of poetry and pathos.

America is the noisiest country that ever existed. One is waked up in the morning, not by the singing of the nightingale, but by the steam whistle. It is surprising that the sound practical sense of the Americans does not reduce this intolerable noise. All Art depends upon exquisite and delicate sensibility, and such continual turmoil must ultimately be destructive of the musical faculty.

There is not so much beauty to be found in American cities as in Oxford, Cambridge, Salisbury or Winchester, where are lovely relics of a beautiful age; but still there is a good deal of beauty to be seen in them now and then, but only where the American has not attempted to create it. Where the Americans have attempted to produce beauty they have signally failed. A remarkable characteristic of the Americans is the manner in which they have applied science to modern life.

This is apparent in the most cursory stroll through New York. In England an inventor is regarded almost as a crazy man, and in too many instances invention ends in disappointment and poverty. In America an inventor is honoured, help is forthcoming, and the exercise of ingenuity, the application of science to the work of man, is there the shortest road to wealth. There is no country in the world where machinery is so lovely as in America.

I have always wished to believe that the line of strength and the line of beauty are one. That wish was realised when I contemplated American machinery. It was not until I had seen the water-works at Chicago that I realised the wonders of machinery; the rise and fall of the steel rods, the symmetrical motion of the great wheels is the most beautifully rhythmic thing I have ever seen.[3] One is impressed in America, but not favourably impressed, by the inordinate size of everything. The country seems to try to bully one into a belief in its power by its impressive bigness.

I was disappointed with Niagara—most people must be disappointed with Niagara. Every American bride is taken there, and the sight of the stupendous waterfall must be one of the earliest, if not the keenest, disappointments in American married life. One sees it under bad conditions, very far away, the point of view not showing the splendour of the water. To appreciate it really one has to see it from underneath the fall, and to do that it is necessary to be dressed in a yellow oil-skin, which is as ugly as a mackintosh—and I hope none of you ever wears one. It is a consolation to know, however, that such an artist as Madame Bernhardt has not only worn that yellow, ugly dress, but has been photographed in it.

Perhaps the most beautiful part of America is the West, to reach which, however, involves a journey by rail of six days, racing along tied to an ugly tin-kettle of a steam engine. I found but poor consolation for this journey in the fact that the boys who infest the cars and sell everything that one can eat—or should not eat—were selling editions of my poems vilely printed on a kind of grey blotting paper, for the low price of ten cents.[4] Calling these boys on one side I told them that though poets like to be popular they desire to be paid, and selling editions of my poems without giving me a profit is dealing a blow at literature which must have a disastrous effect on poetical aspirants. The invariable reply that they made was that they themselves made a profit out of the transaction and that was all they cared about.

It is a popular superstition that in America a visitor is invariably addressed as "Stranger." I was never once addressed as "Stranger." When I went to Texas I was called "Captain"; when I got to the centre of the country I was addressed as "Colonel," and, on arriving at the borders of Mexico, as "General." On the whole, however, "Sir," the old English method of addressing people is the most common.

It is, perhaps, worth while to note that what many people call Americanisms are really old English expressions which have lingered in our colonies while they have been lost in our own country. Many people imagine that the term "I guess," which is so common in America, is purely an American expression, but it was used by John Locke in his work on "The Understanding," just as we now use "I think."[5]

It is in the colonies, and not in the mother country, that the old life of the country really exists. If one wants to realise what English Puritanism is—not at its worst (when it is very bad), but at its best, and then it is not very good—I do not think one can find much of it in England, but much can be found about Boston and Massachusetts. We have got rid of it. America still preserves it, to be, I hope, a short-lived curiosity.

San Francisco is a really beautiful city. China Town, peopled by Chinese labourers, is the most artistic town I have ever come across. The people—strange, melancholy Orientals, whom many people would call common, and they are certainly very poor—have determined that they will have nothing about them that is not beautiful. In the Chinese restaurant, where these navvies meet to have supper in the evening, I found them drinking tea out of china cups as delicate as the petals of a rose-leaf, whereas at the gaudy hotels I was supplied with a delf cup an inch and a half thick. When the Chinese bill was presented it was made out on rice paper, the account being done in Indian ink as fantastically as if an artist had been etching little birds on a fan.

Salt Lake City contains only two buildings of note, the chief being the Tabernacle, which is in the shape of a soup-kettle. It is decorated by the only native artist, and he has treated religious subjects in the naive spirit of the early Florentine painters, representing people of our own day in the dress of the period side by side with people of Biblical history who are clothed in some romantic costume.

The building next in importance is called the Amelia Palace, in honour of one of Brigham Young's wives. When he died the present president of the Mormons stood up in the Tabernacle and said that it had been revealed to him that he was to have the Amelia Palace, and that on this subject there were to be no more revelations of any kind!

From Salt Lake City one travels over the great plains of Colorado and up the Rocky Mountains, on the top of which is Leadville, the richest city in the world. It has also got the reputation of being the roughest, and every man carries a revolver. I was told that if I went there they would be sure to shoot me or my travelling manager. I wrote and told them that nothing that they could do to my travelling manager would intimidate me. They are miners—men working in metals, so I lectured to them on the Ethics of Art. I read them passages from the autobiography of Benvenuto Cellini and they seemed much delighted. I was reproved by my hearers for not having brought him with me. I explained that he had been dead for some little time which elicited the enquiry "Who shot him"? They afterwards took me to a dancing saloon where I saw the only rational method of art criticism I have ever come across. Over the piano was printed a notice:—

PLEASE DO NOT SHOOT THE PIANIST.
HE IS DOING HIS BEST.

The mortality among pianists in that place is marvellous. Then they asked me to supper, and having accepted, I had to descend a mine in a rickety bucket in which it was impossible to be graceful. Having got into the heart of the mountain I had supper, the first course being whisky, the second whisky and the third whisky.

I went to the Theatre to lecture and I was informed that just before I went there two men had been seized for committing a murder, and in that theatre they had been brought on to the stage at eight o'clock in the evening, and then and there tried and executed before a crowded audience. But I found these miners very charming and not at all rough.

Among the more elderly inhabitants of the South I found a melancholy tendency to date every event of importance by the late war. "How beautiful the moon is to-night," I once remarked to a gentleman who was standing next to me. "Yes," was his reply, "but you should have seen it before the war."

So infinitesimal did I find the knowledge of Art, west of the Rocky Mountains, that an art patron—one who in his day had been a miner—actually sued the railroad company for damages because the plaster cast of Venus of Milo, which he had imported from Paris, had been delivered minus the arms. And, what is more surprising still, he gained his case and the damages.

Pennsylvania, with its rocky gorges and woodland scenery, reminded me of Switzerland. The prairie reminded me of a piece of blotting-paper.

The Spanish and French have left behind them memorials in the beauty of their names. All the cities that have beautiful names derive them from the Spanish or the French. The English people give intensely ugly names to places. One place had such an ugly name that I refused to lecture there. It was called Grigsville. Supposing I had founded a school of Art there—fancy "Early Grigsville." Imagine a School of Art teaching "Grigsville Renaissance."

As for slang I did not hear much of it, though a young lady who had changed her clothes after an afternoon dance did say that "after the heel kick she shifted her day goods."

American youths are pale and precocious, or sallow and supercilious, but American girls are pretty and charming—little oases of pretty unreasonableness in a vast desert of practical common-sense.

Every American girl is entitled to have twelve young men devoted to her. They remain her slaves and she rules them with charming nonchalance.

The men are entirely given to business; they have, as they say, their brains in front of their heads. They are also exceedingly acceptive of new ideas. Their education is practical. We base the education of children entirely on books, but we must give a child a mind before we can instruct the mind. Children have a natural antipathy to books—handicraft should be the basis of education. Boys and girls should be taught to use their hands to make something, and they would be less apt to destroy and be mischievous.

In going to America one learns that poverty is not a necessary accompaniment to civilisation. There at any rate is a country that has no trappings, no pageants and no gorgeous ceremonies. I saw only two processions—one was the Fire Brigade preceded by the Police, the other was the Police preceded by the Fire Brigade.

Every man when he gets to the age of twenty-one is allowed a vote, and thereby immediately acquires his political education. The Americans are the best politically educated people in the world. It is well worth one's while to go to a country which can teach us the beauty of the word FREEDOM and the value of the thing LIBERTY.

COLLEGE WRITING 1: REFLECTION WITHIN THE TEXT

Write your own Impressions—of a place of your own choosing. That is, choose two places, one that you feel comfortable with and that you know very well, and another that you don't feel comfortable in, one that you don't know very well. Now, enter the place in that you don't know well, and report on it in the style of Oscar Wilde's "Impressions of America."

COLLEGE WRITING 2: RESEARCH OUTSIDE THE TEXT

Research America in the 1880s. Choose an aspect of Wilde's impressions and explain it—that is—perhaps the fashions of the time, or the noise, or the education. Write about the development of that thing until that point in time, and explain the difference from what Wilde was used to in England.

IDEAS AND VALUES: CONNECT THE TEXT

» Oscar Wilde writes in "Impressions of America" about the strange differences both good and bad between England and its former colony, the United States; W.E.B. Du Bois writes in "Of Our Spiritual Strivings" that "the words I longed for, and all their dazzling opportunities, were theirs, not mine," and in Gilman's "Yellow Wallpaper", the main character, having found herself on the "wrong side," of matrimony, country living, and her husband's medical opinion, gives us her unique perspective as well. What does perspective mean— how is it formed? What makes a perspective unique? What makes a perspective important, or worthwhile to understand? How does one get the perspective of another—or is it even possible to see through the eyes of another?

» In Philip K. Dick's "The Gun" culture is the one treasure that "the dragon guards," but in Nathanial Hawthorne's "Earth's Holocaust," culture is merely fuel for the fire, while in Wilde's "Impressions of America" culture is neither here nor there, but a category of different perspectives, perhaps a tool to be used one way or another, in practicality or fashion—as he doesn't enter into geography ("latitude or longitude"), economics ("the value of its dry goods"), or politics.

» But what is culture? What is its value—ultimately? Is it a way of life? A relic of the past? Does it hold us back, or does it tell us who we are? What relationship should we strike towards culture itself—? And what care should we take to understand its origins, if any at all?

» Humankind has invented the Internet, the telephone, the motor vehicle, air travel, the atomic bomb… Look at Oscar Wilde's "Impressions of America," and his focus on "practical education" and the beauty of American engineering—and then move to "The Gun," when an alien ship approaches Earth but cannot reach it because of Earth's engineering, and then "The Machine Stops," a world in which "the machine" is all that matters—not human progress—but the progress of "the machine." And finally "Earth's Holocaust," in which the people of the world decide to burn everything—all ideas—all progress, all technology. What roll does technological progress play, and what roll should technology play in the progress of mankind? How would you define progress?

Of Our Spiritual Strivings

By W.E.B. Du Bois

3,125 WORDS. 18 MINUTES.
READING LEVEL: GRADE 12.2

O water, voice of my heart, crying in the sand,
All night long crying with a mournful cry,
As I lie and listen, and cannot understand
The voice of my heart in my side or the voice of the sea,
O water, crying for rest, is it I, is it I?
All night long the water is crying to me.
Unresting water, there shall never be rest
Till the last moon droop and the last tide fail,
And the fire of the end begin to burn in the west;
And the heart shall be weary and wonder and cry like the sea,
All life long crying without avail,
As the water all night long is crying to me.

ARTHUR SYMONS

Between me and the other world there is ever an unasked question: unasked by some through feelings of delicacy; by others through the difficulty of rightly framing it. All, nevertheless, flutter round it. They approach me in a half-hesitant sort of way, eye me curiously or compassionately, and then, instead of saying directly, How does it feel to be a problem? they say, I know an excellent colored man in my town; or, I fought at Mechanicsville; or, Do not these Southern outrages make your blood boil? At these I smile, or am interested, or reduce the boiling to a simmer, as the occasion may require. To the real question, How does it feel to be a problem? I answer seldom a word.

And yet, being a problem is a strange experience,—peculiar even for one who has never been anything else, save perhaps in babyhood and in Europe. It is in the early days of rollicking boyhood that the revelation first bursts upon one, all in a day, as it were. I remember well when the shadow swept across me. I was a little thing, away up in the hills of New England, where the dark Housatonic winds between Hoosac and Taghkanic to the sea. In a wee wooden schoolhouse, something put it into the boys' and girls' heads to buy gorgeous visiting-cards—ten cents a package—and exchange. The exchange was merry, till one girl, a tall newcomer, refused my card,—refused it peremptorily, with a glance. Then it dawned upon me with a certain suddenness that I was different from the others; or like, mayhap, in heart and life and longing, but shut out from their world by a vast veil. I had thereafter no desire to tear down that veil, to creep through; I held all beyond it in common contempt, and lived above it in a region of blue sky and great wandering shadows. That sky was bluest when I could beat my mates at examination-time, or beat them at a foot-race, or even beat their stringy heads. Alas, with the years all this fine contempt began to fade; for the words I longed for, and all their dazzling opportunities, were theirs, not mine. But they should not keep these prizes, I said; some, all, I would wrest from them. Just how I would do it I could never decide: by reading law, by healing the sick, by telling the wonderful tales that swam in my head,—some way. With other black boys the strife was not so fiercely sunny: their youth shrunk into tasteless sycophancy, or into silent hatred of the pale world about them and mocking distrust of everything white; or wasted itself in a bitter cry, Why did God make me an outcast and a stranger in mine own house? The shades of the prison-house closed round about us all: walls strait and stubborn to the whitest, but relentlessly narrow, tall, and unscalable to sons of night who must plod darkly on in resignation, or beat unavailing palms against the stone, or steadily, half hopelessly, watch the streak of blue above.

After the Egyptian and Indian, the Greek and Roman, the Teuton and Mongolian, the Negro is a sort of seventh son, born with a veil, and gifted with second-sight in this American world,—a world which yields him no true self-consciousness, but only lets him see himself through the revelation of the other world. It is a peculiar sensation, this double-consciousness, this sense of always looking at one's self through the eyes of others, of measuring one's soul by the tape of a world that looks on in amused contempt and pity. One ever feels his twoness,—an American, a Negro; two souls, two thoughts, two unreconciled strivings; two warring ideals in one dark body, whose dogged strength alone keeps it from being torn asunder.

The history of the American Negro is the history of this strife,—this longing to attain self-conscious manhood, to merge his double self into a better and truer self. In this merging he wishes neither of the older selves to be lost. He would not Africanize America, for America has too much to teach the world and Africa. He would not bleach his Negro soul in a flood of white Americanism, for he knows that Negro blood has a message for the world. He simply wishes to make it possible for a man to be both a Negro and an American, without being cursed and spit upon by his fellows, without having the doors of Opportunity closed roughly in his face.

This, then, is the end of his striving: to be a co-worker in the kingdom of culture, to escape both death and isolation, to husband and use his best powers and his latent genius. These powers of body and mind have in the past been strangely wasted, dispersed, or forgotten. The shadow of a mighty Negro past flits through the tale of Ethiopia the Shadowy and of Egypt the Sphinx. Through history, the powers of single black men flash here and there like falling stars, and die sometimes before the world has rightly gauged their brightness. Here in America, in the few days since Emancipation, the black man's turning hither and thither in hesitant and doubtful striving has often made his very strength to lose effectiveness, to seem like absence of power, like weakness. And yet it is not weakness,—it is the contradiction of double aims. The double-aimed struggle of the black artisan—on the one hand to escape white contempt for a nation of mere hewers of wood and drawers of water, and on the other hand to plough and nail and dig for a poverty-stricken horde— could only result in making him a poor craftsman, for he had but half a heart in either cause. By the poverty and ignorance of his people, the Negro minister or doctor was tempted toward quackery and demagogy; and by the criticism of the other world, toward ideals that made him ashamed of his lowly tasks. The would-be black savant was confronted by the paradox that the knowledge his people needed was a twice-told tale to his white neighbors, while the knowledge which would teach the white world was Greek to his own flesh and blood. The innate love of harmony and beauty that set the ruder souls of his people a-dancing and a-singing raised but confusion and doubt in the soul of the black artist; for the beauty revealed to him was the soul-beauty of a race which his larger audience despised, and he could not articulate the message of another people. This waste of double aims, this seeking to satisfy two unreconciled ideals, has wrought sad havoc with the courage and faith and deeds of ten thousand thousand people,—has sent them often wooing false gods and invoking false means of salvation, and at times has even seemed about to make them ashamed of themselves.

Away back in the days of bondage they thought to see in one divine event the end of all doubt and disappointment; few men ever worshipped Freedom with half such unquestioning faith as did the American Negro for two centuries. To him, so far as he thought and dreamed, slavery was indeed the sum of all villainies, the cause of all sorrow, the root of all prejudice; Emancipation was the key to a promised land of sweeter beauty than ever stretched before the eyes of wearied Israelites. In song and exhortation swelled one refrain—Liberty; in his tears and curses the God he implored had Freedom in his right hand. At last it came,—suddenly, fearfully, like a dream. With one wild carnival of blood and passion came the message in his own plaintive cadences:—

"Shout, O children!
Shout, you're free!
For God has bought your liberty!"

Years have passed away since then,—ten, twenty, forty; forty years of national life, forty years of renewal and development, and yet the swarthy spectre sits in its accustomed seat at the Nation's feast. In vain do we cry to this our vastest social problem:—

"Take any shape but that, and my firm nerves
Shall never tremble!"

The Nation has not yet found peace from its sins; the freedman has not yet found in freedom his promised land. Whatever of good may have come in these years of change, the shadow of a deep disappointment rests upon the Negro people,—a disappointment all the more bitter because the unattained ideal was unbounded save by the simple ignorance of a lowly people.

The first decade was merely a prolongation of the vain search for freedom, the boon that seemed ever barely to elude their grasp,—like a tantalizing will-o'-the-wisp, maddening and misleading the headless host. The holocaust of war, the terrors of the Ku-Klux Klan, the lies of carpet-baggers, the disorganization of industry, and the contradictory advice of friends and foes, left the bewildered serf with no new watchword beyond the old cry for freedom. As the time flew, however, he began to grasp a new idea. The ideal of liberty demanded for its attainment powerful means, and these the Fifteenth Amendment gave him. The ballot, which before he had looked upon as a visible sign of freedom, he now regarded as the chief means of gaining and perfecting the liberty with which war had partially endowed him. And why not? Had not votes made war and emancipated millions? Had not votes enfranchised the freedmen? Was anything impossible to a power that had done all this? A million black men started with renewed zeal to vote themselves into the kingdom. So the decade flew away, the revolution of 1876 came, and left the half-free serf weary, wondering, but still inspired. Slowly but steadily, in the following years, a new vision began gradually to replace the dream of political power,—a powerful movement, the rise of another ideal to guide the unguided, another pillar of fire by night after a clouded day. It was the ideal of "book-learning"; the curiosity, born of compulsory ignorance, to know and test the power of the cabalistic letters of the white man, the longing to know. Here at last seemed to have been discovered the mountain path to Canaan; longer than the highway of Emancipation and law, steep and rugged, but straight, leading to heights high enough to overlook life.

Up the new path the advance guard toiled, slowly, heavily, doggedly; only those who have watched and guided the faltering feet, the misty minds, the dull understandings, of the dark pupils of these schools know how faithfully, how piteously, this people strove to learn. It was weary work. The cold statistician wrote down the inches of progress here and there, noted also where here and there a foot had slipped or some one had fallen. To the tired climbers, the horizon was ever dark, the mists were often cold, the Canaan was always dim and far away. If, however, the vistas disclosed as yet no goal, no resting-place, little but flattery and criticism, the journey at least gave leisure for reflection and self-examination; it changed the child of Emancipation to the youth with dawning self-consciousness, self-realization, self-respect. In those sombre forests of his striving his own soul rose before him, and he saw himself,—darkly as through a veil; and yet he saw in himself some faint revelation of his power, of his mission. He began to have a dim feeling that, to attain his place in the world, he must be himself, and not another. For the first time he sought to analyze the burden he bore upon his back, that dead-weight of social degradation partially masked behind a half-named Negro problem. He felt his poverty; without a cent, without a home, without land, tools, or savings, he had entered into competition with rich, landed, skilled neighbors. To be a poor man is hard, but to be a poor race in a land of dollars is the very bottom of hardships. He felt the weight of his ignorance,—not simply of letters, but of life, of business, of the humanities; the accumulated sloth and shirking and awkwardness of decades and centuries shackled his hands and feet. Nor was his burden all poverty and ignorance. The red stain of bastardy, which two centuries of systematic legal defilement of Negro women had stamped upon his race, meant not only the loss of ancient African chastity, but also the hereditary weight of a mass of corruption from white adulterers, threatening almost the obliteration of the Negro home.

A people thus handicapped ought not to be asked to race with the world, but rather allowed to give all its time and thought to its own social problems. But alas! while sociologists gleefully count his bastards and his prostitutes, the very soul of the toiling, sweating black man is darkened by the shadow of a vast despair. Men call the shadow prejudice, and learnedly explain it as the natural defence of culture against barbarism, learning against ignorance, purity against crime, the "higher" against the "lower" races. To which the Negro cries Amen! and swears that to so much of this strange prejudice as is founded on just homage to civilization, culture, righteousness, and progress, he humbly bows and meekly does obeisance. But before that nameless prejudice that leaps beyond all this he stands helpless, dismayed, and well-nigh speechless; before that personal disrespect and mockery, the ridicule and systematic humiliation, the distortion of fact and wanton license of fancy, the cynical ignoring of the better and the boisterous welcoming of the worse, the all-pervading desire to inculcate disdain for everything black, from Toussaint to the devil,—before this there rises a sickening despair that would disarm and discourage any nation save that black host to whom "discouragement" is an unwritten word.

But the facing of so vast a prejudice could not but bring the inevitable self-questioning, self-disparagement, and lowering of ideals which ever accompany repression and breed in an atmosphere of contempt and hate. Whisperings and portents came home upon the four winds: Lo! we are diseased and dying, cried the dark hosts; we cannot write, our voting is vain; what need of education, since we must always cook and serve? And the Nation echoed and enforced this self-criticism, saying: Be content to be servants, and nothing more; what need of higher culture for half-men? Away with the black man's ballot, by force or fraud,—and behold the suicide of a race! Nevertheless, out of the evil came something of good,— the more careful adjustment of education to real life, the clearer perception of the Negroes' social responsibilities, and the sobering realization of the meaning of progress.

So dawned the time of Sturm und Drang: storm and stress to-day rocks our little boat on the mad waters of the world-sea; there is within and without the sound of conflict, the burning of body and rending of soul; inspiration strives with doubt, and faith with vain questionings. The bright ideals of the past,—physical freedom, political power, the training of brains and the training of hands,—all these in turn have waxed and waned, until even the last grows dim and overcast. Are they all wrong,— all false? No, not that, but each alone was over-simple and incomplete,— the dreams of a credulous race-childhood, or the fond imaginings of the other world which does not know and does not want to know our power. To be really true, all these ideals must be melted and welded into one. The training of the schools we need to-day more than ever,—the training of deft hands, quick eyes and ears, and above all the broader, deeper, higher culture of gifted minds and pure hearts. The power of the ballot we need in sheer self-defence,—else what shall save us from a second slavery? Freedom, too, the long-sought, we still seek,—the freedom of life and limb, the freedom to work and think, the freedom to love and aspire. Work, culture, liberty,—all these we need, not singly but together, not successively but together, each growing and aiding each, and all striving toward that vaster ideal that swims before the Negro people, the ideal of human brotherhood, gained through the unifying ideal of Race; the ideal of fostering and developing the traits and talents of the Negro, not in opposition to or contempt for other races, but rather in large conformity to the greater ideals of the American Republic, in order that some day on American soil two world-races may give each to each those characteristics both so sadly lack. We the darker ones come even now not altogether empty-handed: there are to-day no truer exponents of the pure human spirit of the Declaration of Independence than the American Negroes; there is no true American music but the wild sweet melodies of the Negro slave; the American fairy tales and folklore are Indian and African; and, all in all, we black men seem the sole oasis of simple faith and reverence in a dusty desert of dollars and smartness. Will America be poorer if she replace her brutal dyspeptic blundering with light-hearted but determined Negro humility? or her coarse and cruel wit with loving jovial good-humor? or her vulgar music with the soul of the Sorrow Songs?

Merely a concrete test of the underlying principles of the great republic is the Negro Problem, and the spiritual striving of the freedmen's sons is the travail of souls whose burden is almost beyond the measure of their strength, but who bear it in the name of an historic race, in the name of this the land of their fathers' fathers, and in the name of human opportunity.

COLLEGE WRITING 1: REFLECTION WITHIN THE TEXT

Consider W.E.B Du Bois's spiritual striving as your own. Put yourself in his shoes—write as if you are the problem in your society: what do you do? What do you tell yourself? How do you design your life—your self image—your relationships, to survive? How do you get along in a society that regards your very existence as "a problem"?

COLLEGE WRITING 2: RESEARCH OUTSIDE THE TEXT

Research life for black Americans 40 years after emancipation, but 60 years before the Civil Rights Movement. What's changed? What's the same? Has institutional racism been solved? Has equality been achieved? How does life for black Americans at the turn of the 20th century compare to the turn of the 21st century?

IDEAS AND VALUES: CONNECT THE TEXT

»   In Akutagawa's short story "Rashōmon" the ex-servant of a samurai struggles with whether or not to become a thief, and in Virginia Woolf's "The New Dress," Mabel is absolutely consumed with the question of her appearance in her new dress, and the judgments of those who surround her, and in W.E.B. Du Bois's "Of Our Spiritual Strivings" he writes, "It dawned upon me with a certain suddenness that I was different from the others; or like, mayhap, in heart and life and longing, but shut out from their world by a vast veil." In these three texts there are three extremely different accounts of a struggle for identity—of that question of sameness and of quality of a person. What can be said for all of them? What makes them different? What can be made of this struggle for identity—why is it important—is it?

»   Swift's "A Modest Proposal" Chesnutt's "The Sheriff's Children" and W.E.B. Du Bois's "Of Our Spiritual Strivings," explore the concepts of compassion and empathy—the ability to imagine what it's like to be another person, or the unwillingness to do so. How do the problems in each of the texts compare? What happens when an individual, or group of people, are classified as a "problems"? How should society deal with societal problems? How does it deal with the problems in these three texts? What is the nature of people as problem—is it even fair to think of a person as a problem? What does it do to a person to call them a problem?

»   Oscar Wilde writes in "Impressions of America" about the strange differences both good and bad between England and its former colony, the United States; W.E.B. Du Bois writes in "Of Our Spiritual Strivings" that "the words I longed for, and all their dazzling opportunities, were theirs, not mine," and in Gilman's "Yellow Wallpaper", the main character, having found herself on the "wrong side," of matrimony, country living, and her husband's medical opinion, gives us her unique perspective as well. What does perspective mean— how is it formed? What makes a perspective unique? What makes a perspective important, or worthwhile to understand? How does one get the perspective of another—or is it even possible to see through the eyes of another?

»   What is a stereotype? Do you consider the " Cowboy," the "Easterner" or the "Swede" in Crane's "The Blue Hotel" stereotypes? How about the children in Swift's "A Modest Proposal"? Lastly, what use of stereotypes has Du Bois's in "Of Our Spiritual Strivings" found necessary to make his points? How do the stereotypes help the reader to better understand the characters or topics discussed in these writings? Do we need stereotypes to help aid in our understanding of ourselves and others?

Porcelain and Pink

By F. Scott Fitzgerald

3,107 WORDS. 18 MINUTES.
READING LEVEL: GRADE 7.6

A room in the down-stairs of a summer cottage. High around the wall runs an art frieze of a fisherman with a pile of nets at his feet and a ship on a crimson ocean, a fisherman with a pile of nets at his feet and a ship on a crimson ocean, a fisherman with a pile of nets at his feet and so on. In one place on the frieze there is an overlapping—here we have half a fisherman with half a pile of nets at his foot, crowded damply against half a ship on half a crimson ocean. The frieze is not in the plot, but frankly it fascinates me. I could continue indefinitely, but I am distracted by one of the two objects in the room—a blue porcelain bath-tub. It has character, this bath-tub. It is not one of the new racing bodies, but is small with a high tonneau and looks as if it were going to jump; discouraged, however, by the shortness of its legs, it has submitted to its environment and to its coat of sky-blue paint. But it grumpily refuses to allow any patron completely to stretch his legs—which brings us neatly to the second object in the room:

It is a girl—clearly an appendage to the bath-tub, only her head and throat—beautiful girls have throats instead of necks—and a suggestion of shoulder appearing above the side. For the first ten minutes of the play the audience is engrossed in wondering if she really is playing the game fairly and hasn't any clothes on or whether it is being cheated and she is dressed.

The girl's name is JULIE MARVIS. From the proud way she sits up in the bath-tub we deduce that she is not very tall and that she carries herself well. When she smiles, her upper lip rolls a little and reminds you of an Easter Bunny. She is within whispering distance of twenty years old.

One thing more—above and to the right of the bath-tub is a window. It is narrow and has a wide sill; it lets in much sunshine, but effectually prevents any one who looks in from seeing the bath-tub. You begin to suspect the plot?

We open, conventionally enough, with a song, but, as the startled gasp of the audience quite drowns out the first half, we will give only the last of it:

JULIE: (In an airy sophrano—enthusiastico)

When Caesar did the Chicago

He was a graceful child,

Those sacred chickens

Just raised the dickens

The Vestal Virgins went wild.

Whenever the Nervii got nervy

He gave them an awful razz

They shook is their shoes

With the Consular blues

The Imperial Roman Jazz

(During the wild applause that follows JULIE modestly moves her arms and makes waves on the surface of the water—at least we suppose she does. Then the door on the left opens and LOIS MARVIS enters, dressed but carrying garments and towels. LOIS is a year older than JULIE and is nearly her double in face and voice, but in her clothes and expression are the marks of the conservative. Yes, you've guessed it. Mistaken identity is the old rusty pivot upon which the plot turns.)

LOIS: (Starting) Oh, 'scuse me. I didn't know you were here.

JULIE: Oh, hello. I'm giving a little concert—

LOIS: (Interrupting) Why didn't you lock the door?

JULIE: Didn't I?

LOIS: Of course you didn't. Do you think I just walked through it?

JULIE: I thought you picked the lock, dearest.

LOIS: You're so careless.

JULIE: No. I'm happy as a garbage-man's dog and I'm giving a little concert.

LOIS: (Severely) Grow up!

JULIE: (Waving a pink arm around the room) The walls reflect the sound, you see. That's why there's something very beautiful about singing in a bath-tub. It gives an effect of surpassing loveliness. Can I render you a selection?

LOIS: I wish you'd hurry out of the tub.

JULIE: (Shaking her head thoughtfully) Can't be hurried. This is my kingdom at present, Godliness.

LOIS: Why the mellow name?

JULIE: Because you're next to Cleanliness. Don't throw anything please!

LOIS: How long will you be?

JULIE: (After some consideration) Not less than fifteen nor more than twenty-five minutes.

LOIS: As a favor to me will you make it ten?

JULIE: (Reminiscing) Oh, Godliness, do you remember a day in the chill of last January when one Julie, famous for her Easter-rabbit smile, was going out and there was scarcely any hot water and young Julie had just filled the tub for her own little self when the wicked sister came and did bathe herself therein, forcing the young Julie to perform her ablutions with cold cream—which is expensive and a darn lot of troubles?

LOIS: (Impatiently) Then you won't hurry?

JULIE: Why should I?

LOIS: I've got a date.

JULIE: Here at the house?

LOIS: None of your business.

(JULIE shrugs the visible tips of her shoulders and stirs the water into ripples.)

JULIE: So be it.

LOIS: Oh, for Heaven's sake, yes! I have a date here, at the house— in a way.

JULIE: In a way?

LOIS: He isn't coming in. He's calling for me and we're walking.

JULIE: (Raising her eyebrows) Oh, the plot clears. It's that literary Mr. Calkins. I thought you promised mother you wouldn't invite him in.

LOIS: (Desperately) She's so idiotic. She detests him because he's just got a divorce. Of course she's had more expedience than I have, but—

JULIE: (Wisely) Don't let her kid you! Experience is the biggest gold brick in the world. All older people have it for sale.

LOIS: I like him. We talk literature.

JULIE: Oh, so that's why I've noticed all these weighty, books around the house lately.

LOIS: He lends them to me.

JULIE: Well, you've got to play his game. When in Rome do as the Romans would like to do. But I'm through with books. I'm all educated.

LOIS: You're very inconsistent—last summer you read every day.

JULIE: If I were consistent I'd still be living on warm milk out of a bottle.

LOIS: Yes, and probably my bottle. But I like Mr. Calkins.

JULIE: I never met him.

LOIS: Well, will you hurry up?

JULIE: Yes. (After a pause) I wait till the water gets tepid and then I let in more hot.

LOIS: (Sarcastically) How interesting!

JULIE: 'Member when we used to play "soapo"?

LOIS: Yes—and ten years old. I'm really quite surprised that you don't play it still.

JULIE: I do. I'm going to in a minute.

LOIS: Silly game.

JULIE: (Warmly) No, it isn't. It's good for the nerves. I'll bet you've forgotten how to play it.

LOIS: (Defiantly) No, I haven't. You—you get the tub all full of soapsuds and then you get up on the edge and slide down.

JULIE: (Shaking her head scornfully) Huh! That's only part of it. You've got to slide down without touching your hand or feet—

LOIS:(Impatiently) Oh, Lord! What do I care? I wish we'd either stop coming here in the summer or else get a house with two bath-tubs.

JULIE: You can buy yourself a little tin one, or use the hose——

LOIS: Oh, shut up!

JULIE: (Irrelevantly) Leave the towel.

LOIS: What?

JULIE: Leave the towel when you go.

LOIS: This towel?

JULIE: (Sweetly) Yes, I forgot my towel.

LOIS: (Looking around for the first time) Why, you idiot! You haven't even a kimono.

JULIE: (Also looking around) Why, so I haven't.

LOIS: (Suspicion growing on her) How did you get here?

JULIE: (Laughing) I guess I—I guess I whisked here. You know—a white form whisking down the stairs and—

LOIS: (Scandalized) Why, you little wretch. Haven't you any pride or self-respect?

JULIE: Lots of both. I think that proves it. I looked very well. I really am rather cute in my natural state.

LOIS: Well, you—

JULIE: (Thinking aloud) I wish people didn't wear any clothes. I guess I ought to have been a pagan or a native or something.

LOIS: You're a—

JULIE: I dreamt last night that one Sunday in church a small boy brought in a magnet that attracted cloth. He attracted the clothes right off of everybody; put them in an awful state; people were crying and shrieking and carrying on as if they'd just discovered their skins for the first time. Only I didn't care. So I just laughed. I had to pass the collection plate because nobody else would.

LOIS: (Who has turned a deaf ear to this speech) Do you mean to tell me that if I hadn't come you'd have run back to your room—un—unclothed?

JULIE: Au naturel is so much nicer.

LOIS: Suppose there had been some one in the living-room.

JULIE: There never has been yet.

LOIS: Yet! Good grief! How long—

JULIE: Besides, I usually have a towel.

LOIS: (Completely overcome) Golly! You ought to be spanked. I hope, you get caught. I hope there's a dozen ministers in the living-room when you come out—and their wives, and their daughters.

JULIE: There wouldn't be room for them in the living-room, answered Clean Kate of the Laundry District.

LOIS: All right. You've made your own—bath-tub; you can lie in it.

(LOIS starts determinedly for the door.)

JULIE: (In alarm) Hey! Hey! I don't care about the k'mono, but I want the towel. I can't dry myself on a piece of soap and a wet wash-rag.

LOIS: (Obstinately). I won't humor such a creature. You'll have to dry yourself the best way you can. You can roll on the floor like the animals do that don't wear any clothes.

JULIE: (Complacent again) All right. Get out!

LOIS: (Haughtily) Huh!

(JULIE turns on the cold water and with her finger directs a parabolic stream at LOIS. LOIS retires quickly, slamming the door after her. JULIE laughs and turns off the water)

JULIE: (Singing)

When the Arrow-collar man

Meets the D'jer-kiss girl

On the smokeless Sante Fé

Her Pebeco smile

Her Lucile style

De dum da-de-dum one day— (She changes to a whistle and leans forward to turn on the taps, but is startled by three loud banging noises in the pipes. Silence for a moment—then she puts her mouth down near the spigot as if it were a telephone)

JULIE: Hello! (No answer) Are you a plumber? (No answer) Are you the water department? (One loud, hollow bang) What do you want? (No answer) I believe you're a ghost. Are you? (No answer) Well, then, stop banging. (She reaches out and turns on the warm tap. No water flows. Again she puts her mouth down close to the spigot) If you're the plumber that's a mean trick. Turn it on for a fellow. (Two loud, hollow bangs) Don't argue! I want water—water! Water!

(A young man's head appears in the window—a head decorated with a slim mustache and sympathetic eyes. These last stare, and though they can see nothing but many fishermen with nets and much crimson ocean, they decide him to speak)

THE YOUNG MAN: Some one fainted?

JULIE: (Starting up, all ears immediately) Jumping cats!

THE YOUNG MAN: (Helpfully) Water's no good for fits.

JULIE: Fits! Who said anything about fits!

THE YOUNG MAN: You said something about a cat jumping

JULIE: (Decidedly) I did not!

THE YOUNG MAN: Well, we can talk it over later, Are you ready to go out? Or do you still feel that if you go with me just now everybody will gossip?

JULIE: (Smiling) Gossip! Would they? It'd be more than gossip—it'd be a regular scandal.

THE YOUNG MAN: Here, you're going it a little strong. Your family might be somewhat disgruntled—but to the pure all things are suggestive. No one else would even give it a thought, except a few old women. Come on.

JULIE: You don't know what you ask.

THE YOUNG MAN: Do you imagine we'd have a crowd following us?

JULIE: A crowd? There'd be a special, all-steel, buffet train leaving New York hourly.

THE YOUNG MAN: Say, are you house-cleaning?

JULIE: Why?

THE YOUNG MAN: I see all the pictures are off the walls.

JULIE: Why, we never have pictures in this room.

THE YOUNG MAN: Odd, I never heard of a room without pictures or tapestry or panelling or something.

JULIE: There's not even any furniture in here.

THE YOUNG MAN: What a strange house!

JULIE: It depend on the angle you see it from.

THE YOUNG MAN: (Sentimentally) It's so nice talking to you like this—when you're merely a voice. I'm rather glad I can't see you.

JULIE; (Gratefully) So am I.

THE YOUNG MAN: What color are you wearing?

JULIE: (After a critical survey of her shoulders) Why, I guess it's a sort of pinkish white.

THE YOUNG MAN: Is it becoming to you?

JULIE: Very. It's—it's old. I've had it for a long while.

THE YOUNG MAN: I thought you hated old clothes.

JULIE: I do but this was a birthday present and I sort of have to wear it.

THE YOUNG MAN: Pinkish-white. Well I'll bet it's divine. Is it in style?

JULIE: Quite. It's very simple, standard model.

THE YOUNG MAN: What a voice you have! How it echoes! Sometimes I shut my eyes and seem to see you in a far desert island calling for me. And I plunge toward you through the surf, hearing you call as you stand there, water stretching on both sides of you—

(The soap slips from the side of the tub and splashes in. The young man blinks)

YOUNG MAN: What was that? Did I dream it?

JULIE: Yes. You're—you're very poetic, aren't you?

THE YOUNG MAN: (Dreamily) No. I do prose. I do verse only when I am stirred.

JULIE: (Murmuring) Stirred by a spoon—

THE YOUNG MAN: I have always loved poetry. I can remember to this day the first poem I ever learned by heart. It was "Evangeline."

JULIE: That's a fib.

THE YOUNG MAN: Did I say "Evangeline"? I meant "The Skeleton in Armor."

JULIE: I'm a low-brow. But I can remember my first poem. It had one verse:

Parker and Davis
Sittin' on a fence
Tryne to make a dollar
Outa fif-teen cents.

THE YOUNG MAN: (Eagerly) Are you growing fond of literature?

JULIE: If it's not too ancient or complicated or depressing. Same way with people. I usually like 'em not too ancient or complicated or depressing.

THE YOUNG MAN: Of course I've read enormously. You told me last night that you were very fond of Walter Scott.

JULIE: (Considering) Scott? Let's see. Yes, I've read "Ivanhoe" and "The Last of the Mohicans."

THE YOUNG MAN: That's by Cooper.

JULIE: (Angrily) "Ivanhoe" is? You're crazy! I guess I know. I read it.

THE YOUNG MAN: "The Last of the Mohicans" is by Cooper.

JULIE: What do I care! I like O. Henry. I don't see how he ever wrote those stories. Most of them he wrote in prison. "The Ballad of Reading Gaol" he made up in prison.

THE YOUNG MAN: (Biting his lip) Literature—literature! How much it has meant to me!

JULIE: Well, as Gaby Deslys said to Mr. Bergson, with my looks and your brains there's nothing we couldn't do.

THE YOUNG MAN: (Laughing) You certainly are hard to keep up with. One day you're awfully pleasant and the next you're in a mood. If I didn't understand your temperament so well—

JULIE: (Impatiently) Oh, you're one of these amateur charac-
ter-readers, are you? Size people up in five minutes and then look wise
whenever they're mentioned. I hate that sort of thing.

THE YOUNG MAN: I don't boast of sizing you up. You're most
mysterious, I'll admit. JULIE: There's only two mysterious people in
history.

THE YOUNG MAN: Who are they?

JULIE: The Man with the Iron Mask and the fella who says "ug
uh-glug uh-glug uh-glug" when the line is busy.

THE YOUNG MAN: You are mysterious, I love you. You're beautiful, intelligent, and virtuous, and that's the rarest known combination.

JULIE: You're a historian. Tell me if there are any bath-tubs in history. I think they've been frightfully neglected.

THE YOUNG MAN: Bath-tubs! Let's see. Well, Agamemnon was
stabbed in his bath-tub. And Charlotte Corday stabbed Marat in his bath-
tub.

JULIE: (Sighing) Way back there! Nothing new besides the sun, is
there? Why only yesterday I picked up a musical-comedy score that mast
have been at least twenty years old; and there on the cover it said "The
Shimmies of Normandy," but shimmie was spelt the old way, with a "C."

THE YOUNG MAN: I loathe these modern dances. Oh, Lois, I
wish I could see you. Come to the window.

(There is a loud bang in the water-pipe and suddenly the flow starts
from the open taps. Julie turns them off quickly)

THE YOUNG MAN: (Puzzled) What on earth was that?

JULIE: (Ingeniously) I heard something, too.

THE YOUNG MAN: Sounded like running water.

JULIE: Didn't it? Strange like it. As a matter of fact I was filling the
gold-fish bowl.

THE YOUNG MAN: (Still puzzled) What was that banging noise?

JULIE: One of the fish snapping his golden jaws.

THE YOUNG MAN: (With sudden resolution) Lois, I love you. I
am not a mundane man but I am a forger—

JULIE: (Interested at once) Oh, how fascinating.

THE YOUNG MAN:—a forger ahead. Lois, I want you.

JULIE: (Skeptically) Huh! What you really want is for the world to
come to attention and stand there till you give "Rest!"

THE YOUNG MAN: Lois I—Lois I—

(*He stops as Lois opens the door, comes in, and bangs it behind her. She looks peevishly at* JULIE *and then suddenly catches sight of the young man in the window*)

LOIS: (In horror) Mr. Calkins!

THE YOUNG MAN: (Surprised) Why I thought you said you were wearing pinkish white!

(*After one despairing stare* LOIS *shrieks, throws up her hands in surrender, and sinks to the floor.*)

THE YOUNG MAN: (In great alarm) Good Lord! She's fainted! I'll be right in.

(JULIE'S eyes light on the towel which has slipped from LOIS'S inert hand.)

JULIE: In that case I'll be right out.

(*She puts her hands on the side of the tub to lift herself out and a murmur, half gasp, half sigh, ripples from the audience. A Belasco midnight comes quickly down and blots out the stage.*)

CURTAIN.

COLLEGE WRITING 1: REFLECTION WITHIN THE TEXT

Fitzgerald's "Porcelain and Pink" is ultimately a story about being ones self and a woman in the 1920's. There were a number of expectations about being a woman in the 1920s—and a number of those expectations being thrown out with the bathwater. How have expectations changed since your parent's generation? Write a one scene play in which you do something that your parents would not do when they were your age. Make it backfire on you in the same way it does in "Porcelain and Pink".

COLLEGE WRITING 2: RESEARCH OUTSIDE THE TEXT

Research "the roaring twenties." How did it come by that name? What were women "up to" at that time? What were the important political issues of the time concerning women? Bring what you find back to "Porcelain in Pink," and consider whether this changes how you view the behavior of the main character.

IDEAS AND VALUES: CONNECT THE TEXT

» What meaning is there in a color? Why are stop signs red? What is the color of sadness? Why do we wrap little boys in blue and girls in pink? Why do brides wear white on their wedding day? What is the significance of the title colors in their respective stories: "The Yellow Wallpaper," by Gilman, "Porcelain and Pink," by Fitzgerald, and "The Blue Hotel," by Crane? Could different colors have been used without changing these stories?

» Absurdity is the quality of being illogical, unreasonable, or just plain ridiculous. But absurdity often has a logic of its own—and in real life, as in literature, people end up in situations, and doing things, both noble and tragic, that can be characterized as absurd. How can this be? In Twain's "The Stolen White Elephant," the caretaker of a priceless White Elephant is led on a wild goose chase, and seems to have been swindled of all his savings by a fantastic detective agency. In "Porcelain and Pink," the main character finds herself in the nude among her date that afternoon, and matter-of-factly, renounces the norms of her society, and in Swift's essay "A Modest Proposal," the author offers a solution to a looming problem in Ireland of hungry and illiterate children—to eat them. Each of these texts touches upon aspects of the absurd. How are they the same? How are they different? What is the quality of their absurdity—that is—what makes them absurd? And are they truly—or can you find a hint of reason in any of them?

»　How is the truth manipulated in Crane's "The Blue Hotel," Fitzgerald's "Porcelain and Pink," and Twain's "The Stolen White Elephant"? How does the reader know what is true in each story? What is the truth in each story? Who relies on the truth in each story? Who relies on the perversion of truth? What are the stakes? What is truth? Why do humans have a concept of truth—if our surroundings are self evident? Should one always strive to be truthful?

A Modest Proposal

*For preventing the children of poor people in Ireland, from being a
burden on their parents or country, and for making them beneficial to the
publick.*

By Jonathan Swift

3,416 WORDS. 19 MINUTES.
READING LEVEL: GRADE 16

It is a melancholy object to those, who walk through this great town,
or travel in the country, when they see the streets, the roads and cabbin-
doors crowded with beggars of the female sex, followed by three, four,
or six children, all in rags, and importuning every passenger for an alms.
These mothers instead of being able to work for their honest livelihood,
are forced to employ all their time in stroling to beg sustenance for their
helpless infants who, as they grow up, either turn thieves for want of
work, or leave their dear native country, to fight for the Pretender in
Spain, or sell themselves to the Barbadoes.

I think it is agreed by all parties, that this prodigious number of
children in the arms, or on the backs, or at the heels of their mothers,
and frequently of their fathers, is in the present deplorable state of the
kingdom, a very great additional grievance; and therefore whoever could
find out a fair, cheap and easy method of making these children sound
and useful members of the common-wealth, would deserve so well of the
publick, as to have his statue set up for a preserver of the nation.

But my intention is very far from being confined to provide only
for the children of professed beggars: it is of a much greater extent, and
shall take in the whole number of infants at a certain age, who are born of
parents in effect as little able to support them, as those who demand our
charity in the streets.

As to my own part, having turned my thoughts for many years,
upon this important subject, and maturely weighed the several schemes
of our projectors, I have always found them grossly mistaken in their
computation. It is true, a child just dropt from its dam, may be supported

by her milk, for a solar year, with little other nourishment: at most not above the value of two shillings, which the mother may certainly get, or the value in scraps, by her lawful occupation of begging; and it is exactly at one year old that I propose to provide for them in such a manner, as, instead of being a charge upon their parents, or the parish, or wanting food and raiment for the rest of their lives, they shall, on the contrary, contribute to the feeding, and partly to the cloathing of many thousands.

There is likewise another great advantage in my scheme, that it will prevent those voluntary abortions, and that horrid practice of women murdering their bastard children, alas! too frequent among us, sacrificing the poor innocent babes, I doubt, more to avoid the expence than the shame, which would move tears and pity in the most savage and inhuman breast.

The number of souls in this kingdom being usually reckoned one million and a half, of these I calculate there may be about two hundred thousand couple whose wives are breeders; from which number I subtract thirty thousand couple, who are able to maintain their own children, (although I apprehend there cannot be so many, under the present distresses of the kingdom) but this being granted, there will remain an hundred and seventy thousand breeders. I again subtract fifty thousand, for those women who miscarry, or whose children die by accident or disease within the year. There only remain an hundred and twenty thousand children of poor parents annually born. The question therefore is, How this number shall be reared, and provided for? which, as I have already said, under the present situation of affairs, is utterly impossible by all the methods hitherto proposed. For we can neither employ them in handicraft or agriculture; they neither build houses, (I mean in the country) nor cultivate land: they can very seldom pick up a livelihood by stealing till they arrive at six years old; except where they are of towardly parts, although I confess they learn the rudiments much earlier; during which time they can however be properly looked upon only as proba-tioners: As I have been informed by a principal gentleman in the county of Cavan, who protested to me, that he never knew above one or two instances under the age of six, even in a part of the kingdom so renowned for the quickest proficiency in that art.

I am assured by our merchants, that a boy or a girl before twelve years old, is no saleable commodity, and even when they come to this age, they will not yield above three pounds, or three pounds and half a crown at most, on the exchange; which cannot turn to account either to the parents or kingdom, the charge of nutriments and rags having been at least four times that value.

I shall now therefore humbly propose my own thoughts, which I hope will not be liable to the least objection.

I have been assured by a very knowing American of my acquaintance in London, that a young healthy child well nursed, is, at a year old, a most delicious nourishing and wholesome food, whether stewed, roasted, baked, or boiled; and I make no doubt that it will equally serve in a fricasie, or a ragoust.

I do therefore humbly offer it to publick consideration, that of the hundred and twenty thousand children, already computed, twenty thousand may be reserved for breed, whereof only one fourth part to be males; which is more than we allow to sheep, black cattle, or swine, and my reason is, that these children are seldom the fruits of marriage, a circumstance not much regarded by our savages, therefore, one male will be sufficient to serve four females. That the remaining hundred thousand may, at a year old, be offered in sale to the persons of quality and fortune, through the kingdom, always advising the mother to let them suck plentifully in the last month, so as to render them plump, and fat for a good table. A child will make two dishes at an entertainment for friends, and when the family dines alone, the fore or hind quarter will make a reasonable dish, and seasoned with a little pepper or salt, will be very good boiled on the fourth day, especially in winter.

I have reckoned upon a medium, that a child just born will weigh 12 pounds, and in a solar year, if tolerably nursed, encreaseth to 28 pounds.

I grant this food will be somewhat dear, and therefore very proper for landlords, who, as they have already devoured most of the parents, seem to have the best title to the children.

Infant's flesh will be in season throughout the year, but more plentiful in March, and a little before and after; for we are told by a grave author, an eminent French physician, that fish being a prolifick dyet, there are more children born in Roman Catholick countries about nine months after Lent, the markets will be more glutted than usual, because the number of Popish infants, is at least three to one in this kingdom, and therefore it will have one other collateral advantage, by lessening the number of Papists among us.

I have already computed the charge of nursing a beggar's child (in which list I reckon all cottagers, labourers, and four-fifths of the farmers) to be about two shillings per annum, rags included; and I believe no gentleman would repine to give ten shillings for the carcass of a good fat child, which, as I have said, will make four dishes of excellent nutritive meat, when he hath only some particular friend, or his own family to dine with him. Thus the squire will learn to be a good landlord, and grow popular among his tenants, the mother will have eight shillings neat profit, and be fit for work till she produces another child.

Those who are more thrifty (as I must confess the times require) may flea the carcass; the skin of which, artificially dressed, will make admirable gloves for ladies, and summer boots for fine gentlemen.

As to our City of Dublin, shambles may be appointed for this purpose, in the most convenient parts of it, and butchers we may be assured will not be wanting; although I rather recommend buying the children alive, and dressing them hot from the knife, as we do roasting pigs.

A very worthy person, a true lover of his country, and whose virtues I highly esteem, was lately pleased, in discoursing on this matter, to offer a refinement upon my scheme. He said, that many gentlemen of this kingdom, having of late destroyed their deer, he conceived that the want of venison might be well supply'd by the bodies of young lads and maidens, not exceeding fourteen years of age, nor under twelve; so great a number of both sexes in every country being now ready to starve for want of work and service: And these to be disposed of by their parents if alive, or otherwise by their nearest relations. But with due deference to so excellent a friend, and so deserving a patriot, I cannot be altogether in his sentiments; for as to the males, my American acquaintance assured me from frequent experience, that their flesh was generally tough and lean, like that of our school-boys, by continual exercise, and their taste disagreeable, and to fatten them would not answer the charge. Then as to the females, it would, I think, with humble submission, be a loss to the publick, because they soon would become breeders themselves: And besides, it is not improbable that some scrupulous people might be apt to censure such a practice, (although indeed very unjustly) as a little bordering upon cruelty, which, I confess, hath always been with me the strongest objection against any project, how well soever intended.

But in order to justify my friend, he confessed, that this expedient was put into his head by the famous Salmanaazor, a native of the island Formosa, who came from thence to London, above twenty years ago, and in conversation told my friend, that in his country, when any young person happened to be put to death, the executioner sold the carcass to persons of quality, as a prime dainty; and that, in his time, the body of a plump girl of fifteen, who was crucified for an attempt to poison the Emperor, was sold to his imperial majesty's prime minister of state, and other great mandarins of the court in joints from the gibbet, at four hundred crowns. Neither indeed can I deny, that if the same use were made of several plump young girls in this town, who without one single groat to their fortunes, cannot stir abroad without a chair, and appear at a play-house and assemblies in foreign fineries which they never will pay for; the kingdom would not be the worse.

Some persons of a desponding spirit are in great concern about that vast number of poor people, who are aged, diseased, or maimed; and I have been desired to employ my thoughts what course may be taken, to ease the nation of so grievous an incumbrance. But I am not in the least pain upon that matter, because it is very well known, that they are every day dying, and rotting, by cold and famine, and filth, and vermin, as fast as can be reasonably expected. And as to the young labourers, they are now in almost as hopeful a condition. They cannot get work, and consequently pine away from want of nourishment, to a degree, that if at any time they are accidentally hired to common labour, they have not strength to perform it, and thus the country and themselves are happily delivered from the evils to come.

I have too long digressed, and therefore shall return to my subject. I think the advantages by the proposal which I have made are obvious and many, as well as of the highest importance.

For first, as I have already observed, it would greatly lessen the number of Papists, with whom we are yearly over-run, being the principal breeders of the nation, as well as our most dangerous enemies, and who stay at home on purpose with a design to deliver the kingdom to the Pretender, hoping to take their advantage by the absence of so many good

Protestants, who have chosen rather to leave their country, than stay at home and pay tithes against their conscience to an episcopal curate.

Secondly, The poorer tenants will have something valuable of their own, which by law may be made liable to a distress, and help to pay their landlord's rent, their corn and cattle being already seized, and money a thing unknown.

Thirdly, Whereas the maintainance of an hundred thousand children, from two years old, and upwards, cannot be computed at less than ten shillings a piece per annum, the nation's stock will be thereby encreased fifty thousand pounds per annum, besides the profit of a new dish, introduced to the tables of all gentlemen of fortune in the kingdom, who have any refinement in taste. And the money will circulate among our selves, the goods being entirely of our own growth and manufacture.

Fourthly, The constant breeders, besides the gain of eight shillings sterling per annum by the sale of their children, will be rid of the charge of maintaining them after the first year.

Fifthly, This food would likewise bring great custom to taverns, where the vintners will certainly be so prudent as to procure the best receipts for dressing it to perfection; and consequently have their houses frequented by all the fine gentlemen, who justly value themselves upon their knowledge in good eating; and a skilful cook, who understands how to oblige his guests, will contrive to make it as expensive as they please.

Sixthly, This would be a great inducement to marriage, which all wise nations have either encouraged by rewards, or enforced by laws and penalties. It would encrease the care and tenderness of mothers towards their children, when they were sure of a settlement for life to the poor babes, provided in some sort by the publick, to their annual profit instead of expence. We should soon see an honest emulation among the married women, which of them could bring the fattest child to the market. Men would become as fond of their wives, during the time of their pregnancy, as they are now of their mares in foal, their cows in calf, or sow when they are ready to farrow; nor offer to beat or kick them (as is too frequent a practice) for fear of a miscarriage.

Many other advantages might be enumerated. For instance, the addition of some thousand carcasses in our exportation of barrel'd beef: the propagation of swine's flesh, and improvement in the art of making good bacon, so much wanted among us by the great destruction of pigs, too frequent at our tables; which are no way comparable in taste or magnificence to a well grown, fat yearly child, which roasted whole will make a considerable figure at a Lord Mayor's feast, or any other publick entertainment. But this, and many others, I omit, being studious of brevity.

Supposing that one thousand families in this city, would be constant customers for infants flesh, besides others who might have it at merry meetings, particularly at weddings and christenings, I compute that Dublin would take off annually about twenty thousand carcasses; and the rest of the kingdom (where probably they will be sold somewhat cheaper) the remaining eighty thousand.

I can think of no one objection, that will possibly be raised against this proposal, unless it should be urged, that the number of people will be thereby much lessened in the kingdom. This I freely own, and 'twas indeed one principal design in offering it to the world. I desire the reader will observe, that I calculate my remedy for this one individual Kingdom of Ireland, and for no other that ever was, is, or, I think, ever can be upon Earth. Therefore let no man talk to me of other expedients: Of taxing our absentees at five shillings a pound: Of using neither cloaths, nor houshold furniture, except what is of our own growth and manufacture: Of utterly rejecting the materials and instruments that promote foreign luxury: Of curing the expensiveness of pride, vanity, idleness, and gaming in our women: Of introducing a vein of parsimony, prudence and temperance: Of learning to love our country, wherein we differ even from Laplanders, and the inhabitants of Topinamboo: Of quitting our animosities and factions, nor acting any longer like the Jews, who were murdering one another at the very moment their city was taken: Of being a little cautious not to sell our country and consciences for nothing: Of teaching landlords to have at least one degree of mercy towards their tenants. Lastly, of putting a spirit of honesty, industry, and skill into our shop-keepers, who, if a resolution could now be taken to buy only our native goods, would immediately unite to cheat and exact upon us in the price, the measure, and the goodness, nor could ever yet be brought to make one fair proposal of just dealing, though often and earnestly invited to it.

Therefore I repeat, let no man talk to me of these and the like expedients, 'till he hath at least some glympse of hope, that there will ever be some hearty and sincere attempt to put them into practice.

But, as to my self, having been wearied out for many years with offering vain, idle, visionary thoughts, and at length utterly despairing of success, I fortunately fell upon this proposal, which, as it is wholly new, so it hath something solid and real, of no expence and little trouble, full in our own power, and whereby we can incur no danger in disobliging England. For this kind of commodity will not bear exportation, and flesh being of too tender a consistence, to admit a long continuance in salt, although perhaps I could name a country, which would be glad to eat up our whole nation without it.

After all, I am not so violently bent upon my own opinion, as to reject any offer, proposed by wise men, which shall be found equally innocent, cheap, easy, and effectual. But before something of that kind shall be advanced in contradiction to my scheme, and offering a better, I desire the author or authors will be pleased maturely to consider two points. First, As things now stand, how they will be able to find food and raiment for a hundred thousand useless mouths and backs. And secondly, There being a round million of creatures in humane figure throughout this kingdom, whose whole subsistence put into a common stock, would leave them in debt two million of pounds sterling, adding those who are beggars by profession, to the bulk of farmers, cottagers and labourers, with their wives and children, who are beggars in effect; I desire those politicians who dislike my overture, and may perhaps be so bold to attempt an answer, that they will first ask the parents of these mortals, whether they would not at this day think it a great happiness to have been sold for food at a year old, in the manner I prescribe, and thereby have avoided such a perpetual scene of misfortunes, as they have since gone through, by the oppression of landlords, the impossibility of paying rent without money or trade, the want of common sustenance, with neither house nor cloaths to cover them from the inclemencies of the weather, and the most inevitable prospect of intailing the like, or greater miseries, upon their breed for ever.

I profess, in the sincerity of my heart, that I have not the least personal interest in endeavouring to promote this necessary work, having no other motive than the publick good of my country, by advancing our trade, providing for infants, relieving the poor, and giving some pleasure to the rich. I have no children, by which I can propose to get a single penny; the youngest being nine years old, and my wife past child-bearing.

COLLEGE WRITING 1: REFLECTION WITHIN THE TEXT

Identify a problem that is personal but also political. It could be a problem of yours, or a problem for your school, your parents, your employer, or a friend.

In the style of Jonathan Swift, write a tongue in cheek "modest proposal" to fix this ill. Swift's proposal is satire—that means he doesn't really believe we should go about eating starving children. He is satirizing the callousness of certain members of his society and their political views, by taking them to the extreme.

COLLEGE WRITING 2: RESEARCH OUTSIDE THE TEXT

Research Ireland in 1729. Look at the situation to which Jonathan Swift was referring. Research the policies and prevalent attitudes towards the Irish in England at the time, and consider why Swift thought it necessary to write such a scathing and satirical essay.

IDEAS AND VALUES: CONNECT THE TEXT

» Absurdity is the quality of being illogical, unreasonable, or just plain ridiculous. But absurdity often has a logic of its own—and in real life, as in literature, people end up in situations, and doing things, both noble and tragic, that can be characterized as absurd. How can this be? In Twain's "The Stolen White Elephant," the caretaker of a priceless White Elephant is led on a wild goose chase, and seems to have been swindled of all his savings by a fantastic detective agency. In "Porcelain and Pink," the main character finds herself in the nude among her date that afternoon, and matter-of-factly, renounces the norms of her society, and in Swift's essay "A Modest Proposal," the author offers a solution to a looming problem in Ireland of hungry and illiterate children—to eat them. Each of these texts touches upon aspects of the absurd. How are they the same? How are they different? What is the quality of their absurdity—that is—what makes them absurd? And are they truly—or can you find a hint of reason in any of them?

» Swift's "A Modest Proposal" Chesnutt's "The Sheriff's Children" and W.E.B. Du Bois's "Of Our Spiritual Strivings," explore the concepts of compassion and empathy—the ability to imagine what it's like to be another person, or the unwillingness to do so. How do the problems in each of the texts compare? What happens when an individual, or group of people, are classified as a "problems"? How should society deal with societal problems? How does it deal with the problems in these three texts? What is the nature of people as problem—is it even fair to think of a person as a problem? What does it do to a person to call them a problem?

» What is a stereotype? Do you consider the " Cowboy," the "Easterner" or the "Swede" in Crane's "The Blue Hotel" stereotypes? How about the children in Swift's "A Modest Proposal"? Lastly, what use of stereotypes has Du Bois's in "Of Our Spiritual Strivings" found necessary to make his points? How do the stereotypes help the reader to better understand the characters or topics discussed in these writings? Do we need stereotypes to help aid in our understanding of ourselves and others?

Wakefield

By Nathaniel Hawthorne

3,472 WORDS. 19 MINUTES.
READING LEVEL: GRADE 12

In some old magazine or newspaper I recollect a story, told as truth, of a man—let us call him Wakefield—who absented himself for a long time from his wife. The fact, thus abstractedly stated, is not very uncommon, nor, without a proper distinction of circumstances, to be condemned either as naughty or nonsensical. Howbeit, this, though far from the most aggravated, is perhaps the strangest instance on record of marital delinquency, and, moreover, as remarkable a freak as may be found in the whole list of human oddities. The wedded couple lived in London. The man, under pretence of going a journey, took lodgings in the next street to his own house, and there, unheard of by his wife or friends and without the shadow of a reason for such self-banishment, dwelt upward of twenty years. During that period he beheld his home every day, and frequently the forlorn Mrs. Wakefield. And after so great a gap in his matrimonial felicity—when his death was reckoned certain, his estate settled, his name dismissed from memory and his wife long, long ago resigned to her autumnal widowhood—he entered the door one evening quietly as from a day's absence, and became a loving spouse till death.

This outline is all that I remember. But the incident, though of the purest originality, unexampled, and probably never to be repeated, is one, I think, which appeals to the general sympathies of mankind. We know, each for himself, that none of us would perpetrate such a folly, yet feel as if some other might. To my own contemplations, at least, it has often recurred, always exciting wonder, but with a sense that the story must be true and a conception of its hero's character. Whenever any subject so forcibly affects the mind, time is well spent in thinking of it. If the reader choose, let him do his own meditation; or if he prefer to ramble with me through the twenty years of Wakefield's vagary, I bid him welcome, trusting that there will be a pervading spirit and a moral, even should we fail to find them, done up neatly and condensed into the final sentence. Thought has always its efficacy and every striking incident its moral.

What sort of a man was Wakefield? We are free to shape out our own idea and call it by his name. He was now in the meridian of life; his matrimonial affections, never violent, were sobered into a calm, habitual sentiment; of all husbands, he was likely to be the most constant, because a certain sluggishness would keep his heart at rest wherever it might be placed. He was intellectual, but not actively so; his mind occupied itself in long and lazy musings that tended to no purpose or had not vigor to attain it; his thoughts were seldom so energetic as to seize hold of words. Imagination, in the proper meaning of the term, made no part of Wakefield's gifts. With a cold but not depraved nor wandering heart, and a mind never feverish with riotous thoughts nor perplexed with originality, who could have anticipated that our friend would entitle himself to a foremost place among the doers of eccentric deeds? Had his acquaintances been asked who was the man in London the surest to perform nothing to-day which should be remembered on the morrow, they would have thought of Wakefield. Only the wife of his bosom might have hesitated. She, without having analyzed his character, was partly aware of a quiet selfishness that had rusted into his inactive mind; of a peculiar sort of vanity, the most uneasy attribute about him; of a disposition to craft which had seldom produced more positive effects than the keeping of petty secrets hardly worth revealing; and, lastly, of what she called a little strangeness sometimes in the good man. This latter quality is indefinable, and perhaps non-existent.

Let us now imagine Wakefield bidding adieu to his wife. It is the dusk of an October evening. His equipment is a drab greatcoat, a hat covered with an oil-cloth, top-boots, an umbrella in one hand and a small portmanteau in the other. He has informed Mrs. Wakefield that he is to take the night-coach into the country. She would fain inquire the length of his journey, its object and the probable time of his return, but, indulgent to his harmless love of mystery, interrogates him only by a look. He tells her not to expect him positively by the return-coach nor to be alarmed should he tarry three or four days, but, at all events, to look for him at supper on Friday evening. Wakefield, himself, be it considered, has no suspicion of what is before him. He holds out his hand; she gives her own and meets his parting kiss in the matter-of-course way of a ten years' matrimony, and forth goes the middle-aged Mr. Wakefield, almost resolved to perplex his good lady by a whole week's absence. After the door has closed behind him, she perceives it thrust partly open and a vision of her husband's face through the aperture, smiling on her and gone in a moment. For the time this little incident is dismissed without a thought, but long afterward, when she has been more years a widow than a wife, that smile recurs and flickers across all her reminiscences of Wakefield's visage. In her many musings she surrounds the original smile with a multitude of fantasies which make it strange and awful; as, for instance, if she imagines him in a coffin, that parting look is frozen on his pale features; or if she dreams of him in heaven, still his blessed spirit wears a quiet and crafty smile. Yet for its sake, when all others have given him up for dead, she sometimes doubts whether she is a widow.

But our business is with the husband. We must hurry after him along the street ere he lose his individuality and melt into the great mass of London life. It would be vain searching for him there. Let us follow close at his heels, therefore, until, after several superfluous turns and doublings, we find him comfortably established by the fireside of a small apartment previously bespoken. He is in the next street to his own and at his journey's end. He can scarcely trust his good-fortune in having got thither unperceived, recollecting that at one time he was delayed by the throng in the very focus of a lighted lantern, and again there were footsteps that seemed to tread behind his own, distinct from the multitudinous tramp around him, and anon he heard a voice shouting afar and fancied that it called his name. Doubtless a dozen busybodies had been watching him and told his wife the whole affair.

Poor Wakefield! little knowest thou thine own insignificance in this great world. No mortal eye but mine has traced thee. Go quietly to thy bed, foolish man, and on the morrow, if thou wilt be wise, get thee home to good Mrs. Wakefield and tell her the truth. Remove not thyself even for a little week from thy place in her chaste bosom. Were she for a single moment to deem thee dead or lost or lastingly divided from her, thou wouldst be woefully conscious of a change in thy true wife for ever after. It is perilous to make a chasm in human affections—not that they gape so long and wide, but so quickly close again.

Almost repenting of his frolic, or whatever it may be termed, Wakefield lies down betimes, and, starting from his first nap, spreads forth his arms into the wide and solitary waste of the unaccustomed bed, "No," thinks he, gathering the bedclothes about him; "I will not sleep alone another night." In the morning he rises earlier than usual and sets himself to consider what he really means to do. Such are his loose and rambling modes of thought that he has taken this very singular step with the consciousness of a purpose, indeed, but without being able to define it sufficiently for his own contemplation. The vagueness of the project and the convulsive effort with which he plunges into the execution of it are equally characteristic of a feeble-minded man. Wakefield sifts his ideas, however, as minutely as he may, and finds himself curious to know the progress of matters at home—how his exemplary wife will endure her widowhood of a week, and, briefly, how the little sphere of creatures and circumstances in which he was a central object will be affected by his removal. A morbid vanity, therefore, lies nearest the bottom of the affair. But how is he to attain his ends? Not, certainly, by keeping close in this comfortable lodging, where, though he slept and awoke in the next street to his home, he is as effectually abroad as if the stage-coach had been whirling him away all night. Yet should he reappear, the whole project is knocked in the head. His poor brains being hopelessly puzzled with this dilemma, he at length ventures out, partly resolving to cross the head of the street and send one hasty glance toward his forsaken domicile. Habit—for he is a man of habits—takes him by the hand and guides him, wholly unaware, to his own door, where, just at the critical moment, he is aroused by the scraping of his foot upon the step.—Wakefield, whither are you going?

At that instant his fate was turning on the pivot. Little dreaming of the doom to which his first backward step devotes him, he hurries away, breathless with agitation hitherto unfelt, and hardly dares turn his head at the distant corner. Can it be that nobody caught sight of him? Will not the whole household—the decent Mrs. Wakefield, the smart maid-servant and the dirty little footboy—raise a hue-and-cry through London streets in pursuit of their fugitive lord and master? Wonderful escape! He gathers courage to pause and look homeward, but is perplexed with a sense of change about the familiar edifice such as affects us all when, after a separation of months or years, we again see some hill or lake or work of art with which we were friends of old. In ordinary cases this indescribable impression is caused by the comparison and contrast between our imperfect reminiscences and the reality. In Wakefield the magic of a single night has wrought a similar transformation, because in that brief period a great moral change has been effected. But this is a secret from himself. Before leaving the spot he catches a far and momentary glimpse of his wife passing athwart the front window with her face turned toward the head of the street. The crafty nincompoop takes to his heels, scared with the idea that among a thousand such atoms of mortality her eye must have detected him. Right glad is his heart, though his brain be somewhat dizzy, when he finds himself by the coal-fire of his lodgings.

So much for the commencement of this long whim-wham. After the initial conception and the stirring up of the man's sluggish temperament to put it in practice, the whole matter evolves itself in a natural train. We may suppose him, as the result of deep deliberation, buying a new wig of reddish hair and selecting sundry garments, in a fashion unlike his customary suit of brown, from a Jew's old-clothes bag. It is accomplished: Wakefield is another man. The new system being now established, a retrograde movement to the old would be almost as difficult as the step that placed him in his unparalleled position. Furthermore, he is rendered obstinate by a sulkiness occasionally incident to his temper and brought on at present by the inadequate sensation which he conceives to have been produced in the bosom of Mrs. Wakefield. He will not go back until she be frightened half to death. Well, twice or thrice has she passed before his sight, each time with a heavier step, a paler cheek and more anxious brow, and in the third week of his non-appearance he detects a portent of evil entering the house in the guise of an apothecary. Next day the knocker is muffled. Toward nightfall comes the chariot of a physician and deposits its big-wigged and solemn burden at Wakefield's door, whence after a quarter of an hour's visit he emerges, perchance the herald of a funeral. Dear woman! will she die?

By this time Wakefield is excited to something like energy of feeling, but still lingers away from his wife's bedside, pleading with his conscience that she must not be disturbed at such a juncture. If aught else restrains him, he does not know it. In the course of a few weeks she gradually recovers. The crisis is over; her heart is sad, perhaps, but quiet, and, let him return soon or late, it will never be feverish for him again. Such ideas glimmer through the mist of Wakefield's mind and render him indistinctly conscious that an almost impassable gulf divides his hired apartment from his former home. "It is but in the next street," he sometimes says. Fool! it is in another world. Hitherto he has put off his return from one particular day to another; henceforward he leaves the precise time undetermined—not to-morrow; probably next week; pretty soon. Poor man! The dead have nearly as much chance of revisiting their earthly homes as the self-banished Wakefield.

Would that I had a folio to write, instead of an article of a dozen pages! Then might I exemplify how an influence beyond our control lays its strong hand on every deed which we do and weaves its consequences into an iron tissue of necessity.

Wakefield is spellbound. We must leave him for ten years or so to haunt around his house without once crossing the threshold, and to be faithful to his wife with all the affection of which his heart is capable, while he is slowly fading out of hers. Long since, it must be remarked, he has lost the perception of singularity in his conduct.

Now for a scene. Amid the throng of a London street we distinguish a man, now waxing elderly, with few characteristics to attract careless observers, yet bearing in his whole aspect the handwriting of no common fate for such as have the skill to read it. He is meagre; his low and narrow forehead is deeply wrinkled; his eyes, small and lustreless, sometimes wander apprehensively about him, but oftener seem to look inward. He bends his head and moves with an indescribable obliquity of gait, as if unwilling to display his full front to the world. Watch him long enough to see what we have described, and you will allow that circumstances—which often produce remarkable men from Nature's ordinary handiwork—have produced one such here. Next, leaving him to sidle along the footwalk, cast your eyes in the opposite direction, where a portly female considerably in the wane of life, with a prayer-book in her hand, is proceeding to yonder church. She has the placid mien of settled widowhood. Her regrets have either died away or have become so essential to her heart that they would be poorly exchanged for joy. Just as the lean man and well-conditioned woman are passing a slight obstruction occurs and brings these two figures directly in contact. Their hands touch; the pressure of the crowd forces her bosom against his shoulder; they stand face to face, staring into each other's eyes. After a ten years' separation thus Wakefield meets his wife. The throng eddies away and carries them asunder. The sober widow, resuming her former pace, proceeds to church, but pauses in the portal and throws a perplexed glance along the street. She passes in, however, opening her prayer-book as she goes.

And the man? With so wild a face that busy and selfish London stands to gaze after him he hurries to his lodgings, bolts the door and throws himself upon the bed. The latent feelings of years break out; his feeble mind acquires a brief energy from their strength; all the miserable strangeness of his life is revealed to him at a glance, and he cries out passionately, "Wakefield, Wakefield! You are mad!" Perhaps he was so. The singularity of his situation must have so moulded him to itself that, considered in regard to his fellow-creatures and the business of life, he could not be said to possess his right mind. He had contrived—or, rather, he had happened—to dissever himself from the world, to vanish, to give up his place and privileges with living men without being admitted among the dead. The life of a hermit is nowise parallel to his. He was in the bustle of the city as of old, but the crowd swept by and saw him not; he was, we may figuratively say, always beside his wife and at his hearth, yet must never feel the warmth of the one nor the affection of the other. It was Wakefield's unprecedented fate to retain his original share of human sympathies and to be still involved in human interests, while he had lost his reciprocal influence on them. It would be a most curious speculation to trace out the effect of such circumstances on his heart and intellect separately and in unison. Yet, changed as he was, he would seldom be conscious of it, but deem himself the same man as ever; glimpses of the truth, indeed, would come, but only for the moment, and still he would keep saying, "I shall soon go back," nor reflect that he had been saying so for twenty years.

I conceive, also, that these twenty years would appear in the retrospect scarcely longer than the week to which Wakefield had at first limited his absence. He would look on the affair as no more than an interlude in the main business of his life. When, after a little while more, he should deem it time to re-enter his parlor, his wife would clap her hands for joy on beholding the middle-aged Mr. Wakefield. Alas, what a mistake! Would Time but await the close of our favorite follies, we should be young men—all of us—and till Doomsday.

One evening, in the twentieth year since he vanished, Wakefield is taking his customary walk toward the dwelling which he still calls his own. It is a gusty night of autumn, with frequent showers that patter down upon the pavement and are gone before a man can put up his umbrella. Pausing near the house, Wakefield discerns through the parlor-windows of the second floor the red glow and the glimmer and fitful flash of a comfortable fire. On the ceiling appears a grotesque shadow of good Mrs. Wakefield. The cap, the nose and chin and the broad waist form an admirable caricature, which dances, moreover, with the up-flickering and down-sinking blaze almost too merrily for the shade of an elderly widow. At this instant a shower chances to fall, and is driven by the unmannerly gust full into Wakefield's face and bosom. He is quite penetrated with its autumnal chill. Shall he stand wet and shivering here, when his own hearth has a good fire to warm him and his own wife will run to fetch the gray coat and small-clothes which doubtless she has kept carefully in the closet of their bedchamber? No; Wakefield is no such fool. He ascends the steps—heavily, for twenty years have stiffened his legs since he came down, but he knows it not.—Stay, Wakefield! Would you go to the sole home that is left you? Then step into your grave.—The door opens. As he passes in we have a parting glimpse of his visage, and recognize the crafty smile which was the precursor of the little joke that he has ever since been playing off at his wife's expense. How unmercifully has he quizzed the poor woman! Well, a good night's rest to Wakefield!

This happy event—supposing it to be such—could only have occurred at an unpremeditated moment. We will not follow our friend across the threshold. He has left us much food for thought, a portion of which shall lend its wisdom to a moral and be shaped into a figure. Amid the seeming confusion of our mysterious world individuals are so nicely adjusted to a system, and systems to one another and to a whole, that by stepping aside for a moment a man exposes himself to a fearful risk of losing his place for ever. Like Wakefield, he may become, as it were, the outcast of the universe.

can never return to normal at home.

COLLEGE WRITING 1: REFLECTION WITHIN THE TEXT

» Think about Wakefield's wife's response to him leaving. How did she feel when he was first missing and how did her feelings change as time passed? What state of mind is she in at the moment of his arrival? How would she deal with all of her emotions from the past 20 years? From the wife's perspective add an additional scene at the end of "Wakefield", after he returns.

» Find a news story about someone that you find strange. In the style of Hawthorne's "Wakefield" explore what happened from that persons's point of view. Write a story that ends where the news story begins.

Choose 1

COLLEGE WRITING 2: RESEARCH OUTSIDE THE TEXT

» Research a factual account of a person who intentionally disappeared from their own life. Why did the person leave? Did they return? How did the people they left behind react? Compare the text you found to Wakefield. How are Wakefield and the person from your research the same? How do they differ? How does Hawthorne's telling of Wakefield's story compare to the text you found? Does one help you understand the other? Why, or why not?

» Find a news story about an individual's actions that you find inexplicible. In the style of Hawthorne's "Wakefield" explore and explain what happened from the point of view of the person involved. Write a narrative that starts with the beginning of their story and ends at the point when the news story is written.

IDEAS AND VALUES: CONNECT THE TEXT

» How do the outcasts in Hawthorne's "Wakefield," Woolf's "The New Dress," and Chesnutt's "The Sheriff's Children" differ? How are they the same? Why are the characters outcasts? Who casts them out? How does society view each of the outcasts in these stories? What kind of society would cast these people out?

» What is independence in Conrad's "One Day More", Hawthorne's

"Wakefield", and Forester's "The Machine Stops"? What are the consequences of independence, for not only the individual but for society? Can a balance be struck between independence and the needs of a community?

An Occurrence at Owl Creek Bridge

By Ambrose Bierce

3,772 WORDS. 21 MINUTES.
READING LEVEL: GRADE 10.3

1

A man stood upon a railroad bridge in northern Alabama, looking down into the swift water twenty feet below. The man's hands were
behind his back, the wrists bound with a cord. A rope closely encircled his
neck. It was attached to a stout cross-timber above his head and the slack
fell to the level of his knees. Some loose boards laid upon the ties support-
ing the rails of the railway supplied a footing for him and his executioners—two private soldiers of the Federal army, directed by a sergeant
who in civil life may have been a deputy sheriff. At a short remove upon
the same temporary platform was an officer in the uniform of his rank,
armed. He was a captain. A sentinel at each end of the bridge stood with
his rifle in the position known as "support," that is to say, vertical in front
of the left shoulder, the hammer resting on the forearm thrown straight
across the chest—a formal and unnatural position, enforcing an erect
carriage of the body. It did not appear to be the duty of these two men to
know what was occurring at the center of the bridge; they merely blockaded the two ends of the foot planking that traversed it.

Beyond one of the sentinels nobody was in sight; the railroad ran
straight away into a forest for a hundred yards, then, curving, was lost
to view. Doubtless there was an outpost farther along. The other bank of
the stream was open ground—a gentle slope topped with a stockade of
vertical tree trunks, loopholed for rifles, with a single embrasure through
which protruded the muzzle of a brass cannon commanding the bridge.
Midway up the slope between the bridge and fort were the spectators—a
single company of infantry in line, at "parade rest," the butts of their rifles
on the ground, the barrels inclining slightly backward against the right
shoulder, the hands crossed upon the stock. A lieutenant stood at the
right of the line, the point of his sword upon the ground, his left hand

resting upon his right. Excepting the group of four at the center of the bridge, not a man moved. The company faced the bridge, staring stonily, motionless. The sentinels, facing the banks of the stream, might have been statues to adorn the bridge. The captain stood with folded arms, silent, observing the work of his subordinates, but making no sign. Death is a dignitary who when he comes announced is to be received with formal manifestations of respect, even by those most familiar with him. In the code of military etiquette silence and fixity are forms of deference.

The man who was engaged in being hanged was apparently about thirty-five years of age. He was a civilian, if one might judge from his habit, which was that of a planter. His features were good—a straight nose, firm mouth, broad forehead, from which his long, dark hair was combed straight back, falling behind his ears to the collar of his well fitting frock coat. He wore a moustache and pointed beard, but no whiskers; his eyes were large and dark gray, and had a kindly expression which one would hardly have expected in one whose neck was in the hemp. Evidently this was no vulgar assassin. The liberal military code makes provision for hanging many kinds of persons, and gentlemen are not excluded.

The preparations being complete, the two private soldiers stepped aside and each drew away the plank upon which he had been standing. The sergeant turned to the captain, saluted and placed himself immediately behind that officer, who in turn moved apart one pace. These movements left the condemned man and the sergeant standing on the two ends of the same plank, which spanned three of the cross-ties of the bridge. The end upon which the civilian stood almost, but not quite, reached a fourth. This plank had been held in place by the weight of the captain; it was now held by that of the sergeant. At a signal from the former the latter would step aside, the plank would tilt and the condemned man go down between two ties. The arrangement commended itself to his judgement as simple and effective. His face had not been covered nor his eyes bandaged. He looked a moment at his "unsteadfast footing," then let his gaze wander to the swirling water of the stream racing madly beneath his feet. A piece of dancing driftwood caught his attention and his eyes followed it down the current. How slowly it appeared to move! What a sluggish stream!

He closed his eyes in order to fix his last thoughts upon his wife and children. The water, touched to gold by the early sun, the brooding mists under the banks at some distance down the stream, the fort, the soldiers, the piece of drift—all had distracted him. And now he became conscious of a new disturbance. Striking through the thought of his dear ones was sound which he could neither ignore nor understand, a sharp, distinct, metallic percussion like the stroke of a blacksmith's hammer upon the anvil; it had the same ringing quality. He wondered what it was, and whether immeasurably distant or near by— it seemed both. Its recurrence was regular, but as slow as the tolling of a death knell. He awaited each new stroke with impatience and—he knew not why—apprehension. The intervals of silence grew progressively longer; the delays became maddening. With their greater infrequency the sounds increased in strength and sharpness. They hurt his ear like the thrust of a knife; he feared he would shriek. What he heard was the ticking of his watch.

He unclosed his eyes and saw again the water below him. "If I could free my hands," he thought, "I might throw off the noose and spring into the stream. By diving I could evade the bullets and, swimming vigorously, reach the bank, take to the woods and get away home. My home, thank God, is as yet outside their lines; my wife and little ones are still beyond the invader's farthest advance."

As these thoughts, which have here to be set down in words, were flashed into the doomed man's brain rather than evolved from it the captain nodded to the sergeant. The sergeant stepped aside.

2

Peyton Farquhar was a well to do planter, of an old and highly respected Alabama family. Being a slave owner and like other slave owners a politician, he was naturally an original secessionist and ardently devoted to the Southern cause. Circumstances of an imperious nature, which it is unnecessary to relate here, had prevented him from taking service with that gallant army which had fought the disastrous campaigns ending with the fall of Corinth, and he chafed under the inglorious restraint, longing for the release of his energies, the larger life of the soldier, the opportunity for distinction. That opportunity, he felt, would come, as it comes to all in wartime. Meanwhile he did what he could. No service was too humble for him to perform in the aid of the South, no adventure too perilous for him to undertake if consistent with the character of a civilian who was at heart a soldier, and who in good faith and without too much qualification assented to at least a part of the frankly villainous dictum that all is fair in love and war.

One evening while Farquhar and his wife were sitting on a rustic bench near the entrance to his grounds, a gray-clad soldier rode up to the gate and asked for a drink of water. Mrs. Farquhar was only too happy to serve him with her own white hands. While she was fetching the water her husband approached the dusty horseman and inquired eagerly for news from the front.

"The Yanks are repairing the railroads," said the man, "and are getting ready for another advance. They have reached the Owl Creek bridge, put it in order and built a stockade on the north bank. The commandant has issued an order, which is posted everywhere, declaring that any civilian caught interfering with the railroad, its bridges, tunnels, or trains will be summarily hanged. I saw the order."

"How far is it to the Owl Creek bridge?" Farquhar asked.

"About thirty miles."

"Is there no force on this side of the creek?"

"Only a picket post half a mile out, on the railroad, and a single sentinel at this end of the bridge."

"Suppose a man—a civilian and student of hanging—should elude the picket post and perhaps get the better of the sentinel," said Farquhar, smiling, "what could he accomplish?"

The soldier reflected. "I was there a month ago," he replied. "I observed that the flood of last winter had lodged a great quantity of drift-wood against the wooden pier at this end of the bridge. It is now dry and would burn like tinder."

The lady had now brought the water, which the soldier drank. He thanked her ceremoniously, bowed to her husband and rode away. An hour later, after nightfall, he repassed the plantation, going northward in the direction from which he had come. He was a Federal scout.

3

As Peyton Farquhar fell straight downward through the bridge he lost consciousness and was as one already dead. From this state he was awakened—ages later, it seemed to him—by the pain of a sharp pres-sure upon his throat, followed by a sense of suffocation. Keen, poignant agonies seemed to shoot from his neck downward through every fiber of his body and limbs. These pains appeared to flash along well defined lines of ramification and to beat with an inconceivably rapid periodicity. They seemed like streams of pulsating fire heating him to an intolerable temperature. As to his head, he was conscious of nothing but a feeling of fullness—of congestion. These sensations were unaccompanied by thought. The intellectual part of his nature was already effaced; he had power only to feel, and feeling was torment. He was conscious of motion. Encompassed in a luminous cloud, of which he was now merely the fiery heart, without material substance, he swung through unthinkable arcs of oscillation, like a vast pendulum. Then all at once, with terrible sudden-ness, the light about him shot upward with the noise of a loud splash; a frightful roaring was in his ears, and all was cold and dark. The power of thought was restored; he knew that the rope had broken and he had fallen into the stream. There was no additional strangulation; the noose about his neck was already suffocating him and kept the water from his lungs. To die of hanging at the bottom of a river!—the idea seemed to him ludi-crous. He opened his eyes in the darkness and saw above him a gleam of light, but how distant, how inaccessible! He was still sinking, for the light became fainter and fainter until it was a mere glimmer. Then it began to grow and brighten, and he knew that he was rising toward the surface—knew it with reluctance, for he was now very comfortable. "To be hanged and drowned," he thought, "that is not so bad; but I do not wish to be shot. No; I will not be shot; that is not fair."

He was not conscious of an effort, but a sharp pain in his wrist apprised him that he was trying to free his hands. He gave the struggle his attention, as an idler might observe the feat of a juggler, without interest in the outcome. What splendid effort!—what magnificent, what superhuman strength! Ah, that was a fine endeavor! Bravo! The cord fell away; his arms parted and floated upward, the hands dimly seen on each side in the growing light. He watched them with a new interest as first one and then the other pounced upon the noose at his neck. They tore it away and thrust it fiercely aside, its undulations resembling those of a water snake. "Put it back, put it back!" He thought he shouted these words to his hands, for the undoing of the noose had been succeeded by the direst pang that he had yet experienced. His neck ached horribly; his brain was on fire, his heart, which had been fluttering faintly, gave a great leap, trying to force itself out at his mouth. His whole body was racked and wrenched with an insupportable anguish! But his disobedient hands gave no heed to the command. They beat the water vigorously with quick, downward strokes, forcing him to the surface. He felt his head emerge; his eyes were blinded by the sunlight; his chest expanded convulsively, and with a supreme and crowning agony his lungs engulfed a great draught of air, which instantly he expelled in a shriek!

He was now in full possession of his physical senses. They were, indeed, preternaturally keen and alert. Something in the awful disturbance of his organic system had so exalted and refined them that they made record of things never before perceived. He felt the ripples upon his face and heard their separate sounds as they struck. He looked at the forest on the bank of the stream, saw the individual trees, the leaves and the veining of each leaf—he saw the very insects upon them: the locusts, the brilliant bodied flies, the gray spiders stretching their webs from twig to twig. He noted the prismatic colors in all the dewdrops upon a million blades of grass. The humming of the gnats that danced above the eddies of the stream, the beating of the dragon flies' wings, the strokes of the water spiders' legs, like oars which had lifted their boat—all these made audible music. A fish slid along beneath his eyes and he heard the rush of its body parting the water.

He had come to the surface facing down the stream; in a moment the visible world seemed to wheel slowly round, himself the pivotal point, and he saw the bridge, the fort, the soldiers upon the bridge, the captain, the sergeant, the two privates, his executioners. They were in silhouette against the blue sky. They shouted and gesticulated, pointing at him. The captain had drawn his pistol, but did not fire; the others were unarmed. Their movements were grotesque and horrible, their forms gigantic.

Suddenly he heard a sharp report and something struck the water smartly within a few inches of his head, spattering his face with spray. He heard a second report, and saw one of the sentinels with his rifle at his shoulder, a light cloud of blue smoke rising from the muzzle. The man in the water saw the eye of the man on the bridge gazing into his own through the sights of the rifle. He observed that it was a gray eye and remembered having read that gray eyes were keenest, and that all famous marksmen had them. Nevertheless, this one had missed.

A counter-swirl had caught Farquhar and turned him half round; he was again looking at the forest on the bank opposite the fort. The sound of a clear, high voice in a monotonous singsong now rang out behind him and came across the water with a distinctness that pierced and subdued all other sounds, even the beating of the ripples in his ears. Although no soldier, he had frequented camps enough to know the dread significance of that deliberate, drawling, aspirated chant; the lieutenant on shore was taking a part in the morning's work. How coldly and pitilessly—with what an even, calm intonation, presaging, and enforcing tranquility in the men—with what accurately measured interval fell those cruel words:

"Company! . . . Attention! . . . Shoulder arms! . . . Ready!. . . Aim! . . . Fire!"

Farquhar dived—dived as deeply as he could. The water roared in his ears like the voice of Niagara, yet he heard the dull thunder of the volley and, rising again toward the surface, met shining bits of metal, singularly flattened, oscillating slowly downward. Some of them touched him on the face and hands, then fell away, continuing their descent. One lodged between his collar and neck; it was uncomfortably warm and he snatched it out.

As he rose to the surface, gasping for breath, he saw that he had been a long time under water; he was perceptibly farther downstream—nearer to safety. The soldiers had almost finished reloading; the metal ramrods flashed all at once in the sunshine as they were drawn from the barrels, turned in the air, and thrust into their sockets. The two sentinels fired again, independently and ineffectually.

The hunted man saw all this over his shoulder; he was now swimming vigorously with the current. His brain was as energetic as his arms and legs; he thought with the rapidity of lightning:

"The officer," he reasoned, "will not make that martinet's error a second time. It is as easy to dodge a volley as a single shot. He has probably already given the command to fire at will. God help me, I cannot dodge them all!"

An appalling splash within two yards of him was followed by a loud, rushing sound, DIMINUENDO, which seemed to travel back through the air to the fort and died in an explosion which stirred the very river to its deeps! A rising sheet of water curved over him, fell down upon him, blinded him, strangled him! The cannon had taken an hand in the game. As he shook his head free from the commotion of the smitten water he heard the deflected shot humming through the air ahead, and in an instant it was cracking and smashing the branches in the forest beyond.

"They will not do that again," he thought; "the next time they will use a charge of grape. I must keep my eye upon the gun; the smoke will apprise me—the report arrives too late; it lags behind the missile. That is a good gun."

Suddenly he felt himself whirled round and round—spinning like a top. The water, the banks, the forests, the now distant bridge, fort and men, all were commingled and blurred. Objects were represented by their colors only; circular horizontal streaks of color—that was all he saw. He had been caught in a vortex and was being whirled on with a velocity of advance and gyration that made him giddy and sick. In few moments he was flung upon the gravel at the foot of the left bank of the stream—the southern bank—and behind a projecting point which concealed him from his enemies. The sudden arrest of his motion, the abrasion of one of his hands on the gravel, restored him, and he wept with delight. He dug his fingers into the sand, threw it over himself in handfuls and audibly bless-ed it. It looked like diamonds, rubies, emeralds; he could think of nothing beautiful which it did not resemble. The trees upon the bank were giant garden plants; he noted a definite order in their arrangement, inhaled the fragrance of their blooms. A strange roseate light shone through the spaces among their trunks and the wind made in their branches the music of AEolian harps. He had not wish to perfect his escape—he was content to remain in that enchanting spot until retaken.

A whiz and a rattle of grapeshot among the branches high above his head roused him from his dream. The baffled cannoneer had fired him a random farewell. He sprang to his feet, rushed up the sloping bank, and plunged into the forest.

All that day he traveled, laying his course by the rounding sun. The forest seemed interminable; nowhere did he discover a break in it, not even a woodman's road. He had not known that he lived in so wild a region. There was something uncanny in the revelation.

By nightfall he was fatigued, footsore, famished. The thought of his wife and children urged him on. At last he found a road which led him in what he knew to be the right direction. It was as wide and straight as a city street, yet it seemed untraveled. No fields bordered it, no dwell-ing anywhere. Not so much as the barking of a dog suggested human habitation. The black bodies of the trees formed a straight wall on both sides, terminating on the horizon in a point, like a diagram in a lesson in perspective. Overhead, as he looked up through this rift in the wood, shone great golden stars looking unfamiliar and grouped in strange constellations. He was sure they were arranged in some order which had a secret and malign significance. The wood on either side was full of singular noises, among which—once, twice, and again—he distinctly heard whispers in an unknown tongue.

His neck was in pain and lifting his hand to it found it horribly swollen. He knew that it had a circle of black where the rope had bruised it. His eyes felt congested; he could no longer close them. His tongue was swollen with thirst; he relieved its fever by thrusting it forward from between his teeth into the cold air. How softly the turf had carpeted the untraveled avenue—he could no longer feel the roadway beneath his feet!

Doubtless, despite his suffering, he had fallen asleep while walking, for now he sees another scene—perhaps he has merely recovered from a delirium. He stands at the gate of his own home. All is as he left it, and all bright and beautiful in the morning sunshine. He must have traveled the entire night. As he pushes open the gate and passes up the wide white walk, he sees a flutter of female garments; his wife, looking fresh and cool and sweet, steps down from the veranda to meet him. At the bottom of the steps she stands waiting, with a smile of ineffable joy, an attitude of matchless grace and dignity. Ah, how beautiful she is! He springs forwards with extended arms. As he is about to clasp her he feels a stunning blow upon the back of the neck; a blinding white light blazes all about him with a sound like the shock of a cannon—then all is darkness and silence!

Peyton Farquhar was dead; his body, with a broken neck, swung gently from side to side beneath the timbers of the Owl Creek bridge.

COLLEGE WRITING 1: REFLECTION WITHIN THE TEXT

Imagine joining something to gain recognition. Imagine that you don't totally believe in the cause. How do you feel participating in something that you do not truly believe in? What happens? What becomes of you—and your relationships. Do you regret it? Write a story, like Farquhar's delusion of escape, in which you somehow get out of the consequences of joining.

COLLEGE WRITING 2: RESEARCH OUTSIDE THE TEXT

In Bierce's "Occurrence at Owl Creek Bridge," Peyton Farquhar attempts to sabotage a Union Army supply line. Like Payton, people choose to fight for their countries in times of war, even though there is a risk of dying. What could possibly convince someone to gamble with their life? Or is that not how soldiers see it? Do all soldiers fully believe that they could die?

Research how recruits are convinced to risk their lives. Does the way in which we talk about war, and the causes being fought for, affect the soldier's expectations?

IDEAS AND VALUES: CONNECT THE TEXT

» In Jack London's "To Build A Fire" the main character is faced with the necessity of building a fire to ensure his survival. Yet his need for fire is determined by earlier choices he made. In Ambrose Bierce's "Occurrence at Owl Creek Bridge" Peyton Farquhar is fighting to escape his situation in order to survive—but again, his earlier choices are what led to his hanging. In Ryunosuke Akutagawa's "Rashōmon" Rashōmon must make a choice that will determine his ability to survive after he is let go a servant due only to the economic situation of his master. His conversation with the wig-maker leads him to his decision. How do each of these characters survive? What specific elements affects each of their ability to survive? What choices do the characters face that affect their ability to survive? What sacrifices are worth making in order to survive? Why are the characters willing and able, or not, to make these choices?

»   In Twain's "The War Prayer" he writes that "The country was up in arms, the war was on, in every breast burned the holy fire of patriotism," when a stranger mounts the stage, declares himself the messenger of God, and explains what the people's "War Prayer" truly means for the enemy. In "Occurrence at Owl Creek Bridge," Peyton Farquhar seems to be the "enemy," the one that doesn't belong—and finally in "The Machine Stops," E.M. Forester writes about a different kind of belonging—not to a nation, but to a way of life; to a machine not unlike today's Internet. These are three different views of belonging; what does it mean to belong? What is it for? What is the "other side" of belonging? In order for one to belong, must there be others who do not belong? What effect does it have, and why do humans do it? Is belonging ultimately a good, or a bad thing?

»   How does the thought of glory motivate the characters in Mark Twain's "The War Prayer," Ambrose Bierce's "Occurrence at Owl Creek Bridge," and Twain's "The Stolen White Elephant"? Does glory motivate people to do good? Is one man's glory another man's glory as well? What is glory, after all?

The New Dress

By Virginia Woolf

3,211 WORDS. 18 MINUTES.
READING LEVEL: GRADE 11.2

Mabel had her first serious suspicion that something was wrong as she took her cloak off and Mrs. Barnet, while handing her the mirror and touching the brushes and thus drawing her attention, perhaps rather markedly, to all the appliances for tidying and improving hair, complexion, clothes, which existed on the dressing table, confirmed the suspicion—that it was not right, not quite right, which growing stronger as she went upstairs and springing at her, with conviction as she greeted Clarissa Dalloway, she went straight to the far end of the room, to a shaded corner where a looking-glass hung and looked. No! It was not RIGHT. And at once the misery which she always tried to hide, the profound dissatisfaction—the sense she had had, ever since she was a child, of being inferior to other people—set upon her, relentlessly, remorselessly, with an intensity which she could not beat off, as she would when she woke at night at home, by reading Borrow or Scott; for oh these men, oh these women, all were thinking—"What's Mabel wearing? What a fright she looks! What a hideous new dress!"—their eyelids flickering as they came up and then their lids shutting rather tight. It was her own appalling inadequacy; her cowardice; her mean, water-sprinkled blood that depressed her. And at once the whole of the room where, for ever so many hours, she had planned with the little dressmaker how it was to go, seemed sordid, repulsive; and her own drawing-room so shabby, and herself, going out, puffed up with vanity as she touched the letters on the hall table and said: "How dull!" to show off—all this now seemed unutterably silly, paltry, and provincial. All this had been absolutely destroyed, shown up, exploded, the moment she came into Mrs. Dalloway's drawing-room.

What she had thought that evening when, sitting over the teacups, Mrs. Dalloway's invitation came, was that, of course, she could not be fashionable. It was absurd to pretend it even—fashion meant cut, meant style, meant thirty guineas at least—but why not be original? Why not be herself, anyhow? And, getting up, she had taken that old fashion book of her mother's, a Paris fashion book of the time of the Empire, and had thought how much prettier, more dignified, and more womanly they were then, and so set herself—oh, it was foolish—trying to be like them, pluming herself in fact, upon being modest and old-fashioned, and very charming, giving herself up, no doubt about it, to an orgy of self-love, which deserved to be chastised, and so rigged herself out like this.

But she dared not look in the glass. She could not face the whole horror—the pale yellow, idiotically old-fashioned silk dress with its long skirt and its high sleeves and its waist and all the things that looked so charming in the fashion book, but not on her, not among all these ordinary people. She felt like a dressmaker's dummy standing there, for young people to stick pins into.

"But, my dear, it's perfectly charming!" Rose Shaw said, looking her up and down with that little satirical pucker of the lips which she expected—Rose herself being dressed in the height of the fashion, precisely like everybody else, always.

We are all like flies trying to crawl over the edge of the saucer, Mabel thought, and repeated the phrase as if she were crossing herself, as if she were trying to find some spell to annul this pain, to make this agony endurable. Tags of Shakespeare, lines from books she had read ages ago, suddenly came to her when she was in agony, and she repeated them over and over again. "Flies trying to crawl," she repeated. If she could say that over often enough and make herself see the flies, she would become numb, chill, frozen, dumb. Now she could see flies crawling slowly out of a saucer of milk with their wings stuck together; and she strained and strained (standing in front of the looking-glass, listening to Rose Shaw) to make herself see Rose Shaw and all the other people there as flies, trying to hoist themselves out of something, or into something, meagre, insignificant, toiling flies. But she could not see them like that, not other people. She saw herself like that—she was a fly, but the others were dragonflies, butterflies, beautiful insects, dancing, fluttering, skimming, while she alone dragged herself up out of the saucer. (Envy and spite, the most detestable of the vices, were her chief faults.)

"I feel like some dowdy, decrepit, horribly dingy old fly," she said, making Robert Haydon stop just to hear her say that, just to reassure herself by furbishing up a poor weak-kneed phrase and so showing how detached she was, how witty, that she did not feel in the least out of anything. And, of course, Robert Haydon answered something, quite polite, quite insincere, which she saw through instantly, and said to herself, directly he went (again from some book), "Lies, lies, lies!" For a party makes things either much more real, or much less real, she thought; she saw in a flash to the bottom of Robert Haydon's heart; she saw through everything. She saw the truth. THIS was true, this drawing-room, this self, and the other false. Miss Milan's little workroom was really terribly hot, stuffy, sordid. It smelt of clothes and cabbage cooking; and yet, when Miss Milan put the glass in her hand, and she looked at herself with the dress on, finished, an extraordinary bliss shot through her heart. Suffused with light, she sprang into existence. Rid of cares and wrinkles, what she had dreamed of herself was there—a beautiful woman. just for a second (she had not dared look longer, Miss Milan wanted to know about the length of the skirt), there looked at her, framed in the scrolloping mahogany, a grey-white, mysteriously smiling, charming girl, the core of herself, the soul of herself; and it was not vanity only, not only self-love that made her think it good, tender, and true. Miss Milan said that the skirt could not well be longer; if anything the skirt, said Miss Milan, puckering her forehead, considering with all her wits about her, must be shorter; and she felt, suddenly, honestly, full of love for Miss Milan, much, much fonder of Miss Milan than of any one in the whole world, and could have cried for pity that she should be crawling on the floor with her mouth full of pins, and her face red and her eyes bulging—that one human being should be doing this for another, and she saw them all as human beings merely, and herself going off to her party, and Miss Milan pulling the cover over the canary's cage, or letting him pick a hemp-seed from between her lips, and the thought of it, of this side of human nature and its patience and its endurance and its being content with such miserable, scanty, sordid, little pleasures filled her eyes with tears.

And now the whole thing had vanished. The dress, the room, the love, the pity, the scrolloping looking-glass, and the canary's cage—all had vanished, and here she was in a corner of Mrs. Dalloway's drawing-room, suffering tortures, woken wide awake to reality.

But it was all so paltry, weak-blooded, and petty-minded to care so much at her age with two children, to be still so utterly dependent on people's opinions and not have principles or convictions, not to be able to say as other people did, "There's Shakespeare! There's death! We're all weevils in a captain's biscuit"—or whatever it was that people did say.

She faced herself straight in the glass; she pecked at her left shoulder; she issued out into the room, as if spears were thrown at her yellow dress from all sides. But instead of looking fierce or tragic, as Rose Shaw would have done—Rose would have looked like Boadicea—she looked foolish and self-conscious, and simpered like a schoolgirl and slouched across the room, positively slinking, as if she were a beaten mongrel, and looked at a picture, an engraving. As if one went to a party to look at a picture! Everybody knew why she did it—it was from shame, from humiliation.

"Now the fly's in the saucer," she said to herself, "right in the middle, and can't get out, and the milk," she thought, rigidly staring at the picture, "is sticking its wings together."

"It's so old-fashioned," she said to Charles Burt, making him stop (which by itself he hated) on his way to talk to some one else.

She meant, or she tried to make herself think that she meant, that it was the picture and not her dress, that was old-fashioned. And one word of praise, one word of affection from Charles would have made all the difference to her at the moment. If he had only said, "Mabel, you're looking charming to-night!" it would have changed her life. But then she ought to have been truthful and direct. Charles said nothing of the kind, of course. He was malice itself. He always saw through one, especially if one were feeling particularly mean, paltry, or feeble-minded.

"Mabel's got a new dress!" he said, and the poor fly was absolutely shoved into the middle of the saucer. Really, he would like her to drown, she believed. He had no heart, no fundamental kindness, only a veneer of friendliness. Miss Milan was much more real, much kinder. If only one could feel that and stick to it, always. "Why," she asked herself—replying to Charles much too pertly, letting him see that she was out of temper, or "ruffled" as he called it ("Rather ruffled?" he said and went on to laugh at her with some woman over there)—"Why," she asked herself, "can't I feel one thing always, feel quite sure that Miss Milan is right, and Charles wrong and stick to it, feel sure about the canary and pity and love and not be whipped all round in a second by coming into a room full of people?" It was her odious, weak, vacillating character again, always giving at the critical moment and not being seriously interested in conchology, etymology, botany, archeology, cutting up potatoes and watching them fructify like Mary Dennis, like Violet Searle.

Then Mrs. Holman, seeing her standing there, bore down upon her. Of course a thing like a dress was beneath Mrs. Holman's notice, with her family always tumbling downstairs or having the scarlet fever. Could Mabel tell her if Elmthorpe was ever let for August and September? Oh, it was a conversation that bored her unutterably!—it made her furious to be treated like a house agent or a messenger boy, to be made use of. Not to have value, that was it, she thought, trying to grasp something hard, something real, while she tried to answer sensibly about the bathroom and the south aspect and the hot water to the top of the house; and all the time she could see little bits of her yellow dress in the round look-ing-glass which made them all the size of boot-buttons or tadpoles; and it was amazing to think how much humiliation and agony and self-loathing and effort and passionate ups and downs of feeling were contained in a thing the size of a threepenny bit. And what was still odder, this thing, this Mabel Waring, was separate, quite disconnected; and though Mrs. Holman (the black button) was leaning forward and telling her how her eldest boy had strained his heart running, she could see her, too, quite detached in the looking-glass, and it was impossible that the black dot, leaning forward, gesticulating, should make the yellow dot, sitting soli-tary, self-centred, feel what the black dot was feeling, yet they pretended.

"So impossible to keep boys quiet"—that was the kind of thing one said.

And Mrs. Holman, who could never get enough sympathy and snatched what little there was greedily, as if it were her right (but she deserved much more for there was her little girl who had come down this morning with a swollen knee-joint), took this miserable offering and looked at it suspiciously, grudgingly, as if it were a halfpenny when it ought to have been a pound and put it away in her purse, must put up with it, mean and miserly though it was, times being hard, so very hard; and on she went, creaking, injured Mrs. Holman, about the girl with the swollen joints. Ah, it was tragic, this greed, this clamour of human beings, like a row of cormorants, barking and flapping their wings for sympa-thy—it was tragic, could one have felt it and not merely pretended to feel it!

But in her yellow dress to-night she could not wring out one drop more; she wanted it all, all for herself. She knew (she kept on looking into the glass, dipping into that dreadfully showing-up blue pool) that she was condemned, despised, left like this in a backwater, because of her being like this a feeble, vacillating creature; and it seemed to her that the yellow dress was a penance which she had deserved, and if she had been dressed like Rose Shaw, in lovely, clinging green with a ruffle of swansdown, she would have deserved that; and she thought that there was no escape for her—none whatever. But it was not her fault altogether, after all. It was being one of a family of ten; never having money enough, always skimping and paring; and her mother carrying great cans, and the lino-leum worn on the stair edges, and one sordid little domestic tragedy after another—nothing catastrophic, the sheep farm failing, but not utterly; her eldest brother marrying beneath him but not very much—there was no romance, nothing extreme about them all. They petered out respectably in seaside resorts; every watering-place had one of her aunts even now asleep in some lodging with the front windows not quite facing the sea. That was so like them—they had to squint at things always. And she had done the same—she was just like her aunts. For all her dreams of living in India, married to some hero like Sir Henry Lawrence, some empire builder (still the sight of a native in a turban filled her with romance), she had failed utterly. She had married Hubert, with his safe, permanent underling's job in the Law Courts, and they managed tolerably in a smallish house, without proper maids, and hash when she was alone or just bread and butter, but now and then—Mrs. Holman was off, thinking her the most dried-up, unsympathetic twig she had ever met, absurdly dressed, too, and would tell every one about Mabel's fantastic appearance—now and then, thought Mabel Waring, left alone on the blue sofa, punching the cushion in order to look occupied, for she would not join Charles Burt and Rose Shaw, chattering like magpies and perhaps laughing at her by the fire-place—now and then, there did come to her delicious moments, reading the other night in bed, for instance, or down by the sea on the sand in the sun, at Easter—let her recall it—a great tuft of pale sand-grass standing all twisted like a shock of spears against the sky, which was blue like a smooth china egg, so firm, so hard, and then the melody of the waves— "Hush, hush," they said, and the children's shouts paddling—yes, it was a divine moment, and there she lay, she felt, in the hand of the Goddess who was the world; rather a hard-hearted, but very beautiful Goddess, a little lamb laid on the altar (one did think these silly things, and it didn't matter so long as one never said them). And also with Hubert sometimes she had quite unexpectedly—carving the mutton for Sunday lunch, for no reason, opening a letter, coming into a room—divine moments, when she said to herself (for she would never say this to anybody else), "This is it. This has happened. This is it!" And the other way about it was equally surprising—that is, when everything was arranged—music, weather, holidays, every reason for happiness was there—then nothing happened at all. One wasn't happy. It was flat, just flat, that was all.

Her wretched self again, no doubt! She had always been a fretful, weak, unsatisfactory mother, a wobbly wife, lolling about in a kind of twilight existence with nothing very clear or very bold, or more one thing than another, like all her brothers and sisters, except perhaps Herbert—they were all the same poor water-veined creatures who did nothing. Then in the midst of this creeping, crawling life, suddenly she was on the crest of a wave. That wretched fly—where had she read the story that kept coming into her mind about the fly and the saucer?—struggled out. Yes, she had those moments. But now that she was forty, they might come more and more seldom. By degrees she would cease to struggle any more. But that was deplorable! That was not to be endured! That made her feel ashamed of herself!

She would go to the London Library to-morrow. She would find some wonderful, helpful, astonishing book, quite by chance, a book by a clergyman, by an American no one had ever heard of; or she would walk down the Strand and drop, accidentally, into a hall where a miner was telling about the life in the pit, and suddenly she would become a new person. She would be absolutely transformed. She would wear a uniform; she would be called Sister Somebody; she would never give a thought to clothes again. And for ever after she would be perfectly clear about Charles Burt and Miss Milan and this room and that room; and it would be always, day after day, as if she were lying in the sun or carving the mutton. It would be it!

So she got up from the blue sofa, and the yellow button in the looking-glass got up too, and she waved her hand to Charles and Rose to show them she did not depend on them one scrap, and the yellow button moved out of the looking-glass, and all the spears were gathered into her breast as she walked towards Mrs. Dalloway and said "Good night."

"But it's too early to go," said Mrs. Dalloway, who was always so charming.

"I'm afraid I must," said Mabel Waring. "But," she added in her weak, wobbly voice which only sounded ridiculous when she tried to strengthen it, "I have enjoyed myself enormously."

'I have enjoyed myself," she said to Mr. Dalloway, whom she met on the stairs.

"Lies, lies, lies!" she said to herself, going downstairs, and "Right in the saucer!" she said to herself as she thanked Mrs. Barnet for helping her and wrapped herself, round and round and round, in the Chinese cloak she had worn these twenty years.

COLLEGE WRITING 1: REFLECTION WITHIN THE TEXT

Insert yourself into the party, and knowing the anxiety that Mabel feels about her new dress—say something to her. While you're at it, write a letter to Mrs. Barnet, explaining exactly the situation with Mabel, and what Mrs. Barnet could do differently—if anything—for her young friend Mabel.

COLLEGE WRITING 2: RESEARCH OUTSIDE THE TEXT

Research the role of women leading up to the 1920s. How had it evolved and why had it evolved to that point? What were the economic and social pressures that affected women in America at that time? Using your research explain Mabel's behavior and perspective.

IDEAS AND VALUES: CONNECT THE TEXT

» How do the outcasts in Hawthorne's "Wakefield," Woolf's "The New Dress," and Chesnutt's "The Sheriff's Children" differ? How are they the same? Why are the characters outcasts? Who casts them out? How does society view each of the outcasts in these stories? What kind of society would cast these people out?

» In Akutagawa's short story "Rashōmon" the ex-servant of a samurai struggles with whether or not to become a thief, and in Virginia Woolf's "The New Dress," Mabel is absolutely consumed with the question of her appearance in her new dress, and the judgments of those who surround her, and in W.E.B. Du Bois's "Of Our Spiritual Strivings" he writes, "It dawned upon me with a certain suddenness that I was different from the others; or like, mayhap, in heart and life and longing, but shut out from their world by a vast veil." In these three texts there are three extremely different accounts of a struggle for identity—of that question of sameness and of quality of a person. What can be said for all of them? What makes them different? What can be made of this struggle for identity—why is it important—is it?

» In Gilman's "The Yellow Wallpaper" the main character believes she can see a woman living in the walls, and in Woolf's "The Dress" a young woman obsesses over her appearance, and lastly in Conrad's "One Day

More", Captain Hagbeard is said to be crazy, as he always believes that his son will return "tomorrow," even after his son has returned today! But what is the nature of what we call "mental illness?" Is it an illness, like the common cold—do we "catch it" from the air? Or does it form some other way? Is there an environmental aspect to mental illnesses, or are we merely born destined to be sane or...ill?

The Star

By H.G. Wells

4,457 WORDS. 25 MINUTES.
READING LEVEL: GRADE 11.1

It was on the first day of the new year that the announcement was made, almost simultaneously from three observatories, that the motion of the planet Neptune, the outermost of all the planets that wheel about the sun, had become very erratic. Ogilvy had already called attention to a suspected retardation in its velocity in December. Such a piece of news was scarcely calculated to interest a world the greater portion of whose inhabitants were unaware of the existence of the planet Neptune, nor outside the astronomical profession did the subsequent discovery of a faint remote speck of light in the region of the perturbed planet cause any very great excitement. Scientific people, however, found the intelligence remarkable enough, even before it became known that the new body was rapidly growing larger and brighter, that its motion was quite different from the orderly progress of the planets, and that the deflection of Neptune and its[38] satellite was becoming now of an unprecedented kind.

Few people without a training in science can realise the huge isolation of the solar system. The sun with its specks of planets, its dust of planetoids, and its impalpable comets, swims in a vacant immensity that almost defeats the imagination. Beyond the orbit of Neptune there is space, vacant so far as human observation has penetrated, without warmth or light or sound, blank emptiness, for twenty million times a million miles. That is the smallest estimate of the distance to be traversed before the very nearest of the stars is attained. And, saving a few comets more unsubstantial than the thinnest flame, no matter had ever to human knowledge crossed this gulf of space, until early in the twentieth century this strange wanderer appeared. A vast mass of matter it was, bulky, heavy, rushing without warning out of the black mystery of the sky into the radiance of the sun. By the second day it was clearly visible to any decent instrument, as a speck with a barely sensible diameter, in the constellation Leo near Regulus. In a little while an opera glass could attain it.

On the third day of the new year the newspaper readers of two hemispheres were made aware for the first time of the real importance of this unusual apparition in the heavens. "A Planetary Collision," one London paper headed the news, and proclaimed Duchaine's opinion that this strange new planet would probably collide with Neptune. The leader writers enlarged upon the topic. So that in most of the capitals of the world, on January 3rd, there was an expectation, however vague of some imminent phenomenon in the sky; and as the night followed the sunset round the globe, thousands of men turned their eyes skyward to see—the old familiar stars just as they had always been.

Until it was dawn in London and Pollux setting and the stars overhead grown pale. The Winter's dawn it was, a sickly filtering accumulation of daylight, and the light of gas and candles shone yellow in the windows to show where people were astir. But the yawning policeman saw the thing, the busy crowds in the markets stopped agape, workmen going to their work betimes, milkmen, the drivers of news-carts, dissipation going home jaded and pale, homeless wanderers, sentinels on their beats, and in the country, labourers trudging afield, poachers slinking home, all over the dusky quickening country it could be seen—and out at sea by seamen watching for the day—a great white star, come suddenly into the westward sky!

Brighter it was than any star in our skies; brighter than the evening star at its brightest. It still glowed out white and large, no mere twinkling spot of light, but a small round clear shining disc, an hour after the day had come. And where science has not reached, men stared and feared, telling one another of the wars and pestilences that are foreshadowed by these fiery signs in the Heavens. Sturdy Boers, dusky Hottentots, Gold Coast negroes, Frenchmen, Spaniards, Portuguese, stood in the warmth of the sunrise watching the setting of this strange new star.

And in a hundred observatories there had been suppressed excitement, rising almost to shouting pitch, as the two remote bodies had rushed together, and a hurrying to and fro, to gather photographic apparatus and spectroscope, and this appliance and that, to record this novel astonishing sight, the destruction of a world. For it was a world, a sister planet of our earth, far greater than our earth indeed, that had so suddenly flashed into flaming death. Neptune it was, had been struck, fairly and squarely, by the strange planet from outer space and the heat of the concussion had incontinently turned two solid globes into one vast mass of incandescence. Round the world that day, two hours before the dawn, went the pallid great white star, fading only as it sank westward and the sun mounted above it. Everywhere men marvelled at it, but of all those who saw it none could have marvelled more than those sailors, habitual watchers of the stars, who far away at sea had heard nothing of its advent and saw it now rise like a pigmy moon and climb zenithward and hang overhead and sink westward with the passing of the night.

And when next it rose over Europe everywhere were crowds of watchers on hilly slopes, on house-roofs, in open spaces, staring eastward for the rising of the great new star. It rose with a white glow in front of it, like the glare of a white fire, and those who had seen it come into existence the night before cried out at the sight of it. "It is larger," they cried. "It is brighter!" And, indeed the moon a quarter full and sinking in the west was in its apparent size beyond comparison, but scarcely in all its breadth had it as much brightness now as the little circle of the strange new star.

"It is brighter!" cried the people clustering in the streets. But in the dim observatories the watchers held their breath and peered at one another. "It is nearer," they said. "Nearer!"

And voice after voice repeated, "It is nearer," and the clicking telegraph took that up, and it trembled along telephone wires, and in a thousand cities grimy compositors fingered the type. "It is nearer." Men writing in offices, struck with a strange realisation, flung down their pens, men talking in a thousand places suddenly came upon a grotesque possibility in those words, "It is nearer." It hurried along awakening streets, it was shouted down the frost-stilled ways of quiet villages, men who had read these things from the throbbing tape stood in yellow-lit doorways shouting the news to the passers-by. "It is nearer." Pretty women, flushed and glittering, heard the news told jestingly between the dances, and feigned an intelligent interest they did not feel. "Nearer! Indeed. How curious! How very, very clever people must be to find out things like that!"

Lonely tramps faring through the wintry night murmured those words to comfort themselves—looking skyward. "It has need to be nearer, for the night's as cold as charity. Don't seem much warmth from it if it is nearer, all the same."

"What is a new star to me?" cried the weeping woman kneeling beside her dead.

The schoolboy, rising early for his examination work, puzzled it out for himself—with the great white star, shining broad and bright through the frost-flowers of his window. "Centrifugal, centripetal," he said, with his chin on his fist. "Stop a planet in its flight, rob it of its centrifugal force, what then? Centripetal has it, and down it falls into the sun! And this—!"

"Do we come in the way? I wonder—"

The light of that day went the way of its brethren, and with the later watches of the frosty darkness rose the strange star again. And it was now so bright that the waxing moon seemed but a pale yellow ghost of itself, hanging huge in the sunset. In a South African city a great man had married, and the streets were alight to welcome his return with his bride. "Even the skies have illuminated," said the flatterer. Under Capricorn, two negro lovers, daring the wild beasts and evil spirits, for love of one another, crouched together in a cane brake where the fire-flies hovered. "That is our star," they whispered, and felt strangely comforted by the sweet brilliance of its light.

The master mathematician sat in his private room and pushed the papers from him. His calculations were already finished. In a small white phial there still remained a little of the drug that had kept him awake and active for four long nights. Each day, serene, explicit, patient as ever, he had given his lecture to his students, and then had come back at once to this momentous calculation. His face was grave, a little drawn and hectic from his drugged activity. For some time he seemed lost in thought. Then he went to the window, and the blind went up with a click. Half way up the sky, over the clustering roofs, chimneys and steeples of the city, hung the star.

He looked at it as one might look into the eyes of a brave enemy. "You may kill me," he said after a silence. "But I can hold you—and all the universe for that matter—in the grip of this little brain. I would not change. Even now."

He looked at the little phial. "There will be no need of sleep again," he said. The next day at noon, punctual to the minute, he entered his lecture theatre, put his hat on the end of the table as his habit was, and carefully selected a large piece of chalk. It was a joke among his students that he could not lecture without that piece of chalk to fumble in his fingers, and once he had been stricken to impotence by their hiding his supply. He came and looked under his grey eyebrows at the rising tiers of young fresh faces, and spoke with his accustomed studied commonness of phrasing. "Circumstances have arisen—circumstances beyond my control," he said and paused, "which will debar me from completing the course I had designed. It would seem, gentlemen, if I may put the thing clearly and briefly, that—Man has lived in vain."

The students glanced at one another. Had they heard aright? Mad? Raised eyebrows and grinning lips there were, but one or two faces remained intent upon his calm grey-fringed face. "It will be interesting," he was saying, "to devote this morning to an exposition, so far as I can make it clear to you, of the calculations that have led me to this conclusion. Let us assume—"

He turned towards the blackboard, meditating a diagram in the way that was usual to him. "What was that about 'lived in vain?'" whispered one student to another. "Listen," said the other, nodding towards the lecturer.

And presently they began to understand.

That night the star rose later, for its proper eastward motion had carried it some way across Leo towards Virgo, and its brightness was so great that the sky became a luminous blue as it rose, and every star was hidden in its turn, save only Jupiter near the zenith, Capella, Aldebaran, Sirius and the pointers of the Bear. It was very white and beautiful. In many parts of the world that night a pallid halo encircled it about. It was perceptibly larger; in the clear refractive sky of the tropics it seemed as if it were nearly a quarter the size of the moon. The frost was still on the ground in England, but the world was as brightly lit as if it were midsummer moonlight. One could see to read quite ordinary print by that cold clear light, and in the cities the lamps burnt yellow and wan.

And everywhere the world was awake that night, and throughout Christendom a sombre murmur hung in the keen air over the countryside like the belling of bees in the heather, and this murmurous tumult grew to a clangour in the cities. It was the tolling of the bells in a million belfry towers and steeples, summoning the people to sleep no more, to sin no more, but to gather in their churches and pray. And overhead, growing larger and brighter, as the earth rolled on its way and the night passed, rose the dazzling star.

And the streets and houses were alight in all the cities, the shipyards glared, and whatever roads led to high country were lit and crowded all night long. And in all the seas about the civilised lands, ships with throbbing engines, and ships with bellying sails, crowded with men and living creatures, were standing out to ocean and the north. For already the warning of the master mathematician had been telegraphed all over the world, and translated into a hundred tongues. The new planet and Neptune, locked in a fiery embrace, were whirling headlong, ever faster and faster towards the sun. Already every second this blazing mass flew a hundred miles, and every second its terrific velocity increased. As it flew now, indeed, it must pass a hundred million of miles wide of the earth and scarcely affect it. But near its destined path, as yet only slightly perturbed, spun the mighty planet Jupiter and his moons sweeping splendid round the sun. Every moment now the attraction between the fiery star and the greatest of the planets grew stronger. And the result of that attraction? Inevitably Jupiter would be deflected from its orbit into an elliptical path, and the burning star, swung by his attraction wide of its sunward rush, would "describe a curved path" and perhaps collide with, and certainly pass very close to, our earth. "Earthquakes, volcanic outbreaks, cyclones, sea waves, floods, and a steady rise in temperature to I know not what limit"—so prophesied the master mathematician.

And overhead, to carry out his words, lonely and cold and livid, blazed the star of the coming doom.

To many who stared at it that night until their eyes ached, it seemed that it was visibly approaching. And that night, too, the weather changed, and the frost that had gripped all Central Europe and France and England softened towards a thaw.

But you must not imagine because I have spoken of people praying through the night and people going aboard ships and people fleeing towards mountainous country that the whole world was already in a terror because of the star. As a matter of fact, use and wont still ruled the world, and save for the talk of idle moments and the splendour of the night, nine human beings out of ten were still busy at their common occupations. In all the cities the shops, save one here and there, opened and closed at their proper hours, the doctor and the undertaker plied their trades, the workers gathered in the factories, soldiers drilled, scholars studied, lovers sought one another, thieves lurked and fled, politicians planned their schemes. The presses of the newspapers roared through the nights, and many a priest of this church and that would not open his holy building to further what he considered a foolish panic. The newspapers insisted on the lesson of the year 1000—for then, too, people had anticipated the end. The star was no star—mere gas—a comet; and were it a star it could not possibly strike the earth. There was no precedent for such a thing. Common sense was sturdy everywhere, scornful, jesting, a little inclined to persecute the obdurate fearful. That night, at seven-fifteen by Greenwich time, the star would be at its nearest to Jupiter. Then the world would see the turn things would take. The master mathematician's grim warnings were treated by many as so much mere elaborate self-advertisement. Common sense at last, a little heated by argument, signified its unalterable convictions by going to bed. So, too, barbarism and savagery, already tired of the novelty, went about their nightly business, and save for a howling dog here and there, the beast world left the star unheeded.

And yet, when at last the watchers in the European States saw the star rise, an hour later it is true, but no larger than it had been the night before, there were still plenty awake to laugh at the master mathematician—to take the danger as if it had passed.

But hereafter the laughter ceased. The star grew—it grew with a terrible steadiness hour after hour, a little larger each hour, a little nearer the midnight zenith, and brighter and brighter, until it had turned night into a second day. Had it come straight to the earth instead of in a curved path, had it lost no velocity to Jupiter, it must have leapt the intervening gulf in a day, but as it was it took five days altogether to come by our planet. The next night it had become a third the size of the moon before it set to English eyes, and the thaw was assured. It rose over America near the size of the moon, but blinding white to look at, and hot; and a breath of hot wind blew now with its rising and gathering strength, and in Virginia, and Brazil, and down the St. Lawrence valley, it shone intermittently through a driving reek of thunder-clouds, flickering violet lightning, and hail unprecedented. In Manitoba was a thaw and devastating floods. And upon all the mountains of the earth the snow and ice began to melt that night, and all the rivers coming out of high country flowed thick and turbid, and soon—in their upper reaches—with swirling trees and the bodies of beasts and men. They rose steadily, steadily in the ghostly brilliance, and came trickling over their banks at last, behind the flying population of their valleys.

And along the coast of Argentina and up the South Atlantic the tides were higher than had ever been in the memory of man, and the storms drove the waters in many cases scores of miles inland, drowning whole cities. And so great grew the heat during the night that the rising of the sun was like the coming of a shadow. The earthquakes began and grew until all down America from the Arctic Circle to Cape Horn, hillsides were sliding, fissures were opening, and houses and walls crumbling to destruction. The whole side of Cotopaxi slipped out in one vast convulsion, and a tumult of lava poured out so high and broad and swift and liquid that in one day it reached the sea.

So the star, with the wan moon in its wake, marched across the Pacific, trailed the thunderstorms like the hem of a robe, and the growing tidal wave that toiled behind it, frothing and eager, poured over island and island and swept them clear of men. Until that wave came at last—in a blinding light and with the breath of a furnace, swift and terrible it came—a wall of water, fifty feet high, roaring hungrily, upon the long coasts of Asia, and swept inland across the plains of China. For a space the star, hotter now and larger and brighter than the sun in its strength, showed with pitiless brilliance the wide and populous country; towns and villages with their pagodas and trees, roads, wide cultivated fields, millions of sleepless people staring in helpless terror at the incandescent sky; and then, low and growing, came the murmur of the flood. And thus it was with millions of men that night—a flight nowhither, with limbs heavy with heat and breath fierce and scant, and the flood like a wall swift and white behind. And then death.

China was lit glowing white, but over Japan and Java and all the islands of Eastern Asia the great star was a ball of dull red fire because of the steam and smoke and ashes the volcanoes were spouting forth to salute its coming. Above was the lava, hot gases and ash, and below the seething floods, and the whole earth swayed and rumbled with the earthquake shocks. Soon the immemorial snows of Thibet and the Himalaya were melting and pouring down by ten million deepening converging channels upon the plains of Burmah and Hindostan. The tangled summits of the Indian jungles were aflame in a thousand places, and below the hurrying waters around the stems were dark objects that still struggled feebly and reflected the blood-red tongues of fire. And in a rudderless confusion a multitude of men and women fled down the broad river-ways to that one last hope of men—the open sea.

Larger grew the star, and larger, hotter, and brighter with a terrible swiftness now. The tropical ocean had lost its phosphorescence, and the whirling steam rose in ghostly wreaths from the black waves that plunged incessantly, speckled with storm-tossed ships.

And then came a wonder. It seemed to those who in Europe watched for the rising of the star that the world must have ceased its rotation. In a thousand open spaces of down and upland the people who had fled thither from the floods and the falling houses and sliding slopes of hill watched for that rising in vain. Hour followed hour through a terrible suspense, and the star rose not. Once again men set their eyes upon the old constellations they had counted lost to them forever. In England it was hot and clear overhead, though the ground quivered perpetually, but in the tropics, Sirius and Capella and Aldebaran showed through a veil of steam. And when at last the great star rose near ten hours late, the sun rose close upon it, and in the centre of its white heart was a disc of black.

Over Asia it was the star had begun to fall behind the movement of the sky, and then suddenly, as it hung over India, its light had been veiled. All the plain of India from the mouth of the Indus to the mouths of the Ganges was a shallow waste of shining water that night, out of which rose temples and palaces, mounds and hills, black with people. Every minaret was a clustering mass of people, who fell one by one into the turbid waters, as heat and terror overcame them. The whole land seemed a-wailing, and suddenly there swept a shadow across that furnace of despair, and a breath of cold wind, and a gathering of clouds, out of the cooling air. Men looking up, near blinded, at the star, saw that a black disc was creeping across the light. It was the moon, coming between the star and the earth. And even as men cried to God at this respite, out of the East with a strange inexplicable swiftness sprang the sun. And then star, sun and moon rushed together across the heavens.[55]

So it was that presently, to the European watchers, star and sun rose close upon each other, drove headlong for a space and then slower, and at last came to rest, star and sun merged into one glare of flame at the zenith of the sky. The moon no longer eclipsed the star but was lost to sight in the brilliance of the sky. And though those who were still alive regarded it for the most part with that dull stupidity that hunger, fatigue, heat and despair engender, there were still men who could perceive the meaning of these signs. Star and earth had been at their nearest, had swung about one another, and the star had passed. Already it was receding, swifter and swifter, in the last stage of its headlong journey downward into the sun.

And then the clouds gathered, blotting out the vision of the sky, the thunder and lightning wove a garment round the world; all over the earth was such a downpour of rain as men had never before seen, and where the volcanoes flared red against the cloud canopy there descended torrents of mud. Everywhere the waters were pouring off the land, leaving mud-silted ruins, and the earth littered like a storm-worn beach with all that had floated, and the dead bodies of the men and brutes, its children. For days the water streamed off the land, sweeping away soil and trees and houses in the way, and piling huge dykes and scooping out Titanic gullies over the country side. Those were the days of darkness that followed the star and the heat. All through them, and for many weeks and months, the earthquakes continued.

But the star had passed, and men, hunger-driven and gathering courage only slowly, might creep back to their ruined cities, buried granaries, and sodden fields. Such few ships as had escaped the storms of that time came stunned and shattered and sounding their way cautious-ly through the new marks and shoals of once familiar ports. And as the storms subsided men perceived that everywhere the days were hotter than of yore, and the sun larger, and the moon, shrunk to a third of its former size, took now fourscore days between its new and new.

But of the new brotherhood that grew presently among men, of the saving of laws and books and machines, of the strange change that had come over Iceland and Greenland and the shores of Baffin's Bay, so that the sailors coming there presently found them green and gracious, and could scarce believe their eyes, this story does not tell. Nor of the movement of mankind now that the earth was hotter, northward and southward towards the poles of the earth. It concerns itself only with the coming and the passing of the Star.

The Martian astronomers—for there are astronomers on Mars, although they are very different beings from men—were naturally profoundly interested by these things. They saw them from their own standpoint of course. "Considering the mass and temperature of the missile that was flung through our solar system into the sun," one wrote, "it is astonishing what a little damage the earth, which it missed so narrowly, has sustained. All the familiar continental markings and the masses of the seas remain intact, and indeed the only difference seems to be a shrinkage of the white discolouration (supposed to be frozen water) round either pole." Which only shows how small the vastest of human catastrophes may seem, at a distance of a few million miles.

COLLEGE WRITING 1: REFLECTION WITHIN THE TEXT

You are the mathematician from the story. What do you do? Do you tell anyone? Do you tell everyone? What do you and your family and loved ones do? Do you merely go about your life, and hope for the best? Do you go feverish with anticipation and try to fix the problem? Do you embark on a crime spree and hope that all possibility of your punishment will be destroyed? Tell the story.

COLLEGE WRITING 2: RESEARCH OUTSIDE THE TEXT

Research a cataclysmic event. It could be something in the future—like the super-volcano under Yellowstone, or perhaps the fault off the West Coast of the United States, or man made climate change—or perhaps if you are so inclined the coming Rapture. Research the "preparation" that certain people are making for this event. You could also research previous events—wildfires, earthquakes, mudslides and tidal waves, droughts, floods and the like—and tell us what happened, what preparation had been made for these potential events, and how effective the preparation was, or will be.

IDEAS AND VALUES: CONNECT THE TEXT

In H.G. Wells's "The Star" a mathematician predicts that a celestial body that has collided with Neptune will approach Earth and all manner of nature will wreak havoc on mankind, while in Jack London's "To Build a Fire," the man fails to appreciate the dangers of his surroundings, and finally in "The Machine Stops" a whole society has shut themselves away from "the surface," choosing rather to experience life as indirectly as possible. In these stories we have three visions of man's relationship to nature; what unites them? What makes them different? Is nature a force to be conquered, bent to man's will? Is nature a god to be feared, or even worshipped? Is mankind something set apart from nature—or are we nature as well?

The Gun

By Philip K. Dick

4,816 WORDS. 27 MINUTES.
READING LEVEL: GRADE 6.9

Nothing moved or stirred. Everything was silent, dead. Only the gun showed signs of life ... and the trespassers had wrecked that for all time. The return journey to pick up the treasure would be a cinch ... they smiled.

1

The Captain peered into the eyepiece of the telescope. He adjusted the focus quickly.

"It was an atomic fission we saw, all right," he said presently. He sighed and pushed the eyepiece away. "Any of you who wants to look may do so. But it's not a pretty sight." `

"Let me look," Tance the archeologist said. He bent down to look, squinting. "Good Lord!" He leaped violently back, knocking against Dorle, the Chief Navigator.

"Why did we come all this way, then?" Dorle asked, looking around at the other men. "There's no point even in landing. Let's go back at once."

"Perhaps he's right," the biologist murmured. "But I'd like to look for myself, if I may." He pushed past Tance and peered into the sight.

He saw a vast expanse, an endless surface of gray, stretching to the edge of the planet. At first he thought it was water but after a moment he realized that it was slag, pitted, fused slag, broken only by hills of rock jutting up at intervals. Nothing moved or stirred. Everything was silent, dead.

"I see," Fomar said, backing away from the eyepiece. "Well, I won't find any legumes there." He tried to smile, but his lips stayed unmoved. He stepped away and stood by himself, staring past the others.

"I wonder what the atmospheric sample will show," Tance said.

"I think I can guess," the Captain answered. "Most of the atmosphere is poisoned. But didn't we expect all this? I don't see why we're so surprised. A fission visible as far away as our system must be a terrible thing."

He strode off down the corridor, dignified and expressionless. They watched him disappear into the control room.

As the Captain closed the door the young woman turned. "What did the telescope show? Good or bad?"

"Bad. No life could possibly exist. Atmosphere poisoned, water vaporized, all the land fused."

"Could they have gone underground?"

The Captain slid back the port window so that the surface of the planet under them was visible. The two of them stared down, silent and disturbed. Mile after mile of unbroken ruin stretched out, blackened slag, pitted and scarred, and occasional heaps of rock.

Suddenly Nasha jumped. "Look! Over there, at the edge. Do you see it?"

They stared. Something rose up, not rock, not an accidental formation. It was round, a circle of dots, white pellets on the dead skin of the planet. A city? Buildings of some kind?

"Please turn the ship," Nasha said excitedly. She pushed her dark hair from her face. "Turn the ship and let's see what it is!"

The ship turned, changing its course. As they came over the white dots the Captain lowered the ship, dropping it down as much as he dared. "Piers," he said. "Piers of some sort of stone. Perhaps poured artificial stone. The remains of a city."

"Oh, dear," Nasha murmured. "How awful." She watched the ruins disappear behind them. In a half-circle the white squares jutted from the slag, chipped and cracked, like broken teeth.

"There's nothing alive," the Captain said at last. "I think we'll go right back; I know most of the crew want to. Get the Government Receiving Station on the sender and tell them what we found, and that we—"

2

He staggered.

The first atomic shell had struck the ship, spinning it around. The Captain fell to the floor, crashing into the control table. Papers and instruments rained down on him. As he started to his feet the second shell struck. The ceiling cracked open, struts and girders twisted and bent. The ship shuddered, falling suddenly down, then righting itself as automatic controls took over.

The Captain lay on the floor by the smashed control board. In the corner Nasha struggled to free herself from the debris.

Outside the men were already sealing the gaping leaks in the side of the ship, through which the precious air was rushing, dissipating into the void beyond. "Help me!" Dorle was shouting. "Fire over here, wiring ignited." Two men came running. Tance watched helplessly, his eyeglasses broken and bent.

"So there is life here, after all," he said, half to himself. "But how could—"

"Give us a hand," Fomar said, hurrying past. "Give us a hand, we've got to land the ship!"

It was night. A few stars glinted above them, winking through the drifting silt that blew across the surface of the planet.

Dorle peered out, frowning. "What a place to be stuck in." He resumed his work, hammering the bent metal hull of the ship back into place. He was wearing a pressure suit; there were still many small leaks, and radioactive particles from the atmosphere had already found their way into the ship.

Nasha and Fomar were sitting at the table in the control room, pale and solemn, studying the inventory lists.

"Low on carbohydrates," Fomar said. "We can break down the stored fats if we want to, but—"

"I wonder if we could find anything outside." Nasha went to the window. "How uninviting it looks." She paced back and forth, very slender and small, her face dark with fatigue. "What do you suppose an exploring party would find?"

Fomar shrugged. "Not much. Maybe a few weeds growing in cracks here and there. Nothing we could use. Anything that would adapt to this environment would be toxic, lethal."

Nasha paused, rubbing her cheek. There was a deep scratch there, still red and swollen. "Then how do you explain—*it*? According to your theory the inhabitants must have died in their skins, fried like yams. But who fired on us? Somebody detected us, made a decision, aimed a gun."

"And gauged distance," the Captain said feebly from the cot in the corner. He turned toward them. "That's the part that worries me. The first shell put us out of commission, the second almost destroyed us. They were well aimed, perfectly aimed. We're not such an easy target."

"True." Fomar nodded. "Well, perhaps we'll know the answer before we leave here. What a strange situation! All our reasoning tells us that no life could exist; the whole planet burned dry, the atmosphere itself gone, completely poisoned."

"The gun that fired the projectiles survived," Nasha said. "Why not people?"

"It's not the same. Metal doesn't need air to breathe. Metal doesn't get leukemia from radioactive particles. Metal doesn't need food and water."

There was silence.

"A paradox," Nasha said. "Anyhow, in the morning I think we should send out a search party. And meanwhile we should keep on trying to get the ship in condition for the trip back."

"It'll be days before we can take off," Fomar said. "We should keep every man working here. We can't afford to send out a party."

Nasha smiled a little. "We'll send you in the first party. Maybe you can discover—what was it you were so interested in?"

"Legumes. Edible legumes."

"Maybe you can find some of them. Only—"

"Only what?"

"Only watch out. They fired on us once without even knowing who we were or what we came for. Do you suppose that they fought with each other? Perhaps they couldn't imagine anyone being friendly, under any circumstances. What a strange evolutionary trait, inter-species warfare. Fighting within the race!"

"We'll know in the morning," Fomar said. "Let's get some sleep."

3

The sun came up chill and austere. The three people, two men and a woman, stepped through the port, dropping down on the hard ground below.

"What a day," Dorle said grumpily. "I said how glad I'd be to walk on firm ground again, but—"

"Come on," Nasha said. "Up beside me. I want to say something to you. Will you excuse us, Tance?"

Tance nodded gloomily. Dorle caught up with Nasha. They walked together, their metal shoes crunching the ground underfoot. Nasha glanced at him.

"Listen. The Captain is dying. No one knows except the two of us. By the end of the day-period of this planet he'll be dead. The shock did something to his heart. He was almost sixty, you know."

Dorle nodded. "That's bad. I have a great deal of respect for him. You will be captain in his place, of course. Since you're vice-captain now—"

"No. I prefer to see someone else lead, perhaps you or Fomar. I've been thinking over the situation and it seems to me that I should declare myself mated to one of you, whichever of you wants to be captain. Then I could devolve the responsibility."

"Well, I don't want to be captain. Let Fomar do it."

Nasha studied him, tall and blond, striding along beside her in his pressure suit. "I'm rather partial to you," she said. "We might try it for a time, at least. But do as you like. Look, we're coming to something."

They stopped walking, letting Tance catch up. In front of them was some sort of a ruined building. Dorle stared around thoughtfully.

"Do you see? This whole place is a natural bowl, a huge valley. See how the rock formations rise up on all sides, protecting the floor. Maybe some of the great blast was deflected here."

They wandered around the ruins, picking up rocks and fragments. "I think this was a farm," Tance said, examining a piece of wood. "This was part of a tower windmill."

"Really?" Nasha took the stick and turned it over. "Interesting. But let's go; we don't have much time."

"Look," Dorle said suddenly. "Off there, a long way off. Isn't that something?" He pointed.

Nasha sucked in her breath. "The white stones."

"What?"

Nasha looked up at Dorle. "The white stones, the great broken teeth. We saw them, the Captain and I, from the control room." She touched Dorle's arm gently. "That's where they fired from. I didn't think we had landed so close."

"What is it?" Tance said, coming up to them. "I'm almost blind without my glasses. What do you see?"

"The city. Where they fired from."

"Oh." All three of them stood together. "Well, let's go," Tance said. "There's no telling what we'll find there." Dorle frowned at him.

"Wait. We don't know what we would be getting into. They must have patrols. They probably have seen us already, for that matter."

"They probably have seen the ship itself," Tance said. "They probably know right now where they can find it, where they can blow it up. So what difference does it make whether we go closer or not?"

"That's true," Nasha said. "If they really want to get us we haven't a chance. We have no armaments at all; you know that."

"I have a hand weapon." Dorle nodded. "Well, let's go on, then. I suppose you're right, Tance."

"But let's stay together," Tance said nervously. "Nasha, you're going too fast."

Nasha looked back. She laughed. "If we expect to get there by nightfall we must go fast."

4

They reached the outskirts of the city at about the middle of the afternoon. The sun, cold and yellow, hung above them in the colorless sky. Dorle stopped at the top of a ridge overlooking the city.

"Well, there it is. What's left of it."

There was not much left. The huge concrete piers which they had noticed were not piers at all, but the ruined foundations of buildings. They had been baked by the searing heat, baked and charred almost to the ground. Nothing else remained, only this irregular circle of white squares, perhaps four miles in diameter.

Dorle spat in disgust. "More wasted time. A dead skeleton of a city, that's all."

"But it was from here that the firing came," Tance murmured. "Don't forget that."

"And by someone with a good eye and a great deal of experience," Nasha added. "Let's go."

They walked into the city between the ruined buildings. No one spoke. They walked in silence, listening to the echo of their footsteps.

"It's macabre," Dorle muttered. "I've seen ruined cities before but they died of old age, old age and fatigue. This was killed, seared to death. This city didn't die—it was murdered."

"I wonder what the city was called," Nasha said. She turned aside, going up the remains of a stairway from one of the foundations. "Do you think we might find a signpost? Some kind of plaque?"

She peered into the ruins.

"There's nothing there," Dorle said impatiently. "Come on."

"Wait." Nasha bent down, touching a concrete stone. "There's something inscribed on this."

"What is it?" Tance hurried up. He squatted in the dust, running his gloved fingers over the surface of the stone. "Letters, all right." He took a writing stick from the pocket of his pressure suit and copied the inscription on a bit of paper. Dorle glanced over his shoulder. The inscription was:

FRANKLIN APARTMENTS

"That's this city," Nasha said softly. "That was its name."

Tance put the paper in his pocket and they went on. After a time Dorle said, "Nasha, you know, I think we're being watched. But don't look around."

The woman stiffened. "Oh? Why do you say that? Did you see something?"

"No. I can feel it, though. Don't you?"

Nasha smiled a little. "I feel nothing, but perhaps I'm more used to being stared at." She turned her head slightly. "Oh!"

Dorle reached for his hand weapon. "What is it? What do you see?" Tance had stopped dead in his tracks, his mouth half open.

"The gun," Nasha said. "It's the gun."

"Look at the size of it. The size of the thing." Dorle unfastened his hand weapon slowly. "That's it, all right."

The gun was huge. Stark and immense it pointed up at the sky, a mass of steel and glass, set in a huge slab of concrete. Even as they watched the gun moved on its swivel base, whirring underneath. A slim vane turned with the wind, a network of rods atop a high pole.

"It's alive," Nasha whispered. "It's listening to us, watching us."

The gun moved again, this time clockwise. It was mounted so that it could make a full circle. The barrel lowered a trifle, then resumed its original position.

"But who fires it?" Tance said.

Dorle laughed. "No one. No one fires it."

They stared at him. "What do you mean?"

"It fires itself."

They couldn't believe him. Nasha came close to him, frowning, looking up at him. "I don't understand. What do you mean, it fires itself?"

"Watch, I'll show you. Don't move." Dorle picked up a rock from the ground. He hesitated a moment and then tossed the rock high in the air. The rock passed in front of the gun. Instantly the great barrel moved, the vanes contracted.

5

The rock fell to the ground. The gun paused, then resumed its calm swivel, its slow circling.

"You see," Dorle said, "it noticed the rock, as soon as I threw it up in the air. It's alert to anything that flies or moves above the ground level. Probably it detected us as soon as we entered the gravitational field of the planet. It probably had a bead on us from the start. We don't have a chance. It knows all about the ship. It's just waiting for us to take off again."

"I understand about the rock," Nasha said, nodding. "The gun noticed it, but not us, since we're on the ground, not above. It's only designed to combat objects in the sky. The ship is safe until it takes off again, then the end will come."

"But what's this gun for?" Tance put in. "There's no one alive here. Everyone is dead."

"It's a machine," Dorle said. "A machine that was made to do a job. And it's doing the job. How it survived the blast I don't know. On it goes, waiting for the enemy. Probably they came by air in some sort of projectiles."

"The enemy," Nasha said. "Their own race. It is hard to believe that they really bombed themselves, fired at themselves."

"Well, it's over with. Except right here, where we're standing. This one gun, still alert, ready to kill. It'll go on until it wears out."

"And by that time we'll be dead," Nasha said bitterly.

"There must have been hundreds of guns like this," Dorle murmured. "They must have been used to the sight, guns, weapons, uniforms. Probably they accepted it as a natural thing, part of their lives, like eating and sleeping. An institution, like the church and the state. Men trained to fight, to lead armies, a regular profession. Honored, respected."

Tance was walking slowly toward the gun, peering nearsightedly up at it. "Quite complex, isn't it? All those vanes and tubes. I suppose this is some sort of a telescopic sight." His gloved hand touched the end of a long tube.

Instantly the gun shifted, the barrel retracting. It swung—

"Don't move!" Dorle cried. The barrel swung past them as they stood, rigid and still. For one terrible moment it hesitated over their heads, clicking and whirring, settling into position. Then the sounds died out and the gun became silent.

Tance smiled foolishly inside his helmet. "I must have put my finger over the lens. I'll be more careful." He made his way up onto the circular slab, stepping gingerly behind the body of the gun. He disappeared from view.

"Where did he go?" Nasha said irritably. "He'll get us all killed."

"Tance, come back!" Dorle shouted. "What's the matter with you?"

"In a minute." There was a long silence. At last the archeologist appeared. "I think I've found something. Come up and I'll show you."

"What is it?"

"Dorle, you said the gun was here to keep the enemy off. I think I know why they wanted to keep the enemy off."

They were puzzled.

"I think I've found what the gun is supposed to guard. Come and give me a hand."

"All right," Dorle said abruptly. "Let's go." He seized Nasha's hand. "Come on. Let's see what he's found. I thought something like this might happen when I saw that the gun was—"

"Like what?" Nasha pulled her hand away. "What are you talking about? You act as if you knew what he's found."

"I do." Dorle smiled down at her. "Do you remember the legend that all races have, the myth of the buried treasure, and the dragon, the serpent that watches it, guards it, keeping everyone away?"

She nodded. "Well?"

Dorle pointed up at the gun.

"That," he said, "is the dragon. Come on."

6

Between the three of them they managed to pull up the steel cover and lay it to one side. Dorle was wet with perspiration when they finished.

"It isn't worth it," he grunted. He stared into the dark yawning hole. "Or is it?"

Nasha clicked on her hand lamp, shining the beam down the stairs. The steps were thick with dust and rubble. At the bottom was a steel door.

"Come on," Tance said excitedly. He started down the stairs. They watched him reach the door and pull hopefully on it without success. "Give a hand!"

"All right." They came gingerly after him. Dorle examined the door. It was bolted shut, locked. There was an inscription on the door but he could not read it.

"Now what?" Nasha said.

Dorle took out his hand weapon. "Stand back. I can't think of any other way." He pressed the switch. The bottom of the door glowed red. Presently it began to crumble. Dorle clicked the weapon off. "I think we can get through. Let's try."

The door came apart easily. In a few minutes they had carried it away in pieces and stacked the pieces on the first step. Then they went on, flashing the light ahead of them.

They were in a vault. Dust lay everywhere, on everything, inches thick. Wood crates lined the walls, huge boxes and crates, packages and containers. Tance looked around curiously, his eyes bright.

"What exactly are all these?" he murmured. "Something valuable, I would think." He picked up a round drum and opened it. A spool fell to the floor, unwinding a black ribbon. He examined it, holding it up to the light.

"Look at this!"

They came around him. "Pictures," Nasha said. "Tiny pictures."

"Records of some kind." Tance closed the spool up in the drum again. "Look, hundreds of drums." He flashed the light around. "And those crates. Let's open one."

Dorle was already prying at the wood. The wood had turned brittle and dry. He managed to pull a section away.

It was a picture. A boy in a blue garment, smiling pleasantly, staring ahead, young and handsome. He seemed almost alive, ready to move toward them in the light of the hand lamp. It was one of them, one of the ruined race, the race that had perished.

For a long time they stared at the picture. At last Dorle replaced the board.

"All these other crates," Nasha said. "More pictures. And these drums. What are in the boxes?"

"This is their treasure," Tance said, almost to himself. "Here are their pictures, their records. Probably all their literature is here, their stories, their myths, their ideas about the universe."

"And their history," Nasha said. "We'll be able to trace their development and find out what it was that made them become what they were."

Dorle was wandering around the vault. "Odd," he murmured. "Even at the end, even after they had begun to fight they still knew, someplace down inside them, that their real treasure was this, their books and pictures, their myths. Even after their big cities and buildings and industries were destroyed they probably hoped to come back and find this. After everything else was gone."

"When we get back home we can agitate for a mission to come here," Tance said. "All this can be loaded up and taken back. We'll be leaving about—"

He stopped.

"Yes," Dorle said dryly. "We'll be leaving about three day-periods from now. We'll fix the ship, then take off. Soon we'll be home, that is, if nothing happens. Like being shot down by that—"

"Oh, stop it!" Nasha said impatiently. "Leave him alone. He's right: all this must be taken back home, sooner or later. We'll have to solve the problem of the gun. We have no choice."

Dorle nodded. "What's your solution, then? As soon as we leave the ground we'll be shot down." His face twisted bitterly. "They've guarded their treasure too well. Instead of being preserved it will lie here until it rots. It serves them right."

"How?"

"Don't you see? This was the only way they knew, building a gun and setting it up to shoot anything that came along. They were so certain that everything was hostile, the enemy, coming to take their possessions away from them. Well, they can keep them."

Nasha was deep in thought, her mind far away. Suddenly she gasped. "Dorle," she said. "What's the matter with us? We have no problem. The gun is no menace at all."

The two men stared at her.

"No menace?" Dorle said. "It's already shot us down once. And as soon as we take off again—"

"Don't you see?" Nasha began to laugh. "The poor foolish gun, it's completely harmless. Even I could deal with it alone."

"You?"

Her eyes were flashing. "With a crowbar. With a hammer or a stick of wood. Let's go back to the ship and load up. Of course we're at its mercy in the air: that's the way it was made. It can fire into the sky, shoot down anything that flies. But that's all! Against something on the ground it has no defenses. Isn't that right?"

Dorle nodded slowly. "The soft underbelly of the dragon. In the legend, the dragon's armor doesn't cover its stomach." He began to laugh. "That's right. That's perfectly right."

"Let's go, then," Nasha said. "Let's get back to the ship. We have work to do here."

7

It was early the next morning when they reached the ship. During the night the Captain had died, and the crew had ignited his body, according to custom. They had stood solemnly around it until the last ember died. As they were going back to their work the woman and the two men appeared, dirty and tired, still excited.

And presently, from the ship, a line of people came, each carrying something in his hands. The line marched across the gray slag, the eternal expanse of fused metal. When they reached the weapon they all fell on the gun at once, with crowbars, hammers, anything that was heavy and hard.

The telescopic sights shattered into bits. The wiring was pulled out, torn to shreds. The delicate gears were smashed, dented.

Finally the warheads themselves were carried off and the firing pins removed.

The gun was smashed, the great weapon destroyed. The people went down into the vault and examined the treasure. With its metal-armored guardian dead there was no danger any longer. They studied the pictures, the films, the crates of books, the jeweled crowns, the cups, the statues.

At last, as the sun was dipping into the gray mists that drifted across the planet they came back up the stairs again. For a moment they stood around the wrecked gun looking at the unmoving outline of it.

156

Then they started back to the ship. There was still much work to be done. The ship had been badly hurt, much had been damaged and lost. The important thing was to repair it as quickly as possible, to get it into the air.

With all of them working together it took just five more days to make it spaceworthy.

8

Nasha stood in the control room, watching the planet fall away behind them. She folded her arms, sitting down on the edge of the table.

"What are you thinking?" Dorle said.

"I? Nothing."

"Are you sure?"

"I was thinking that there must have been a time when this planet was quite different, when there was life on it."

"I suppose there was. It's unfortunate that no ships from our system came this far, but then we had no reason to suspect intelligent life until we saw the fission glow in the sky."

"And then it was too late."

"Not quite too late. After all, their possessions, their music, books, their pictures, all of that will survive. We'll take them home and study them, and they'll change us. We won't be the same afterwards. Their sculpturing, especially. Did you see the one of the great winged creature, without a head or arms? Broken off, I suppose. But those wings— It looked very old. It will change us a great deal."

"When we come back we won't find the gun waiting for us," Nasha said. "Next time it won't be there to shoot us down. We can land and take the treasure, as you call it." She smiled up at Dorle. "You'll lead us back there, as a good captain should."

"Captain?" Dorle grinned. "Then you've decided."

Nasha shrugged. "Fomar argues with me too much. I think, all in all, I really prefer you."

"Then let's go," Dorle said. "Let's go back home."

The ship roared up, flying over the ruins of the city. It turned in a huge arc and then shot off beyond the horizon, heading into outer space.

9

Down below, in the center of the ruined city, a single half-broken detector vane moved slightly, catching the roar of the ship. The base of the great gun throbbed painfully, straining to turn. After a moment a red warning light flashed on down inside its destroyed works.

And a long way off, a hundred miles from the city, another warning light flashed on, far underground. Automatic relays flew into action. Gears turned, belts whined. On the ground above a section of metal slag slipped back. A ramp appeared.

A moment later a small cart rushed to the surface.

The cart turned toward the city. A second cart appeared behind it. It was loaded with wiring cables. Behind it a third cart came, loaded with telescopic tube sights. And behind came more carts, some with relays, some with firing controls, some with tools and parts, screws and bolts, pins and nuts. The final one contained atomic warheads.

The carts lined up behind the first one, the lead cart. The lead cart started off, across the frozen ground, bumping calmly along, followed by the others. Moving toward the city.

To the damaged gun.

COLLEGE WRITING 1: REFLECTION WITHIN THE TEXT

Imagine you are an inhabitant of Franklin Apartments. Describe the final days of your civilization. What did you put in the vault, and why? Include at least one personal item.

COLLEGE WRITING 2: RESEARCH OUTSIDE THE TEXT

Research the most credible threat to humanity. What is it? Is it external, or internal? Given this threat what is the best method to preserving the world's various cultural artifacts?

IDEAS AND VALUES: CONNECT THE TEXT

» In Philip K. Dick's "The Gun" culture is the one treasure that "the dragon guards," but in Nathanial Hawthorne's "Earth's Holocaust," culture is merely fuel for the fire, while in Wilde's "Impressions of America" culture is neither here nor there, but a category of different perspectives, perhaps a tool to be used one way or another, in practicality or fashion—as he doesn't enter into geography ("latitude or longitude"), economics ("the value of its dry goods"), or politics. But what is culture? What is its value—ultimately? Is it a way of life? A relic of the past? Does it hold us back, or does it tell us who we are? What relationship should we strike towards culture itself—? And what care should we take to understand its origins, if any at all?

» Humankind has invented the Internet, the telephone, the motor vehicle, air travel, the atomic bomb... Look at Oscar Wilde's "Impressions of America," and his focus on "practical education" and the beauty of American engineering—and then move to "The Gun," when an alien ship approaches Earth but cannot reach it because of Earth's engineering, and then "The Machine Stops," a world in which "the machine" is all that matters—not human progress—but the progress of "the machine." And finally "Earth's Holocaust," in which the people of the world decide to burn everything—all ideas—all progress, all technology. What roll does technological progress play, and what roll should technology play in the progress of mankind? How would you define progress?

The Yellow Wallpaper

By Charlotte Perkins Gilman

6,127 WORDS. 34 MINUTES.
READING LEVEL: GRADE 8.3

It is very seldom that mere ordinary people like John and myself secure ancestral halls for the summer.

A colonial mansion, a hereditary estate, I would say a haunted house, and reach the height of romantic felicity—but that would be asking too much of fate!

Still I will proudly declare that there is something queer about it.

Else, why should it be let so cheaply? And why have stood so long untenanted?

John laughs at me, of course, but one expects that in marriage.

John is practical in the extreme. He has no patience with faith, an intense horror of superstition, and he scoffs openly at any talk of things not to be felt and seen and put down in figures.

John is a physician, and PERHAPS—(I would not say it to a living soul, of course, but this is dead paper and a great relief to my mind)—PERHAPS that is one reason I do not get well faster.

You see he does not believe I am sick!

And what can one do?

If a physician of high standing, and one's own husband, assures friends and relatives that there is really nothing the matter with one but temporary nervous depression—a slight hysterical tendency—what is one to do?

My brother is also a physician, and also of high standing, and he says the same thing.

So I take phosphates or phosphites—whichever it is, and tonics, and journeys, and air, and exercise, and am absolutely forbidden to "work" until I am well again.

Personally, I disagree with their ideas.

Personally, I believe that congenial work, with excitement and change, would do me good.

But what is one to do?

I did write for a while in spite of them; but it DOES exhaust me a good deal—having to be so sly about it, or else meet with heavy opposition.

I sometimes fancy that in my condition if I had less opposition and more society and stimulus—but John says the very worst thing I can do is to think about my condition, and I confess it always makes me feel bad.

So I will let it alone and talk about the house.

The most beautiful place! It is quite alone, standing well back from the road, quite three miles from the village. It makes me think of English places that you read about, for there are hedges and walls and gates that lock, and lots of separate little houses for the gardeners and people.

There is a DELICIOUS garden! I never saw such a garden—large and shady, full of box-bordered paths, and lined with long grape-covered arbors with seats under them.

There were greenhouses, too, but they are all broken now.

There was some legal trouble, I believe, something about the heirs and coheirs; anyhow, the place has been empty for years.

That spoils my ghostliness, I am afraid, but I don't care—there is something strange about the house—I can feel it.

I even said so to John one moonlight evening, but he said what I felt was a DRAUGHT, and shut the window.

I get unreasonably angry with John sometimes. I'm sure I never used to be so sensitive. I think it is due to this nervous condition.

But John says if I feel so, I shall neglect proper self-control; so I take pains to control myself—before him, at least, and that makes me very tired.

I don't like our room a bit. I wanted one downstairs that opened on the piazza and had roses all over the window, and such pretty old-fashioned chintz hangings! but John would not hear of it.

He said there was only one window and not room for two beds, and no near room for him if he took another.

He is very careful and loving, and hardly lets me stir without special direction.

I have a schedule prescription for each hour in the day; he takes all care from me, and so I feel basely ungrateful not to value it more.

He said we came here solely on my account, that I was to have perfect rest and all the air I could get. "Your exercise depends on your strength, my dear," said he, "and your food somewhat on your appetite; but air you can absorb all the time." So we took the nursery at the top of the house.

It is a big, airy room, the whole floor nearly, with windows that look all ways, and air and sunshine galore. It was nursery first and then playroom and gymnasium, I should judge; for the windows are barred for little children, and there are rings and things in the walls.

The paint and paper look as if a boys' school had used it. It is stripped off—the paper—in great patches all around the head of my bed, about as far as I can reach, and in a great place on the other side of the room low down. I never saw a worse paper in my life.

One of those sprawling flamboyant patterns committing every artistic sin.

It is dull enough to confuse the eye in following, pronounced enough to constantly irritate and provoke study, and when you follow the lame uncertain curves for a little distance they suddenly commit suicide—plunge off at outrageous angles, destroy themselves in unheard of contradictions.

The color is repellent, almost revolting; a smouldering unclean yellow, strangely faded by the slow-turning sunlight.

It is a dull yet lurid orange in some places, a sickly sulphur tint in others.

No wonder the children hated it! I should hate it myself if I had to live in this room long.

There comes John, and I must put this away,—he hates to have me write a word.

We have been here two weeks, and I haven't felt like writing before, since that first day.

I am sitting by the window now, up in this atrocious nursery, and there is nothing to hinder my writing as much as I please, save lack of strength.

John is away all day, and even some nights when his cases are serious.

I am glad my case is not serious!

But these nervous troubles are dreadfully depressing.

John does not know how much I really suffer. He knows there is no REASON to suffer, and that satisfies him.

Of course it is only nervousness. It does weigh on me so not to do my duty in any way!

I meant to be such a help to John, such a real rest and comfort, and here I am a comparative burden already!

Nobody would believe what an effort it is to do what little I am able,—to dress and entertain, and order things.

It is fortunate Mary is so good with the baby. Such a dear baby!

And yet I CANNOT be with him, it makes me so nervous.

I suppose John never was nervous in his life. He laughs at me so about this wall-paper!

At first he meant to repaper the room, but afterwards he said that I was letting it get the better of me, and that nothing was worse for a nervous patient than to give way to such fancies.

He said that after the wall-paper was changed it would be the heavy bedstead, and then the barred windows, and then that gate at the head of the stairs, and so on.

"You know the place is doing you good," he said, "and really, dear, I don't care to renovate the house just for a three months' rental."

"Then do let us go downstairs," I said, "there are such pretty rooms there."

Then he took me in his arms and called me a blessed little goose, and said he would go down to the cellar, if I wished, and have it whitewashed into the bargain.

But he is right enough about the beds and windows and things.

It is an airy and comfortable room as any one need wish, and, of course, I would not be so silly as to make him uncomfortable just for a whim.

I'm really getting quite fond of the big room, all but that horrid paper.

Out of one window I can see the garden, those mysterious deepshaded arbors, the riotous old-fashioned flowers, and bushes and gnarly trees.

Out of another I get a lovely view of the bay and a little private wharf belonging to the estate. There is a beautiful shaded lane that runs down there from the house. I always fancy I see people walking in these numerous paths and arbors, but John has cautioned me not to give way to fancy in the least. He says that with my imaginative power and habit of story-making, a nervous weakness like mine is sure to lead to all manner of excited fancies, and that I ought to use my will and good sense to check the tendency. So I try.

I think sometimes that if I were only well enough to write a little it would relieve the press of ideas and rest me.

But I find I get pretty tired when I try.

It is so discouraging not to have any advice and companionship about my work. When I get really well, John says we will ask Cousin Henry and Julia down for a long visit; but he says he would as soon put fireworks in my pillow-case as to let me have those stimulating people about now.

I wish I could get well faster.

But I must not think about that. This paper looks to me as if it KNEW what a vicious influence it had!

There is a recurrent spot where the pattern lolls like a broken neck and two bulbous eyes stare at you upside down.

I get positively angry with the impertinence of it and the everlastingness. Up and down and sideways they crawl, and those absurd, unblinking eyes are everywhere. There is one place where two breadths didn't match, and the eyes go all up and down the line, one a little higher than the other.

I never saw so much expression in an inanimate thing before, and we all know how much expression they have! I used to lie awake as a child and get more entertainment and terror out of blank walls and plain furniture than most children could find in a toy store.

I remember what a kindly wink the knobs of our big, old bureau used to have, and there was one chair that always seemed like a strong friend.

I used to feel that if any of the other things looked too fierce I could always hop into that chair and be safe.

The furniture in this room is no worse than inharmonious, however, for we had to bring it all from downstairs. I suppose when this was used as a playroom they had to take the nursery things out, and no wonder! I never saw such ravages as the children have made here.

The wall-paper, as I said before, is torn off in spots, and it sticketh closer than a brother—they must have had perseverance as well as hatred.

Then the floor is scratched and gouged and splintered, the plaster itself is dug out here and there, and this great heavy bed which is all we found in the room, looks as if it had been through the wars.

But I don't mind it a bit—only the paper.

There comes John's sister. Such a dear girl as she is, and so careful of me! I must not let her find me writing.

She is a perfect and enthusiastic housekeeper, and hopes for no better profession. I verily believe she thinks it is the writing which made me sick!

But I can write when she is out, and see her a long way off from these windows.

There is one that commands the road, a lovely shaded winding road, and one that just looks off over the country. A lovely country, too, full of great elms and velvet meadows.

This wall-paper has a kind of sub-pattern in a different shade, a particularly irritating one, for you can only see it in certain lights, and not clearly then.

But in the places where it isn't faded and where the sun is just so—I can see a strange, provoking, formless sort of figure, that seems to skulk about behind that silly and conspicuous front design.

There's sister on the stairs!

Well, the Fourth of July is over! The people are gone and I am tired out. John thought it might do me good to see a little company, so we just had mother and Nellie and the children down for a week.

Of course I didn't do a thing. Jennie sees to everything now.

But it tired me all the same.

John says if I don't pick up faster he shall send me to Weir Mitchell in the fall.

But I don't want to go there at all. I had a friend who was in his hands once, and she says he is just like John and my brother, only more so!

Besides, it is such an undertaking to go so far.

I don't feel as if it was worth while to turn my hand over for anything, and I'm getting dreadfully fretful and querulous.

I cry at nothing, and cry most of the time.

Of course I don't when John is here, or anybody else, but when I am alone.

And I am alone a good deal just now. John is kept in town very often by serious cases, and Jennie is good and lets me alone when I want her to.

So I walk a little in the garden or down that lovely lane, sit on the porch under the roses, and lie down up here a good deal.

I'm getting really fond of the room in spite of the wall-paper. Perhaps BECAUSE of the wall-paper.

It dwells in my mind so!

I lie here on this great immovable bed—it is nailed down, I believe—and follow that pattern about by the hour. It is as good as gymnastics, I assure you. I start, we'll say, at the bottom, down in the corner over there where it has not been touched, and I determine for the thousandth time that I WILL follow that pointless pattern to some sort of a conclusion.

I know a little of the principle of design, and I know this thing was not arranged on any laws of radiation, or alternation, or repetition, or symmetry, or anything else that I ever heard of.

It is repeated, of course, by the breadths, but not otherwise.

Looked at in one way each breadth stands alone, the bloated curves and flourishes—a kind of "debased Romanesque" with delirium tremens—go waddling up and down in isolated columns of fatuity.

But, on the other hand, they connect diagonally, and the sprawling outlines run off in great slanting waves of optic horror, like a lot of wallowing seaweeds in full chase.

The whole thing goes horizontally, too, at least it seems so, and I exhaust myself in trying to distinguish the order of its going in that direction.

They have used a horizontal breadth for a frieze, and that adds wonderfully to the confusion.

There is one end of the room where it is almost intact, and there, when the crosslights fade and the low sun shines directly upon it, I can almost fancy radiation after all,—the interminable grotesques seem to form around a common centre and rush off in headlong plunges of equal distraction.

It makes me tired to follow it. I will take a nap I guess.

I don't know why I should write this.

I don't want to.

I don't feel able.

166

And I know John would think it absurd. But I MUST say what I feel and think in some way—it is such a relief!

But the effort is getting to be greater than the relief.

Half the time now I am awfully lazy, and lie down ever so much.

John says I musn't lose my strength, and has me take cod liver oil and lots of tonics and things, to say nothing of ale and wine and rare meat.

Dear John! He loves me very dearly, and hates to have me sick. I tried to have a real earnest reasonable talk with him the other day, and tell him how I wish he would let me go and make a visit to Cousin Henry and Julia.

But he said I wasn't able to go, nor able to stand it after I got there; and I did not make out a very good case for myself, for I was crying before I had finished.

It is getting to be a great effort for me to think straight. Just this nervous weakness I suppose.

And dear John gathered me up in his arms, and just carried me upstairs and laid me on the bed, and sat by me and read to me till it tired my head.

He said I was his darling and his comfort and all he had, and that I must take care of myself for his sake, and keep well.

He says no one but myself can help me out of it, that I must use my will and self-control and not let any silly fancies run away with me.

There's one comfort, the baby is well and happy, and does not have to occupy this nursery with the horrid wall-paper.

If we had not used it, that blessed child would have! What a fortunate escape! Why, I wouldn't have a child of mine, an impressionable little thing, live in such a room for worlds.

I never thought of it before, but it is lucky that John kept me here after all, I can stand it so much easier than a baby, you see.

Of course I never mention it to them any more—I am too wise,—but I keep watch of it all the same.

There are things in that paper that nobody knows but me, or ever will.

Behind that outside pattern the dim shapes get clearer every day.

It is always the same shape, only very numerous.

And it is like a woman stooping down and creeping about behind that pattern. I don't like it a bit. I wonder—I begin to think—I wish John would take me away from here!

It is so hard to talk with John about my case, because he is so wise, and because he loves me so.

But I tried it last night.

It was moonlight. The moon shines in all around just as the sun does.

I hate to see it sometimes, it creeps so slowly, and always comes in by one window or another.

John was asleep and I hated to waken him, so I kept still and watched the moonlight on that undulating wall-paper till I felt creepy.

The faint figure behind seemed to shake the pattern, just as if she wanted to get out.

I got up softly and went to feel and see if the paper DID move, and when I came back John was awake.

"What is it, little girl?" he said. "Don't go walking about like that— you'll get cold."

I though it was a good time to talk, so I told him that I really was not gaining here, and that I wished he would take me away.

"Why darling!" said he, "our lease will be up in three weeks, and I can't see how to leave before.

"The repairs are not done at home, and I cannot possibly leave town just now. Of course if you were in any danger, I could and would, but you really are better, dear, whether you can see it or not. I am a doctor, dear, and I know. You are gaining flesh and color, your appetite is better, I feel really much easier about you."

"I don't weigh a bit more," said I, "nor as much; and my appetite may be better in the evening when you are here, but it is worse in the morning when you are away!"

"Bless her little heart!" said he with a big hug, "she shall be as sick as she pleases! But now let's improve the shining hours by going to sleep, and talk about it in the morning!"

"And you won't go away?" I asked gloomily.

"Why, how can I, dear? It is only three weeks more and then we will take a nice little trip of a few days while Jennie is getting the house ready. Really dear you are better!"

"Better in body perhaps—" I began, and stopped short, for he sat up straight and looked at me with such a stern, reproachful look that I could not say another word.

"My darling," said he, "I beg of you, for my sake and for our child's sake, as well as for your own, that you will never for one instant let that idea enter your mind! There is nothing so dangerous, so fascinating, to a temperament like yours. It is a false and foolish fancy. Can you not trust me as a physician when I tell you so?"

So of course I said no more on that score, and we went to sleep before long. He thought I was asleep first, but I wasn't, and lay there for hours trying to decide whether that front pattern and the back pattern really did move together or separately.

On a pattern like this, by daylight, there is a lack of sequence, a defiance of law, that is a constant irritant to a normal mind.

The color is hideous enough, and unreliable enough, and infuriating enough, but the pattern is torturing.

You think you have mastered it, but just as you get well underway in following, it turns a back-somersault and there you are. It slaps you in the face, knocks you down, and tramples upon you. It is like a bad dream.

The outside pattern is a florid arabesque, reminding one of a fungus. If you can imagine a toadstool in joints, an interminable string of toadstools, budding and sprouting in endless convolutions—why, that is something like it.

That is, sometimes!

There is one marked peculiarity about this paper, a thing nobody seems to notice but myself, and that is that it changes as the light changes.

When the sun shoots in through the east window—I always watch for that first long, straight ray—it changes so quickly that I never can quite believe it.

That is why I watch it always.

By moonlight—the moon shines in all night when there is a moon—I wouldn't know it was the same paper.

At night in any kind of light, in twilight, candle light, lamplight, and worst of all by moonlight, it becomes bars! The outside pattern I mean, and the woman behind it is as plain as can be.

I didn't realize for a long time what the thing was that showed behind, that dim sub-pattern, but now I am quite sure it is a woman.

By daylight she is subdued, quiet. I fancy it is the pattern that keeps her so still. It is so puzzling. It keeps me quiet by the hour.

I lie down ever so much now. John says it is good for me, and to sleep all I can.

Indeed he started the habit by making me lie down for an hour after each meal.

It is a very bad habit I am convinced, for you see I don't sleep.

And that cultivates deceit, for I don't tell them I'm awake—O no!

The fact is I am getting a little afraid of John.

He seems very queer sometimes, and even Jennie has an inexplicable look.

It strikes me occasionally, just as a scientific hypothesis,—that perhaps it is the paper!

I have watched John when he did not know I was looking, and come into the room suddenly on the most innocent excuses, and I've caught him several times LOOKING AT THE PAPER! And Jennie too. I caught Jennie with her hand on it once.

She didn't know I was in the room, and when I asked her in a quiet, a very quiet voice, with the most restrained manner possible, what she was doing with the paper—she turned around as if she had been caught stealing, and looked quite angry—asked me why I should frighten her so!

Then she said that the paper stained everything it touched, that she had found yellow smooches on all my clothes and John's, and she wished we would be more careful!

Did not that sound innocent? But I know she was studying that pattern, and I am determined that nobody shall find it out but myself!

Life is very much more exciting now than it used to be. You see I have something more to expect, to look forward to, to watch. I really do eat better, and am more quiet than I was.

John is so pleased to see me improve! He laughed a little the other day, and said I seemed to be flourishing in spite of my wall-paper.

I turned it off with a laugh. I had no intention of telling him it was BECAUSE of the wall-paper—he would make fun of me. He might even want to take me away.

I don't want to leave now until I have found it out. There is a week more, and I think that will be enough.

I'm feeling ever so much better! I don't sleep much at night, for it is so interesting to watch developments; but I sleep a good deal in the daytime.

In the daytime it is tiresome and perplexing.

There are always new shoots on the fungus, and new shades of yellow all over it. I cannot keep count of them, though I have tried conscientiously.

It is the strangest yellow, that wall-paper! It makes me think of all the yellow things I ever saw—not beautiful ones like buttercups, but old foul, bad yellow things.

But there is something else about that paper—the smell! I noticed it the moment we came into the room, but with so much air and sun it was not bad. Now we have had a week of fog and rain, and whether the windows are open or not, the smell is here.

It creeps all over the house.

I find it hovering in the dining-room, skulking in the parlor, hiding in the hall, lying in wait for me on the stairs.

It gets into my hair.

Even when I go to ride, if I turn my head suddenly and surprise it—there is that smell!

Such a peculiar odor, too! I have spent hours in trying to analyze it, to find what it smelled like.

It is not bad—at first, and very gentle, but quite the subtlest, most enduring odor I ever met.

In this damp weather it is awful, I wake up in the night and find it hanging over me.

It used to disturb me at first. I thought seriously of burning the house—to reach the smell.

But now I am used to it. The only thing I can think of that it is like is the COLOR of the paper! A yellow smell.

There is a very funny mark on this wall, low down, near the mopboard. A streak that runs round the room. It goes behind every piece of furniture, except the bed, a long, straight, even SMOOCH, as if it had been rubbed over and over.

I wonder how it was done and who did it, and what they did it for. Round and round and round—round and round and round—it makes me dizzy!

I really have discovered something at last.

Through watching so much at night, when it changes so, I have finally found out.

The front pattern DOES move—and no wonder! The woman behind shakes it!

Sometimes I think there are a great many women behind, and sometimes only one, and she crawls around fast, and her crawling shakes it all over.

Then in the very bright spots she keeps still, and in the very shady spots she just takes hold of the bars and shakes them hard.

And she is all the time trying to climb through. But nobody could climb through that pattern—it strangles so; I think that is why it has so many heads.

They get through, and then the pattern strangles them off and turns them upside down, and makes their eyes white!

If those heads were covered or taken off it would not be half so bad.

I think that woman gets out in the daytime!

And I'll tell you why—privately—I've seen her!

I can see her out of every one of my windows!

It is the same woman, I know, for she is always creeping, and most women do not creep by daylight.

I see her on that long road under the trees, creeping along, and when a carriage comes she hides under the blackberry vines.

I don't blame her a bit. It must be very humiliating to be caught creeping by daylight!

I always lock the door when I creep by daylight. I can't do it at night, for I know John would suspect something at once.

And John is so queer now, that I don't want to irritate him. I wish he would take another room! Besides, I don't want anybody to get that woman out at night but myself.

I often wonder if I could see her out of all the windows at once.

But, turn as fast as I can, I can only see out of one at one time.

And though I always see her, she MAY be able to creep faster than I can turn!

I have watched her sometimes away off in the open country, creeping as fast as a cloud shadow in a high wind.

If only that top pattern could be gotten off from the under one! I mean to try it, little by little.

I have found out another funny thing, but I shan't tell it this time! It does not do to trust people too much.

There are only two more days to get this paper off, and I believe John is beginning to notice. I don't like the look in his eyes.

And I heard him ask Jennie a lot of professional questions about me. She had a very good report to give.

She said I slept a good deal in the daytime.

John knows I don't sleep very well at night, for all I'm so quiet!

He asked me all sorts of questions, too, and pretended to be very loving and kind.

As if I couldn't see through him!

Still, I don't wonder he acts so, sleeping under this paper for three months.

It only interests me, but I feel sure John and Jennie are secretly affected by it.

Hurrah! This is the last day, but it is enough. John is to stay in town over night, and won't be out until this evening.

Jennie wanted to sleep with me—the sly thing! but I told her I should undoubtedly rest better for a night all alone.

That was clever, for really I wasn't alone a bit! As soon as it was moonlight and that poor thing began to crawl and shake the pattern, I got up and ran to help her.

I pulled and she shook, I shook and she pulled, and before morning we had peeled off yards of that paper.

A strip about as high as my head and half around the room.

And then when the sun came and that awful pattern began to laugh at me, I declared I would finish it to-day!

We go away to-morrow, and they are moving all my furniture down again to leave things as they were before.

Jennie looked at the wall in amazement, but I told her merrily that I did it out of pure spite at the vicious thing.

She laughed and said she wouldn't mind doing it herself, but I must not get tired.

How she betrayed herself that time!

But I am here, and no person touches this paper but me—not ALIVE!

She tried to get me out of the room—it was too patent! But I said it was so quiet and empty and clean now that I believed I would lie down again and sleep all I could; and not to wake me even for dinner—I would call when I woke.

So now she is gone, and the servants are gone, and the things are gone, and there is nothing left but that great bedstead nailed down, with the canvas mattress we found on it.

We shall sleep downstairs to-night, and take the boat home to-morrow.

I quite enjoy the room, now it is bare again.

How those children did tear about here!

This bedstead is fairly gnawed!

But I must get to work.

I have locked the door and thrown the key down into the front path.

I don't want to go out, and I don't want to have anybody come in, till John comes.

I want to astonish him.

I've got a rope up here that even Jennie did not find. If that woman does get out, and tries to get away, I can tie her!

But I forgot I could not reach far without anything to stand on!

This bed will NOT move!

I tried to lift and push it until I was lame, and then I got so angry I bit off a little piece at one corner—but it hurt my teeth.

Then I peeled off all the paper I could reach standing on the floor. It sticks horribly and the pattern just enjoys it! All those strangled heads and bulbous eyes and waddling fungus growths just shriek with derision!

I am getting angry enough to do something desperate. To jump out of the window would be admirable exercise, but the bars are too strong even to try.

Besides I wouldn't do it. Of course not. I know well enough that a step like that is improper and might be misconstrued.

I don't like to LOOK out of the windows even—there are so many of those creeping women, and they creep so fast.

I wonder if they all come out of that wall-paper as I did?

174

But I am securely fastened now by my well-hidden rope—you don't get ME out in the road there!

I suppose I shall have to get back behind the pattern when it comes night, and that is hard!

It is so pleasant to be out in this great room and creep around as I please!

I don't want to go outside. I won't, even if Jennie asks me to.

For outside you have to creep on the ground, and everything is green instead of yellow.

But here I can creep smoothly on the floor, and my shoulder just fits in that long smooch around the wall, so I cannot lose my way.

Why there's John at the door!

It is no use, young man, you can't open it!

How he does call and pound!

Now he's crying for an axe.

It would be a shame to break down that beautiful door!

"John dear!" said I in the gentlest voice, "the key is down by the front steps, under a plantain leaf!"

That silenced him for a few moments.

Then he said—very quietly indeed, "Open the door, my darling!"

"I can't," said I. "The key is down by the front door under a plantain leaf!"

And then I said it again, several times, very gently and slowly, and said it so often that he had to go and see, and he got it of course, and came in. He stopped short by the door.

"What is the matter?" he cried. "For God's sake, what are you doing!"

I kept on creeping just the same, but I looked at him over my shoulder.

"I've got out at last," said I, "in spite of you and Jane. And I've pulled off most of the paper, so you can't put me back!"

Now why should that man have fainted? But he did, and right across my path by the wall, so that I had to creep over him every time!

COLLEGE WRITING 1: REFLECTION WITHIN THE TEXT

You've been diagnosed with melancholia. Who in your life would you be forced to turn to for advice? Why would you be expected to trust this person?

Imagine that this person asks you to stay in your room, and speak to no one for a week. They take away your phone, computer, TV. You have no music to listen to or books to read.

Your room has a bed, a table and chair, and no other objects. Describe what the room looks like. What color is it? What does that color mean? What would you do to pass the time? Write a story similar to "The Yellow Wallpaper" of going mad in isolation.

COLLEGE WRITING 2: RESEARCH OUTSIDE THE TEXT

Research medical views of women in the 1890s. What is the scientific rationale, at that time, for the treatments John prescribes for the narrator? Were his views held by the majority of people at the time? What were some of the other opinions of the time? Using what you've learned from your research, write a piece from John's perspective that explains and defends his medical treatment of the narrator.

IDEAS AND VALUES: CONNECT THE TEXT

» In London's "To Build A Fire" the main character is always referred to as "the man," or simply "he." In Gilman's "The Yellow Wallpaper" the narrator never directly gives us her name, while her husband refers to her only as: "blessed little goose," "Darling," "his darling," and "little girl." In Crane's "The Blue Hotel" there are the characters of the Easterner, the Cowboy, the Swede, and the Gambler, but also Pat and Johnnie Scully. What is the nature of anonymity? What do the anonymous characters in these stories have in common? Between these texts, does anonymity seem to be a good thing? Are the anonymous characters the most powerful, or fortunate characters in their respective stories? Ultimately why are some characters named and others not?

» What meaning is there in a color? Why are stop signs red? What is the color of sadness? Why do we wrap little boys in blue and girls in pink? Why do brides wear white on their wedding day? What is the significance of the title colors in their respective stories: "The Yellow Wallpaper," by Gilman, "Porcelain and Pink," by Fitzgerald, and "The Blue Hotel," by Crane? Could different colors have been used without changing these stories?

»   In Chopin's "Story of an Hour" Louise Mallard's marriage seems to have ended abruptly with a sudden "railroad accident," and we find her in her room, celebrating her newfound freedom, while in "The Yellow Wallpaper," the narrator's husband uses his role as patriarch and physician to prescribe his wife's country home into a prison. Lastly, in E.M. Forester's "The Machine Stops," Kuno's mother, Vashti becomes increasingly alarmed at her son's rejection of their underground culture, as he derides her unquestioning fealty to the machine as mere worship—and eventually he reveals to her his will to live on the surface. In these three texts there is a force that holds captive one or more person; consider these forces individually, and explore how they operate, their functions, how they came into being, and what good or evil they do. What is the essence of captivity? Why does it exist? Is it pure cruelty—or is there something else?

»   Oscar Wilde writes in "Impressions of America" about the strange differences both good and bad between England and its former colony, the United States; W.E.B. Du Bois writes in "Of Our Spiritual Strivings" that "the words I longed for, and all their dazzling opportunities, were theirs, not mine," and in Gilman's "Yellow Wallpaper", the main character, having found herself on the "wrong side," of matrimony, country living, and her husband's medical opinion, gives us her unique perspective as well. What does perspective mean— how is it formed? What makes a perspective unique? What makes a perspective important, or worthwhile to understand? How does one get the perspective of another—or is it even possible to see through the eyes of another?

The Sheriff's Children

By Charles Chesnutt

6,813 WORDS. 38 MINUTES.
READING LEVEL: GRADE 10.2

Branson County, North Carolina, is in a sequestered district of one of the staidest and most conservative States of the Union. Society in Branson County is almost primitive in its simplicity. Most of the white people own the farms they till, and even before the war there were no very wealthy families to force their neighbors, by comparison, into the category of "poor whites."

To Branson County, as to most rural communities in the South, the war is the one historical event that overshadows all others. It is the era from which all local chronicles are dated,—births, deaths, marriages, storms, freshets. No description of the life of any Southern community would be perfect that failed to emphasize the all pervading influence of the great conflict.

Yet the fierce tide of war that had rushed through the cities and along the great highways of the country had comparatively speaking but slightly disturbed the sluggish current of life in this region, remote from railroads and navigable streams. To the north in Virginia, to the west in Tennessee, and all along the seaboard the war had raged; but the thunder of its cannon had not disturbed the echoes of Branson County, where the loudest sounds heard were the crack of some hunter's rifle, the baying of some deep-mouthed hound, or the yodel of some tuneful negro on his way through the pine forest. To the east, Sherman's army had passed on its march to the sea; but no straggling band of "bummers" had penetrated the confines of Branson County. The war, it is true, had robbed the county of the flower of its young manhood; but the burden of taxation, the doubt and uncertainty of the conflict, and the sting of ultimate defeat, had been borne by the people with an apathy that robbed misfortune of half its sharpness.

The nearest approach to town life afforded by Branson County is found in the little village of Troy, the county seat, a hamlet with a population of four or five hundred.

Ten years make little difference in the appearance of these remote Southern towns. If a railroad is built through one of them, it infuses some enterprise; the social corpse is galvanized by the fresh blood of civilization that pulses along the farthest ramifications of our great system of commercial highways. At the period of which I write, no railroad had come to Troy. If a traveler, accustomed to the bustling life of cities, could have ridden through Troy on a summer day, he might easily have fancied himself in a deserted village. Around him he would have seen weather-beaten houses, innocent of paint, the shingled roofs in many instances covered with a rich growth of moss. Here and there he would have met a razor-backed hog lazily rooting his way along the principal thoroughfare; and more than once he would probably have had to disturb the slumbers of some yellow dog, dozing away the hours in the ardent sunshine, and reluctantly yielding up his place in the middle of the dusty road.

On Saturdays the village presented a somewhat livelier appearance, and the shade trees around the court house square and along Front Street served as hitching-posts for a goodly number of horses and mules and stunted oxen, belonging to the farmer-folk who had come in to trade at the two or three local stores.

A murder was a rare event in Branson County. Every well-informed citizen could tell the number of homicides committed in the county for fifty years back, and whether the slayer, in any given instance, had escaped, either by flight or acquittal, or had suffered the penalty of the law. So, when it became known in Troy early one Friday morning in summer, about ten years after the war, that old Captain Walker, who had served in Mexico under Scott, and had left an arm on the field of Gettysburg, had been foully murdered during the night, there was intense excitement in the village. Business was practically suspended, and the citizens gathered in little groups to discuss the murder, and speculate upon the identity of the murderer. It transpired from testimony at the coroner's inquest, held during the morning, that a strange mulatto had been seen going in the direction of Captain Walker's house the night before, and had been met going away from Troy early Friday morning, by a farmer on his way to town. Other circumstances seemed to connect the stranger with the crime. The sheriff organized a posse to search for him, and early in the evening, when most of the citizens of Troy were at supper, the suspected man was brought in and lodged in the county jail.

By the following morning the news of the capture had spread to the farthest limits of the county. A much larger number of people than usual came to town that Saturday,—bearded men in straw hats and blue home-spun shirts, and butternut trousers of great amplitude of material and vagueness of outline; women in homespun frocks and slat-bonnets, with faces as expressionless as the dreary sandhills which gave them a meagre sustenance.

The murder was almost the sole topic of conversation. A steady stream of curious observers visited the house of mourning, and gazed upon the rugged face of the old veteran, now stiff and cold in death; and more than one eye dropped a tear at the remembrance of the cheery smile, and the joke—sometimes superannuated, generally feeble, but always good-natured—with which the captain had been wont to greet his acquaintances. There was a growing sentiment of anger among these stern men, toward the murderer who had thus cut down their friend, and a strong feeling that ordinary justice was too slight a punishment for such a crime.

Toward noon there was an informal gathering of citizens in Dan Tyson's store.

"I hear it 'lowed that Square Kyahtah's too sick ter hol' co'te this evenin'," said one, "an' that the purlim'nary hearin' 'll haf ter go over 'tel nex' week."

A look of disappointment went round the crowd.

"Hit 's the durndes', meanes' murder ever committed in this caoun-ty," said another, with moody emphasis.

"I s'pose the n——- 'lowed the Cap'n had some green-backs," observed a third speaker.

"The Cap'n," said another, with an air of superior information, "has left two bairls of Confedrit money, which he 'spected 'ud be good some day er nuther."

This statement gave rise to a discussion of the speculative value of Confederate money; but in a little while the conversation returned to the murder.

"Hangin' air too good fer the murderer," said one; "he oughter be burnt, stidier bein' hung."

There was an impressive pause at this point, during which a jug of moonlight whiskey went the round of the crowd.

"Well," said a round-shouldered farmer, who, in spite of his peace-able expression and faded gray eye, was known to have been one of the most daring followers of a rebel guerrilla chieftain, "what air yer gwine ter do about it? Ef you fellers air gwine ter set down an' let a wuthless n———kill the bes' white man in Branson, an' not say nuthin' ner do nuthin', *I'll* move outen the caounty."

This speech gave tone and direction to the rest of the conversation. Whether the fear of losing the round-shouldered farmer operated to bring about the result or not is immaterial to this narrative; but, at all events, the crowd decided to lynch the negro. They agreed that this was the least that could be done to avenge the death of their murdered friend, and that it was a becoming way in which to honor his memory. They had some vague notions of the majesty of the law and the rights of the citizen, but in the passion of the moment these sunk into oblivion; a white man had been killed by a negro.

"The Cap'n was an ole sodger," said one of his friends solemnly. "He 'll sleep better when he knows that a co'te-martial has be'n hilt an' jestice done."

By agreement the lynchers were to meet at Tyson's store at five o'clock in the afternoon, and proceed thence to the jail, which was situated down the Lumberton Dirt Road (as the old turnpike antedating the plank-road was called), about half a mile south of the court-house. When the preliminaries of the lynching had been arranged, and a committee appointed to manage the affair, the crowd dispersed, some to go to their dinners, and some to secure recruits for the lynching party.

It was twenty minutes to five o'clock, when an excited negro, panting and perspiring, rushed up to the back door of Sheriff Campbell's dwelling, which stood at a little distance from the jail and somewhat farther than the latter building from the court-house. A turbaned colored woman came to the door in response to the negro's knock.

"Hoddy, Sis' Nance."

"Hoddy, Brer Sam."

"Is de shurff in," inquired the negro.

"Yas, Brer Sam, he 's eatin' his dinner," was the answer.

"Will yer ax 'im ter step ter de do' a minute, Sis' Nance?"

The woman went into the dining-room, and a moment later the sheriff came to the door. He was a tall, muscular man, of a ruddier complexion than is usual among Southerners. A pair of keen, deep-set gray eyes looked out from under bushy eyebrows, and about his mouth was a masterful expression, which a full beard, once sandy in color, but now profusely sprinkled with gray, could not entirely conceal. The day was hot; the sheriff had discarded his coat and vest, and had his white shirt open at the throat.

"What do you want, Sam?" he inquired of the negro, who stood hat in hand, wiping the moisture from his face with a ragged shirt-sleeve.

"Shurff, dey gwine ter hang de pris'ner w'at 's lock' up in de jail. Dey 're comin' dis a-way now. I wuz layin' down on a sack er corn down at de sto', behine a pile er flour-bairls, w'en I hearn Doc' Cain en Kunnel Wright talkin' erbout it. I slip' outen de back do', en run here as fas' as I could. I hearn you say down ter de sto' once't dat you would n't let nobody take a pris'ner 'way fum you widout walkin' over yo' dead body, en I thought I 'd let you know 'fo' dey come, so yer could pertec' de pris'ner."

The sheriff listened calmly, but his face grew firmer, and a determined gleam lit up his gray eyes. His frame grew more erect, and he unconsciously assumed the attitude of a soldier who momentarily expects to meet the enemy face to face.

"Much obliged, Sam," he answered. "I 'll protect the prisoner. Who 's coming?"

"I dunno who-all *is* comin'," replied the negro. "Dere 's Mistah McSwayne, en Doc' Cain, en Maje' McDonal', en Kunnel Wright, en a heap er yuthers. I wuz so skeered I done furgot mo' d'n half un em. I spec' dey mus' be mos' here by dis time, so I 'll git outen de way, fer I don' want nobody fer ter think I wuz mix' up in dis business." The negro glanced nervously down the road toward the town, and made a movement as if to go away.

"Won't you have some dinner first?" asked the sheriff.

The negro looked longingly in at the open door, and sniffed the appetizing odor of boiled pork and collards.

"I ain't got no time fer ter tarry, Shurff," he said, "but Sis' Nance mought gin me sump'n I could kyar in my han' en eat on de way."

A moment later Nancy brought him a huge sandwich of split corn-pone, with a thick slice of fat bacon inserted between the halves, and a couple of baked yams. The negro hastily replaced his ragged hat on his head, dropped the yams in the pocket of his capacious trousers, and, taking the sandwich in his hand, hurried across the road and disappeared in the woods beyond.

The sheriff reëntered the house, and put on his coat and hat. He then took down a double-barreled shotgun and loaded it with buckshot. Filling the chambers of a revolver with fresh cartridges, he slipped it into the pocket of the sack-coat which he wore.

A comely young woman in a calico dress watched these proceedings with anxious surprise.

"Where are you going, father?" she asked. She had not heard the conversation with the negro.

"I am goin' over to the jail," responded the sheriff. "There 's a mob comin' this way to lynch the n——- we 've got locked up. But they won't do it," he added, with emphasis.

"Oh, father! don't go!" pleaded the girl, clinging to his arm; "they 'll shoot you if you don't give him up."

"You never mind me, Polly," said her father reassuringly, as he gently unclasped her hands from his arm. "I 'll take care of myself and the prisoner, too. There ain't a man in Branson County that would shoot me. Besides, I have faced fire too often to be scared away from my duty. You keep close in the house," he continued, "and if any one disturbs you just use the old horse-pistol in the top bureau drawer. It 's a little old-fashioned, but it did good work a few years ago."

The young girl shuddered at this sanguinary allusion, but made no further objection to her father's departure.

The sheriff of Branson was a man far above the average of the community in wealth, education, and social position. His had been one of the few families in the county that before the war had owned large estates and numerous slaves. He had graduated at the State University at Chapel Hill, and had kept up some acquaintance with current literature and advanced thought. He had traveled some in his youth, and was looked up to in the county as an authority on all subjects connected with the outer world. At first an ardent supporter of the Union, he had opposed the secession movement in his native State as long as opposition availed to stem the tide of public opinion. Yielding at last to the force of circumstances, he had entered the Confederate service rather late in the war, and served with distinction through several campaigns, rising in time to the rank of colonel. After the war he had taken the oath of allegiance, and had been chosen by the people as the most available candidate for the office of sheriff, to which he had been elected without opposition. He had filled the office for several terms, and was universally popular with his constituents.

Colonel or Sheriff Campbell, as he was indifferently called, as the military or civil title happened to be most important in the opinion of the person addressing him, had a high sense of the responsibility attaching to his office. He had sworn to do his duty faithfully, and he knew what his duty was, as sheriff, perhaps more clearly than he had apprehended it in other passages of his life. It was, therefore, with no uncertainty in regard to his course that he prepared his weapons and went over to the jail. He had no fears for Polly's safety.

The sheriff had just locked the heavy front door of the jail behind him when a half dozen horsemen, followed by a crowd of men on foot, came round a bend in the road and drew near the jail. They halted in front of the picket fence that surrounded the building, while several of the committee of arrangements rode on a few rods farther to the sheriff's house. One of them dismounted and rapped on the door with his riding-whip.

"Is the sheriff at home?" he inquired.

"No, he has just gone out," replied Polly, who had come to the door.

"We want the jail keys," he continued.

"They are not here," said Polly. "The sheriff has them himself." Then she added, with assumed indifference, "He is at the jail now."

The man turned away, and Polly went into the front room, from which she peered anxiously between the slats of the green blinds of a window that looked toward the jail. Meanwhile the messenger returned to his companions and announced his discovery. It looked as though the sheriff had learned of their design and was preparing to resist it.

One of them stepped forward and rapped on the jail door.

"Well, what is it?" said the sheriff, from within.

"We want to talk to you, Sheriff," replied the spokesman.

There was a little wicket in the door; this the sheriff opened, and answered through it.

"All right, boys, talk away. You are all strangers to me, and I don't know what business you can have." The sheriff did not think it necessary to recognize anybody in particular on such an occasion; the question of identity sometimes comes up in the investigation of these extra-judicial executions.

"We 're a committee of citizens and we want to get into the jail."

"What for? It ain't much trouble to get into jail. Most people want to keep out."

The mob was in no humor to appreciate a joke, and the sheriff's witticism fell dead upon an unresponsive audience.

"We want to have a talk with the n———- that killed Cap'n Walker."

"You can talk to that n———- in the court-house, when he 's brought out for trial. Court will be in session here next week. I know what you fellows want, but you can't get my prisoner to-day. Do you want to take the bread out of a poor man's mouth? I get seventy-five cents a day for keeping this prisoner, and he 's the only one in jail. I can't have my family suffer just to please you fellows."

One or two young men in the crowd laughed at the idea of Sheriff Campbell's suffering for want of seventy-five cents a day; but they were frowned into silence by those who stood near them.

"Ef yer don't let us in," cried a voice, "we 'll bu's' the do' open."

"Bust away," answered the sheriff, raising his voice so that all could hear. "But I give you fair warning. The first man that tries it will be filled with buckshot. I 'm sheriff of this county; I know my duty, and I mean to do it."

"What 's the use of kicking, Sheriff," argued one of the leaders of the mob. "The n———- is sure to hang anyhow; he richly deserves it; and we 've got to do something to teach the n———-s their places, or white people won't be able to live in the county."

"There 's no use talking, boys," responded the sheriff. "I 'm a white man outside, but in this jail I 'm sheriff; and if this n———- 's to be hung in this county, I propose to do the hanging. So you fellows might as well right-about-face, and march back to Troy. You 've had a pleasant trip, and the exercise will be good for you. You know *me*. I 've got powder and ball, and I 've faced fire before now, with nothing between me and the enemy, and I don't mean to surrender this jail while I 'm able to shoot." Having thus announced his determination, the sheriff closed and fastened the wicket, and looked around for the best position from which to defend the building.

The crowd drew off a little, and the leaders conversed together in low tones.

The Branson County jail was a small, two-story brick building, strongly constructed, with no attempt at architectural ornamentation. Each story was divided into two large cells by a passage running from front to rear. A grated iron door gave entrance from the passage to each of the four cells. The jail seldom had many prisoners in it, and the lower windows had been boarded up. When the sheriff had closed the wicket, he ascended the steep wooden stairs to the upper floor. There was no window at the front of the upper passage, and the most available position from which to watch the movements of the crowd below was the front window of the cell occupied by the solitary prisoner.

The sheriff unlocked the door and entered the cell. The prisoner was crouched in a corner, his yellow face, blanched with terror, looking ghastly in the semi-darkness of the room. A cold perspiration had gathered on his forehead, and his teeth were chattering with affright.

"For God's sake, Sheriff," he murmured hoarsely, "don't let 'em lynch me; I did n't kill the old man."

The sheriff glanced at the cowering wretch with a look of mingled contempt and loathing.

"Get up," he said sharply. "You will probably be hung sooner or later, but it shall not be to-day, if I can help it. I 'll unlock your fetters, and if I can't hold the jail, you 'll have to make the best fight you can. If I 'm shot, I 'll consider my responsibility at an end."

There were iron fetters on the prisoner's ankles, and handcuffs on his wrists. These the sheriff unlocked, and they fell clanking to the floor.

"Keep back from the window," said the sheriff. "They might shoot if they saw you."

The sheriff drew toward the window a pine bench which formed a part of the scanty furniture of the cell, and laid his revolver upon it. Then he took his gun in hand, and took his stand at the side of the window where he could with least exposure of himself watch the movements of the crowd below.

The lynchers had not anticipated any determined resistance. Of course they had looked for a formal protest, and perhaps a sufficient show of opposition to excuse the sheriff in the eye of any stickler for legal formalities. They had not however come prepared to fight a battle, and no one of them seemed willing to lead an attack upon the jail. The leaders of the party conferred together with a good deal of animated gesticulation, which was visible to the sheriff from his outlook, though the distance was too great for him to hear what was said. At length one of them broke away from the group, and rode back to the main body of the lynchers, who were restlessly awaiting orders.

"Well, boys," said the messenger, "we 'll have to let it go for the present. The sheriff says he 'll shoot, and he 's got the drop on us this time. There ain't any of us that want to follow Cap'n Walker jest yet. Besides, the sheriff is a good fellow, and we don't want to hurt 'im. But," he added, as if to reassure the crowd, which began to show signs of disappointment, "the n——- might as well say his prayers, for he ain't got long to live."

There was a murmur of dissent from the mob, and several voices insisted that an attack be made on the jail. But pacific counsels finally prevailed, and the mob sullenly withdrew.

The sheriff stood at the window until they had disappeared around the bend in the road. He did not relax his watchfulness when the last one was out of sight. Their withdrawal might be a mere feint, to be followed by a further attempt. So closely, indeed, was his attention drawn to the outside, that he neither saw nor heard the prisoner creep stealthily across the floor, reach out his hand and secure the revolver which lay on the bench behind the sheriff, and creep as noiselessly back to his place in the corner of the room.

A moment after the last of the lynching party had disappeared there was a shot fired from the woods across the road; a bullet whistled by the window and buried itself in the wooden casing a few inches from where the sheriff was standing. Quick as thought, with the instinct born of a semi-guerrilla army experience, he raised his gun and fired twice at the point from which a faint puff of smoke showed the hostile bullet to have been sent. He stood a moment watching, and then rested his gun against the window, and reached behind him mechanically for the other weapon. It was not on the bench. As the sheriff realized this fact, he turned his head and looked into the muzzle of the revolver.

"Stay where you are, Sheriff," said the prisoner, his eyes glistening, his face almost ruddy with excitement.

The sheriff mentally cursed his own carelessness for allowing him to be caught in such a predicament. He had not expected anything of the kind. He had relied on the negro's cowardice and subordination in the presence of an armed white man as a matter of course. The sheriff was a brave man, but realized that the prisoner had him at an immense disadvantage. The two men stood thus for a moment, fighting a harmless duel with their eyes.

"Well, what do you mean to do?" asked the sheriff with apparent calmness.

"To get away, of course," said the prisoner, in a tone which caused the sheriff to look at him more closely, and with an involuntary feeling of apprehension; if the man was not mad, he was in a state of mind akin to madness, and quite as dangerous. The sheriff felt that he must speak the prisoner fair, and watch for a chance to turn the tables on him. The keen-eyed, desperate man before him was a different being altogether from the groveling wretch who had begged so piteously for life a few minutes before.

At length the sheriff spoke:——

"Is this your gratitude to me for saving your life at the risk of my own? If I had not done so, you would now be swinging from the limb of some neighboring tree."

"True," said the prisoner, "you saved my life, but for how long? When you came in, you said Court would sit next week. When the crowd went away they said I had not long to live. It is merely a choice of two ropes."

"While there 's life there 's hope," replied the sheriff. He uttered this commonplace mechanically, while his brain was busy in trying to think out some way of escape. "If you are innocent you can prove it."

The mulatto kept his eye upon the sheriff. "I did n't kill the old man," he replied; "but I shall never be able to clear myself. I was at his house at nine o'clock. I stole from it the coat that was on my back when I was taken. I would be convicted, even with a fair trial, unless the real murderer were discovered beforehand."

The sheriff knew this only too well. While he was thinking what argument next to use, the prisoner continued:——

"Throw me the keys—no, unlock the door."

The sheriff stood a moment irresolute. The mulatto's eye glittered ominously. The sheriff crossed the room and unlocked the door leading into the passage.

188

"Now go down and unlock the outside door."

The heart of the sheriff leaped within him. Perhaps he might make a dash for liberty, and gain the outside. He descended the narrow stairs, the prisoner keeping close behind him.

The sheriff inserted the huge iron key into the lock. The rusty bolt yielded slowly. It still remained for him to pull the door open.

"Stop!" thundered the mulatto, who seemed to divine the sheriff's purpose. "Move a muscle, and I 'll blow your brains out."

The sheriff obeyed; he realized that his chance had not yet come.

"Now keep on that side of the passage, and go back upstairs."

Keeping the sheriff under cover of the revolver, the mulatto followed him up the stairs. The sheriff expected the prisoner to lock him into the cell and make his own escape. He had about come to the conclusion that the best thing he could do under the circumstances was to submit quietly, and take his chances of recapturing the prisoner after the alarm had been given. The sheriff had faced death more than once upon the battlefield. A few minutes before, well armed, and with a brick wall between him and them he had dared a hundred men to fight; but he felt instinctively that the desperate man confronting him was not to be trifled with, and he was too prudent a man to risk his life against such heavy odds. He had Polly to look after, and there was a limit beyond which devotion to duty would be quixotic and even foolish.

"I want to get away," said the prisoner, "and I don't want to be captured; for if I am I know I will be hung on the spot. I am afraid," he added somewhat reflectively, "that in order to save myself I shall have to kill you."

"Good God!" exclaimed the sheriff in involuntary terror; "you would not kill the man to whom you owe your own life."

"You speak more truly than you know," replied the mulatto. "I indeed owe my life to you."

The sheriff started, he was capable of surprise, even in that moment of extreme peril. "Who are you?" he asked in amazement.

"Tom, Cicely's son," returned the other. He had closed the door and stood talking to the sheriff through the grated opening. "Don't you remember Cicely—Cicely whom you sold, with her child, to the specula-tor on his way to Alabama?"

The sheriff did remember. He had been sorry for it many a time since. It had been the old story of debts, mortgages, and bad crops. He had quarreled with the mother. The price offered for her and her child had been unusually large, and he had yielded to the combination of anger and pecuniary stress.

"Good God!" he gasped, "you would not murder your own father?"

"My father?" replied the mulatto. "It were well enough for me to claim the relationship, but it comes with poor grace from you to ask anything by reason of it. What father's duty have you ever performed for me? Did you give me your name, or even your protection? Other white men gave their colored sons freedom and money, and sent them to the free States. *You* sold *me* to the rice swamps."

"I at least gave you the life you cling to," murmured the sheriff.

"Life?" said the prisoner, with a sarcastic laugh. "What kind of a life? You gave me your own blood, your own features,—no man need look at us together twice to see that,—and you gave me a black mother. Poor wretch! She died under the lash, because she had enough womanhood to call her soul her own. You gave me a white man's spirit, and you made me a slave, and crushed it out."

"But you are free now," said the sheriff. He had not doubted, could not doubt, the mulatto's word. He knew whose passions coursed beneath that swarthy skin and burned in the black eyes opposite his own. He saw in this mulatto what he himself might have become had not the safe-guards of parental restraint and public opinion been thrown around him.

"Free to do what?" replied the mulatto. "Free in name, but despised and scorned and set aside by the people to whose race I belong far more than to my mother's."

"There are schools," said the sheriff. "You have been to school." He had noticed that the mulatto spoke more eloquently and used better language than most Branson County people.

"I have been to school, and dreamed when I went that it would work some marvelous change in my condition. But what did I learn? I learned to feel that no degree of learning or wisdom will change the color of my skin and that I shall always wear what in my own country is a badge of degradation. When I think about it seriously I do not care particularly for such a life. It is the animal in me, not the man, that flees the gallows. I owe you nothing," he went on, "and expect nothing of you; and it would be no more than justice if I should avenge upon you my mother's wrongs and my own. But still I hate to shoot you; I have never yet taken human life—for I did *not* kill the old captain. Will you promise to give no alarm and make no attempt to capture me until morning, if I do not shoot?"

So absorbed were the two men in their colloquy and their own tumultuous thoughts that neither of them had heard the door below move upon its hinges. Neither of them had heard a light step come stealthily up the stairs, nor seen a slender form creep along the darkening passage toward the mulatto.

The sheriff hesitated. The struggle between his love of life and his sense of duty was a terrific one. It may seem strange that a man who could sell his own child into slavery should hesitate at such a moment, when his life was trembling in the balance. But the baleful influence of human slavery poisoned the very fountains of life, and created new standards of right. The sheriff was conscientious; his conscience had merely been warped by his environment. Let no one ask what his answer would have been; he was spared the necessity of a decision.

"Stop," said the mulatto, "you need not promise. I could not trust you if you did. It is your life for mine; there is but one safe way for me; you must die."

He raised his arm to fire, when there was a flash—a report from the passage behind him. His arm fell heavily at his side, and the pistol dropped at his feet.

The sheriff recovered first from his surprise, and throwing open the door secured the fallen weapon. Then seizing the prisoner he thrust him into the cell and locked the door upon him; after which he turned to Polly, who leaned half-fainting against the wall, her hands clasped over her heart.

"Oh, father, I was just in time!" she cried hysterically, and, wildly sobbing, threw herself into her father's arms.

"I watched until they all went away," she said. "I heard the shot from the woods and I saw you shoot. Then when you did not come out I feared something had happened, that perhaps you had been wounded. I got out the other pistol and ran over here. When I found the door open, I knew something was wrong, and when I heard voices I crept upstairs, and reached the top just in time to hear him say he would kill you. Oh, it was a narrow escape!"

When she had grown somewhat calmer, the sheriff left her standing there and went back into the cell. The prisoner's arm was bleeding from a flesh wound. His bravado had given place to a stony apathy. There was no sign in his face of fear or disappointment or feeling of any kind. The sheriff sent Polly to the house for cloth, and bound up the prisoner's wound with a rude skill acquired during his army life.

"I 'll have a doctor come and dress the wound in the morning," he said to the prisoner. "It will do very well until then, if you will keep quiet. If the doctor asks you how the wound was caused, you can say that you were struck by the bullet fired from the woods. It would do you no good to have it known that you were shot while attempting to escape."

The prisoner uttered no word of thanks or apology, but sat in sullen silence. When the wounded arm had been bandaged, Polly and her father returned to the house.

The sheriff was in an unusually thoughtful mood that evening. He put salt in his coffee at supper, and poured vinegar over his pancakes. To many of Polly's questions he returned random answers. When he had gone to bed he lay awake for several hours.

In the silent watches of the night, when he was alone with God, there came into his mind a flood of unaccustomed thoughts. An hour or two before, standing face to face with death, he had experienced a sensation similar to that which drowning men are said to feel—a kind of clarifying of the moral faculty, in which the veil of the flesh, with its obscuring passions and prejudices, is pushed aside for a moment, and all the acts of one's life stand out, in the clear light of truth, in their correct proportions and relations,—a state of mind in which one sees himself as God may be supposed to see him. In the reaction following his rescue, this feeling had given place for a time to far different emotions. But now, in the silence of midnight, something of this clearness of spirit returned to the sheriff. He saw that he had owed some duty to this son of his,—that neither law nor custom could destroy a responsibility inherent in the nature of mankind. He could not thus, in the eyes of God at least, shake off the consequences of his sin. Had he never sinned, this wayward spirit would never have come back from the vanished past to haunt him. As these thoughts came, his anger against the mulatto died away, and in its place there sprang up a great pity. The hand of parental authority might have restrained the passions he had seen burning in the prisoner's eyes when the desperate

192

man spoke the words which had seemed to doom his father to death. The sheriff felt that he might have saved this fiery spirit from the slough of slavery; that he might have sent him to the free North, and given him there, or in some other land, an opportunity to turn to usefulness and honorable pursuits the talents that had run to crime, perhaps to madness; he might, still less, have given this son of his the poor simulacrum of liberty which men of his caste could possess in a slave-holding community; or least of all, but still something, he might have kept the boy on the plantation, where the burdens of slavery would have fallen lightly upon him.

The sheriff recalled his own youth. He had inherited an honored name to keep untarnished; he had had a future to make; the picture of a fair young bride had beckoned him on to happiness. The poor wretch now stretched upon a pallet of straw between the brick walls of the jail had none of these things,—no name, no father, no mother—in the true meaning of motherhood,—and until the past few years no possible future, and then one vague and shadowy in its outline, and dependent for form and substance upon the slow solution of a problem in which there were many unknown quantities.

From what he might have done to what he might yet do was an easy transition for the awakened conscience of the sheriff. It occurred to him, purely as a hypothesis, that he might permit his prisoner to escape; but his oath of office, his duty as sheriff, stood in the way of such a course, and the sheriff dismissed the idea from his mind. He could, however, investigate the circumstances of the murder, and moveHeaven and earth to discover the real criminal, for he no longer doubted the prisoner's innocence; he could employ counsel for the accused, and perhaps influence public opinion in his favor. An acquittal once secured, some plan could be devised by which the sheriff might in some degree atone for his crime against this son of his—against society—against God.

When the sheriff had reached this conclusion he fell into an unquiet slumber, from which he awoke late the next morning.

He went over to the jail before breakfast and found the prisoner lying on his pallet, his face turned to the wall; he did not move when the sheriff rattled the door.

"Good-morning," said the latter, in a tone intended to waken the prisoner.

There was no response. The sheriff looked more keenly at the recumbent figure; there was an unnatural rigidity about its attitude.

He hastily unlocked the door and, entering the cell, bent over the prostrate form. There was no sound of breathing; he turned the body over—it was cold and stiff. The prisoner had torn the bandage from his wound and bled to death during the night. He had evidently been dead several hours.

COLLEGE WRITING 1: REFLECTION WITHIN THE TEXT

Chesnutt's "The Sheriff's Children" is as much about race, slavery, and corruption as it is about belonging; look at the title of the story—it is not "The Sheriff's Son," or "The Sheriff's Child," but "The Sheriff's Children". Why? Why did Chesnutt choose to give the Sheriff a daughter, and to include her in the title? What does she have to do with the sheriff's son?

Consider—what would have happened if the son had not allowed himself to die in that prison cell. Imagine if he had been acquitted and saved as was the sheriff's plan. Imagine the best possible outcome—that they make amends and the sheriff offers to take his son back into his home. Then what?

COLLEGE WRITING 2: RESEARCH OUTSIDE THE TEXT

What is belonging—and why do humans do it? Why do humans form groups, and socialize? Why do groups cast certain members out—even if they've done nothing wrong, committed no crimes, and contribute to the survival of the group? What is the significance between identity and group membership in human social relations?

IDEAS AND VALUES: CONNECT THE TEXT

»   How do the outcasts in Hawthorne's "Wakefield," Woolf's "The New Dress," and Chesnutt's "The Sheriff's Children" differ? How are they the same? Why are the characters outcasts? Who casts them out? How does society view each of the outcasts in these stories? What kind of society would cast these people out?

»   Swift's "A Modest Proposal" Chesnutt's "The Sheriff's Children" and W.E.B. Du Bois's "Of Our Spiritual Strivings," explore the concepts of compassion and empathy—the ability to imagine what it's like to be another person, or the unwillingness to do so. How do the problems in each of the texts compare? What happens when an individual, or group of people, are classified as a "problems"? How should society deal with societal problems? How does it deal with the problems in these three texts? What is the nature of people as problem—is it even fair to think of a person as a problem? What does it do to a person to call them a problem?

» In Chesnutt's "The Sheriff's Children," Twain's "The Stolen White Elephant," and Twain's "The War Prayer" there exists forms of conformity and nonconformity. What is conformity—is it one's actions, one's thoughts, more, less? And how is it determined what conforming is and what isn't? Why does one conform in the first place? Why would one choose to not conform? Look at the challenges faced by the nonconformists in these stories: are the nonconformists successful? What challenges do they face?

The Stolen White Elephant

by Mark Twain

6,766 WORDS. 38 MINUTES.
READING LEVEL: GRADE 10.2

1

The following curious history was related to me by a chance railway acquaintance. He was a gentleman more than seventy years of age, and his thoroughly good and gentle face and earnest and sincere manner imprinted the unmistakable stamp of truth upon every statement which fell from his lips. He said:

You know in what reverence the royal white elephant of Siam is held by the people of that country. You know it is sacred to kings, only kings may possess it, and that it is, indeed, in a measure even superior to kings, since it receives not merely honor but worship. Very well; five years ago, when the troubles concerning the frontier line arose between Great Britain and Siam, it was presently manifest that Siam had been in the wrong. Therefore every reparation was quickly made, and the British representative stated that he was satisfied and the past should be forgotten. This greatly relieved the King of Siam, and partly as a token of gratitude, but partly also, perhaps, to wipe out any little remaining vestige of unpleasantness which England might feel toward him, he wished to send the Queen a present—the sole sure way of propitiating an enemy, according to Oriental ideas. This present ought not only to be a royal one, but transcendently royal. Wherefore, what offering could be so meet as that of a white elephant? My position in the Indian civil service was such that I was deemed peculiarly worthy of the honor of conveying the present to her Majesty. A ship was fitted out for me and my servants and the officers and attendants of the elephant, and in due time I arrived in New York harbor and placed my royal charge in admirable quarters in Jersey City. It was necessary to remain awhile in order to recruit the animal's health before resuming the voyage.

All went well during a fortnight—then my calamities began. The white elephant was stolen! I was called up at dead of night and informed of this fearful misfortune. For some moments I was beside myself with terror and anxiety; I was helpless. Then I grew calmer and collected my faculties. I soon saw my course—for, indeed, there was but the one course for an intelligent man to pursue. Late as it was, I flew to New York and got a policeman to conduct me to the headquarters of the detective force. Fortunately I arrived in time, though the chief of the force, the celebrated Inspector Blunt was just on the point of leaving for his home. He was a man of middle size and compact frame, and when he was thinking deeply he had a way of knitting his brows and tapping his forehead reflectively with his finger, which impressed you at once with the conviction that you stood in the presence of a person of no common order. The very sight of him gave me confidence and made me hopeful. I stated my errand. It did not flurry him in the least; it had no more visible effect upon his iron self-possession than if I had told him somebody had stolen my dog. He motioned me to a seat, and said, calmly:

"Allow me to think a moment, please."

So saying, he sat down at his office table and leaned his head upon his hand. Several clerks were at work at the other end of the room; the scratching of their pens was all the sound I heard during the next six or seven minutes. Meantime the inspector sat there, buried in thought. Finally he raised his head, and there was that in the firm lines of his face which showed me that his brain had done its work and his plan was made. Said he—and his voice was low and impressive:

"This is no ordinary case. Every step must be warily taken; each step must be made sure before the next is ventured. And secrecy must be observed—secrecy profound and absolute. Speak to no one about the matter, not even the reporters. I will take care of them; I will see that they get only what it may suit my ends to let them know." He touched a bell; a youth appeared. "Alaric, tell the reporters to remain for the present." The boy retired. "Now let us proceed to business—and systematically. Nothing can be accomplished in this trade of mine without strict and minute method."

He took a pen and some paper. "Now—name of the elephant?"

"Hassan Ben Ali Ben Selim Abdallah Mohammed Moisé Alhammal Jamsetjejeebhoy Dhuleep Sultan Ebu Bhudpoor."

"Very well. Given name?"

"Jumbo."

"Very well. Place of birth?"

"The capital city of Siam."

"Parents living?"

"No—dead."

"Had they any other issue besides this one?"

"None. He was an only child."

"Very well. These matters are sufficient under that head. Now please describe the elephant, and leave out no particular, however insignificant—that is, insignificant from your point of view. To men in my profession there are no insignificant particulars; they do not exist."

I described, he wrote. When I was done, he said:

"Now listen. If I have made any mistakes, correct me."

He read as follows:

"Height, 19 feet; length from apex of forehead to insertion of tail, 26 feet; length of trunk, 16 feet; length of tail, 6 feet; total length, including trunk, and tail, 48 feet; length of tusks, 9 1/2 feet; ears keeping with these dimensions; footprint resembles the mark left when one up-ends a barrel in the snow; color of the elephant, a dull white; has a hole the size of a plate in each ear for the insertion of jewelry and possesses the habit in a remarkable degree of squirting water upon spectators and of maltreating with his trunk not only such persons as he is acquainted with, but even entire strangers; limps slightly with his right hind leg, and has a small scar in his left armpit caused by a former boil; had on, when stolen, a castle containing seats for fifteen persons, and a gold-cloth saddle-blanket the size of an ordinary carpet."

There were no mistakes. The inspector touched the bell, handed the description to Alaric, and said:

"Have fifty thousand copies of this printed at once and mailed to every detective office and pawnbroker's shop on the continent." Alaric retired. "There—so far, so good. Next, I must have a photograph of the property."

I gave him one. He examined it critically, and said:

"It must do, since we can do no better; but he has his trunk curled up and tucked into his mouth. That is unfortunate, and is calculated to mislead, for of course he does not usually have it in that position." He touched his bell.

"Alaric, have fifty thousand copies of this photograph made the first thing in the morning, and mail them with the descriptive circulars."

Alaric retired to execute his orders. The inspector said:

"It will be necessary to offer a reward, of course. Now as to the amount?"

"What sum would you suggest?"

"To begin with, I should say—well, twenty-five thousand dollars. It is an intricate and difficult business; there are a thousand avenues of escape and opportunities of concealment. These thieves have friends and pals everywhere—"

"Bless me, do you know who they are?"

The wary face, practised in concealing the thoughts and feelings within, gave me no token, nor yet the replying words, so quietly uttered:

"Never mind about that. I may, and I may not. We generally gather a pretty shrewd inkling of who our man is by the manner of his work and the size of the game he goes after. We are not dealing with a pickpocket or a hall thief now, make up your mind to that. This property was not 'lifted' by a novice. But, as I was saying, considering the amount of travel which will have to be done, and the diligence with which the thieves will cover up their traces as they move along, twenty-five thousand may be too small a sum to offer, yet I think it worth while to start with that."

So we determined upon that figure as a beginning. Then this man, whom nothing escaped which could by any possibility be made to serve as a clue, said:

"There are cases in detective history to show that criminals have been detected through peculiarities, in their appetites. Now, what does this elephant eat, and how much?"

"Well, as to what he eats—he will eat anything. He will eat a man, he will eat a Bible—he will eat anything between a man and a Bible."

"Good very good, indeed, but too general. Details are necessary— details are the only valuable things in our trade. Very well—as to men. At one meal—or, if you prefer, during one day—how man men will he eat, if fresh?"

"He would not care whether they were fresh or not; at a single meal he would eat five ordinary men."

"Very good; five men; we will put that down. What nationalities would he prefer?"

"He is indifferent about nationalities. He prefers acquaintances, but is not prejudiced against strangers."

"Very good. Now, as to Bibles. How many Bibles would he eat at a meal?"

"He would eat an entire edition."

"It is hardly succinct enough. Do you mean the ordinary octavo, or the family illustrated?"

"I think he would be indifferent to illustrations that is, I think he would not value illustrations above simple letterpress."

"No, you do not get my idea. I refer to bulk. The ordinary octavo Bible weighs about two pounds and a half, while the great quarto with the illustrations weighs ten or twelve. How many Dore Bibles would he eat at a meal?"

"If you knew this elephant, you could not ask. He would take what they had."

"Well, put it in dollars and cents, then. We must get at it somehow. The Dore costs a hundred dollars a copy, Russia leather, beveled."

"He would require about fifty thousand dollars worth—say an edition of five hundred copies."

"Now that is more exact. I will put that down. Very well; he likes men and Bibles; so far, so good. What else will he eat? I want particulars."

"He will leave Bibles to eat bricks, he will leave bricks to eat bottles, he will leave bottles to eat clothing, he will leave clothing to eat cats, he will leave cats to eat oysters, he will leave oysters to eat ham, he will leave ham to eat sugar, he will leave sugar to eat pie, he will leave pie to eat potatoes, he will leave potatoes to eat bran; he will leave bran to eat hay, he will leave hay to eat oats, he will leave oats to eat rice, for he was mainly raised on it. There is nothing whatever that he will not eat but European butter, and he would eat that if he could taste it."

"Very good. General quantity at a meal—say about—"

"Well, anywhere from a quarter to half a ton."

"And he drinks—"

"Everything that is fluid. Milk, water, whisky, molasses, castor oil, camphene, carbolic acid—it is no use to go into particulars; whatever fluid occurs to you set it down. He will drink anything that is fluid, except European coffee."

"Very good. As to quantity?"

"Put it down five to fifteen barrels—his thirst varies; his other appetites do not."

"These things are unusual. They ought to furnish quite good clues toward tracing him."

He touched the bell.

"Alaric; summon Captain Burns."

Burns appeared. Inspector Blunt unfolded the whole matter to him, detail by detail. Then he said in the clear, decisive tones of a man whose plans are clearly defined in his head and who is accustomed to command:

"Captain Burns, detail Detectives Jones, Davis, Halsey, Bates, and Hackett to shadow the elephant."

"Yes, sir."

"Detail Detectives Moses, Dakin, Murphy, Rogers, Tupper, Higgins, and Bartholomew to shadow the thieves."

"Yes, sir."

"Place a strong guard—A guard of thirty picked men, with a relief of thirty—over the place from whence the elephant was stolen, to keep strict watch there night and day, and allow none to approach—except reporters—without written authority from me."

"Yes, sir."

"Place detectives in plain clothes in the railway; steamship, and ferry depots, and upon all roadways leading out of Jersey City, with orders to search all suspicious persons."

"Yes, sir."

"Furnish all these men with photograph and accompanying description of the elephant, and instruct them to search all trains and outgoing ferryboats and other vessels."

"Yes, sir."

"If the elephant should be found, let him be seized, and the information forwarded to me by telegraph."

"Yes, sir."

"Let me be informed at once if any clues should be found—footprints of the animal, or anything of that kind."

"Yes, sir."

"Get an order commanding the harbor police to patrol the frontages vigilantly."

"Yes, sir."

"Despatch detectives in plain clothes over all the railways, north as far as Canada, west as far as Ohio, south as far as Washington."

"Yes, sir."

"Place experts in all the telegraph offices to listen to all messages; and let them require that all cipher despatches be interpreted to them."

"Yes, sir."

"Let all these things be done with the utmost's secrecy—mind, the most impenetrable secrecy."

"Yes, sir."

"Report to me promptly at the usual hour."

"Yes, Sir."

"Go!"

"Yes, sir."

He was gone.

Inspector Blunt was silent and thoughtful a moment, while the fire in his eye cooled down and faded out. Then he turned to me and said in a placid voice:

"I am not given to boasting, it is not my habit; but—we shall find the elephant."

I shook him warmly by the hand and thanked him; and I FELT my thanks, too. The more I had seen of the man the more I liked him and the more I admired him and marveled over the mysterious wonders of his profession. Then we parted for the night, and I went home with a far happier heart than I had carried with me to his office.

2

Next morning it was all in the newspapers, in the minutest detail. It even had additions—consisting of Detective This, Detective That, and Detective The Other's "Theory" as to how the robbery was done, who the robbers were, and whither they had flown with their booty. There were eleven of these theories, and they covered all the possibilities; and this single fact shows what independent thinkers detectives are. No two theories were alike, or even much resembled each other, save in one striking particular, and in that one all the other eleven theories were absolutely agreed. That was, that although the rear of my building was torn out and the only door remained locked, the elephant had not been removed through the rent, but by some other (undiscovered) outlet. All agreed that the robbers had made that rent only to mislead the detectives. That never would have occurred to me or to any other layman, perhaps, but it had not deceived the detectives for a moment. Thus, what I had supposed was the only thing that had no mystery about it was in fact the very thing I had gone furthest astray in. The eleven theories all named the supposed robbers, but no two named the same robbers; the total number of suspected persons was thirty-seven. The various newspaper accounts all closed with the most important opinion of all—that of Chief Inspector Blunt. A portion of this statement read as follows:

The chief knows who the two principals are, namely, "Brick" Duffy and "Red" McFadden. Ten days before the robbery was achieved he was already aware that it was to be attempted, and had quietly proceeded to shadow these two noted villains; but unfortunately on the night in question their track was lost, and before it could be found again the bird was flown—that is, the elephant.

Duffy and McFadden are the boldest scoundrels in the profession; the chief has reasons for believing that they are the men who stole the stove out of the detective headquarters on a bitter night last winter—in consequence of which the chief and every detective present were in the hands of the physicians before morning, some with frozen feet, others with frozen fingers, ears, and other members.

When I read the first half of that I was more astonished than ever at the wonderful sagacity of this strange man. He not only saw everything in the present with a clear eye, but even the future could not be hidden from him. I was soon at his office, and said I could not help wishing he had had those men arrested, and so prevented the trouble and loss; but his reply was simple and unanswerable:

"It is not our province to prevent crime, but to punish it. We cannot punish it until it is committed."

I remarked that the secrecy with which we had begun had been marred by the newspapers; not only all our facts but all our plans and purposes had been revealed; even all the suspected persons had been named; these would doubtless disguise themselves now, or go into hiding.

"Let them. They will find that when I am ready for them my hand will descend upon them, in their secret places, as unerringly as the hand of fate. As to the newspapers, we must keep in with them. Fame, reputation, constant public mention—these are the detective's bread and butter. He must publish his facts, else he will be supposed to have none; he must publish his theory, for nothing is so strange or striking as a detective's theory, or brings him so much wondering respect; we must publish our plans, for these the journals insist upon having, and we could not deny them without offending. We must constantly show the public what we are doing, or they will believe we are doing nothing. It is much pleasanter to have a newspaper say, 'Inspector Blunt's ingenious and extraordinary theory is as follows,' than to have it say some harsh thing, or, worse still, some sarcastic one."

"I see the force of what you say. But I noticed that in one part of your remarks in the papers this morning you refused to reveal your opinion upon a certain minor point."

"Yes, we always do that; it has a good effect. Besides, I had not formed any opinion on that point, anyway."

I deposited a considerable sum of money with the inspector, to meet current expenses, and sat down to wait for news. We were expecting the telegrams to begin to arrive at any moment now. Meantime I reread the newspapers and also our descriptive circular, and observed that our twenty-five thousand dollars reward seemed to be offered only to detectives. I said I thought it ought to be offered to anybody who would catch the elephant. The inspector said:

"It is the detectives who will find the elephant; hence the reward will go to the right place. If other people found the animal, it would only be by watching the detectives and taking advantage of clues and indications stolen from them, and that would entitle the detectives to the reward, after all. The proper office of a reward is to stimulate the men who deliver up their time and their trained sagacities to this sort of work, and not to confer benefits upon chance citizens who stumble upon a capture without having earned the benefits by their own merits and labors."

This was reasonable enough, certainly. Now the telegraphic machine in the corner began to click, and the following despatch was the result:

FLOWER STATION, N. Y., 7.30 A.M. Have got a clue. Found a succession of deep tracks across a farm near here. Followed them two miles east without result; think elephant went west. Shall now shadow him in that direction. DARLEY, Detective.

"Darley's one of the best men on the force," said the inspector. "We shall hear from him again before long."

Telegram No. 2 came:

BARKER'S, N. J., 7.40 A.M. Just arrived. Glass factory broken open here during night, and eight hundred bottles taken. Only water in large quantity near here is five miles distant. Shall strike for there. Elephant will be thirsty. Bottles were empty. BAKER, Detective.

"That promises well, too," said the inspector.

"I told you the creature's appetites would not be bad clues."

Telegram No. 3:

TAYLORVILLE, L. I. 8.15 A.M. A haystack near here disappeared during night. Probably eaten. Have got a clue, and am off. HUBBARD, Detective.

"How he does move around!" said the inspector "I knew we had a difficult job on hand, but we shall catch him yet."

FLOWER STATION, N. Y., 9 A.M. Shadowed the tracks three miles westward. Large, deep, and ragged. Have just met a farmer who says they are not elephant-tracks. Says they are holes where he dug up saplings for shade-trees when ground was frozen last winter. Give me orders how to proceed. DARLEY, Detective.

"Aha! a confederate of the thieves! The thing, grows warm," said the inspector.

He dictated the following telegram to Darley:

Arrest the man and force him to name his pals. Continue to follow the tracks to the Pacific, if necessary. Chief BLUNT.

Next telegram:

CONEY POINT, PA., 8.45 A.M. Gas office broken open here during night and three months' unpaid gas bills taken. Have got a clue and am away. MURPHY, Detective.

"Heavens!" said the inspector; "would he eat gas bills?"

"Through ignorance—yes; but they cannot support life. At least, unassisted."

Now came this exciting telegram:

IRONVILLE, N. Y., 9.30 A.M. Just arrived. This village in consternation. Elephant passed through here at five this morning. Some say he went east some say west, some north, some south—but all say they did not wait to notice, particularly. He killed a horse; have secured a piece of it for a clue. Killed it with his trunk; from style of blow, think he struck it left-handed. From position in which horse lies, think elephant traveled northward along line of Berkley Railway. Has four and a half hours' start, but I move on his track at once. HAWES, Detective

I uttered exclamations of joy. The inspector was as self-contained as a graven image. He calmly touched his bell.

"Alaric, send Captain Burns here."

Burns appeared.

"How many men are ready for instant orders?"

"Ninety-six, sir."

"Send them north at once. Let them concentrate along the line of the Berkley road north of Ironville."

"Yes, sir."

"Let them conduct their movements with the utmost secrecy. As fast as others are at liberty, hold them for orders."

"Yes, sir."

"Go!"

"Yes, sir."

Presently came another telegram:

SAGE CORNERS, N. Y., 10.30. Just arrived. Elephant passed through here at 8.15. All escaped from the town but a policeman. Apparently elephant did not strike at policeman, but at the lamp-post. Got both. I have secured a portion of the policeman as clue.   STUMM, Detective.

"So the elephant has turned westward," said the inspector. "However, he will not escape, for my men are scattered all over that region."

The next telegram said:

GLOVER'S, 11.15 Just arrived. Village deserted, except sick and aged. Elephant passed through three-quarters of an hour ago. The anti-temperance mass-meeting was in session; he put his trunk in at a window and washed it out with water from cistern. Some swallowed it—since dead; several drowned. Detectives Cross and O'Shaughnessy were passing through town, but going south—so missed elephant. Whole region for many miles around in terror—people flying from their homes. Wherever they turn they meet elephant, and many are killed. BRANT, Detective.

I could have shed tears, this havoc so distressed me. But the inspector only said:

"You see—we are closing in on him. He feels our presence; he has turned eastward again."

Yet further troublous news was in store for us. The telegraph brought this:

HOGANSPORT, 12.19. Just arrived. Elephant passed through half an hour ago, creating wildest fright and excitement. Elephant raged around streets; two plumbers going by, killed one—other escaped. Regret general.   O'FLAHERTY, Detective.

"Now he is right in the midst of my men," said the inspector. "Nothing can save him."

A succession of telegrams came from detectives who were scattered through New Jersey and Pennsylvania, and who were following clues consisting of ravaged barns, factories, and Sunday-school libraries, with high hopes-hopes amounting to certainties, indeed. The inspector said:

"I wish I could communicate with them and order them north, but that is impossible. A detective only visits a telegraph office to send his report; then he is off again, and you don't know where to put your hand on him."

Now came this despatch:

BRIDGEPORT, CT., 12.15. Barnum offers rate of $4,000 a year for exclusive privilege of using elephant as traveling advertising medium from now till detectives find him. Wants to paste circus-posters on him. Desires immediate answer.   BOGGS, Detective.

"That is perfectly absurd!" I exclaimed.

"Of course it is," said the inspector. "Evidently Mr. Barnum, who thinks he is so sharp, does not know me—but I know him."

Then he dictated this answer to the despatch:

Mr. Barnum's offer declined. Make it $7,000 or nothing.   Chief BLUNT.

"There. We shall not have to wait long for an answer. Mr. Barnum is not at home; he is in the telegraph office—it is his way when he has business on hand. Inside of three—"

Done.—P. T. BARNUM.

So interrupted the clicking telegraphic instrument. Before I could make a comment upon this extraordinary episode, the following despatch carried my thoughts into another and very distressing channel:

BOLIVIA, N. Y., 12.50. Elephant arrived here from the south and passed through toward the forest at 11.50, dispersing a funeral on the way, and diminishing the mourners by two. Citizens fired some small cannonballs into him, and then fled. Detective Burke and I arrived ten minutes later, from the north, but mistook some excavations for footprints, and so lost a good deal of time; but at last we struck the right trail and followed it to the woods. We then got down on our hands and knees and continued to keep a sharp eye on the track, and so shadowed it into the brush. Burke was in advance. Unfortunately the animal had stopped to rest; therefore, Burke having his head down, intent upon the track, butted up against the elephant's hind legs before he was aware of his vicinity. Burke instantly arose to his feet, seized the tail, and exclaimed joyfully, "I claim the re—" but got no further, for a single blow of the huge trunk laid the brave fellow's fragments low in death. I fled rearward, and the elephant turned and shadowed me to the edge of the wood, making tremendous speed, and I should inevitably have been lost, but that the remains of the funeral providentially intervened again and diverted his attention. I have just learned that nothing of that funeral is now left; but this is no loss, for there is abundance of material for another. Meantime, the elephant has disappeared again.   MULROONEY, Detective.

We heard no news except from the diligent and confident detectives scattered about New Jersey, Pennsylvania, Delaware, and Virginia—who were all following fresh and encouraging clues—until shortly after 2 P.M., when this telegram came:

BAXTER CENTER, 2.15. Elephant been here, plastered over with circus-bills, and he broke up a revival, striking down and damaging many who were on the point of entering upon a better life. Citizens penned him up and established a guard. When Detective Brown and I arrived, some time after, we entered inclosure and proceeded to identify elephant by photograph and description. All marks tallied exactly except one, which we could not see—the boil-scar under armpit. To make sure, Brown crept under to look, and was immediately brained—that is, head crushed and destroyed, though nothing issued from debris. All fled so did elephant, striking right and left with much effect. Has escaped, but left bold blood-track from cannon-wounds. Rediscovery certain. He broke southward, through a dense forest.   BRENT, Detective.

That was the last telegram. At nightfall a fog shut down which was so dense that objects but three feet away could not be discerned. This lasted all night. The ferry-boats and even the omnibuses had to stop running.

Next morning the papers were as full of detective theories as before; they had all our tragic facts in detail also, and a great many more which they had received from their telegraphic correspondents. Column after column was occupied, a third of its way down, with glaring head-lines, which it made my heart sick to read. Their general tone was like this:

THE WHITE ELEPHANT AT LARGE! HE MOVES UPON HIS FATAL MARCH! WHOLE VILLAGES DESERTED BY THEIR FRIGHT-STRICKEN OCCUPANTS! PALE TERROR GOES BEFORE HIM, DEATH AND DEVASTATION FOLLOW AFTER! AFTER THESE, THE DETECTIVES! BARNS DESTROYED, FACTORIES GUTTED, HARVESTS DEVOURED, PUBLIC ASSEMBLAGES DISPERSED, ACCOMPANIED BY SCENES OF CARNAGE IMPOSSIBLE TO DESCRIBE! THEORIES OF THIR-TY-FOUR OF THE MOST DISTINGUISHED DETECTIVES ON THE FORCE! THEORY OF CHIEF BLUNT!

"There!" said Inspector Blunt, almost betrayed into excitement, "this is magnificent! This is the greatest windfall that any detective organization ever had. The fame of it will travel to the ends of the earth, and endure to the end of time, and my name with it."

But there was no joy for me. I felt as if I had committed all those red crimes, and that the elephant was only my irresponsible agent. And how the list had grown! In one place he had "interfered with an election and killed five repeaters." He had followed this act with the destruction of two pool fellows, named O'Donohue and McFlannigan, who had "found a refuge in the home of the oppressed of all lands only the day before, and were in the act of exercising for the first time the noble right of American citizens at the polls, when stricken down by the relentless hand of the Scourge of Siam." In another, he had "found a crazy sensation-preacher preparing his next season's heroic attacks on the dance, the theater, and other things which can't strike back, and had stepped on him." And in still another place he had "killed a lightning-rod agent." And so the list went on, growing redder and redder, and more and more heartbreaking. Sixty persons had been killed, and two hundred and forty wounded. All the accounts bore just testimony to the activity and devotion of the detectives, and all closed with the remark that "three hundred thousand citizens and four detectives saw the dread creature, and two of the latter he destroyed."

I dreaded to hear the telegraphic instrument begin to click again. By and by the messages began to pour in, but I was happily disappointed in their nature. It was soon apparent that all trace of the elephant was lost. The fog had enabled him to search out a good hiding-place unobserved. Telegrams from the most absurdly distant points reported that a dim vast mass had been glimpsed there through the fog at such and such an hour, and was "undoubtedly the elephant." This dim vast mass had been glimpsed in New Haven, in New Jersey, in Pennsylvania, in interior New York, in Brooklyn, and even in the city of New York itself! But in all cases the dim vast mass had vanished quickly and left no trace. Every detective of the large force scattered over this huge extent of country sent his hourly report, and each and every one of them had a clue, and was shadowing something, and was hot upon the heels of it.

But the day passed without other result.

The next day the same.

The next just the same.

The newspaper reports began to grow monotonous with facts that amounted to nothing, clues which led to nothing, and theories which had nearly exhausted the elements which surprise and delight and dazzle.

By advice of the inspector I doubled the reward.

Four more dull days followed. Then came a bitter blow to the poor, hard-working detectives—the journalists declined to print their theories, and coldly said, "Give us a rest."

Two weeks after the elephant's disappearance I raised the reward to seventy-five thousand dollars by the inspector's advice. It was a great sum, but I felt that I would rather sacrifice my whole private fortune than lose my credit with my government. Now that the detectives were in adversity, the newspapers turned upon them, and began to fling the most stinging sarcasms at them. This gave the minstrels an idea, and they dressed themselves as detectives and hunted the elephant on the stage in the most extravagant way. The caricaturists made pictures of detectives scanning the country with spy-glasses, while the elephant, at their backs, stole apples out of their pockets. And they made all sorts of ridiculous pictures of the detective badge—you have seen that badge printed in gold on the back of detective novels no doubt, it is a wide-staring eye, with the legend, "WE NEVER SLEEP." When detectives called for a drink, the would-be facetious barkeeper resurrected an obsolete form of expression and said, "Will you have an eye-opener?" All the air was thick with sarcasms.

But there was one man who moved calm, untouched, unaffected, through it all. It was that heart of oak, the chief inspector. His brave eye never drooped, his serene confidence never wavered. He always said:

"Let them rail on; he laughs best who laughs last."

My admiration for the man grew into a species of worship. I was at his side always. His office had become an unpleasant place to me, and now became daily more and more so. Yet if he could endure it I meant to do so also—at least, as long as I could. So I came regularly, and stayed— the only outsider who seemed to be capable of it. Everybody wondered how I could; and often it seemed to me that I must desert, but at such times I looked into that calm and apparently unconscious face, and held my ground.

About three weeks after the elephant's disappearance I was about to say, one morning, that I should have to strike my colors and retire, when the great detective arrested the thought by proposing one more superb and masterly move.

This was to compromise with the robbers. The fertility of this man's invention exceeded anything I have ever seen, and I have had a wide intercourse with the world's finest minds. He said he was confident he could compromise for one hundred thousand dollars and recover the elephant. I said I believed I could scrape the amount together, but what would become of the poor detectives who had worked so faithfully? He said:

"In compromises they always get half."

This removed my only objection. So the inspector wrote two notes, in this form:

DEAR MADAM,—Your husband can make a large sum of money (and be entirely protected from the law) by making an immediate, appointment with me.   Chief BLUNT.

He sent one of these by his confidential messenger to the "reputed wife" of Brick Duffy, and the other to the reputed wife of Red McFadden.

Within the hour these offensive answers came:

YE OWLD FOOL: brick McDuffys bin ded 2 yere.   BRIDGET MAHONEY.

CHIEF BAT,—Red McFadden is hung and in heving 18 month. Any Ass but a detective know that.   MARY O'HOOLIGAN.

212

"I had long suspected these facts," said the inspector; "this testimony proves the unerring accuracy of my instinct."

The moment one resource failed him he was ready with another. He immediately wrote an advertisement for the morning papers, and I kept a copy of it:

A.—xwblv.242 N. Tjnd—fz328wmlg. Ozpo,—; 2m! ogw. Mum

He said that if the thief was alive this would bring him to the usual rendezvous. He further explained that the usual rendezvous was a place where all business affairs between detectives and criminals were conducted. This meeting would take place at twelve the next night.

We could do nothing till then, and I lost no time in getting out of the office, and was grateful indeed for the privilege.

At eleven the next night I brought one hundred thousand dollars in bank-notes and put them into the chief's hands, and shortly afterward he took his leave, with the brave old undimmed confidence in his eye. An almost intolerable hour dragged to a close; then I heard his welcome tread, and rose gasping and tottered to meet him. How his fine eyes flamed with triumph! He said:

"We've compromised! The jokers will sing a different tune to-morrow! Follow me!"

He took a lighted candle and strode down into the vast vaulted basement where sixty detectives always slept, and where a score were now playing cards to while the time. I followed close after him. He walked swiftly down to the dim remote end of the place, and just as I succumbed to the pangs of suffocation and was swooning away he stumbled and fell over the outlying members of a mighty object, and I heard him exclaim as he went down:

"Our noble profession is vindicated. Here is your elephant!"

I was carried to the office above and restored with carbolic acid. The whole detective force swarmed in, and such another season of triumphant rejoicing ensued as I had never witnessed before. The reporters were called, baskets of champagne were opened, toasts were drunk, the hand-shakings and congratulations were continuous and enthusiastic. Naturally the chief was the hero of the hour, and his happiness was so complete and had been so patiently and worthily and bravely won that it made me happy to see it, though I stood there a homeless beggar, my priceless charge dead, and my position in my country's service lost to me through what would always seem my fatally careless execution of a great trust. Many an eloquent eye testified its deep admiration for the chief, and many a detective's voice murmured, "Look at him—just the king of the profession; only give him a clue, it's all he wants, and there ain't anything hid that he can't find." The dividing of the fifty thousand dollars made great pleasure; when it was finished the chief made a little speech while he put his share in his pocket, in which he said, "Enjoy it, boys, for you've earned it; and, more than that, you've earned for the detective profession undying fame."

A telegram arrived, which read:

MONROE, MICH., 10 P.M. First time I've struck a telegraph office in over three weeks. Have followed those footprints, horseback, through the woods, a thousand miles to here, and they get stronger and bigger and fresher every day. Don't worry-inside of another week I'll have the elephant. This is dead sure. DARLEY, Detective.

The chief ordered three cheers for "Darley, one of the finest minds on the force," and then commanded that he be telegraphed to come home and receive his share of the reward.

So ended that marvelous episode of the stolen elephant. The newspapers were pleasant with praises once more, the next day, with one contemptible exception. This sheet said, "Great is the detective! He may be a little slow in finding a little thing like a mislaid elephant he may hunt him all day and sleep with his rotting carcass all night for three weeks, but he will find him at last if he can get the man who mislaid him to show him the place!"

Poor Hassan was lost to me forever. The cannonshots had wounded him fatally, he had crept to that unfriendly place in the fog, and there, surrounded by his enemies and in constant danger of detection, he had wasted away with hunger and suffering till death gave him peace.

The compromise cost me one hundred thousand dollars; my detective expenses were forty-two thousand dollars more; I never applied for a place again under my government; I am a ruined man and a wanderer in the earth, but my admiration for that man, whom I believe to be the greatest detective the world has ever produced, remains undimmed to this day, and will so remain unto the end.

COLLEGE WRITING 1: REFLECTION WITHIN THE TEXT

Have you ever asked someone to help you—and found that the help was worse than the original problem? Have you ever lost something and discovered that it was under your nose the entire time! It seems like Twain's "A Stolen White Elephant," is in part about common sense and the absurdity of ready-made solutions; compose your own "White Elephant," but this time with the trappings and circumstances of your life.

COLLEGE WRITING 2: RESEARCH OUTSIDE THE TEXT

Research Siam in the 1880s. Where is it—what do we call it today? Is Twain's story based in truth? Or is completely made up—right down to the King of Siam love for his white elephant? What was the state of police detectives, and private detectives, at the time Twain wrote this? Had detective fiction become popular at this point in American literature? Was his work meant to make fun of other popular authors at the time? If so, which ones (and why)?

IDEAS AND VALUES: CONNECT THE TEXT

» Absurdity is the quality of being illogical, unreasonable, or just plain ridiculous. But absurdity often has a logic of its own—and in real life, as in literature, people end up in situations, and doing things, both noble and tragic, that can be characterized as absurd. How can this be? In Twain's "The Stolen White Elephant," the caretaker of a priceless White Elephant is led on a wild goose chase, and seems to have been swindled of all his savings by a fantastic detective agency. In "Porcelain and Pink," the main character finds herself in the nude among her date that afternoon, and matter-of-factly, renounces the norms of her society, and in Swift's essay "A Modest Proposal," the author offers a solution to a looming problem in Ireland of hungry and illiterate children—to eat them. Each of these texts touches upon aspects of the absurd. How are they the same? How are they different? What is the quality of their absurdity—that is—what makes them absurd? And are they truly—or can you find a hint of reason in any of them?

» How does the thought of glory motivate the characters in Mark

Twain's "The War Prayer," Ambrose Bierce's "Occurrence at Owl Creek Bridge," and Twain's "The Stolen White Elephant"? Does glory motivate people to do good? Is one man's glory another man's glory as well? What is glory, after all?

» In Chesnutt's "The Sheriff's Children," Twain's "The Stolen White Elephant," and Twain's "The War Prayer" there exists forms of conformity and nonconformity. What is conformity—is it one's actions, one's thoughts, more, less? And how is it determined what conforming is and what isn't? Why does one conform in the first place? Why would one choose to not conform? Look at the challenges faced by the nonconformists in these stories: are the nonconformists successful? What challenges do they face?

» How is the truth manipulated in Crane's "The Blue Hotel," Fitzgerald's "Porcelain and Pink," and Twain's "The Stolen White Elephant"? How does the reader know what is true in each story? What is the truth in each story? Who relies on the truth in each story? Who relies on the perversion of truth? What are the stakes? What is truth? Why do humans have a concept of truth—if our surroundings are self evident? Should one always strive to be truthful?

To Build a Fire

By Jack London

7,103 WORDS. 39 MINUTES.
READING LEVEL: GRADE 8.8

Day had broken cold and grey, exceedingly cold and grey, when the man turned aside from the main Yukon trail and climbed the high earth-bank, where a dim and little-travelled trail led eastward through the fat spruce timberland. It was a steep bank, and he paused for breath at the top, excusing the act to himself by looking at his watch. It was nine o'clock. There was no sun nor hint of sun, though there was not a cloud in the sky. It was a clear day, and yet there seemed an intangible pall over the face of things, a subtle gloom that made the day dark, and that was due to the absence of sun. This fact did not worry the man. He was used to the lack of sun. It had been days since he had seen the sun, and he knew that a few more days must pass before that cheerful orb, due south, would just peep above the sky-line and dip immediately from view.

The man flung a look back along the way he had come. The Yukon lay a mile wide and hidden under three feet of ice. On top of this ice were as many feet of snow. It was all pure white, rolling in gentle undulations where the ice-jams of the freeze-up had formed. North and south, as far as his eye could see, it was unbroken white, save for a dark hair-line that curved and twisted from around the spruce-covered island to the south, and that curved and twisted away into the north, where it disappeared behind another spruce-covered island. This dark hair-line was the trail—the main trail—that led south five hundred miles to the Chilcoot Pass, Dyea, and salt water; and that led north seventy miles to Dawson, and still on to the north a thousand miles to Nulato, and finally to St. Michael on Bering Sea, a thousand miles and half a thousand more.

But all this—the mysterious, far-reaching hairline trail, the absence of sun from the sky, the tremendous cold, and the strangeness and weirdness of it all—made no impression on the man. It was not because he was long used to it. He was a new-comer in the land, a *chechaquo*, and this was his first winter. The trouble with him was that he was without imagination. He was quick and alert in the things of life, but only in the things, and not in the significances. Fifty degrees below zero meant eighty odd degrees of frost. Such fact impressed him as being cold and uncomfortable, and that was all. It did not lead him to meditate upon his frailty as a creature of temperature, and upon man's frailty in general, able only to live within certain narrow limits of heat and cold; and from there on it did not lead him to the conjectural field of immortality and man's place in the universe. Fifty degrees below zero stood for a bite of frost that hurt and that must be guarded against by the use of mittens, ear-flaps, warm moccasins, and thick socks. Fifty degrees below zero was to him just precisely fifty degrees below zero. That there should be anything more to it than that was a thought that never entered his head.

As he turned to go on, he spat speculatively. There was a sharp, explosive crackle that startled him. He spat again. And again, in the air, before it could fall to the snow, the spittle crackled. He knew that at fifty below spittle crackled on the snow, but this spittle had crackled in the air. Undoubtedly it was colder than fifty below—how much colder he did not know. But the temperature did not matter. He was bound for the old claim on the left fork of Henderson Creek, where the boys were already. They had come over across the divide from the Indian Creek country, while he had come the roundabout way to take a look at the possibilities of getting out logs in the spring from the islands in the Yukon. He would be in to camp by six o'clock; a bit after dark, it was true, but the boys would be there, a fire would be going, and a hot supper would be ready. As for lunch, he pressed his hand against the protruding bundle under his jacket. It was also under his shirt, wrapped up in a handkerchief and lying against the naked skin. It was the only way to keep the biscuits from freezing. He smiled agreeably to himself as he thought of those biscuits, each cut open and sopped in bacon grease, and each enclosing a generous slice of fried bacon.

He plunged in among the big spruce trees. The trail was faint. A foot of snow had fallen since the last sled had passed over, and he was glad he was without a sled, travelling light. In fact, he carried nothing but the lunch wrapped in the handkerchief. He was surprised, however, at the cold. It certainly was cold, he concluded, as he rubbed his numbed nose and cheek-bones with his mittened hand. He was a warm-whiskered man, but the hair on his face did not protect the high cheek-bones and the eager nose that thrust itself aggressively into the frosty air.

At the man's heels trotted a dog, a big native husky, the proper wolf-dog, grey-coated and without any visible or temperamental difference from its brother, the wild wolf. The animal was depressed by the tremendous cold. It knew that it was no time for travelling. Its instinct told it a truer tale than was told to the man by the man's judgment. In reality, it was not merely colder than fifty below zero; it was colder than sixty below, than seventy below. It was seventy-five below zero. Since the freezing-point is thirty-two above zero, it meant that one hundred and seven degrees of frost obtained. The dog did not know anything about thermometers. Possibly in its brain there was no sharp consciousness of a condition of very cold such as was in the man's brain. But the brute had its instinct. It experienced a vague but menacing apprehension that subdued it and made it slink along at the man's heels, and that made it question eagerly every unwonted movement of the man as if expecting him to go into camp or to seek shelter somewhere and build a fire. The dog had learned fire, and it wanted fire, or else to burrow under the snow and cuddle its warmth away from the air.

The frozen moisture of its breathing had settled on its fur in a fine powder of frost, and especially were its jowls, muzzle, and eyelashes whitened by its crystalled breath. The man's red beard and moustache were likewise frosted, but more solidly, the deposit taking the form of ice and increasing with every warm, moist breath he exhaled. Also, the man was chewing tobacco, and the muzzle of ice held his lips so rigidly that he was unable to clear his chin when he expelled the juice. The result was that a crystal beard of the colour and solidity of amber was increasing its length on his chin. If he fell down it would shatter itself, like glass, into brittle fragments. But he did not mind the appendage. It was the penalty all tobacco-chewers paid in that country, and he had been out before in two cold snaps. They had not been so cold as this, he knew, but by the spirit thermometer at Sixty Mile he knew they had been registered at fifty below and at fifty-five.

He held on through the level stretch of woods for several miles, crossed a wide flat of nigger-heads, and dropped down a bank to the frozen bed of a small stream. This was Henderson Creek, and he knew he was ten miles from the forks. He looked at his watch. It was ten o'clock. He was making four miles an hour, and he calculated that he would arrive at the forks at half-past twelve. He decided to celebrate that event by eating his lunch there.

The dog dropped in again at his heels, with a tail drooping discouragement, as the man swung along the creek-bed. The furrow of the old sled-trail was plainly visible, but a dozen inches of snow covered the marks of the last runners. In a month no man had come up or down that silent creek. The man held steadily on. He was not much given to thinking, and just then particularly he had nothing to think about save that he would eat lunch at the forks and that at six o'clock he would be in camp with the boys. There was nobody to talk to and, had there been, speech would have been impossible because of the ice-muzzle on his mouth. So he continued monotonously to chew tobacco and to increase the length of his amber beard.

Once in a while the thought reiterated itself that it was very cold and that he had never experienced such cold. As he walked along he rubbed his cheek-bones and nose with the back of his mittened hand. He did this automatically, now and again changing hands. But rub as he would, the instant he stopped his cheek-bones went numb, and the following instant the end of his nose went numb. He was sure to frost his cheeks; he knew that, and experienced a pang of regret that he had not devised a nose-strap of the sort Bud wore in cold snaps. Such a strap passed across the cheeks, as well, and saved them. But it didn't matter much, after all. What were frosted cheeks? A bit painful, that was all; they were never serious.

Empty as the man's mind was of thoughts, he was keenly observant, and he noticed the changes in the creek, the curves and bends and timber-jams, and always he sharply noted where he placed his feet. Once, coming around a bend, he shied abruptly, like a startled horse, curved away from the place where he had been walking, and retreated several paces back along the trail. The creek he knew was frozen clear to the bottom—no creek could contain water in that arctic winter—but he knew also that there were springs that bubbled out from the hillsides and ran along under the snow and on top the ice of the creek. He knew that the coldest snaps never froze these springs, and he knew likewise their danger. They were traps. They hid pools of water under the snow that might be three inches deep, or three feet. Sometimes a skin of ice half an inch thick covered them, and in turn was covered by the snow. Sometimes there were alternate layers of water and ice-skin, so that when one broke through he kept on breaking through for a while, sometimes wetting himself to the waist.

That was why he had shied in such panic. He had felt the give under his feet and heard the crackle of a snow-hidden ice-skin. And to get his feet wet in such a temperature meant trouble and danger. At the very least it meant delay, for he would be forced to stop and build a fire, and under its protection to bare his feet while he dried his socks and moccasins. He stood and studied the creek-bed and its banks, and decided that the flow of water came from the right. He reflected awhile, rubbing his nose and cheeks, then skirted to the left, stepping gingerly and testing the footing for each step. Once clear of the danger, he took a fresh chew of tobacco and swung along at his four-mile gait.

In the course of the next two hours he came upon several similar traps. Usually the snow above the hidden pools had a sunken, candied appearance that advertised the danger. Once again, however, he had a close call; and once, suspecting danger, he compelled the dog to go on in front. The dog did not want to go. It hung back until the man shoved it forward, and then it went quickly across the white, unbroken surface. Suddenly it broke through, floundered to one side, and got away to firmer footing. It had wet its forefeet and legs, and almost immediately the water that clung to it turned to ice. It made quick efforts to lick the ice off its legs, then dropped down in the snow and began to bite out the ice that had formed between the toes. This was a matter of instinct. To permit the ice to remain would mean sore feet. It did not know this. It merely obeyed the mysterious prompting that arose from the deep crypts of its being. But the man knew, having achieved a judgment on the subject, and he removed the mitten from his right hand and helped tear out the ice-particles. He did not expose his fingers more than a minute, and was astonished at the swift numbness that smote them. It certainly was cold. He pulled on the mitten hastily, and beat the hand savagely across his chest.

At twelve o'clock the day was at its brightest. Yet the sun was too far south on its winter journey to clear the horizon. The bulge of the earth intervened between it and Henderson Creek, where the man walked under a clear sky at noon and cast no shadow. At half-past twelve, to the minute, he arrived at the forks of the creek. He was pleased at the speed he had made. If he kept it up, he would certainly be with the boys by six.

He unbuttoned his jacket and shirt and drew forth his lunch. The action consumed no more than a quarter of a minute, yet in that brief moment the numbness laid hold of the exposed fingers. He did not put the mitten on, but, instead, struck the fingers a dozen sharp smashes against his leg. Then he sat down on a snow-covered log to eat. The sting that followed upon the striking of his fingers against his leg ceased so quickly that he was startled, he had had no chance to take a bite of biscuit. He struck the fingers repeatedly and returned them to the mitten, baring the other hand for the purpose of eating. He tried to take a mouthful, but the ice-muzzle prevented. He had forgotten to build a fire and thaw out. He chuckled at his foolishness, and as he chuckled he noted the numbness creeping into the exposed fingers. Also, he noted that the stinging which had first come to his toes when he sat down was already passing away. He wondered whether the toes were warm or numbed. He moved them inside the moccasins and decided that they were numbed.

He pulled the mitten on hurriedly and stood up. He was a bit frightened. He stamped up and down until the stinging returned into the feet. It certainly was cold, was his thought. That man from Sulphur Creek had spoken the truth when telling how cold it sometimes got in the country. And he had laughed at him at the time! That showed one must not be too sure of things. There was no mistake about it, it was cold. He strode up and down, stamping his feet and threshing his arms, until reassured by the returning warmth. Then he got out matches and proceeded to make a fire. From the undergrowth, where high water of the previous spring had lodged a supply of seasoned twigs, he got his firewood. Working carefully from a small beginning, he soon had a roaring fire, over which he thawed the ice from his face and in the protection of which he ate his biscuits. For the moment the cold of space was outwitted. The dog took satisfaction in the fire, stretching out close enough for warmth and far enough away to escape being singed.

When the man had finished, he filled his pipe and took his comfortable time over a smoke. Then he pulled on his mittens, settled the ear-flaps of his cap firmly about his ears, and took the creek trail up the left fork. The dog was disappointed and yearned back toward the fire. This man did not know cold. Possibly all the generations of his ancestry had been ignorant of cold, of real cold, of cold one hundred and seven degrees below freezing-point. But the dog knew; all its ancestry knew, and it had inherited the knowledge. And it knew that it was not good to walk abroad in such fearful cold. It was the time to lie snug in a hole in the snow and wait for a curtain of cloud to be drawn across the face of outer space whence this cold came. On the other hand, there was keen intimacy between the dog and the man. The one was the toil-slave of the other, and the only caresses it had ever received were the caresses of the whip-lash and of harsh and menacing throat-sounds that threatened the whip-lash. So the dog made no effort to communicate its apprehension to the man. It was not concerned in the welfare of the man; it was for its own sake that it yearned back toward the fire. But the man whistled, and spoke to it with the sound of whip-lashes, and the dog swung in at the man's heels and followed after.

The man took a chew of tobacco and proceeded to start a new amber beard. Also, his moist breath quickly powdered with white his moustache, eyebrows, and lashes. There did not seem to be so many springs on the left fork of the Henderson, and for half an hour the man saw no signs of any. And then it happened. At a place where there were no signs, where the soft, unbroken snow seemed to advertise solidity beneath, the man broke through. It was not deep. He wetted himself half-way to the knees before he floundered out to the firm crust.

He was angry, and cursed his luck aloud. He had hoped to get into camp with the boys at six o'clock, and this would delay him an hour, for he would have to build a fire and dry out his foot-gear. This was imperative at that low temperature—he knew that much; and he turned aside to the bank, which he climbed. On top, tangled in the underbrush about the trunks of several small spruce trees, was a high-water deposit of dry firewood—sticks and twigs principally, but also larger portions of seasoned branches and fine, dry, last-year's grasses. He threw down several large pieces on top of the snow. This served for a foundation and prevented the young flame from drowning itself in the snow it otherwise would melt. The flame he got by touching a match to a small shred of birch-bark that he took from his pocket. This burned even more readily than paper. Placing it on the foundation, he fed the young flame with wisps of dry grass and with the tiniest dry twigs.

He worked slowly and carefully, keenly aware of his danger. Gradually, as the flame grew stronger, he increased the size of the twigs with which he fed it. He squatted in the snow, pulling the twigs out from their entanglement in the brush and feeding directly to the flame. He knew there must be no failure. When it is seventy-five below zero, a man must not fail in his first attempt to build a fire—that is, if his feet are wet. If his feet are dry, and he fails, he can run along the trail for half a mile and restore his circulation. But the circulation of wet and freezing feet cannot be restored by running when it is seventy-five below. No matter how fast he runs, the wet feet will freeze the harder.

All this the man knew. The old-timer on Sulphur Creek had told him about it the previous fall, and now he was appreciating the advice. Already all sensation had gone out of his feet. To build the fire he had been forced to remove his mittens, and the fingers had quickly gone numb. His pace of four miles an hour had kept his heart pumping blood to the surface of his body and to all the extremities. But the instant he stopped, the action of the pump eased down. The cold of space smote the unprotected tip of the planet, and he, being on that unprotected tip, received the full force of the blow. The blood of his body recoiled before it. The blood was alive, like the dog, and like the dog it wanted to hide away and cover itself up from the fearful cold. So long as he walked four miles an hour, he pumped that blood, willy-nilly, to the surface; but now it ebbed away and sank down into the recesses of his body. The extremities were the first to feel its absence. His wet feet froze the faster, and his exposed fingers numbed the faster, though they had not yet begun to freeze. Nose and cheeks were already freezing, while the skin of all his body chilled as it lost its blood.

But he was safe. Toes and nose and cheeks would be only touched by the frost, for the fire was beginning to burn with strength. He was feeding it with twigs the size of his finger. In another minute he would be able to feed it with branches the size of his wrist, and then he could remove his wet foot-gear, and, while it dried, he could keep his naked feet warm by the fire, rubbing them at first, of course, with snow. The fire was a success. He was safe. He remembered the advice of the old-timer on Sulphur Creek, and smiled. The old-timer had been very serious in laying down the law that no man must travel alone in the Klondike after fifty below. Well, here he was; he had had the accident; he was alone; and he had saved himself. Those old-timers were rather womanish, some of them, he thought. All a man had to do was to keep his head, and he was all right. Any man who was a man could travel alone. But it was surprising, the rapidity with which his cheeks and nose were freezing. And he had not thought his fingers could go lifeless in so short a time. Lifeless they were, for he could scarcely make them move together to grip a twig, and they seemed remote from his body and from him. When he touched a twig, he had to look and see whether or not he had hold of it. The wires were pretty well down between him and his finger-ends.

All of which counted for little. There was the fire, snapping and crackling and promising life with every dancing flame. He started to untie his moccasins. They were coated with ice; the thick German socks were like sheaths of iron half-way to the knees; and the mocassin strings were like rods of steel all twisted and knotted as by some conflagration. For a moment he tugged with his numbed fingers, then, realizing the folly of it, he drew his sheath-knife.

But before he could cut the strings, it happened. It was his own fault or, rather, his mistake. He should not have built the fire under the spruce tree. He should have built it in the open. But it had been easier to pull the twigs from the brush and drop them directly on the fire. Now the tree under which he had done this carried a weight of snow on its boughs. No wind had blown for weeks, and each bough was fully freighted. Each time he had pulled a twig he had communicated a slight agitation to the tree—an imperceptible agitation, so far as he was concerned, but an agitation sufficient to bring about the disaster. High up in the tree one bough capsized its load of snow. This fell on the boughs beneath, capsizing them. This process continued, spreading out and involving the whole tree. It grew like an avalanche, and it descended without warning upon the man and the fire, and the fire was blotted out! Where it had burned was a mantle of fresh and disordered snow.

The man was shocked. It was as though he had just heard his own sentence of death. For a moment he sat and stared at the spot where the fire had been. Then he grew very calm. Perhaps the old-timer on Sulphur Creek was right. If he had only had a trail-mate he would have been in no danger now. The trail-mate could have built the fire. Well, it was up to him to build the fire over again, and this second time there must be no failure. Even if he succeeded, he would most likely lose some toes. His feet must be badly frozen by now, and there would be some time before the second fire was ready.

Such were his thoughts, but he did not sit and think them. He was busy all the time they were passing through his mind, he made a new foundation for a fire, this time in the open; where no treacherous tree could blot it out. Next, he gathered dry grasses and tiny twigs from the high-water flotsam. He could not bring his fingers together to pull them out, but he was able to gather them by the handful. In this way he got many rotten twigs and bits of green moss that were undesirable, but it was the best he could do. He worked methodically, even collecting an armful of the larger branches to be used later when the fire gathered strength. And all the while the dog sat and watched him, a certain yearning wistfulness in its eyes, for it looked upon him as the fire-provider, and the fire was slow in coming.

When all was ready, the man reached in his pocket for a second piece of birch-bark. He knew the bark was there, and, though he could not feel it with his fingers, he could hear its crisp rustling as he fumbled for it. Try as he would, he could not clutch hold of it. And all the time, in his consciousness, was the knowledge that each instant his feet were freezing. This thought tended to put him in a panic, but he fought against it and kept calm. He pulled on his mittens with his teeth, and threshed his arms back and forth, beating his hands with all his might against his sides. He did this sitting down, and he stood up to do it; and all the while the dog sat in the snow, its wolf-brush of a tail curled around warmly over its forefeet, its sharp wolf-ears pricked forward intently as it watched the man. And the man as he beat and threshed with his arms and hands, felt a great surge of envy as he regarded the creature that was warm and secure in its natural covering.

After a time he was aware of the first far-away signals of sensation in his beaten fingers. The faint tingling grew stronger till it evolved into a stinging ache that was excruciating, but which the man hailed with satisfaction. He stripped the mitten from his right hand and fetched forth the birch-bark. The exposed fingers were quickly going numb again. Next he brought out his bunch of sulphur matches. But the tremendous cold had already driven the life out of his fingers. In his effort to separate one match from the others, the whole bunch fell in the snow. He tried to pick it out of the snow, but failed. The dead fingers could neither touch nor clutch. He was very careful. He drove the thought of his freezing feet; and nose, and cheeks, out of his mind, devoting his whole soul to the matches. He watched, using the sense of vision in place of that of touch, and when he saw his fingers on each side the bunch, he closed them—that is, he willed to close them, for the wires were drawn, and the fingers did not obey. He pulled the mitten on the right hand, and beat it fiercely against his knee. Then, with both mittened hands, he scooped the bunch of matches, along with much snow, into his lap. Yet he was no better off.

After some manipulation he managed to get the bunch between the heels of his mittened hands. In this fashion he carried it to his mouth. The ice crackled and snapped when by a violent effort he opened his mouth. He drew the lower jaw in, curled the upper lip out of the way, and scraped the bunch with his upper teeth in order to separate a match. He succeeded in getting one, which he dropped on his lap. He was no better off. He could not pick it up. Then he devised a way. He picked it up in his teeth and scratched it on his leg. Twenty times he scratched before he succeeded in lighting it. As it flamed he held it with his teeth to the birch-bark. But the burning brimstone went up his nostrils and into his lungs, causing him to cough spasmodically. The match fell into the snow and went out.

The old-timer on Sulphur Creek was right, he thought in the moment of controlled despair that ensued: after fifty below, a man should travel with a partner. He beat his hands, but failed in exciting any sensation. Suddenly he bared both hands, removing the mittens with his teeth. He caught the whole bunch between the heels of his hands. His arm-muscles not being frozen enabled him to press the hand-heels tightly against the matches. Then he scratched the bunch along his leg. It flared into flame, seventy sulphur matches at once! There was no wind to blow them out. He kept his head to one side to escape the strangling fumes, and held the blazing bunch to the birch-bark. As he so held it, he became aware of sensation in his hand. His flesh was burning. He could smell it. Deep down below the surface he could feel it. The sensation developed into pain that grew acute. And still he endured it, holding the flame of the matches clumsily to the bark that would not light readily because his own burning hands were in the way, absorbing most of the flame.

At last, when he could endure no more, he jerked his hands apart. The blazing matches fell sizzling into the snow, but the birch-bark was alight. He began laying dry grasses and the tiniest twigs on the flame. He could not pick and choose, for he had to lift the fuel between the heels of his hands. Small pieces of rotten wood and green moss clung to the twigs, and he bit them off as well as he could with his teeth. He cherished the flame carefully and awkwardly. It meant life, and it must not perish. The withdrawal of blood from the surface of his body now made him begin to shiver, and he grew more awkward. A large piece of green moss fell squarely on the little fire. He tried to poke it out with his fingers, but his shivering frame made him poke too far, and he disrupted the nucleus of the little fire, the burning grasses and tiny twigs separating and scattering. He tried to poke them together again, but in spite of the tenseness of the effort, his shivering got away with him, and the twigs were hopelessly scattered. Each twig gushed a puff of smoke and went out. The fire-provider had failed. As he looked apathetically about him, his eyes chanced on the dog, sitting across the ruins of the fire from him, in the snow, making restless, hunching movements, slightly lifting one forefoot and then the other, shifting its weight back and forth on them with wistful eagerness.

The sight of the dog put a wild idea into his head. He remembered the tale of the man, caught in a blizzard, who killed a steer and crawled inside the carcass, and so was saved. He would kill the dog and bury his hands in the warm body until the numbness went out of them. Then he could build another fire. He spoke to the dog, calling it to him; but in his voice was a strange note of fear that frightened the animal, who had never known the man to speak in such way before. Something was the matter, and its suspicious nature sensed danger,—it knew not what danger but somewhere, somehow, in its brain arose an apprehension of the man. It flattened its ears down at the sound of the man's voice, and its restless, hunching movements and the liftings and shiftings of its forefeet became more pronounced but it would not come to the man. He got on his hands and knees and crawled toward the dog. This unusual posture again excited suspicion, and the animal sidled mincingly away.

The man sat up in the snow for a moment and struggled for calmness. Then he pulled on his mittens, by means of his teeth, and got upon his feet. He glanced down at first in order to assure himself that he was really standing up, for the absence of sensation in his feet left him unrelated to the earth. His erect position in itself started to drive the webs of suspicion from the dog's mind; and when he spoke peremptorily, with the sound of whip-lashes in his voice, the dog rendered its customary allegiance and came to him. As it came within reaching distance, the man lost his control. His arms flashed out to the dog, and he experienced genuine surprise when he discovered that his hands could not clutch, that there was neither bend nor feeling in the lingers. He had forgotten for the moment that they were frozen and that they were freezing more and more. All this happened quickly, and before the animal could get away, he encircled its body with his arms. He sat down in the snow, and in this fashion held the dog, while it snarled and whined and struggled.

But it was all he could do, hold its body encircled in his arms and sit there. He realized that he could not kill the dog. There was no way to do it. With his helpless hands he could neither draw nor hold his sheath-knife nor throttle the animal. He released it, and it plunged wildly away, with tail between its legs, and still snarling. It halted forty feet away and surveyed him curiously, with ears sharply pricked forward. The man looked down at his hands in order to locate them, and found them hanging on the ends of his arms. It struck him as curious that one should have to use his eyes in order to find out where his hands were. He began threshing his arms back and forth, beating the mittened hands against his sides. He did this for five minutes, violently, and his heart pumped enough blood up to the surface to put a stop to his shivering. But no sensation was aroused in the hands. He had an impression that they hung like weights on the ends of his arms, but when he tried to run the impression down, he could not find it.

A certain fear of death, dull and oppressive, came to him. This fear quickly became poignant as he realized that it was no longer a mere matter of freezing his fingers and toes, or of losing his hands and feet, but that it was a matter of life and death with the chances against him. This threw him into a panic, and he turned and ran up the creek-bed along the old, dim trail. The dog joined in behind and kept up with him. He ran blindly, without intention, in fear such as he had never known in his life. Slowly, as he ploughed and floundered through the snow, he began to see things again—the banks of the creek, the old timber-jams, the leafless aspens, and the sky. The running made him feel better. He did not shiver. Maybe, if he ran on, his feet would thaw out; and, anyway, if he ran far enough, he would reach camp and the boys. Without doubt he would lose some fingers and toes and some of his face; but the boys would take care of him, and save the rest of him when he got there. And at the same time there was another thought in his mind that said he would never get to the camp and the boys; that it was too many miles away, that the freezing had too great a start on him, and that he would soon be stiff and dead. This thought he kept in the background and refused to consider. Sometimes it pushed itself forward and demanded to be heard, but he thrust it back and strove to think of other things.

It struck him as curious that he could run at all on feet so frozen that he could not feel them when they struck the earth and took the weight of his body. He seemed to himself to skim along above the surface and to have no connection with the earth. Somewhere he had once seen a winged Mercury, and he wondered if Mercury felt as he felt when skimming over the earth.

His theory of running until he reached camp and the boys had one flaw in it: he lacked the endurance. Several times he stumbled, and finally he tottered, crumpled up, and fell. When he tried to rise, he failed. He must sit and rest, he decided, and next time he would merely walk and keep on going. As he sat and regained his breath, he noted that he was feeling quite warm and comfortable. He was not shivering, and it even seemed that a warm glow had come to his chest and trunk. And yet, when he touched his nose or cheeks, there was no sensation. Running would not thaw them out. Nor would it thaw out his hands and feet. Then the thought came to him that the frozen portions of his body must be extending. He tried to keep this thought down, to forget it, to think of something else; he was aware of the panicky feeling that it caused, and he was afraid of the panic. But the thought asserted itself, and persisted, until it produced a vision of his body totally frozen. This was too much, and he made another wild run along the trail. Once he slowed down to a walk, but the thought of the freezing extending itself made him run again.

And all the time the dog ran with him, at his heels. When he fell down a second time, it curled its tail over its forefeet and sat in front of him facing him curiously eager and intent. The warmth and security of the animal angered him, and he cursed it till it flattened down its ears appeasingly. This time the shivering came more quickly upon the man. He was losing in his battle with the frost. It was creeping into his body from all sides. The thought of it drove him on, but he ran no more than a hundred feet, when he staggered and pitched headlong. It was his last panic. When he had recovered his breath and control, he sat up and entertained in his mind the conception of meeting death with dignity. However, the conception did not come to him in such terms. His idea of it was that he had been making a fool of himself, running around like a chicken with its head cut off—such was the simile that occurred to him. Well, he was bound to freeze anyway, and he might as well take it decently. With this new-found peace of mind came the first glimmerings of drowsiness. A good idea, he thought, to sleep off to death. It was like taking an anæsthetic. Freezing was not so bad as people thought. There were lots worse ways to die.

He pictured the boys finding his body next day. Suddenly he found himself with them, coming along the trail and looking for himself. And, still with them, he came around a turn in the trail and found himself lying in the snow. He did not belong with himself any more, for even then he was out of himself, standing with the boys and looking at himself in the snow. It certainly was cold, was his thought. When he got back to the States he could tell the folks what real cold was. He drifted on from this to a vision of the old-timer on Sulphur Creek. He could see him quite clearly, warm and comfortable, and smoking a pipe.

"You were right, old hoss; you were right," the man mumbled to the old-timer of Sulphur Creek.

Then the man drowsed off into what seemed to him the most comfortable and satisfying sleep he had ever known. The dog sat facing him and waiting. The brief day drew to a close in a long, slow twilight. There were no signs of a fire to be made, and, besides, never in the dog's experience had it known a man to sit like that in the snow and make no fire. As the twilight drew on, its eager yearning for the fire mastered it, and with a great lifting and shifting of forefeet, it whined softly, then flattened its ears down in anticipation of being chidden by the man. But the man remained silent. Later, the dog whined loudly. And still later it crept close to the man and caught the scent of death. This made the animal bristle and back away. A little longer it delayed, howling under the stars that leaped and danced and shone brightly in the cold sky. Then it turned and trotted up the trail in the direction of the camp it knew, where were the other food-providers and fire-providers.

COLLEGE WRITING 1: REFLECTION WITHIN THE TEXT

Remember or imagine a difficult situation you've been in—like the man in Jack London's "To Build a Fire". Imagine not heeding the advice given you and instead doing what you think is best. How does the situation turn out? What advice are you given and why do you not listen to it? What choices do you make and why do you make them?

Would you change anything if you had the opportunity to go back in time?

COLLEGE WRITING 2: RESEARCH OUTSIDE THE TEXT

Research extreme cold weather survival techniques. Beyond the advice given to the man in "To Build a Fire", what else could the man have done to survive his trip? Use only materials and knowledge that would have been available in 1908. Write a How-to-Guide for surviving the trip. Include a list of supplies. You may also include advice from the story.

IDEAS AND VALUES: CONNECT THE TEXT

» In London's "To Build A Fire" the main character is always referred to as "the man," or simply "he." In Gilman's "The Yellow Wallpaper" the narrator never directly gives us her name, while her husband refers to her only as: "blessed little goose," "Darling," "his darling," and "little girl." In Crane's "The Blue Hotel" there are the characters of the Easterner, the Cowboy, the Swede, and the Gambler, but also Pat and Johnnie Scully. What is the nature of anonymity? What do the anonymous characters in these stories have in common? Between these texts, does anonymity seem to be a good thing? Are the anonymous characters the most powerful, or fortunate characters in their respective stories? Ultimately why are some characters named and others not?

» In Jack London's "To Build A Fire" the main character is faced with the necessity of building a fire to ensure his survival. Yet his need for fire is determined by earlier choices he made. In Ambrose Bierce's "Occurrence at Owl Creek Bridge" Peyton Farquhar is fighting to escape his situation in order to survive—but again, his earlier choices are what led to his hanging. In Ryunosuke Akutagawa's "Rashōmon" Rashōmon must make a choice that will determine his ability to survive after he is let go a servant due only to the economic situation of his master. His conversation with the wig-maker leads him to his decision. How do each of these characters survive? What specific elements affects each of their ability to survive? What choices do the characters face that affect their ability to survive? What sacrifices are worth making in order to survive? Why are the characters willing and able, or not, to make these choices?

»   In H.G. Wells's "The Star" a mathematician predicts that a celestial body that has collided with Neptune will approach Earth and all manner of nature will wreak havoc on mankind, while in Jack London's "To Build a Fire," the man fails to appreciate the dangers of his surroundings, and finally in "The Machine Stops" a whole society has shut themselves away from "the surface," choosing rather to experience life as indirectly as possible. In these stories we have three visions of man's relationship to nature; what unites them? What makes them different? Is nature a force to be conquered, bent to man's will? Is nature a god to be feared, or even worshipped? Is mankind something set apart from nature—or are we nature as well?

Earth's Holocaust

By Nathaniel Hawthorne

7,565 WORDS. 42 MINUTES.
READING LEVEL: GRADE 12.9

Once upon a time—but whether in the time past or time to come is a matter of little or no moment—this wide world had become so overburdened with an accumulation of worn-out trumpery, that the inhabitants determined to rid themselves of it by a general bonfire. The site fixed upon at the representation of the insurance companies, and as being as central a spot as any other on the globe, was one of the broadest prairies of the West, where no human habitation would be endangered by the flames, and where a vast assemblage of spectators might commodiously admire the show. Having a taste for sights of this kind, and imagining, likewise, that the illumination of the bonfire might reveal some profundity of moral truth heretofore hidden in mist or darkness, I made it convenient to journey thither and be present. At my arrival, although the heap of condemned rubbish was as yet comparatively small, the torch had already been applied. Amid that boundless plain, in the dusk of the evening, like a far off star alone in the firmament, there was merely visible one tremulous gleam, whence none could have anticipated so fierce a blaze as was destined to ensue. With every moment, however, there came foot-travellers, women holding up their aprons, men on horseback, wheelbarrows, lumbering baggage-wagons, and other vehicles, great and small, and from far and near, laden with articles that were judged fit for nothing but to be burned.

"What materials have been used to kindle the flame?" inquired I of a bystander; for I was desirous of knowing the whole process of the affair from beginning to end.

The person whom I addressed was a grave man, fifty years old or thereabout, who had evidently come thither as a looker-on. He struck me immediately as having weighed for himself the true value of life and its circumstances, and therefore as feeling little personal interest in whatever judgment the world might form of them. Before answering my question, he looked me in the face by the kindling light of the fire.

"O, some very dry combustibles," replied he, "and extremely suitable to the purpose,—no other, in fact, than yesterday's newspapers, last month's magazines, and last year's withered leaves. Here now comes some antiquated trash that will take fire like a handful of shavings."

As he spoke, some rough-looking men advanced to the verge of the bonfire, and threw in, as it appeared, all the rubbish of the herald's office,—the blazonry of coat armor, the crests and devices of illustrious families, pedigrees that extended back, like lines of light, into the mist of the dark ages, together with stars, garters, and embroidered collars, each of which, as paltry a bawble as it might appear to the uninstructed eye, had once possessed vast significance, and was still, in truth, reckoned among the most precious of moral or material facts by the worshippers of the gorgeous past. Mingled with this confused heap, which was tossed into the flames by armfuls at once, were innumerable badges of knighthood, comprising those of all the European sovereignties, and Napoleon's decoration of the Legion of Honor, the ribbons of which were entangled with those of the ancient order of St. Louis. There, too, were the medals of our own Society of Cincinnati, by means of which, as history tells us, an order of hereditary knights came near being constituted out of the king quellers of the Revolution. And besides, there were the patents of nobility of German counts and barons, Spanish grandees, and English peers, from the worm-eaten instruments signed by William the Conqueror down to the bran-new parchment of the latest lord who has received his honors from the fair hand of Victoria.

At sight of the dense volumes of smoke, mingled with vivid jets of flame, that gushed and eddied forth from this immense pile of earthly distinctions, the multitude of plebeian spectators set up a joyous shout, and clapped their hands with an emphasis that made the welkin echo. That was their moment of triumph, achieved, after long ages, over creatures of the same clay and the same spiritual infirmities, who had dared to assume the privileges due only to Heaven's better workmanship. But now there rushed towards the blazing heap a gray-haired man, of stately presence, wearing a coat, from the breast of which a star, or other badge of rank, seemed to have been forcibly wrenched away. He had not the tokens of intellectual power in his face; but still there was the demeanor, the habitual and almost native dignity, of one who had been born to the idea of his own social superiority, and had never felt it questioned till that moment.

"People," cried he, gazing at the ruin of what was dearest to his eyes with grief and wonder, but nevertheless with a degree of stateliness,—"people, what have you done? This fire is consuming all that marked your advance from barbarism, or that could have prevented your relapse thither. We, the men of the privileged orders, were those who kept alive from age to age the old chivalrous spirit; the gentle and generous thought; the higher, the purer, the more refined and delicate life. With the nobles, too, you cast off the poet, the painter, the sculptor,—all the beautiful arts; for we were their patrons, and created the atmosphere in which they flourish. In abolishing the majestic distinctions of rank, society loses not only its grace, but its steadfastness—"

More he would doubtless have spoken; but here there arose an outcry, sportive, contemptuous, and indignant, that altogether drowned the appeal of the fallen nobleman, insomuch that, casting one look of despair at his own half-burned pedigree, he shrunk back into the crowd, glad to shelter himself under his new-found insignificance.

"Let him thank his stars that we have not flung him into the same fire!" shouted a rude figure, spurning the embers with his foot. "And henceforth let no man dare to show a piece of musty parchment as his warrant for lording it over his fellows. If he have strength of arm, well and good; it is one species of superiority. If he have wit, wisdom, courage, force of character, let these attributes do for him what they may; but from this day forward no mortal must hope for place and consideration by reckoning up the mouldy bones of his ancestors. That nonsense is done away."

"And in good time," remarked the grave observer by my side, in a low voice, however, "if no worse nonsense comes in its place; but, at all events, this species of nonsense has fairly lived out its life."

There was little space to muse or moralize over the embers of this time-honored rubbish; for, before it was half burned out, there came another multitude from beyond the sea, bearing the purple robes of royalty, and the crowns, globes, and sceptres of emperors and kings. All these had been condemned as useless bawbles, playthings at best, fit only for the infancy of the world or rods to govern and chastise it in its nonage, but with which universal manhood at its full-grown stature could no longer brook to be insulted. Into such contempt had these regal insignia now fallen that the gilded crown and tinselled robes of the player king from Drury Lane Theatre had been thrown in among the rest, doubtless as a mockery of his brother monarchs on the great stage of the world. It was a strange sight to discern the crown jewels of England glowing and flashing in the midst of the fire. Some of them had been delivered down from the time of the Saxon princes; others were purchased with vast revenues, or perchance ravished from the dead brows of the native potentates of Hindustan; and the whole now blazed with a dazzling lustre, as if a star had fallen in that spot and been shattered into fragments. The splendor of the ruined monarchy had no reflection save in those inestimable precious stones. But enough on this subject. It were but tedious to describe how the Emperor of Austria's mantle was converted to tinder, and how the posts and pillars of the French throne became a heap of coals, which it was impossible to distinguish from those of any other wood. Let me add, however, that I noticed one of the exiled Poles stirring up the bonfire with the Czar of Russia's sceptre, which he afterwards flung into the flames.

"The smell of singed garments is quite intolerable here," observed my new acquaintance, as the breeze enveloped us in the smoke of a royal wardrobe. "Let us get to windward and see what they are doing on the other side of the bonfire."

We accordingly passed around, and were just in time to witness the arrival of a vast procession of Washingtonians,—as the votaries of temperance call themselves nowadays,—accompanied by thousands of the Irish disciples of Father Mathew, with that great apostle at their head. They brought a rich contribution to the bonfire, being nothing less than all the hogsheads and barrels of liquor in the world, which they rolled before them across the prairie.

"Now, my children," cried Father Mathew, when they reached the verge of the fire, "one shove more, and the work is done. And now let us stand off and see Satan deal with his own liquor."

Accordingly, having placed their wooden vessels within reach of the flames, the procession stood off at a safe distance, and soon beheld them burst into a blaze that reached the clouds and threatened to set the sky itself on fire. And well it might; for here was the whole world's stock of spirituous liquors, which, instead of kindling a frenzied light in the eyes of individual topers as of yore, soared upwards with a bewildering gleam that startled all mankind. It was the aggregate of that fierce fire which would otherwise have scorched the hearts of millions. Meantime numberless bottles of precious wine were flung into the blaze, which lapped up the contents as if it loved them, and grew, like other drunkards, the merrier and fiercer for what it quaffed. Never again will the insatiable thirst of the fire-fiend be so pampered. Here were the treasures of famous bon vivants,—liquors that had been tossed on ocean, and mellowed in the sun, and hoarded long in the recesses of the earth,—the pale, the gold, the ruddy juice of whatever vineyards were most delicate,—the entire vintage of Tokay,—all mingling in one stream with the vile fluids of the common pot house, and contributing to heighten the self-same blaze. And while it rose in a gigantic spire that seemed to wave against the arch of the firmament and combine itself with the light of stars, the multitude gave a shout as if the broad earth were exulting in its deliverance from the curse of ages.

But the joy was not universal. Many deemed that human life would be gloomier than ever when that brief illumination should sink down. While the reformers were at work I overheard muttered expostulations from several respectable gentlemen with red noses and wearing gouty shoes; and a ragged worthy, whose face looked like a hearth where the fire is burned out, now expressed his discontent more openly and boldly.

"What is this world good for," said the last toper, "now that we can never be jolly any more? What is to comfort the poor man in sorrow and perplexity? How is he to keep his heart warm against the cold winds of this cheerless earth? And what do you propose to give him in exchange for the solace that you take away? How are old friends to sit together by the fireside without a cheerful glass between them? A plague upon your reformation! It is a sad world, a cold world, a selfish world, a low world, not worth an honest fellow's living in, now that good fellowship is gone forever!"

This harangue excited great mirth among the bystanders; but, preposterous as was the sentiment, I could not help commiserating the forlorn condition of the last toper, whose boon companions had dwindled away from his side, leaving the poor fellow without a soul to countenance him in sipping his liquor, nor indeed any liquor to sip. Not that this was quite the true state of the case; for I had observed him at a critical moment filch a bottle of fourth-proof brandy that fell beside the bonfire and hide it in his pocket.

The spirituous and fermented liquors being thus disposed of, the zeal of the reformers next induced them to replenish the fire with all the boxes of tea and bags of coffee in the world. And now came the planters of Virginia, bringing their crops of tobacco. These, being cast upon the heap of inutility, aggregated it to the size of a mountain, and incensed the atmosphere with such potent fragrance that methought we should never draw pure breath again. The present sacrifice seemed to startle the lovers of the weed more than any that they had hitherto witnessed.

"Well, they've put my pipe out," said an old gentleman, flinging it into the flames in a pet. "What is this world coming to? Everything rich and racy—all the spice of life—is to be condemned as useless. Now that they have kindled the bonfire, if these nonsensical reformers would fling themselves into it, all would be well enough!"

"Be patient," responded a stanch conservative; "it will come to that in the end. They will first fling us in, and finally themselves."

From the general and systematic measures of reform I now turn to consider the individual contributions to this memorable bonfire. In many instances these were of a very amusing character. One poor fellow threw in his empty purse, and another a bundle of counterfeit or insolvable bank-notes. Fashionable ladies threw in their last season's bonnets, together with heaps of ribbons, yellow lace, and much other half-worn milliner's ware, all of which proved even more evanescent in the fire than it had been in the fashion. A multitude of lovers of both sexes—discarded maids or bachelors and couples mutually weary of one another—tossed in bundles of perfumed letters and enamored sonnets. A hack politician, being deprived of bread by the loss of office, threw in his teeth, which happened to be false ones. The Rev. Sydney Smith—having voyaged across the Atlantic for that sole purpose—came up to the bonfire with a bitter grin and threw in certain repudiated bonds, fortified though they were with the broad seal of a sovereign state. A little boy of five years old, in the premature manliness of the present epoch, threw in his playthings; a college graduate, his diploma; an apothecary, ruined by the spread of homeopathy, his whole stock of drugs and medicines; a physician, his library; a parson, his old sermons; and a fine gentleman of the old school, his code of manners, which he had formerly written down for the benefit of the next generation. A widow, resolving on a second marriage, slyly threw in her dead husband's miniature. A young man, jilted by his mistress, would willingly have flung his own desperate heart into the flames, but could find no means to wrench it out of his bosom. An American author, whose works were neglected by the public, threw his pen and paper into the bonfire and betook himself to some less discouraging occupation. It somewhat startled me to overhear a number of ladies, highly respectable in appearance, proposing to fling their gowns and petticoats into the flames, and assume the garb, together with the manners, duties, offices, and responsibilities, of the opposite sex.

What favor was accorded to this scheme I am unable to say, my attention being suddenly drawn to a poor, deceived, and half-delirious girl, who, exclaiming that she was the most worthless thing alive or dead, attempted to cast herself into the fire amid all that wrecked and broken trumpery of the world. A good man, however, ran to her rescue.

"Patience, my poor girl!" said he, as he drew her back from the fierce embrace of the destroying angel. "Be patient, and abide Heaven's will. So long as you possess a living soul, all may be restored to its first freshness. These things of matter and creations of human fantasy are fit for nothing but to be burned when once they have had their day; but your day is eternity!"

"Yes," said the wretched girl, whose frenzy seemed now to have sunk down into deep despondency, "yes, and the sunshine is blotted out of it!"

It was now rumored among the spectators that all the weapons and munitions of war were to be thrown into the bonfire with the exception of the world's stock of gunpowder, which, as the safest mode of disposing of it, had already been drowned in the sea. This intelligence seemed to awaken great diversity of opinion. The hopeful philanthropist esteemed it a token that the millennium was already come; while persons of another stamp, in whose view mankind was a breed of bulldogs, prophesied that all the old stoutness, fervor, nobleness, generosity, and magnanimity of the race would disappear,—these qualities, as they affirmed, requiring blood for their nourishment. They comforted themselves, however, in the belief that the proposed abolition of war was impracticable for any length of time together.

Be that as it might, numberless great guns, whose thunder had long been the voice of battle,—the artillery of the Armada, the battering trains of Marlborough, and the adverse cannon of Napoleon and Wellington,—were trundled into the midst of the fire. By the continual addition of dry combustibles, it had now waxed so intense that neither brass nor iron could withstand it. It was wonderful to behold how these terrible instruments of slaughter melted away like playthings of wax. Then the armies of the earth wheeled around the mighty furnace, with their military music playing triumphant marches,—and flung in their muskets and swords. The standard-bearers, likewise, cast one look upward at their banners, all tattered with shot-holes and inscribed with the names of victorious fields; and, giving them a last flourish on the breeze, they lowered them into the flame, which snatched them upward in its rush towards the clouds. This ceremony being over, the world was left without a single weapon in its hands, except possibly a few old king's arms and rusty swords and other trophies of the Revolution in some of our State armories. And now the drums were beaten and the trumpets brayed all together, as a prelude to the proclamation of universal and eternal peace and the announcement that glory was no longer to be won by blood, but that it would henceforth be the contention of the human race to work out the greatest mutual good, and that beneficence, in the future annals of the earth, would claim the praise of valor. The blessed tidings were accordingly promulgated, and caused infinite rejoicings among those who had stood aghast at the horror and absurdity of war.

But I saw a grim smile pass over the seared visage of a stately old commander,—by his war-worn figure and rich military dress, he might have been one of Napoleon's famous marshals,—who, with the rest of the world's soldiery, had just flung away the sword that had been familiar to his right hand for half a century.

"Ay! ay!" grumbled he. "Let them proclaim what they please; but, in the end, we shall find that all this foolery has only made more work for the armorers and cannon-founders."

"Why, sir," exclaimed I, in astonishment, "do you imagine that the human race will ever so far return on the steps of its past madness as to weld another sword or cast another cannon?"

"There will be no need," observed, with a sneer, one who neither felt benevolence nor had faith in it. "When Cain wished to slay his brother, he was at no loss for a weapon."

"We shall see," replied the veteran commander. "If I am mistaken, so much the better; but in my opinion, without pretending to philosophize about the matter, the necessity of war lies far deeper than these honest gentlemen suppose. What! is there a field for all the petty disputes of individuals? and shall there be no great law court for the settlement of national difficulties? The battle-field is the only court where such suits can be tried."

"You forget, general," rejoined I, "that, in this advanced stage of civilization, Reason and Philanthropy combined will constitute just such a tribunal as is requisite."

"Ah, I had forgotten that, indeed!" said the old warrior, as he limped away.

The fire was now to be replenished with materials that had hitherto been considered of even greater importance to the well-being of society than the warlike munitions which we had already seen consumed. A body of reformers had travelled all over the earth in quest of the machinery by which the different nations were accustomed to inflict the punishment of death. A shudder passed through the multitude as these ghastly emblems were dragged forward. Even the flames seemed at first to shrink away, displaying the shape and murderous contrivance of each in a full blaze of light, which of itself was sufficient to convince mankind of the long and deadly error of human law. Those old implements of cruelty; those horrible monsters of mechanism; those inventions which it seemed to demand something worse than man's natural heart to contrive, and which had lurked in the dusky nooks of ancient prisons, the subject of terror-stricken legend,—were now brought forth to view. Headsmen's axes, with the rust of noble and royal blood upon them, and a vast collection of halters that had choked the breath of plebeian victims, were thrown in together. A shout greeted the arrival of the guillotine, which was thrust forward on the same wheels that had borne it from one to another of the blood-stained streets of Paris. But the loudest roar of applause went up, telling the distant sky of the triumph of the earth's redemption, when the gallows made its appearance. An ill-looking fellow, however, rushed forward, and, putting himself in the path of the reformers, bellowed hoarsely, and fought with brute fury to stay their progress.

It was little matter of surprise, perhaps, that the executioner should thus do his best to vindicate and uphold the machinery by which he himself had his livelihood and worthier individuals their death; but it deserved special note that men of a far different sphere—even of that consecrated class in whose guardianship the world is apt to trust its benevolence—were found to take the hangman's view of the question.

"Stay, my brethren!" cried one of them. "You are misled by a false philanthropy; you know not what you do. The gallows is a Heaven-ordained instrument. Bear it back, then, reverently, and set it up in its old place, else the world will fall to speedy ruin and desolation!"

"Onward! onward!" shouted a leader in the reform. "Into the flames with the accursed instrument of man's bloody policy! How can human law inculcate benevolence and love while it persists in setting up the gallows as its chief symbol? One heave more, good friends, and the world will be redeemed from its greatest error."

A thousand hands, that nevertheless loathed the touch, now lent their assistance, and thrust the ominous burden far, far into the centre of the raging furnace. There its fatal and abhorred image was beheld, first black, then a red coal, then ashes.

"That was well done!" exclaimed I.

"Yes, it was well done," replied, but with less enthusiasm than I expected, the thoughtful observer, who was still at my side,—"well done, if the world be good enough for the measure. Death, however, is an idea that cannot easily be dispensed with in any condition between the primal innocence and that other purity and perfection which perchance we are destined to attain after travelling round the full circle; but, at all events, it is well that the experiment should now be tried."

"Too cold! too cold!" impatiently exclaimed the young and ardent leader in this triumph. "Let the heart have its voice here as well as the intellect. And as for ripeness, and as for progress, let mankind always do the highest, kindest, noblest thing that, at any given period, it has attained the perception of; and surely that thing cannot be wrong nor wrongly timed."

I know not whether it were the excitement of the scene, or whether the good people around the bonfire were really growing more enlightened every instant; but they now proceeded to measures in the full length of which I was hardly prepared to keep them company. For instance, some threw their marriage certificates into the flames, and declared themselves candidates for a higher, holier, and more comprehensive union than that which had subsisted from the birth of time under the form of the connubial tie. Others hastened to the vaults of banks and to the coffers of the rich—all of which were opened to the first comer on this fated occasion—and brought entire bales of paper-money to enliven the blaze, and tons of coin to be melted down by its intensity. Henceforth, they said, universal benevolence, uncoined and exhaustless, was to be the golden currency of the world. At this intelligence the bankers and speculators in the stocks grew pale, and a pickpocket, who had reaped a rich harvest among the crowd, fell down in a deadly fainting fit. A few men of business burned their day-books and ledgers, the notes and obligations of their creditors, and all other evidences of debts due to themselves; while perhaps a somewhat larger number satisfied their zeal for reform with the sacrifice of any uncomfortable recollection of their own indebtment. There was then a cry that the period was arrived when the title-deeds of landed property should be given to the flames, and the whole soil of the earth revert to the public, from whom it had been wrongfully abstracted and most unequally distributed among individuals. Another party demanded that all written constitutions, set forms of government, legislative acts, statute-books, and everything else on which human invention had endeavored to stamp its arbitrary laws, should at once be destroyed, leaving the consummated world as free as the man first created.

Whether any ultimate action was taken with regard to these propositions is beyond my knowledge; for, just then, some matters were in progress that concerned my sympathies more nearly.

"See! see! What heaps of books and pamphlets!" cried a fellow, who did not seem to be a lover of literature. "Now we shall have a glorious blaze!"

"That's just the thing!" said a modern philosopher. "Now we shall get rid of the weight of dead men's thought, which has hitherto pressed so heavily on the living intellect that it has been incompetent to any effectual self-exertion. Well done, my lads! Into the fire with them! Now you are enlightening the world indeed!"

"But what is to become of the trade?" cried a frantic bookseller.

"O, by all means, let them accompany their merchandise," coolly observed an author. "It will be a noble funeral-pile!"

The truth was, that the human race had now reached a stage of progress so far beyond what the wisest and wittiest men of former ages had ever dreamed of, that it would have been a manifest absurdity to allow the earth to be any longer encumbered with their poor achievements in the literary line. Accordingly a thorough and searching investigation had swept the booksellers' shops, hawkers' stands, public and private libraries, and even the little book-shelf by the country fireside, and had brought the world's entire mass of printed paper, bound or in sheets, to swell the already mountain bulk of our illustrious bonfire. Thick, heavy folios, containing the labors of lexicographers, commentators, and encyclopedists, were flung in, and, falling among the embers with a leaden thump, smouldered away to ashes like rotten wood. The small, richly gilt French tomes of the last age, with the hundred volumes of Voltaire among them, went off in a brilliant shower of sparkles and little jets of flame; while the current literature of the same nation burned red and blue, and threw an infernal light over the visages of the spectators, converting them all to the aspect of party-colored fiends. A collection of German stories emitted a scent of brimstone. The English standard authors made excellent fuel, generally exhibiting the properties of sound oak logs. Milton's works, in particular, sent up a powerful blaze, gradually reddening into a coal, which promised to endure longer than almost any other material of the pile. From Shakespeare there gushed a flame of such marvellous splendor that men shaded their eyes as against the sun's meridian glory; nor even when the works of his own elucidators were flung upon him did he cease to flash forth a dazzling radiance from beneath the ponderous heap. It is my belief that he is still blazing as fervidly as ever.

"Could a poet but light a lamp at that glorious flame," remarked I, "he might then consume the midnight oil to some good purpose."

"That is the very thing which modern poets have been too apt to do, or at least to attempt," answered a critic. "The chief benefit to be expected from this conflagration of past literature undoubtedly is, that writers will henceforth be compelled to light their lamps at the sun or stars."

"If they can reach so high," said I; "but that task requires a giant, who may afterwards distribute the light among inferior men. It is not every one that can steal the fire from heaven like Prometheus; but, when once he had done the deed, a thousand hearths were kindled by it."

It amazed me much to observe how indefinite was the proportion between the physical mass of any given author and the property of brilliant and long-continued combustion. For instance, there was not a quarto volume of the last century—nor, indeed, of the present—that could compete in that particular with a child's little gilt-covered book, containing *Mother Goose's Melodies*. *The Life and Death of Tom Thumb* outlasted the biography of Marlborough. An epic, indeed a dozen of them, was converted to white ashes before the single sheet of an old ballad was half consumed. In more than one case, too, when volumes of applauded verse proved incapable of anything better than a stifling smoke, an unregarded ditty of some nameless bard—perchance in the corner of a newspaper—soared up among the stars with a flame as brilliant as their own. Speaking of the properties of flame, methought Shelley's poetry emitted a purer light than almost any other productions of his day, contrasting beautifully with the fitful and lurid gleams and gushes of black vapor that flashed and eddied from the volumes of Lord Byron. As for Tom Moore, some of his songs diffused an odor like a burning pastil.

I felt particular interest in watching the combustion of American authors, and scrupulously noted by my watch the precise number of moments that changed most of them from shabbily printed books to indistinguishable ashes. It would be invidious, however, if not perilous, to betray these awful secrets; so that I shall content myself with observing that it was not invariably the writer most frequent in the public mouth that made the most splendid appearance in the bonfire. I especially remember that a great deal of excellent inflammability was exhibited in a thin volume of poems by Ellery Channing; although, to speak the truth, there were certain portions that hissed and spluttered in a very disagreeable fashion. A curious phenomenon occurred in reference to several writers, native as well as foreign. Their books, though of highly respectable figure, instead of bursting into a blaze or even smouldering out their substance in smoke, suddenly melted away in a manner that proved them to be ice.

If it be no lack of modesty to mention my own works, it must here be confessed that I looked for them with fatherly interest, but in vain. Too probably they were changed to vapor by the first action of the heat; at best, I can only hope that, in their quiet way, they contributed a glimmering spark or two to the splendor of the evening.

"Alas! and woe is me!" thus bemoaned himself a heavy-looking gentleman in green spectacles. "The world is utterly ruined, and there is nothing to live for any longer. The business of my life is snatched from me. Not a volume to be had for love or money!"

"This," remarked the sedate observer beside me, "is a bookworm,—one of those men who are born to gnaw dead thoughts. His clothes, you see, are covered with the dust of libraries. He has no inward fountain of ideas; and, in good earnest, now that the old stock is abolished, I do not see what is to become of the poor fellow. Have you no word of comfort for him?"

"My dear sir," said I to the desperate bookworm, "is not nature better than a book? Is not the human heart deeper than any system of philosophy? Is not life replete with more instruction than past observers have found it possible to write down in maxims? Be of good cheer. The great book of Time is still spread wide open before us; and, if we read it aright, it will be to us a volume of eternal truth."

"O, my books, my books, my precious printed books!" reiterated the forlorn bookworm. "My only reality was a bound volume; and now they will not leave me even a shadowy pamphlet!"

In fact, the last remnant of the literature of all the ages was now descending upon the blazing heap in the shape of a cloud of pamphlets from the press of the New World. These likewise were consumed in the twinkling of an eye, leaving the earth, for the first time since the days of Cadmus, free from the plague of letters,—an enviable field for the authors of the next generation.

"Well, and does anything remain to be done?" inquired I, somewhat anxiously. "Unless we set fire to the earth itself, and then leap boldly off into infinite space, I know not that we can carry reform to any farther point."

"You are vastly mistaken, my good friend," said the observer. "Believe me, the fire will not be allowed to settle down without the addition of fuel that will startle many persons who have lent a willing hand thus far."

Nevertheless there appeared to be a relaxation of effort for a little time, during which, probably, the leaders of the movement were considering what should be done next. In the interval, a philosopher threw his theory into the flames,—a sacrifice which, by those who knew how to estimate it, was pronounced the most remarkable that had yet been made. The combustion, however, was by no means brilliant. Some indefatigable people, scorning to take a moment's ease, now employed themselves in collecting all the withered leaves and fallen boughs of the forest, and thereby recruited the bonfire to a greater height than ever. But this was mere by-play.

"Here comes the fresh fuel that I spoke of," said my companion.

To my astonishment the persons who now advanced into the vacant space around the mountain fire bore surplices and other priestly garments, mitres, crosiers, and a confusion of Popish and Protestant emblems with which it seemed their purpose to consummate the great act of faith. Crosses from the spires of old cathedrals were cast upon the heap with as little remorse as if the reverence of centuries passing in long array beneath the lofty towers had not looked up to them as the holiest of symbols. The font in which infants were consecrated to God, the sacramental vessels whence piety received the hallowed draught, were given to the same destruction. Perhaps it most nearly touched my heart to see among these devoted relics fragments of the humble communion-tables and undecorated pulpits which I recognized as having been torn from the meeting-houses of New England. Those simple edifices might have been permitted to retain all of sacred embellishment that their Puritan founders had bestowed, even though the mighty structure of St. Peter's had sent its spoils to the fire of this terrible sacrifice. Yet I felt that these were but the externals of religion, and might most safely be relinquished by spirits that best knew their deep significance.

"All is well," said I, cheerfully. "The wood-paths shall be the aisles of our cathedral, the firmament itself shall be its ceiling. What needs an earthly roof between the Deity and his worshippers? Our faith can well afford to lose all the drapery that even the holiest men have thrown around it, and be only the more sublime in its simplicity."

"True," said my companion; "but will they pause here?"

The doubt implied in his question was well founded. In the general destruction of books already described, a holy volume, that stood apart from the catalogue of human literature, and yet, in one sense, was at its head, had been spared. But the Titan of innovation,—angel or fiend, double in his nature, and capable of deeds befitting both characters,—at first shaking down only the old and rotten shapes of things, had now, as it appeared, laid his terrible hand upon the main pillars which supported the whole edifice of our moral and spiritual state. The inhabitants of the earth had grown too enlightened to define their faith within a form of words, or to limit the spiritual by any analogy to our material existence. Truths which the heavens trembled at were now but a fable of the world's infancy. Therefore, as the final sacrifice of human error, what else remained to be thrown upon the embers of that awful pile, except the book which, though a celestial revelation to past ages, was but a voice from a lower sphere as regarded the present race of man? It was done! Upon the blazing heap of falsehood and worn-out truth—things that the earth had never needed, or had ceased to need, or had grown childishly weary of—fell the ponderous church Bible, the great old volume that had lain so long on the cushion of the pulpit, and whence the pastor's solemn voice had given holy utterance on so many a Sabbath day. There, likewise, fell the family Bible, which the long-buried patriarch had read to his children,—in prosperity or sorrow, by the fireside and in the summer shade of trees,— and had bequeathed downward as the heirloom of generations. There fell the bosom Bible, the little volume that had been the soul's friend of some sorely tried child of dust, who thence took courage, whether his trial were for life or death, steadfastly confronting both in the strong assurance of immortality.

All these were flung into the fierce and riotous blaze; and then a mighty wind came roaring across the plain with a desolate howl, as if it were the angry lamentation of the earth for the loss of heaven's sunshine; and it shook the gigantic pyramid of flame and scattered the cinders of half-consumed abominations around upon the spectators.

"This is terrible!" said I, feeling that my check grew pale, and seeing a like change in the visages about me.

"Be of good courage yet," answered the man with whom I had so often spoken. He continued to gaze steadily at the spectacle with a singular calmness, as if it concerned him merely as an observer. "Be of good courage, nor yet exult too much; for there is far less both of good and evil in the effect of this bonfire than the world might be willing to believe."

"How can that be?" exclaimed I, impatiently. "Has it not consumed everything? Has it not swallowed up or melted down every human or divine appendage of our mortal state that had substance enough to be acted on by fire? Will there be anything left us to-morrow morning better or worse than a heap of embers and ashes?"

"Assuredly there will," said my grave friend. "Come hither to-morrow morning, or whenever the combustible portion of the pile shall be quite burned out, and you will find among the ashes everything really valuable that you have seen cast into the flames. Trust me, the world of to-morrow will again enrich itself with the gold and diamonds which have been cast off by the world of today. Not a truth is destroyed nor buried so deep among the ashes but it will be raked up at last."

This was a strange assurance. Yet I felt inclined to credit it, the more especially as I beheld among the wallowing flames a copy of the Holy Scriptures, the pages of which, instead of being blackened into tinder, only assumed a more dazzling whiteness as the fingermarks of human imperfection were purified away. Certain marginal notes and commentaries, it is true, yielded to the intensity of the fiery test, but without detriment to the smallest syllable that had flamed from the pen of inspiration.

"Yes; there is the proof of what you say," answered I, turning to the observer; "but if only what is evil can feel the action of the fire, then, surely, the conflagration has been of inestimable utility. Yet, if I understand aright, you intimate a doubt whether the world's expectation of benefit would be realized by it."

"Listen to the talk of these worthies," said he, pointing to a group in front of the blazing pile; "possibly they may teach you something useful, without intending it."

The persons whom he indicated consisted of that brutal and most earthy figure who had stood forth so furiously in defence of the gallows,—the hangman, in short,—together with the last thief and the last murderer, all three of whom were clustered about the last toper. The latter was liberally passing the brandy bottle, which he had rescued from the general destruction of wines and spirits. This little convivial party seemed at the lowest pitch of despondency, as considering that the purified world must needs be utterly unlike the sphere that they had hitherto known, and therefore but a strange and desolate abode for gentlemen of their kidney.

"The best counsel for all of us is," remarked the hangman, "that, as soon as we have finished the last drop of liquor, I help you, my three friends, to a comfortable end upon the nearest tree, and then hang myself on the same bough. This is no world for us any longer."

"Poh, poh, my good fellows!" said a dark-complexioned personage, who now joined the group,—his complexion was indeed fearfully dark, and his eyes glowed with a redder light than that of the bonfire; "be not so cast down, my dear friends; you shall see good days yet. There is one thing that these wiseacres have forgotten to throw into the fire, and without which all the rest of the conflagration is just nothing at all; yes, though they had burned the earth itself to a cinder."

"And what may that be?" eagerly demanded the last murderer.

"What but the human heart itself?" said the dark-visaged stranger, with a portentous grin. "And, unless they hit upon some method of purifying that foul cavern, forth from it will reissue all the shapes of wrong and misery—the same old shapes or worse ones—which they have taken such a vast deal of trouble to consume to ashes. I have stood by this livelong night and laughed in my sleeve at the whole business. O, take my word for it, it will be the old world yet!"

This brief conversation supplied me with a theme for lengthened thought. How sad a truth, if true it were, that man's age-long endeavor for perfection had served only to render him the mockery of the evil principle, from the fatal circumstance of an error at the very root of the matter! The heart, the heart, there was the little yet boundless sphere wherein existed the original wrong of which the crime and misery of this outward world were merely types. Purify that inward sphere, and the many shapes of evil that haunt the outward, and which now seem almost our only realities, will turn to shadowy phantoms and vanish of their own accord; but if we go no deeper than the intellect, and strive, with merely that feeble instrument, to discern and rectify what is wrong, our whole accomplishment will be a dream, so unsubstantial that it matters little whether the bonfire, which I have so faithfully described, were what we choose to call a real event and a flame that would scorch the finger, or only a phosphoric radiance and a parable of my own brain.

COLLEGE WRITING 1: REFLECTION WITHIN THE TEXT

Imagine—that you are about to have a bonfire of your own, and you burn everything that is burned in Hawthorne's "Earth's Holocaust". And after you have emptied your life of every thing that was burned in the story, save the floors and the walls, and enough clothes to cover you, ask yourself: who are you? Are you free? Are you different?

List everything that goes to the fire. What defined you? What entertained you? What tools and toys and necessities did you destroy? Consider what they meant to you—or why you held on to these things in the first place. If you hesitate to get rid of anything, even in your imagination, why?

COLLEGE WRITING 2: RESEARCH OUTSIDE THE TEXT

Consider the character of "the bookworm," as he is described in the text: "one of those men who are born to gnaw dead thoughts. His clothes, you see, are covered with the dust of libraries. He has no inward fountain of ideas." Consider the human drive to preserve—and taken at its extreme—to hoard. Why do humans behave in this manner? Why do we collect things in the first place? Things seem to give humans a feeling of comfort. But why? Research this phenomenon.

IDEAS AND VALUES: CONNECT THE TEXT

In Philip K. Dick's "The Gun" culture is the one treasure that "the dragon guards," but in Nathanial Hawthorne's "Earth's Holocaust," culture is merely fuel for the fire, while in Wilde's "Impressions of America" culture is neither here nor there, but a category of different perspectives, perhaps a tool to be used one way or another, in practicality or fashion—as he doesn't enter into geography ("latitude or longitude"), economics ("the value of its dry goods"), or politics. But what is culture? What is its value—ultimately? Is it a way of life? A relic of the past? Does it hold us back, or does it tell us who we are? What relationship should we strike towards culture itself—? And what care should we take to understand its origins, if any at all?

One Day More

By Joseph Conrad

7,665 WORDS. 43 MINUTES.
READING LEVEL: GRADE 6

CHARACTERS

» Captain Hagberd (a retired coasting skipper).

» Josiah Carvil (formerly a shipbuilder—a widower—blind).

» Harry Hagberd (son of Captain Hagberd, who as a boy ran away from home).

» A Lamplighter. Bessie Carvil (daughter of Josiah Carvil).

SCENE

A small sea port.

To rights two yellow brick cottages belonging to Captain Hagberd, one inhabited by himself the other by the Carvils. A lamp-post in front. The red roofs of the town in the background. A sea-wall to left.

Time: The present-early autumn, towards dusk.

SCENE I.

CURTAIN RISES DISCLOSING CARVIL and Bessie moving away from sea-wall. Bessie about twenty-five. Black dress; black straw hat. A lot of mahogany-coloured hair loosely done up. Pale face. Full figure. Very quiet. Carvil, blind, unwieldy. Reddish whiskers; slow, deep voice produced without effort. Immovable, big face.

Carvil (*Hanging heavily on Bessie's arm*). Careful! Go slow! (*Stops; Bessie waits patiently.*) Want your poor blind father to break his neck? (*Shuffles on.*) In a hurry to get home and start that everlasting yarn with your chum the lunatic?

Bessie. I am not in a hurry to get home, father.

Carvil. Well, then, go steady with a poor blind man. Blind! Helpless! (*Strikes the ground with his stick.*) Never mind! I've had time to make enough money to have ham and eggs for breakfast every morning—thank

God! And thank God, too, for it, girl. You haven't known a single hardship in all the days of your idle life. Unless you think that a blind, helpless
father————-

Bessie. What is there for me to be in a hurry for?

Carvil. What did you say?

Bessie. I said there was nothing for me to hurry home for.

Carvil. There is, tho'. To yarn with a lunatic. Anything to get away
from your duty.

Bessie. Captain Hagberd's talk never hurt you or anybody else.

Carvil. Go on. Stick up for your only friend.

Bessie. Is it my fault that I haven't another soul to speak to?

Carvil (*Snarls*). It's mine, perhaps. Can I help being blind? You fret
because you want to be gadding about—with a helpless man left all alone
at home. Your own father too.

Bessie. I haven't been away from you half a day since mother died.

Carvil (*Viciously*). He's a lunatic, our landlord is. That's what he is.
Has been for years—long before those damned doctors destroyed my
sight for me. (*Growls angrily, then sighs.*)

Bessie. Perhaps Captain Hagberd is not so mad as the town takes
him for.

Carvil. (*Grimly*). Don't everybody know how he came here from the
North to wait till his missing son turns up—here—of all places in the
world. His boy that ran away to sea sixteen years ago and never did give
a sign of life since! Don't I remember seeing people dodge round corners
out of his way when he came along High Street. Seeing him, I tell you.
(*Groan.*) He bothered everybody so with his silly talk of his son being sure
to come back home—next year—next spring—next month————. What
is it by this time, hey?

Bessie. Why talk about it? He bothers no one now.

Carvil. No. They've grown too fly. You've got only to pass a remark
on his sail-cloth coat to make him shut up. All the town knows it. But he's
got you to listen to his crazy talk whenever he chooses. Don't I hear you
two at it, jabber, jabber, mumble, mumble————

Bessie. What is there so mad in keeping up hope?

Carvil (*Scathing scorn*). Not mad! Starving himself to lay money
by—for that son. Filling his house with furniture he won't let anyone
see—for that son. Advertising in the papers every week, these sixteen

254

years—for that son. Not mad! Boy, he calls him. Boy Harry. His boy Harry. His lost boy Harry. Yah! Let him lose his sight to know what real trouble means. And the boy—the man, I should say—must 've been put away safe in Davy Jones's locker for many a year—drowned—food for fishes—dead.... Stands to reason, or he would have been here before, smelling around the old fool's money. (*Shakes Bessie's arm slightly.*) Hey?

Bessie. I don't know. May be.

Carvil (*Bursting out*). Damme if I don't think he ever had a son.

Bessie. Poor man. Perhaps he never had.

Carvil. Ain't that mad enough for you? But I suppose you think it sensible.

Bessie. What does it matter? His talk keeps him up.

Carvil. Aye! And it pleases you. Anything to get away from your poor blind father.... Jabber, jabber—mumble, mumble—till I begin to think you must be as crazy as he is. What do you find to talk about, you two? What's your game?

(*During the scene Carvil and Bessie have crossed stage from L. to R. slowly with stoppages.*)

Bessie. It's warm. Will you sit out for a while?

Carvil (*Viciously*). Yes, I will sit out. (*Insistent.*) But what can be your game? What are you up to? (*They pass through garden gate.*) Because if it's his money you are after————-

Bessie. Father! How can you!

Carvil (*Disregarding her*). To make you independent of your poor blind father, then you are a fool. (*Drops heavily on seat.*) He's too much of a miser to ever make a will—even if he weren't mad.

Bessie. Oh! It never entered my head. I swear it never did.

Carvil. Never did. Hey! Then you are a still bigger fool.... I want to go to sleep! (*Takes off his hat, drops it on ground, and leans his head back against the wall.*)

Bessie. And I have been a good daughter to you. Won't you say that for me?

Carvil (*Very distinctly*). I want—to—go—to—sleep. I'm tired. (*Closes his eyes.*)

(*During that scene Captain Hagberd has been seen hesitating at the back of stage, then running quickly to the door of his cottage. He puts inside*

255

a tin kettle (from under his coat) and comes down to the railing between the two gardens stealthily).

SCENE II.

Carvil seated. Bessie. Captain Hagberd (white beard, sail-cloth jacket).

Bessie (*Knitting*). You've been out this afternoon for quite a long time, haven't you?

Capt. Hagberd (*Eager*). Yes, my dear. (*Slily*) Of course you saw me come back.

Bessie. Oh, yes. I did see you. You had something under your coat.

Capt. H. (*Anxiously*). It was only a kettle, my dear. A tin water-kettle. I am glad I thought of it just in time. (*Winks, nods.*) When a husband gets back from his work he needs a lot of water for a wash. See? (*Dignified.*) Not that Harry'll ever need to do a hand's turn after he comes home... (*Falters—casts stealthy glances on all sides*).... tomorrow.

Bessie (*Looks up, grave*). Captain Hagberd, have you ever thought that perhaps your son will not. . .

Capt. H. (*Paternally*). I've thought of everything, my dear—of everything a reasonable young couple may need for housekeeping. Why, I can hardly turn about in my room up there, the house is that full. (*Rubs his hands with satisfaction .*) For my son Harry—when he comes home. One day more.

Bessie (*Flattering*). Oh, you are a great one for bargains. (*Captain Hagberd delighted .*) But, Captain Hagberd—if—if—you don't know what may happen—if all that home you've got together were to be wasted—for nothing—after all. (*Aside .*) Oh, I can't bring it out.

Capt. H. (*Agitated; flings arms up, stamps feet; stuttering*). What? What d'ye mean? What's going to happen to the things?

Bessie (*Soothing*). Nothing! Nothing! Dust—or moth—you know. Damp, perhaps. You never let anyone into the house . . .

Capt. H. Dust! Damp! (*Has a throaty, gurgling laugh .*) I light the fires and dust the things myself. (*Indignant .*) Let anyone into the house, indeed! What would Harry say! (*Walks up and down his garden hastily with tosses, jings, and jerks of his whole body .*)

Bessie (*With authority .*) Now, then, Captain Hagberd! You know I won't put up with your tantrums. (*Shakes finger at him .*)

256

Capt. H. (*Subdued, but still sulky, with his back to her*). You want to see the things. That's what you're after. Well, no, not even you. Not till Harry has had his first look.

Bessie. Oh, no! I don't. (*Relenting* .) Not till you're willing. (*Smiles at Capt. H., who has turned half round already!*) You mustn't excite yourself. (*Knits* .)

Capt. H. (*Condescending*). And you the only sensible girl for miles and miles around. Can't you trust me? I am a domestic man. Always was, my dear. I hated the sea. People don't know what they let their boys into when they send them to sea. As soon make convicts of them at once. What sort of life is it? Most of your time you don't know what's going on at home. (*Insinuating* .) There's nothing anywhere on earth as good as a home, my dear. (*Pause* .) With a good husband...

Carvil (*Heard from his seat fragmentarily*). There they go... jabber, jabber... mumble, mumble. (*With a groaning effort?*) Helpless!

Capt. H. (*Mutters*). Extravagant ham and eggs fellow. (*Louder* .) Of course it isn't as if he had a son to make a home ready for. Girls are different, my dear. They don't run away, my dear, my dear. (*Agitated* .)

Bessie (*Drops her arms wearily*). No, Captain Hagberd—they don't.

Capt. H. (*Slowly*). I wouldn't let my own flesh and blood go to sea. Not I.

Bessie. And the boy ran away.

Capt. H. (*A little vacantly*). Yes, my only son Harry. (*Rouses himself* .) Coming home to-morrow.

Bessie (*Speaks softly*). Sometimes, Captain Hagberd, a hope turns out false.

Capt. H. (*Uneasy*). What's that got to do with Harry's coming back?

Bessie. It's good to hope for something. But suppose now————— (*Feeling her way* .) Yours is not the only lost son that's never...

Capt. H. Never what! You don't believe he's drowned. (*Crouches, glaring and grasping the rails* .)

Bessie (*Frightened, drops knitting*). Captain Hagberd—don't. (*Catches hold of his shoulders over the railings?*) Don't—my God! He's going out of his mind! (*Cries* .) I didn't mean it! I don't know.

Capt. H. (*Has backed away. An affected burst of laughter*). What nonsense. None of us Hagberds belonged to the sea. All farmers for hundreds of years, (*fraternal and cunning?*) Don't alarm yourself, my dear.

The sea can't get us. Look at me! I didn't get drowned. Moreover, Harry ain't a sailor at all. And if he isn't a sailor, he's bound to come back—to-morrow.

Bessie (*Has been facing him; murmurs*). No. I give it up. He scares me. (*Aloud, sharply*.) Then I would give up that advertising in the papers.

Capt. H. (*Surprised and puzzled*). Why, my dear? Everybody does it. His poor mother and I have been advertising for years and years. But she was an impatient woman. She died.

Bessie. If your son's coming, as—as you say—what's the good of that expense? You had better spend that half-crown on yourself. I believe you don't eat enough.

Capt. H. (*Confused*). But it's the right thing to do. Look at the Sunday papers. Missing relatives on top page—all proper. (*Looks unhappy*.)

Bessie (*Tartly*). Ah, well! I declare I don't know what you live on.

Capt. H. Are you getting impatient, my dear? Don't get impatient—like my poor wife. If she'd only been patient she'd be here. Waiting. Only one day more. (*Pleadingly*.) Don't be impatient, my dear.

Bessie. I've no patience with you sometimes.

Capt. H. (*Flash of lucidity*). Why? What's the matter? (*Sympathetic*.) You're tired out, my dear, that's what it is.

Bessie. Yes, I am. Day after day. (*Stands listless, arms hanging down*.)

Capt. H. (*Timidly*). House dull?

Bessie (*Apathetic*). Yes.

Capt. H. (*As before*). H'm. Wash, cook, scrub. Hey?

Bessie (*As before*). Yes.

Capt. H. (*Pointing stealthily at the sleeping Carvil*). Heavy?

Bessie. (*In a dead voice*). Like a millstone.

(*A silence*.)

Capt. H. (*Burst of indignation*). Why don't that extravagant fellow get you a servant?

Bessie. I don't know.

Capt. H. (*Cheerily*). Wait till Harry comes home. He'll get you one.

Bessie (*Almost hysterical; laughs*). Why, Captain Hagberd, perhaps your son won't even want to look at me—when he comes home.

Capt. H. (*In a great voice*). What! (*Quite low*.) The boy wouldn't dare. (*Rising choler*.) Wouldn't dare to refuse the only sensible girl for miles around. That stubborn jackanapes refuse to marry a girl like you! (*Walks about in a fury* .) You trust me, my dear, my dear, my dear. I'll make him. I'll—I'll ————— (*Splutters* .) Cut him off with a shilling.

Bessie. Hush! (Severe .) You mustn't talk like that. What's this? More of your tantrums?

Capt. H. (*Quite humble*). No, no—this isn't my tantrums—when I don't feel quite well in my head. Only I can't stand this... I've grown as fond of you as if you'd been the wife of my Harry already.

And to be told———— (*Cant restrain himself; shouts* .) Jackanapes!

Bessie. Sh————! Don't you worry! (*Wearily* .)

I must give that up too, I suppose. (*Aloud* .) I didn't mean it, Captain Hagberd.

Capt. H. It's as if I were to have two children to-morrow. My son Harry—and the only sensible girl————. Why, my dear, I couldn't get on without you. We two are reasonable together. The rest of the people in this town are crazy. The way they stare at you. And the grins—they're all on the grin. It makes me dislike to go out. (*Bewildered* .) It seems as if there was something wrong about—somewhere. My dear, is there anything wrong—you who are sensible.. .

Bessie (*Soothingly tender*). No, no, Captain Hagberd. There is nothing wrong about you anywhere.

Carvil (*Lying back*). Bessie! (*Sits up* .) Get my hat, Bessie.... Bessie, my hat.... Bessie.... Bessie. ...

(*At the first sound Bessie picks up and puts away her knitting. She walks towards him, picks up hat, puts it on his head*).

Bessie, my... (*Hat on head; shouting stops* .) Bessie. (*Quietly*). Will you go in, now? Carvil. Help me up. Steady. I'm dizzy. It's the thundery weather. An autumn thunderstorm means a bad gale. Very fierce—and sudden. There will be shipwrecks to-night on our coast.

(*Exit Bessie and Carvil through door of their cottage. It has fallen dusk* .)

Capt. H. (*Picks up spade*). Extravagant fellow! And all this town is mad—perfectly mad. I found them out years ago. Thank God they don't come this way staring and grinning. I can't bear them. I'll never go again into that High Street. (*Agitated* .) Never, never, never. Won't need to after to-morrow. Never! (Flings down spade in passion .)

(*While Hagberd speaks, the bow window of the Carvils is lit up, and Bessie is seen settling her father in a big armchair. Pulls down blind. Enter Lamplighter. Capt. H. picks up the spade and leans forward on it with both hands; very still, watching him light the lamp* .)

Lamplighter (*Jocular*). There! You will be able to dig by lamplight if the fancy takes you.

(*Exit Lamplighter to back* .)

Capt. H. (*Disgusted*). Ough! The people here. . . (*Shudders* .)

Lamplighter's Voice (*Heard loudly beyond the cottages*). Yes, that's the way.

(*Enter Harry from back* .)

SCENE III.

(*Capt. H. Harry. Later Bessie*).

Harry Hagberd (*thirty-one, tall, broad shoulders, shaven face, small moustache. Blue serge suit. Coat open. Grey flannel shirt without collar and tie. No waistcoat. Belt with buckle. Black, soft felt hat, wide-brimmed, worn crushed in the crown and a little on one side. Good nature, recklessness, some swagger in the bearing. Assured, deliberate walk with a heavy tread. Slight roll in the gait. Walks down. Stops, hands in pockets. Looks about. Speaks* .) This must be it. Can't see anything beyond. There's somebody. (*Walks up to Capt. Hagberd's gate?*) Can you tell me... (*Manner changes. Leans elbow on gate?*) Why, you must be Capt. Hagberd himself.

Capt. H. (*In garden, both hands on spade, peering, startled*). Yes, I am.

Harry (*Slowly*). You've been advertising in the papers for your son, I believe.

Capt. H. (*Off his guard, nervous*). Yes. My only boy Harry. He's coming home to-morrow. (*Mumbles* .) For a permanent stay.

Harry (*Surprised*). The devil he is! (*Change of tone?*) My word! You've grown a beard like Father Christmas himself.

Capt. H. (*Impressively*). Go your way. (*Waves one hand loftily?*) What's that to you. Go your way. (*Agitated?*) Go your way.

Harry. There, there. I am not trespassing in the street—where I stand—am I? Tell you what, I fancy there's something wrong about your news. Suppose you let me come in—for a quiet chat, you know.

Capt. H. (*Horrified*). Let you— you come in!

Harry (*Persuasive*). Because I could give you some real information about your son. The—very—latest—tip. If you care to hear.

Capt. H. (*Explodes*). No! I don't care to hear. (*Begins to pace to and fro, spade on shoulder. Gesticulating with his other arm* .) Here's a fellow—a grinning town fellow, who says there's something wrong. (*Fiercely* .) I have got more information than you're aware of. I have all the information I want. I have had it for years—for years—for years—enough to last me till to-morrow! Let you come in, indeed! What would Harry say?

(*Bessie Carvil appears at cottage door with a white wrap on her head and stands in her garden trying to see*).

Bessie. What's the matter?

Capt. H. (*Beside himself*). An information fellow. (*Stumbles* .)

Harry (*Putting out arm to steady him, gravely*). Here! Steady a bit! Seems to me somebody's been trying to get at you. (*Change of tone* .) Hullo! What's this rig you've got on?... Storm canvas coat, by George! (*He gives a frig, throaty laugh* .) Well! You *are* a character!

Capt. H. (*Daunted by the allusion, looks at coat*). I—I wear it for— for the time being. Till—till—to-morrow. (*Shrinks away, spade in hand, to door of his cottage* .)

Bessie (Advancing). And what may you want, sir?

Harry (*Turns to Bessie at once; easy manner*). I'd like to know about this swindle that's going to be sprung on him. I didn't mean to startle the old man. You see, on my way here I dropped into a barber's to get a twopenny shave, and they told me there that he was something of a character. He has been a character all his life.

Bessie (*Wondering*). What swindle?

Capt. H. A grinning fellow! (*Makes sudden dash indoors with the spade. Door slams. Affected gurgling laugh within* .)

SCENE IV.

(*Bessie and Harry. Later Capt. H. from window*).

Harry (*After a short silence*). What on earth's upset him so? What's the meaning of all this fuss? He isn't always like that, is he?

Bessie. I don't know who you are; but I may tell you that his mind has been troubled for years about an only son who ran away from home—a long time ago. Everybody knows that here.

Harry (*Thoughtful*). Troubled—for years! (*Suddenly* .) Well, I am the son.

Bessie (*Steps back*). You! . .. Harry!

Harry (*Amused, dry tone*). Got hold of my name, eh? Been making friends with the old man?

Bessie (*Distressed*). Yes... I... sometimes. . . (*Rapidly!*) He's our land-lord.

Harry (*Scornfully*). Owns both them rabbit hutches, does he? Just a thing he'd be proud of... (*Earnest .*) And now you had better tell me all about that chap who's coming to-morrow. Know anything of him? I reckon there's more than one in that little game. Come! Out with it! (*Chaffing .*) I don't take no... from women.

Bessie (*Bewildered*). Oh! It's so difficult... What had I better do?...

Harry (*Good-humoured*). Make a clean breast of it.

Bessie (*Wildly to herself*). Impossible! (*Starts .*) You don't understand. I must think—see—try to—I, I must have time. Plenty of time.

Harry. What for? Come. Two words. And don't be afraid for your-self. I ain't going to make it a police job. But it's the other fellow that'll get upset when he least expects it. There'll be some fun when he shows his mug here to-morrow. (*Snaps fingers .*) I don't care that for the old man's dollars, but right is right. You shall see me put a head on that coon, whoever he is.

Bessie (*Wrings hands slightly*). What had I better do? (*Suddenly to Harry .*) It's you—you yourself that we—that he's waiting for. It's *you* who are to come to-morrow.

Harry (*Slowly*). Oh! it's me! (*Perplexed .*) There's something there I can't understand. I haven't written ahead or anything. It was my chum who showed me the advertisement with the old boy's address, this very morning—in London.

Bessie (*Anxious*). How can I make it plain to you without... (*Bites her lip, embarrassed .*) Sometimes he talks so strangely.

Harry (*Expectant*). Does he? What about?

Bessie. Only you. And he will stand no contradicting.

Harry. Stubborn. Eh? The old man hasn't changed much from what I can remember. (*They stand looking at each other helplessly .*)

Bessie. He's made up his mind you would come back . . . to-morrow.

Harry. I can't hang about here till morning. Got no money to get a bed. Not a cent. But why won't to-day do?

Bessie. Because you've been too long away.

Harry (*With force*). Look here, they fairly drove me out. Poor mother nagged at me for being idle, and the old man said he would cut my soul out of my body rather than let me go to sea.

Bessie (*Murmurs*). He can bear no contradicting.

Harry (*Continuing*). Well, it looked as tho' he would do it too. So I went. (*Moody .*) It seems to me sometimes I was born to them by a mistake... in that other rabbit hutch of a house.

Bessie (*A little mocking*). And where do you think you ought to have been born by rights?

Harry. In the open—upon a beach—on a windy night.

Bessie (*Faintly*). Ah!

Harry. They were characters, both of them, by George! Shall I try the door?

Bessie. Wait. I must explain to you why it is to-morrow.

Harry. Aye. That you must, or...

(*Window in H.'s cottage runs up .*)

Capt. H.'s Voice (*Above*). A—grinning—information—fellow coming to worry me in my own garden! What next?

(*Window rumbles down .*)

Bessie. Yes. I must. (*Lays hand on Harry's sleeve .*) Let's get further off. Nobody ever comes this way after dark.

Harry (*Careless laugh*). Aye. A good road for a walk with a girl.

(*They turn their backs on audience and move up the stage slowly. Close together. Harry bends his head over Bessie*).

Bessie's Voice (*Beginning eagerly*). People here somehow did not take kindly to him.

Harry's Voice. Aye. Aye. I understand that.

(*They walk slowly back towards the front .*)

Bessie. He was almost ready to starve himself for your sake.

Harry. And I had to starve more than once for his whim.

Bessie. I'm afraid you've a hard heart. (*Remains thoughtful .*)

Harry. What for? For running away? (*Indignant .*) Why, he wanted to make a blamed lawyer's clerk of me.

(From here this scene goes on mainly near and about the street lamp .)

Bessie (*Rousing herself*). What are you? A sailor?

Harry. Anything you like. (*Proudly* .) Sailor enough to be worth my salt on board any craft that swims the seas.

Bessie. He will never, never believe it. He mustn't be contradicted.

Harry. Always liked to have his own way. And you've been encouraging him.

Bessie (*Earnestly*). No!—not in everything—not really!

Harry (*Vexed laugh*). What about that pretty tomorrow notion? I've a hungry chum in London—waiting for me.

Bessie (*Defending herself*). Why should I make the poor old friendless man miserable? I thought you were far away. I thought you were dead. I didn't know but you had never been born. I... I... (*Harry turns to her. She desperately* .) It was easier to believe it myself. (*Carried away* .) And after all it's true. It's come to pass. This is the to-morrow we've been waiting for.

Harry (*Half perfunctorily*). Aye. Anybody can see that your heart is as soft as your voice.

Bessie (*As if unable to keep back the words*). I didn't think you would have noticed my voice.

Harry (*Already inattentive*). H'm. Dashed scrape. This is a queer to-morrow, without any sort of today, as far as I can see. (*Resolutely* .) I must try the door.

Bessie. Well—try, then.

Harry (*From gate looking over shoulder at Bessie*). He ain't likely to fly out at me, is he? I would be afraid of laying my hands on him. The chaps are always telling me I don't know my own strength.

Bessie (*In front*). He's the most harmless creature that ever. ..

Harry. You wouldn't say so if you had seen him walloping me with a hard leather strap. (*Walking up garden* .) I haven't forgotten it in sixteen long years. (*Rat-tat-tat twice* .) Hullo, Dad. (*Bessie intensely expectant. Rat-tat-tat* .) Hullo, Dad—let me in. I am your own Harry. Straight. Your son Harry come back home—a day too soon.

(*Window above rumbles up* .)

Capt. H. (*Seen leaning out, aiming with spade*). Aha! Bessie (*Warningly*). Look out, Harry! (*Spade falls* .) Are you hurt? (*Window rumbles down* .)

Harry (*In the distance*). Only grazed my hat.

Bessie. Thank God! (*Intensely* .) What'll he do now?

Harry (*Comes forward, slamming gate behind him*). Just like old times. Nearly licked the life out of me for wanting to go away, and now I come back he shies a confounded old shovel at my head. (*Fumes. Laughs a little*). I wouldn't care, only poor little Ginger—Ginger's my chum up in London—he will starve while I walk back all the way from here. (*Faces Bessie blankly* .) I spent my last twopence on a shave. ... Out of respect for the old man.

Bessie. I think, if you let me, I could manage to talk him round in a week, maybe.

(*A muffled periodical bellowing had been heard faintly for some time* .)

Harry (*On the alert*). What's this? Who's making this row? Hark! Bessie, Bessie. It's in your house, I believe.

Bessie (*Without stirring, drearily*). It's for me.

Harry (*Discreetly, whispering*). Good voice for a ship's deck in a squall. Your husband? (*Steps out of lamplight* .)

Bessie. No. My father. He's blind. (*Pause*). I'm not married.

(*Bellowings grow louder* .)

Harry. Oh, I say. What's up? Who's murdering him?

Bessie (*Calmly*). I expect he's finished his tea. (*Bellowing continues regularly* .)

Harry. Hadn't you better see to it? You'll have the whole town coming out here presently. (*Bessie moves off* .) I say! (*Bessie stops* .) Couldn't you scare up some bread and butter for me from that tea? I'm hungry. Had no breakfast.

Bessie (*Starts off at the word "hungry," dropping to the ground the white woollen shawl*). I won't be a minute. Don't go away.

Harry (*Alone; picks up shawl absently, and, looking at it spread out in his hands, pronounces slowly*). A—dam'—silly—scrape. (*Pause. Throws shawl on arm. Strolls up and down. Mutters.*) No money to get back. (*Louder* .) Silly little Ginger'll think I've got hold of the pieces and given an old shipmate the go by. One good shove—(*Makes motion of bursting in door with his shoulders*)—would burst that door in—I bet. (*Looks about* .) I wonder where the nearest bobby is! No. They would want to bundle me neck and crop into chokey. (*Shudders* .) Perhaps. It makes me dog sick to think of being locked up. Haven't got the nerve. Not for prison. (*Leans against lamp-post* .) And not a cent for my fare. I wonder if that girl now...

Bessie (Coming hastily forward, plate with bread and meat in hand). I didn't take time to get anything else....

Harry (*Begins to eat*). You're not standing treat to a beggar. My dad is a rich man—you know.

Bessie (*Plate in hand*). You resemble your father.

Harry. I was the very image of him in face from a boy—(*Eats*)—and that's about as far as it goes. He was always one of your domestic characters. He looked sick when he had to go to sea for a fortnight's trip. (*Laughs* .) He was all for house and home.

Bessie. And you? Have you never wished for a home? (*Goes off with empty plate and puts it down hastily on Carvil's bench—out of sight* .)

Harry (*Left in front*). Home! If I found myself shut up in what the old man calls a home, I would kick it down about my ears on the third day—or else go to bed and die before the week was out. Die in a house—ough!

Bessie (*Returning; stops and speaks from garden railing*). And where is it that you would wish to die?

Harry. In the bush, in the sea, on some blamed mountain-top for choice. No such luck, tho', I suppose.

Bessie (*From distance*). Would that be luck? Harry. Yes! For them that make the whole world their home.

Bessie (*Comes forward shyly*). The world's a cold home—they say.

Harry (*A little gloomy*). So it is. When a man's done for.

Bessie. You see! (*Taunting*). And a ship's not so very big after all.

Harry. No. But the sea is great. And then what of the ship! You love her and leave her, Miss—Bessie's your name—isn't it?... I like that name.

Bessie. You like my name! I wonder you remembered it.... That's why, I suppose.

Harry (*Slight swagger in voice*). What's the odds! As long as a fellow has lived. And a voyage isn't a marriage—as we sailors say.

Bessie. So you're not married—(*Movement of Harry*)—to any ship.

Harry (*Soft laugh*). Ship! I've loved and left more of them than I can remember. I've been nearly everything you can think of but a tinker or a soldier; I've been a boundary rider; I've sheared sheep and humped my swag and harpooned a whale; I've rigged ships and skinned dead bullocks and prospected for gold—and turned my back on more money than the old man would have scraped together in his whole life.

Bessie (*Thoughtfully*). I could talk him over in a week.. . .

Harry (*Negligently*). I dare say you could. (*Joking* .) I don't know but what I could make shift to wait if you only promise to talk to me now and then. I've grown quite fond of your voice. I like a right woman's voice.

Bessie (*Averted head*). Quite fond! (*Sharply* .) Talk! Nonsense! Much you'd care. (*Businesslike* .) Of course I would have to sometimes.... (*Thoughtful again* .) Yes. In a week—if—if only I knew you would try to get on with him afterwards.

Harry (*Leaning against lamp-post; growls through his teeth*). More humouring. Ah! well, no! (*Hums significantly*)

   Oh, oh, oh, Rio, . . . And fare thee well My bonnie young girl, We're bound for Rio Grande.

Bessie (*Shivering*). What's this?

Harry. Why! The chorus of an up-anchor tune. Kiss and go. A deep-water ship's good-bye.... You are cold. Here's that thing of yours I've picked up and forgot there on my arm. Turn round a bit. So. (*Wraps her up—commanding* .) Hold the ends together in front.

Bessie (*Softly*). A week is not so very long.

Harry (*Begins violently*). You think that I————-
(*Stops with sidelong look at her* .) I can't dodge about in ditches and live on air and water. Can I? I haven't any money—you know.

Bessie. He's been scraping and saving up for years. All he has is for you, and perhaps...

Harry (*Interrupts*). Yes. If I come to sit on it like a blamed toad in a hole. Thank you.

Bessie (*Angrily*). What did you come for, then?

Harry (*Promptly*). For five quid—(*Pause* .)—after a jolly good spree.

Bessie (*Scathingly*). You and that—that—chum of yours have been drinking.

Harry (*Laughs*). Don't fly out, Miss Bessie—dear. Ginger's not a bad little chap. Can't take care of himself, tho'. Blind three days. (*Serious* .) Don't think I am given that way. Nothing and nobody can get over me unless I like. I can be as steady as a rock.

Bessie (*Murmurs*). Oh! I don't think you are bad.

Harry (*Approvingly*). You're right there. (Impulsive .) Ask the girls all over————-(*Checks himself* .) Ginger, he's long-headed, too, in his way—mind you. He sees the paper this morning, and says he to me, 'Hallo!

Look at that, Harry—loving parent—that's five quid, sure.' So we scraped all our pockets for the fare....

Bessie (*Unbelieving*). You came here for that.

Harry (*Surprised*). What else would I want here? Five quid isn't much to ask for—once in sixteen years. (*Through his teeth with a sidelong look at B.*) And now I am ready to go—for my fare.

Bessie (*Clasping her hands*). Whoever heard a man talk like this before! I can't believe you mean it?

Harry. What? That I would go? You just try and see.

Bessie (*Disregarding him*). Don't you care for anyone? Didn't you ever want anyone in the world to care for you?

Harry. In the world! (*Boastful.*) There's hardly a place you can go in the world where you wouldn't find somebody that did care for Harry Hagberd. (*Pause.*) I'm not of the sort that go about skulking under false names.

Bessie. Somebody—that means a woman.

Harry. Well! And if it did.

Bessie (*Unsteadily*). Oh, I see how it is. You get round them with your soft speeches, your promises, and then...

Harry (*Violently*). Never!

Bessie (*Startled, steps back*). Ah—you never. . .

Harry (*Calm*). Never yet told a lie to a woman.

Bessie. What lie?

Harry. Why, the lie that comes glib to a man's tongue. None of that for me. I leave the sneaking off to them soft-spoken chaps you're thinking of. No! If you love me you take me. And if you take me—why, then, the capstan-song of deep-water ships is sure to settle it all some fine day.

Bessie (*After a short pause, with effort*). It's like your ships, then.

Harry (*Amused*). Exactly, up to now. Or else I wouldn't be here in a silly fix.

Bessie (*Assumed indifference*). Perhaps it's because you've never yet met———- (*Voice fails.*)

Harry (*Negligently*). Maybe. And perhaps never shall.... What's the odds? It's the looking for a thing.... No matter. I love them all—ships and women. The scrapes they got me into, and the scrapes they got me out of—my word! I say, Miss Bessie, what are you thinking of?

Bessie (*Lifts her head*). That you are supposed never to tell a lie.

Harry. Never, eh? You wouldn't be that hard on a chap.

Bessie (Recklessly). Never to a woman, I mean.

Harry. Well, no. (*Serious* .) Never anything that matters. (*Aside* .) I don't seem to get any nearer to my railway fare. (*Leans wearily against the lamppost with a far-off look. B. looks at him* .)

Bessie. Now what are you thinking of?

Harry (*Turns his head; stares at B* .). Well, I was thinking what a fine figure of a girl you are.

Bessie (*Looks away a moment*). Is that true, or is it only one of them that don't matter?

Harry (*Laughing a little*). No! no! That's true. Haven't you ever been told that before? The men...

Bessie. I hardly speak to a soul from year's end to year's end. Father's blind. He don't like strangers, and he can't bear to think of me out of his call. Nobody comes near us much.

Harry (*Absent-minded*). Blind—ah! of course.

Bessie. For years and years . . .

Harry (*Commiserating*). For years and years. In one of them hutches. You are a good daughter. (*Brightening up* .) A fine girl altogether. You seem the sort that makes a good chum to a man in a fix. And there's not a man in this whole town who found you out? I can hardly credit it, Miss Bessie. (*B. shakes her head* .) Man I said! (*Contemptuous* .) A lot of tame rabbits in hutches I call them.... (*Breaks off* .) I say, when's the last train up to London? Can you tell me?

Bessie (*Gazes at him steadily*). What for? You've no money.

Harry. That's just it. (*Leans back against post again* .) Hard luck. (*Insinuating* .) But there was never a time in all my travels that a woman of the right sort did not turn up to help me out of a fix. I don't know why. It's perhaps because they know without telling that I love them all. (*Playful* .) I've almost fallen in love with you, Miss Bessie.

Bessie (*Unsteady laugh*). Why! How you talk! You haven't even seen my face properly. (*One step towards H., as if compelled.*)

Harry (*Bending forward gallantly*). A little pale. It suits some. (*Puts out his hand, catches hold of B.'s arm. Draws her to him* .) Let's see.... Yes, it suits you. (*It's a moment before B. puts up her hands, palms out, and turns away her head* .)

Bessie (*Whispering*). Don't. (*Struggles a little. Released, stands averted* .)

Harry. No offence. (*Stands, back to audience, looking at H.'s cottage* .)

Bessie (*Alone in front; faces audience; whispers*). My voice—my figure—my heart—my face....

(*A silence. B.'s face gradually lights up. Directly H. speaks, expression of hopeful attention* .)

Harry (*From railings*). The old man seems to have gone to sleep waiting for that to-morrow of his.

Bessie. Come away. He sleeps very little.

Harry (*Strolls down*). He has taken an everlasting jamming hitch round the whole business. (*Vexed* .) Cast it loose who may. (*Contemptuous exclamation* .) To-morrow. Pooh! It'll be just another mad today.

Bessie. It's the brooding over his hope that's done it. People teased him so. It's his fondness for you that's troubled his mind.

Harry. Aye. A confounded shovel on the head. The old man had always a queer way of showing his fondness for me.

Bessie. A hopeful, troubled, expecting old man—left alone—all alone.

Harry (*Lower tone*). Did he ever tell you what mother died of?

Bessie. Yes. (*A little bitter* .) From impatience.

Harry (*Makes a gesture with his arm; speaks vaguely but with feeling*). I believe you have been very good to my old man....

Bessie (*Tentative*). Wouldn't you try to be a son to him?

Harry (*Angrily*). No contradicting; is that it? You seem to know my dad pretty well. And so do I. He's dead nuts on having his own way—and I've been used to have my own too long. It's the deuce of a fix.

Bessie. How could it hurt you not to contradict him for a while—and perhaps in time you would get used. ..

Harry (*Interrupts sulkily*). I ain't accustomed to knuckle under. There's a pair of us. Hagberd's both. I ought to be thinking of my train.

Bessie (*Earnestly*). Why? There's no need. Let us get away up the road a little.

Harry (*Through his teeth*). And no money for the fare. (*Looks up* .) Sky's come overcast. Black, too. It'll be a wild, windy night... to walk the high road on. But I and wild nights are old friends wherever the free wind blows.

Bessie (*Entreating*). No need. No need. (*Looks apprehensively at Hagberd's cottage. Takes a couple of steps up as if to draw Harry further off. Harry follows. Both stop.*)

Harry (*After waiting*). What about this tomorrow whim?

Bessie. Leave that to me. Of course all his fancies are not mad. They aren't. (*Pause.*) Most people in this town would think what he had set his mind on quite sensible. If he ever talks to you of it, don't contradict him. It would—it would be dangerous.

Harry (*Surprised*). What would he do?

Bessie. He would—I don't know—something rash.

Harry (*Startled*). To himself?

Bessie. No. It'd be against you—I fear.

Harry (*Sullen*). Let him.

Bessie. Never. Don't quarrel. But perhaps he won't even try to talk to you of it. (*Thinking aloud.*) Who knows what I can do with him in a week! I can, I can, I can—I must.

Harry. Come—what's this sensible notion of his that I mustn't quarrel about?

Bessie (*Turns to Harry, calm, forcible*). If I make him once see that you've come back, he will be as sane as you or I. All his mad notions will be gone. But that other is quite sensible. And you mustn't quarrel over it.

(*Moves up to back of stage. Harry follows a little behind, away from audience.*)

Harry's Voice (*Calm*). Let's hear what it is.

(*Voices cease. Action visible as before. Harry steps back and walks hastily down. Bessie at his elbow, follows with her hands clasped?*)

(*Loud burst of voice.*)

Harry (*Raving to and fro*). No! Expects me—a home. Who wants his home?... What I want is hard work, or an all-fired racket, or more room than there is in the whole of England. Expects me! A man like me—for his rotten money—there ain't enough money in the world to turn me into a blamed tame rabbit in a hutch. (*He stops suddenly before Bessie, arms crossed on breast. Violently.*) Don't you see it?

Bessie (*Terrified, stammering faintly*). Yes. Yes. Don't look at me like this. (*Sudden scream.*) Don't quarrel with him. He's mad!

Harry (*Headlong utterance*). Mad! Not he. He likes his own way. Tie me up by the neck here. Here! Ha! Ha! Ha! (*Louder.*) And the whole world is not a bit too big for me to spread my elbows in, I can tell you—what's your name—Bessie. (*Rising scorn*). Marry! Wants me to marry and settle.... (*Scathingly* .) And as likely as not he has looked out the girl too—dash my soul. Talked to you about it—did he? And do you happen to know the Judy—may I ask?

(*Window in Hagberd's cottage runs up. They start and stand still* .)

Capt. H. (*Above, begins slowly*). A grinning information fellow from a crazy town. (*Voice changes* .) Bessie, I see you. . . .

Bessie (*Shrill*). Captain Hagberd! Say nothing. You don't understand. For heaven's sake don't.

Capt. H. Send him away this minute, or I will tell Harry. They know nothing of Harry in this crazy town. Harry's coming home to-morrow. Do you hear? One day more!

(*Silence* .)

Harry (*Mutters*). Well!—he is a character.

Capt. H. (*Chuckles softly*). Never you fear! The boy shall marry you. (*Sudden anger* .) He'll have to. I'll make him. Or, if not—(*Furious*)—I'll cut him off with a shilling, and leave everything to you. Jackanapes! Let him starve!

(*Window rumbles down* .)

Harry (*Slowly*). So it's you—the girl. It's you! Now I begin to see.... By heavens, you have a heart as soft as your woman's voice.

Bessie (*Half averted, face in hands*). You see! Don't come near me.

Harry (*Makes a step towards her*). I must have another look at your pale face.

Bessie (*Turns unexpectedly and pushes him with both hands; Harry staggers back and stands still; Bessie, fiercely*). Go away.

Harry (*Watching her*). Directly. But women always had to get me out of my scrapes. I am a beggar now, and you must help me out of my scrape.

Bessie (*Who at the word "beggar" had begun fumbling in the pocket of her dress, speaks wildly*). Here it is. Take it. Don't look at me. Don't speak to me!

Harry (*Swaggers up under the lamp; looks at coin in his palm*). Half-a-quid. . .. My fare!

Bessie (*Hands clenched*). Why are you still here?

Harry. Well, you are a fine figure of a girl. My word. I've a good mind to stop—for a week.

Bessie (*Pain and shame*). Oh!.... What are you waiting for? If I had more money I would give it all, all. I would give everything I have to make you go—to make you forget you had ever heard my voice and seen my face. (*Covers face with hands* .)

Harry (*Sombre, watches her*). No fear! I haven't forgotten a single one of you in the world. Some've given me more than money. No matter. You can't buy me in—and you can't buy yourself out. . .

(*Strides towards her. Seizes her arms. Short struggle. Bessie gives way. Hair falls loose. H. kisses her forehead, cheeks, lips, then releases her. Bessie staggers against railings* .)

(Exit Harry; measured walk without haste)

Bessie (*Staring eyes, hair loose, back against railings; calls out*). Harry! (*Gathers up her skirts and runs a little way*) Come back, Harry. (*Staggers forward against lamp-post*) Harry! (*Much lower*) Harry! (*In a whisper*) Take me with you. (*Begins to laugh, at first faintly, then louder.*)

(*Window rumbles up, and Capt. H.'s chuckle mingles with Bessie's laughter, which abruptly stops* .)

Capt. H. (*Goes on chuckling; speaks cautiously*). Is he gone yet, that information fellow? Do you see him anywhere, my dear?

Bessie (*Low and stammering*). N-no, no! (*Totters away from lamp-post*) I don't see him.

Capt. H. (*Anxious*). A grinning vagabond, my dear. Good girl. It's you who drove him away. Good girl.

(*Stage gradually darkens*)

Bessie. Go in; be quiet! You have done harm enough.

Capt. H. (*Alarmed*). Why. Do you hear him yet, my dear?

Bessie (*Sobs, drooping against the railings*). No! No! I don't. I don't hear him any more.

Capt. H. (*Triumphant*). Now we shall be all right, my dear, till our Harry comes home to-morrow. (*Affected gurgling laugh* .)

Bessie (*Distracted*). Be quiet. Shut yourself in. You will make me mad. (Losing control of herself, repeats with rising infection) You make me mad.

(*With despair*) There is no to-morrow! (Sinks to ground near middle railings. Low sobs)

(*Stage darkens perceptibly* .)

Capt. H. (*Above, in a voice suddenly dismayed and shrill*).

What! What do you say, my dear? No to-morrow? (*Broken, very feebly* .) No—to-morrow?

(*Window runs down*)

Carvil (*Heard within, muffled bellowing*). Bessie—Bessie—Bessie—Bessie——— (*At the first call Bessie springs up and begins to stumble blindly towards the door. A faint fash of lightnings followed by a very low rumble of thunder*) You!—Bessie!

CURTAIN

COLLEGE WRITING 1: REFLECTION WITHIN THE TEXT

Look at the blind Josiah Carvil's dependence upon his daughter Bessie Carvil; look at Bessie Carvil's dependence on Captain Hagberd for escape from her father, and look at what Harry Hagberd wants from Bessie Carvil.

In all of these cases each character is both dependent yet wishes for independence at the same time. That is, they need something from someone, yet wish that they didn't.

Compare your dependence to one of the relationships in "One Day More". Perhaps it's a parent, lover, or friend. Ask yourself—is it possible to be completely free of this dependence? Is it possible to manage one's level of dependence, on people in general, or individuals specifically?

COLLEGE WRITING 2: RESEARCH OUTSIDE THE TEXT

Research the notion of "codependence." What is it? How does it manifest in "One Day More"? What is the difference between codependence and dependence? How does it inform your understanding of "One Day More"? Consider the occupations and conditions of the characters in your assessment, and how that affects their relationships.

IDEAS AND VALUES: CONNECT THE TEXT

»   What is independence in Conrad's "One Day More", Hawthorne's "Wakefield", and Forester's "The Machine Stops"? What are the consequences of independence, for not only the individual but for society? Can a balance be struck between independence and the needs of a community?

»   In Gilman's "The Yellow Wallpaper" the main character believes she can see a woman living in the walls, and in Woolf's "The Dress" a young woman obsesses over her appearance, and lastly in Conrad's "One Day More", Captain Hagbeard is said to be crazy, as he always believes that his son will return "tomorrow," even after his son has returned today! But what is the nature of what we call "mental illness?" Is it an illness, like the common cold—do we "catch it" from the air? Or does it form some other way? Is there an environmental aspect to mental illnesses, or are we merely born destined to be sane or...ill?

The Blue Hotel

by Stephen Crane

10,697 WORDS. 1 HOUR.
READING LEVEL: GRADE 8.5

1

The Palace Hotel at Fort Romper was painted a light blue, a shade
that is on the legs of a kind of heron, causing the bird to declare its position against any background. The Palace Hotel, then, was always screaming and howling in a way that made the dazzling winter landscape of
Nebraska seem only a gray swampish hush. It stood alone on the prairie,
and when the snow was falling the town two hundred yards away was
not visible. But when the traveller alighted at the railway station he was
obliged to pass the Palace Hotel before he could come upon the company
of low clapboard houses which composed Fort Romper, and it was not to
be thought that any traveller could pass the Palace Hotel without looking
at it. Pat Scully, the proprietor, had proved himself a master of strategy
when he chose his paints. It is true that on clear days, when the great
trans-continental expresses, long lines of swaying Pullmans, swept through
Fort Romper, passengers were overcome at the sight, and the cult that
knows the brown-reds and the subdivisions of the dark greens of the East
expressed shame, pity, horror, in a laugh. But to the citizens of this prairie
town and to the people who would naturally stop there, Pat Scully had
performed a feat. With this opulence and splendor, these creeds, classes,
egotisms, that streamed through Romper on the rails day after day, they
had no color in common.

As if the displayed delights of such a blue hotel were not sufficiently
enticing, it was Scully's habit to go every morning and evening to meet
the leisurely trains that stopped at Romper and work his seductions upon
any man that he might see wavering, gripsack in hand.

One morning, when a snow-crusted engine dragged its long string of
freight cars and its one passenger coach to the station, Scully performed
the marvel of catching three men. One was a shaky and quick-eyed
Swede, with a great shining cheap valise; one was a tall bronzed cowboy,
who was on his way to a ranch near the Dakota line; one was a little silent

man from the East, who didn't look it, and didn't announce it. Scully practically made them prisoners. He was so nimble and merry and kindly that each probably felt it would be the height of brutality to try to escape. They trudged off over the creaking board sidewalks in the wake of the eager little Irishman. He wore a heavy fur cap squeezed tightly down on his head. It caused his two red ears to stick out stiffly, as if they were made of tin.

At last, Scully, elaborately, with boisterous hospitality, conducted them through the portals of the blue hotel. The room which they entered was small. It seemed to be merely a proper temple for an enormous stove, which, in the centre, was humming with godlike violence. At various points on its surface the iron had become luminous and glowed yellow from the heat. Beside the stove Scully's son Johnnie was playing High-Five with an old farmer who had whiskers both gray and sandy. They were quarrelling. Frequently the old farmer turned his face towards a box of sawdust—colored brown from tobacco juice—that was behind the stove, and spat with an air of great impatience and irritation. With a loud flourish of words Scully destroyed the game of cards, and bustled his son up-stairs with part of the baggage of the new guests. He himself conducted them to three basins of the coldest water in the world. The cowboy and the Easterner burnished themselves fiery-red with this water, until it seemed to be some kind of a metal polish. The Swede, however, merely dipped his fingers gingerly and with trepidation. It was notable that throughout this series of small ceremonies the three travellers were made to feel that Scully was very benevolent. He was conferring great favors upon them. He handed the towel from one to the other with an air of philanthropic impulse.

Afterwards they went to the first room, and, sitting about the stove, listened to Scully's officious clamor at his daughters, who were preparing the mid-day meal. They reflected in the silence of experienced men who tread carefully amid new people. Nevertheless, the old farmer, stationary, invincible in his chair near the warmest part of the stove, turned his face from the sawdust box frequently and addressed a glowing commonplace to the strangers. Usually he was answered in short but adequate sentences by either the cowboy or the Easterner. The Swede said nothing. He seemed to be occupied in making furtive estimates of each man in the room. One might have thought that he had the sense of silly suspicion which comes to guilt. He resembled a badly frightened man.

Later, at dinner, he spoke a little, addressing his conversation entirely to Scully. He volunteered that he had come from New York, where for ten years he had worked as a tailor. These facts seemed to strike Scully as fascinating, and afterwards he volunteered that he had lived at Romper for fourteen years. The Swede asked about the crops and the price of labor. He seemed barely to listen to Scully's extended replies. His eyes continued to rove from man to man.

Finally, with a laugh and a wink, he said that some of these Western communities were very dangerous; and after his statement he straightened his legs under the table, tilted his head, and laughed again, loudly. It was plain that the demonstration had no meaning to the others. They looked at him wondering and in silence.

2

As the men trooped heavily back into the front-room, the two little windows presented views of a turmoiling sea of snow. The huge arms of the wind were making attempts—mighty, circular, futile—to embrace the flakes as they sped. A gate-post like a still man with a blanched face stood aghast amid this profligate fury. In a hearty voice Scully announced the presence of a blizzard. The guests of the blue hotel, lighting their pipes, assented with grunts of lazy masculine contentment. No island of the sea could be exempt in the degree of this little room with its humming stove. Johnnie, son of Scully, in a tone which defined his opinion of his ability as a card-player, challenged the old farmer of both gray and sandy whiskers to a game of High-Five. The farmer agreed with a contemptuous and bitter scoff. They sat close to the stove, and squared their knees under a wide board. The cowboy and the Easterner watched the game with interest. The Swede remained near the window, aloof, but with a countenance that showed signs of an inexplicable excitement.

The play of Johnnie and the gray-beard was suddenly ended by another quarrel. The old man arose while casting a look of heated scorn at his adversary. He slowly buttoned his coat, and then stalked with fabulous dignity from the room. In the discreet silence of all other men the Swede laughed. His laughter rang somehow childish. Men by this time had begun to look at him askance, as if they wished to inquire what ailed him.

A new game was formed jocosely. The cowboy volunteered to become the partner of Johnnie, and they all then turned to ask the Swede to throw in his lot with the little Easterner, He asked some questions about the game, and, learning that it wore many names, and that he had played it when it was under an alias, he accepted the invitation. He strode towards the men nervously, as if he expected to be assaulted. Finally, seated, he gazed from face to face and laughed shrilly. This laugh was so strange that the Easterner looked up quickly, the cowboy sat intent and with his mouth open, and Johnnie paused, holding the cards with still fingers.

Afterwards there was a short silence. Then Johnnie said, "Well, let's get at it. Come on now!" They pulled their chairs forward until their knees were bunched under the board. They began to play, and their interest in the game caused the others to forget the manner of the Swede.

The cowboy was a board-whacker. Each time that he held superior cards he whanged them, one by one, with exceeding force, down upon the improvised table, and took the tricks with a glowing air of prowess and pride that sent thrills of indignation into the hearts of his opponents. A game with a board-whacker in it is sure to become intense. The countenances of the Easterner and the Swede were miserable whenever the cowboy thundered down his aces and kings, while Johnnie, his eyes gleaming with joy, chuckled and chuckled.

Because of the absorbing play none considered the strange ways of the Swede. They paid strict heed to the game. Finally, during a lull caused by a new deal, the Swede suddenly addressed Johnnie: "I suppose there have been a good many men killed in this room." The jaws of the others dropped and they looked at him.

"What in hell are you talking about?" said Johnnie.

The Swede laughed again his blatant laugh, full of a kind of false courage and defiance. "Oh, you know what I mean all right," he answered.

"I'm a liar if I do!" Johnnie protested. The card was halted, and the men stared at the Swede. Johnnie evidently felt that as the son of the proprietor he should make a direct inquiry. "Now, what might you be drivin' at, mister?" he asked. The Swede winked at him. It was a wink full of cunning. His fingers shook on the edge of the board. "Oh, maybe you think I have been to nowheres. Maybe you think I'm a tenderfoot?"

"I don't know nothin' about you," answered Johnnie, "and I don't give a damn where you've been. All I got to say is that I don't know what you're driving at. There hain't never been nobody killed in this room."

The cowboy, who had been steadily gazing at the Swede, then spoke: "What's wrong with you, mister?"

Apparently it seemed to the Swede that he was formidably menaced. He shivered and turned white near the corners of his mouth. He sent an appealing glance in the direction of the little Easterner. During these moments he did not forget to wear his air of advanced pot-valor. "They say they don't know what I mean," he remarked mockingly to the Eastern-er.

The latter answered after prolonged and cautious reflection. "I don't understand you," he said, impassively.

The Swede made a movement then which announced that he thought he had encountered treachery from the only quarter where he had expected sympathy, if not help. "Oh, I see you are all against me. I see—"

The cowboy was in a state of deep stupefaction. "Say." he cried, as he tumbled the deck violently down upon the board "—say, what are you gittin' at, hey?"

The Swede sprang up with the celerity of a man escaping from a snake on the floor. "I don't want to fight!" he shouted. "I don't want to fight!"

The cowboy stretched his long legs indolently and deliberately. His hands were in his pockets. He spat into the sawdust box. "Well, who the hell thought you did?" he inquired.

The Swede backed rapidly towards a corner of the room. His hands were out protectingly in front of his chest, but he was making an obvious struggle to control his fright. "Gentlemen," he quavered, "I suppose I am going to be killed before I can leave this house! I suppose I am going to be killed before I can leave this house!" In his eyes was the dying-swan look. Through the windows could be seen the snow turning blue in the shadow of dusk. The wind tore at the house and some loose thing beat regularly against the clap-boards like a spirit tapping.

A door opened, and Scully himself entered. He paused in surprise as he noted the tragic attitude of the Swede. Then he said, "What's the matter here?"

The Swede answered him swiftly and eagerly: "These men are going to kill me."

"Kill you!" ejaculated Scully. "Kill you! What are you talkin'?"

The Swede made the gesture of a martyr.

Scully wheeled sternly upon his son. "What is this, Johnnie?"

The lad had grown sullen. "Damned if I know," he answered. "I can't make no sense to it." He began to shuffle the cards, fluttering them together with an angry snap. "He says a good many men have been killed in this room, or something like that. And he says he's goin' to be killed here too. I don't know what ails him. He's crazy, I shouldn't wonder."

Scully then looked for explanation to the cowboy, but the cowboy simply shrugged his shoulders.

"Kill you?" said Scully again to the Swede. "Kill you? Man, you're off your nut."

"Oh, I know." burst out the Swede. "I know what will happen. Yes, I'm crazy—yes. Yes, of course, I'm crazy—yes. But I know one thing—" There was a sort of sweat of misery and terror upon his face. "I know I won't get out of here alive."

The cowboy drew a deep breath, as if his mind was passing into the last stages of dissolution. "Well, I'm dog-goned," he whispered to himself.

Scully wheeled suddenly and faced his son. "You've been troublin' this man!"

Johnnie's voice was loud with its burden of grievance. "Why, good Gawd, I ain't done nothin' to 'im."

The Swede broke in. "Gentlemen, do not disturb yourselves. I will leave this house. I will go away because"—he accused them dramatically with his glance—"because I do not want to be killed."

Scully was furious with his son. "Will you tell me what is the matter, you young divil? What's the matter, anyhow? Speak out!"

"Blame it!" cried Johnnie in despair, "don't I tell you I don't know. He—he says we want to kill him, and that's all I know. I can't tell what ails him."

The Swede continued to repeat: "Never mind, Mr. Scully; never-mind. I will leave this house. I will go away, because I do not wish to be killed. Yes, of course, I am crazy—yes. But I know one thing! I will go away. I will leave this house. Never mind, Mr. Scully; never mind. I will go away."

"You will not go 'way," said Scully. "You will not go 'way until I hear the reason of this business. If anybody has troubled you I will take care of him. This is my house. You are under my roof, and I will not allow any peaceable man to be troubled here." He cast a terrible eye upon Johnnie, the cowboy, and the Easterner.

"Never mind, Mr. Scully; never mind. I will go away. I do not wish to be killed." The Swede moved towards the door, which opened upon the stairs. It was evidently his intention to go at once for his baggage.

"No, no," shouted Scully peremptorily; but the white-faced man slid by him and disappeared. "Now," said Scully severely, "what does this mane?"

Johnnie and the cowboy cried together: "Why, we didn't do nothin' to 'im!"

Scully's eyes were cold. "No," he said, "you didn't?"

Johnnie swore a deep oath. "Why this is the wildest loon I ever see. We didn't do nothin' at all. We were jest sittin' here playin' cards, and he—"

The father suddenly spoke to the Easterner. "Mr. Blanc," he asked, "what has these boys been doin'?"

The Easterner reflected again. "I didn't see anything wrong at all," he said at last, slowly.

Scully began to howl. "But what does it mane?" He stared ferociously at his son. "I have a mind to lather you for this, me boy."

Johnnie was frantic. "Well, what have I done?" he bawled at his father.

3

"I think you are tongue-tied," said Scully finally to his son, the cowboy, and the Easterner; and at the end of this scornful sentence he left the room.

Up-stairs the Swede was swiftly fastening the straps of his great valise. Once his back happened to be half turned towards the door, and, hearing a noise there, he wheeled and sprang up, uttering a loud cry. Scully's wrinkled visage showed grimly in the light of the small lamp he carried. This yellow effulgence, streaming upward, colored only his prominent features, and left his eyes, for instance, in mysterious shadow. He resembled a murderer.

"Man! man!" he exclaimed, "have you gone daffy?"

"Oh, no! Oh, no!" rejoined the other. "There are people in this world who know pretty nearly as much as you do—understand?"

For a moment they stood gazing at each other. Upon the Swede's deathly pale checks were two spots brightly crimson and sharply edged, as if they had been carefully painted. Scully placed the light on the table and sat himself on the edge of the bed. He spoke ruminatively. "By cracky, I never heard of such a thing in my life. It's a complete muddle. I can't, for the soul of me, think how you ever got this idea into your head." Presently he lifted his eyes and asked: "And did you sure think they were going to kill you?"

The Swede scanned the old man as if he wished to see into his mind. "I did," he said at last. He obviously suspected that this answer might precipitate an outbreak. As he pulled on a strap his whole arm shook, the elbow wavering like a bit of paper.

Scully banged his hand impressively on the foot-board of the bed. "Why, man, we're goin' to have a line of ilictric street-cars in this town next spring."

"'A line of electric street-cars,'" repeated the Swede, stupidly.

"And," said Scully, "there's a new railroad goin' to be built down from Broken Arm to here. Not to mintion the four churches and the smashin' big brick school-house. Then there's the big factory, too. Why, in two years Romper 'll be a metropolis."

Having finished the preparation of his baggage, the Swede straightened himself. "Mr. Scully," he said, with sudden hardihood, "how much do I owe you?"

"You don't owe me anythin'," said the old man, angrily.

"Yes, I do," retorted the Swede. He took seventy-five cents from his pocket and tendered it to Scully; but the latter snapped his fingers in disdainful refusal. However, it happened that they both stood gazing in a strange fashion at three silver pieces on the Swede's open palm.

"I'll not take your money," said Scully at last. "Not after what's been goin' on here." Then a plan seemed to strike him. "Here," he cried, picking up his lamp and moving towards the door. "Here! Come with me a minute."

"No," said the Swede, in overwhelming alarm.

"Yes," urged the old man. "Come on! I want you to come and see a picter—just across the hall—in my room."

The Swede must have concluded that his hour was come. His jaw dropped and his teeth showed like a dead man's. He ultimately followed Scully across the corridor, but he had the step of one hung in chains.

Scully flashed the light high on the wall of his own chamber. There was revealed a ridiculous photograph of a little girl. She was leaning against a balustrade of gorgeous decoration, and the formidable bang to her hair was prominent. The figure was as graceful as an upright sled-stake, and, withal, it was of the hue of lead. "There," said Scully, tenderly, "that's the picter of my little girl that died. Her name was Carrie. She had the purtiest hair you ever saw! I was that fond of her, she—"

Turning then, he saw that the Swede was not contemplating the picture at all, but, instead, was keeping keen watch on the gloom in the rear.

"Look, man!" cried Scully, heartily. "That's the picter of my little gal that died. Her name was Carrie. And then here's the picter of my oldest boy, Michael. He's a lawyer in Lincoln, an' doin' well. I gave that boy a grand eddycation, and I'm glad for it now. He's a fine boy. Look at 'im now. Ain't he bold as blazes, him there in Lincoln, an honored an' respict-ed gintleman. An honored an' respicted gintleman," concluded Scully with a flourish. And, so saying, he smote the Swede jovially on the back.

The Swede faintly smiled.

"Now," said the old man, "there's only one more thing." He dropped suddenly to the floor and thrust his head beneath the bed. The Swede could hear his muffled voice. "I'd keep it under me piller if it wasn't for that boy Johnnie. Then there's the old woman—Where is it now? I never put it twice in the same place. Ah, now come out with you!"

Presently he backed clumsily from under the bed, dragging with him an old coat rolled into a bundle. "I've fetched him," he muttered. Kneel-ing on the floor, he unrolled the coat and extracted from its heart a large yellow-brown whiskey bottle.

His first maneuver was to hold the bottle up to the light. Reassured, apparently, that nobody had been tampering with it, he thrust it with a generous movement towards the Swede.

The weak-kneed Swede was about to eagerly clutch this element of strength, but he suddenly jerked his hand away and cast a look of horror upon Scully.

"Drink," said the old man affectionately. He had risen to his feet, and now stood facing the Swede.

There was a silence. Then again Scully said: "Drink!"

The Swede laughed wildly. He grabbed the bottle, put it to his mouth, and as his lips curled absurdly around the opening and his throat worked, he kept his glance, burning with hatred, upon the old man's face.

4

After the departure of Scully the three men, with the card-board still upon their knees, preserved for a long time an astounded silence. Then Johnnie said: "That's the dod-dangest Swede I ever see."

"He ain't no Swede," said the cowboy, scornfully.

"Well, what is he then?" cried Johnnie. "What is he then?"

"It's my opinion," replied the cowboy deliberately, "he's some kind of a Dutchman." It was a venerable custom of the country to entitle as Swedes all light-haired men who spoke with a heavy tongue. In consequence the idea of the cowboy was not without its daring. "Yes, sir," he repeated. "It's my opinion this feller is some kind of a Dutchman."

"Well, he says he's a Swede, anyhow," muttered Johnnie, sulkily. He turned to the Easterner: "What do you think, Mr. Blanc?"

"Oh, I don't know," replied the Easterner.

"Well, what do you think makes him act that way?" asked the cowboy.

"Why, he's frightened." The Easterner knocked his pipe against a rim of the stove. "He's clear frightened out of his boots."

"What at?" cried Johnnie and cowboy together.

The Easterner reflected over his answer.

"What at?" cried the others again.

"Oh, I don't know, but it seems to me this man has been reading dime-novels, and he thinks he's right out in the middle of it—the shootin' and stabbin' and all."

"But," said the cowboy, deeply scandalized, "this ain't Wyoming, ner none of them places. This is Nebrasker."

"Yes," added Johnnie, "an' why don't he wait till he gits out West?"

The travelled Easterner laughed. "It isn't different there even—not in these days. But he thinks he's right in the middle of hell."

Johnnie and the cowboy mused long.

"It's awful funny," remarked Johnnie at last.

"Yes," said the cowboy. "This is a queer game. I hope we don't git snowed in, because then we'd have to stand this here man bein' around with us all the time. That wouldn't be no good."

"I wish pop would throw him out," said Johnnie.

Presently they heard a loud stamping on the stairs, accompanied by ringing jokes in the voice of old Scully, and laughter, evidently from the Swede. The men around the stove stared vacantly at each other. "Gosh!" said the cowboy. The door flew open, and old Scully, flushed and anecdotal, came into the room. He was jabbering at the Swede, who followed him, laughing bravely. It was the entry of two roisterers from a banquet-hall.

"Come now," said Scully sharply to the three seated men, "move up and give us a chance at the stove." The cowboy and the Easterner obediently sidled their chairs to make room for the new-comers. Johnnie, however, simply arranged himself in a more indolent attitude, and then remained motionless.

"Come! Git over, there," said Scully.

"Plenty of room on the other side of the stove," said Johnnie.

"Do you think we want to sit in the draught?" roared the father.

But the Swede here interposed with a grandeur of confidence. "No, no. Let the boy sit where he likes," he cried in a bullying voice to the father.

"All right! All right!" said Scully, deferentially. The cowboy and the Easterner exchanged glances of wonder.

The five chairs were formed in a crescent about one side of the stove. The Swede began to talk; he talked arrogantly, profanely, angrily. Johnnie, the cowboy, and the Easterner maintained a morose silence, while old Scully appeared to be receptive and eager, breaking in constantly with sympathetic ejaculations.

Finally the Swede announced that he was thirsty. He moved in his chair, and said that he would go for a drink of water.

"I'll git it for you," cried Scully at once.

"No," said the Swede, contemptuously. "I'll get it for myself." He arose and stalked with the air of an owner off into the executive parts of the hotel.

As soon as the Swede was out of hearing Scully sprang to his feet and whispered intensely to the others: "Up-stairs he thought I was tryin' to poison 'im."

"Say," said Johnnie, "this makes me sick. Why don't you throw 'im out in the snow?"

"Why, he's all right now," declared Scully. "It was only that he was from the East, and he thought this was a tough place. That's all. He's all right now."

The cowboy looked with admiration upon the Easterner. "You were straight," he said. "You were on to that there Dutchman."

"Well," said Johnnie to his father, "he may be all right now, but I don't see it. Other time he was scared, but now he's too fresh."

Scully's speech was always a combination of Irish brogue and idiom, Western twang and idiom, and scraps of curiously formal diction taken from the story-books and newspapers, He now hurled a strange mass of language at the head of his son. "What do I keep? What do I keep? What do I keep?" he demanded, in a voice of thunder. He slapped his knee impressively, to indicate that he himself was going to make reply, and that all should heed. "I keep a hotel," he shouted. "A hotel, do you mind? A guest under my roof has sacred privileges. He is to be intimidated by none. Not one word shall he hear that would prejudice him in favor of goin' away. I'll not have it. There's no place in this here town where they can say they iver took in a guest of mine because he was afraid to stay here." He wheeled suddenly upon the cowboy and the Easterner. "Am I right?"

"Yes, Mr. Scully," said the cowboy, "I think you're right."

"Yes, Mr. Scully," said the Easterner, "I think you're right."

5

At six-o'clock supper, the Swede fizzed like a fire-wheel. He sometimes seemed on the point of bursting into riotous song, and in all his madness he was encouraged by old Scully. The Easterner was incased in reserve; the cowboy sat in wide-mouthed amazement, forgetting to eat, while Johnnie wrathily demolished great plates of food. The daughters of the house, when they were obliged to replenish the biscuits, approached as warily as Indians, and, having succeeded in their purpose, fled with ill-concealed trepidation. The Swede domineered the whole feast, and he gave it the appearance of a cruel bacchanal. He seemed to have grown suddenly taller; he gazed, brutally disdainful, into every face. His voice rang through the room. Once when he jabbed out harpoon-fashion with his fork to pinion a biscuit, the weapon nearly impaled the hand of the Easterner which had been stretched quietly out for the same biscuit.

After supper, as the men filed towards the other room, the Swede smote Scully ruthlessly on the shoulder. "Well, old boy, that was a good, square meal." Johnnie looked hopefully at his father; he knew that shoulder was tender from an old fall; and, indeed, it appeared for a moment as if Scully was going to flame out over the matter, but in the end he smiled a sickly smile and remained silent. The others understood from his manner that he was admitting his responsibility for the Swede's new view-point.

Johnnie, however, addressed his parent in an aside. "Why don't you license somebody to kick you down-stairs?" Scully scowled darkly by way of reply.

When they were gathered about the stove, the Swede insisted on another game of High Five. Scully gently deprecated the plan at first, but the Swede turned a wolfish glare upon him. The old man subsided, and the Swede canvassed the others. In his tone there was always a great threat. The cowboy and the Easterner both remarked indifferently that they would play. Scully said that he would presently have to go to meet the 6.58 train, and so the Swede turned menacingly upon Johnnie. For a moment their glances crossed like blades, and then Johnnie smiled and said, "Yes, I'll play."

They formed a square, with the little board on their knees. The Easterner and the Swede were again partners. As the play went on, it was noticeable that the cowboy was not board-whacking as usual. Meanwhile, Scully, near the lamp, had put on his spectacles and, with an appearance curiously like an old priest, was reading a newspaper. In time he went out to meet the 6.58 train, and, despite his precautions, a gust of polar wind whirled into the room as he opened the door. Besides scattering the cards, it dulled the players to the marrow. The Swede cursed frightfully. When Scully returned, his entrance disturbed a cosey and friendly scene. The Swede again cursed. But presently they were once more intent, their heads bent forward and their hands moving swiftly. The Swede had adopted the fashion of board-whacking.

Scully took up his paper and for a long time remained immersed in matters which were extraordinarily remote from him. The lamp burned badly, and once he stopped to adjust the wick. The newspaper, as he turned from page to page, rustled with a slow and comfortable sound. Then suddenly he heard three terrible words: "You are cheatin'!"

Such scenes often prove that there can be little of dramatic import in environment. Any room can present a tragic front; any room can be comic. This little den was now hideous as a torture-chamber. The new faces of the men themselves had changed it upon the instant. The Swede held a huge fist in front of Johnnie's face, while the latter looked steadily over it into the blazing orbs of his accuser. The Easterner had grown pallid; the cowboy's jaw had dropped in that expression of bovine amazement which was one of his important mannerisms. After the three words, the first sound in the room was made by Scully's paper as it floated forgotten to his feet. His spectacles had also fallen from his nose, but by a clutch he had saved them in air. His hand, grasping the spectacles, now remained poised awkwardly and near his shoulder. He stared at the card-players.

Probably the silence was while a second elapsed. Then, if the floor had been suddenly twitched out from under the men they could not have moved quicker. The five had projected themselves headlong towards a common point. It happened that Johnnie, in rising to hurl himself upon the Swede, had stumbled slightly because of his curiously instinctive care for the cards and the board. The loss of the moment allowed time for the arrival of Scully, and also allowed the cowboy time to give the Swede a great push which sent him staggering back. The men found tongue together, and hoarse shouts of rage, appeal, or fear burst from every throat. The cowboy pushed and jostled feverishly at the Swede, and the Easterner and Scully clung wildly to Johnnie; but, through the smoky air, above the swaying bodies of the peace-compellers, the eyes of the two warriors ever sought each other in glances of challenge that were at once hot and steely.

Of course the board had been overturned, and now the whole company of cards was scattered over the floor, where the boots of the men trampled the fat and painted kings and queens as they gazed with their silly eyes at the war that was waging above them.

Scully's voice was dominating the yells. "Stop now? Stop, I say! Stop, now—"

Johnnie, as he struggled to burst through the rank formed by Scully and the Easterner, was crying, "Well, he says I cheated! He says I cheated! I won't allow no man to say I cheated! If he says I cheated, he's a ——————!"

The cowboy was telling the Swede, "Quit, now! Quit, d'ye hear—"

The screams of the Swede never ceased: "He did cheat! I saw him! I saw him—"

As for the Easterner, he was importuning in a voice that was not heeded: "Wait a moment, can't you? Oh, wait a moment. What's the good of a fight over a game of cards? Wait a moment—"

In this tumult no complete sentences were clear. "Cheat"—"Quit"—"He says"—these fragments pierced the uproar and rang out sharply. It was remarkable that, whereas Scully undoubtedly made the most noise, he was the least heard of any of the riotous band.

Then suddenly there was a great cessation. It was as if each man had paused for breath; and although the room was still lighted with the anger of men, it could be seen that there was no danger of immediate conflict, and at once Johnnie, shouldering his way forward, almost succeeded in confronting the Swede. "What did you say I cheated for? What did you say I cheated for? I don't cheat, and I won't let no man say I do!"

The Swede said, "I saw you! I saw you!"

"Well," cried Johnnie, "I'll fight any man what says I cheat!"

"No, you won't," said the cowboy. "Not here."

"Ah, be still, can't you?" said Scully, coming between them.

The quiet was sufficient to allow the Easterner's voice to be heard. He was repealing, "Oh, wait a moment, can't you? What's the good of a fight over a game of cards? Wait a moment!"

Johnnie, his red face appearing above his father's shoulder, hailed the Swede again. "Did you say I cheated?"

The Swede showed his teeth. "Yes."

"Then," said Johnnie, "we must fight."

"Yes, fight," roared the Swede. He was like a demoniac. "Yes, fight! I'll show you what kind of a man I am! I'll show you who you want to fight! Maybe you think I can't fight! Maybe you think I can't! I'll show you, you skin, you card-sharp! Yes, you cheated! You cheated! You cheated!"

"Well, let's go at it, then, mister," said Johnnie, coolly.

The cowboy's brow was beaded with sweat from his efforts in intercepting all sorts of raids. He turned in despair to Scully. "What are you goin' to do now?"

A change had come over the Celtic visage of the old man. He now seemed all eagerness; his eyes glowed.

"We'll let them fight," he answered, stalwartly. "I can't put up with it any longer. I've stood this damned Swede till I'm sick. We'll let them fight."

6

The men prepared to go out-of-doors. The Easterner was so nervous that he had great difficulty in getting his arms into the sleeves of his new leather coat. As the cowboy drew his fur cap down over his cars his hands trembled. In fact, Johnnie and old Scully were the only ones who displayed no agitation. These preliminaries were conducted without words.

Scully threw open the door. "Well, come on," he said. Instantly a terrific wind caused the flame of the lamp to struggle at its wick, while a puff of black smoke sprang from the chimney-top. The stove was in mid-current of the blast, and its voice swelled to equal the roar of the storm. Some of the scarred and bedabbled cards were caught up from the floor and dashed helplessly against the farther wall. The men lowered their heads and plunged into the tempest as into a sea.

No snow was falling, but great whirls and clouds of flakes, swept up from the ground by the frantic winds, were streaming southward with the speed of bullets. The covered land was blue with the sheen of an unearthly satin, and there was no other hue save where, at the low, black railway station—which seemed incredibly distant—one light gleamed like a tiny jewel. As the men floundered into a thigh deep drift, it was known that the Swede was bawling out something. Scully went to him, put a hand on his shoulder and projected an ear. "What's that you say?" he shouted.

"I say," bawled the Swede again, "I won't stand much show against this gang. I know you'll all pitch on me."

Scully smote him reproachfully on the arm. "Tut, man!" he yelled. The wind tore the words from Scully's lips and scattered them far alee.

"You are all a gang of—" boomed the Swede, but the storm also seized the remainder of this sentence.

Immediately turning their backs upon the wind, the men had swung around a corner to the sheltered side of the hotel. It was the function of the little house to preserve here, amid this great devastation of snow, an irregular V-shape of heavily incrusted grass, which crackled beneath the feet. One could imagine the great drifts piled against the windward side. When the party reached the comparative peace of this spot it was found that the Swede was still bellowing.

"Oh, I know what kind of a thing this is! I know you'll all pitch on me. I can't lick you all!"

Scully turned upon him panther fashion. "You'll not have to whip all of us. You'll have to whip my son Johnnie. An' the man what troubles you durin' that time will have me to dale with."

The arrangements were swiftly made. The two men faced each other, obedient to the harsh commands of Scully, whose face, in the subtly luminous gloom, could be seen set in the austere impersonal lines that are pictured on the countenances of the Roman veterans. The Easterner's teeth were chattering, and he was hopping up and down like a mechanical toy. The cowboy stood rock-like.

The contestants had not stripped off any clothing. Each was in his ordinary attire. Their fists were up, and they eyed each other in a calm that had the elements of leonine cruelty in it.

During this pause, the Easterner's mind, like a film, took lasting impressions of three men—the iron-nerved master of the ceremony; the Swede, pale, motionless, terrible; and Johnnie, serene yet ferocious, brutish yet heroic. The entire prelude had in it a tragedy greater than the tragedy of action, and this aspect was accentuated by the long, mellow cry of the blizzard, as it sped the tumbling and wailing flakes into the black abyss of the south.

"Now!" said Scully.

The two combatants leaped forward and crashed together like bullocks. There was heard the cushioned sound of blows, and of a curse squeezing out from between the tight teeth of one.

As for the spectators, the Easterner's pent-up breath exploded from him with a pop of relief, absolute relief from the tension of the preliminaries. The cowboy bounded into the air with a yowl. Scully was immovable as from supreme amazement and fear at the fury of the fight which he himself had permitted and arranged.

For a time the encounter in the darkness was such a perplexity of flying arms that it presented no more detail than would a swiftly revolving wheel. Occasionally a face, as if illumined by a flash of light, would shine out, ghastly and marked with pink spots. A moment later, the men might have been known as shadows, if it were not for the involuntary utterance of oaths that came from them in whispers.

Suddenly a holocaust of warlike desire caught the cowboy, and he bolted forward with the speed of a broncho. "Go it, Johnnie! go it! Kill him! Kill him!"

Scully confronted him. "Kape back," he said; and by his glance the cowboy could tell that this man was Johnnie's father.

To the Easterner there was a monotony of unchangeable fighting that was an abomination. This confused mingling was eternal to his sense, which was concentrated in a longing for the end, the priceless end. Once the fighters lurched near him, and as he scrambled hastily backward he heard them breathe like men on the rack.

"Kill him, Johnnie! Kill him! Kill him! Kill him!" The cowboy's face was contorted like one of those agony masks in museums.

"Keep still," said Scully, icily.

Then there was a sudden loud grunt, incomplete, cut short, and Johnnie's body swung away from the Swede and fell with sickening heaviness to the grass. The cowboy was barely in time to prevent the mad Swede from flinging himself upon his prone adversary. "No, you don't," said the cowboy, interposing an arm. "Wait a second."

Scully was at his son's side. "Johnnie! Johnnie, me boy!" His voice had a quality of melancholy tenderness. "Johnnie! Can you go on with it?" He looked anxiously down into the bloody, pulpy face of his son.

There was a moment of silence, and then Johnnie answered in his ordinary voice, "Yes, I—it—yes."

Assisted by his father he struggled to his feet. "Wait a bit now till you git your wind," said the old man.

A few paces away the cowboy was lecturing the Swede. "No, you don't! Wait a second!"

The Easterner was plucking at Scully's sleeve. "Oh, this is enough," he pleaded. "This is enough! Let it go as it stands. This is enough!"

"Bill," said Scully, "git out of the road." The cowboy stepped aside. "Now." The combatants were actuated by a new caution as they advanced towards collision. They glared at each other, and then the Swede aimed a lightning blow that carried with it his entire weight. Johnnie was evidently half stupid from weakness, but he miraculously dodged, and his fist sent the over-balanced Swede sprawling.

The cowboy, Scully, and the Easterner burst into a cheer that was like a chorus of triumphant soldiery, but before its conclusion the Swede had scuffled agilely to his feet and come in berserk abandon at his foe. There was another perplexity of flying arms, and Johnnie's body again swung away and fell, even as a bundle might fall from a roof. The Swede instantly staggered to a little wind-waved tree and leaned upon it, breathing like an engine, while his savage and flame-lit eyes roamed from face to face as the men bent over Johnnie. There was a splendor of isolation in his situation at this time which the Easterner felt once when, lifting his eyes from the man on the ground, he beheld that mysterious and lonely figure, waiting.

"Arc you any good yet, Johnnie?" asked Scully in a broken voice.

The son gasped and opened his eyes languidly. After a moment he answered, "No—I ain't—any good—any—more." Then, from shame and bodily ill he began to weep, the tears furrowing down through the bloodstains on his face. "He was too—too—too heavy for me."

Scully straightened and addressed the waiting figure. "Stranger," he said, evenly, "it's all up with our side." Then his voice changed into that vibrant huskiness which is commonly the tone of the most simple and deadly announcements. "Johnnie is whipped."

Without replying, the victor moved off on the route to the front door of the hotel.

The cowboy was formulating new and un-spellable blasphemies. The Easterner was startled to find that they were out in a wind that seemed to come direct from the shadowed arctic floes. He heard again the wail of the snow as it was flung to its grave in the south. He knew now that all this time the cold had been sinking into him deeper and deeper, and he wondered that he had not perished. He felt indifferent to the condition of the vanquished man.

"Johnnie, can you walk?" asked Scully.

"Did I hurt—hurt him any?" asked the son.

"Can you walk, boy? Can you walk?"

294

Johnnie's voice was suddenly strong. There was a robust impatience in it. "I asked you whether I hurt him any!"

"Yes, yes, Johnnie," answered the cowboy, consolingly; "he's hurt a good deal."

They raised him from the ground, and as soon as he was on his feet he went tottering off, rebuffing all attempts at assistance. When the party rounded the corner they were fairly blinded by the pelting of the snow. It burned their faces like fire. The cowboy carried Johnnie through the drift to the door. As they entered some cards again rose from the floor and beat against the wall.

The Easterner rushed to the stove. He was so profoundly chilled that he almost dared to embrace the glowing iron. The Swede was not in the room. Johnnie sank into a chair, and, folding his arms on his knees, buried his face in them. Scully, warming one foot and then the other at a rim of the stove, muttered to himself with Celtic mournfulness. The cowboy had removed his fur cap, and with a dazed and rueful air he was running one hand through his tousled locks. From overhead they could hear the creaking of boards, as the Swede tramped here and there in his room.

The sad quiet was broken by the sudden flinging open of a door that led towards the kitchen. It was instantly followed by an inrush of women. They precipitated themselves upon Johnnie amid a chorus of lamentation. Before they carried their prey off to the kitchen, there to be bathed and harangued with that mixture of sympathy and abuse which is a feat of their sex, the mother straightened herself and fixed old Scully with an eye of stern reproach. "Shame be upon you, Patrick Scully!" she cried. "Your own son, too. Shame be upon you!"

"There, now! Be quiet, now!" said the old man, weakly.

"Shame be upon you, Patrick Scully!" The girls, rallying to this slogan, sniffed disdainfully in the direction of those trembling accomplices, the cowboy and the Easterner. Presently they bore Johnnie away, and left the three men to dismal reflection.

7

"I'd like to fight this here Dutchman myself," said the cowboy, breaking a long silence.

Scully wagged his head sadly. "No, that wouldn't do. It wouldn't be right. It wouldn't be right."

"Well, why wouldn't it?" argued the cowboy. "I don't see no harm in it."

"No," answered Scully, with mournful heroism. "It wouldn't be right. It was Johnnie's fight, and now we mustn't whip the man just because he whipped Johnnie."

"Yes, that's true enough," said the cowboy; "but—he better not get fresh with me, because I couldn't stand no more of it."

"You'll not say a word to him," commanded Scully, and even then they heard the tread of the Swede on the stairs. His entrance was made theatric. He swept the door back with a bang and swaggered to the middle of the room. No one looked at him. "Well," he cried, insolently, at Scully, "I s'pose you'll tell me now how much I owe you?"

The old man remained stolid. "You don't owe me nothin'."

"Huh!" said the Swede, "huh! Don't owe 'im nothin'."

The cowboy addressed the Swede. "Stranger, I don't see how you come to be so gay around here."

Old Scully was instantly alert. "Stop!" he shouted, holding his hand forth, fingers upward. "Bill, you shut up!"

The cowboy spat carelessly into the sawdust box. "I didn't say a word, did I?" he asked.

"Mr. Scully," called the Swede, "how much do I owe you?" It was seen that he was attired for departure, and that he had his valise in his hand.

"You don't owe me nothin'," repeated Scully in his same imperturbable way.

"Huh!" said the Swede. "I guess you're right. I guess if it was any way at all, you'd owe me somethin'. That's what I guess." He turned to the cowboy. "'Kill him! Kill him! Kill him!'" he mimicked, and then guffawed victoriously. "'Kill him!'" He was convulsed with ironical humor.

But he might have been jeering the dead. The three men were immovable and silent, staring with glassy eyes at the stove.

The Swede opened the door and passed into the storm, giving one derisive glance backward at the still group.

As soon as the door was closed, Scully and the cowboy leaped to their feet and began to curse. They trampled to and fro, waving their arms and smashing into the air with their fists. "Oh, but that was a hard minute!" wailed Scully. "That was a hard minute! Him there leerin' and scoffin'! One bang at his nose was worth forty dollars to me that minute! How did you stand it, Bill?"

"How did I stand it?" cried the cowboy in a quivering voice. "How did I stand it? Oh!"

The old man burst into sudden brogue. "I'd loike to take that Swade," he wailed, "and hould 'im down on a shtone flure and bate 'im to a jelly wid a shtick!"

The cowboy groaned in sympathy. "I'd like to git him by the neck and ha-ammer him "—he brought his hand down on a chair with a noise like a pistol-shot—"hammer that there Dutchman until he couldn't tell himself from a dead coyote!"

"I'd bate 'im until he—"

"I'd show him some things—"

And then together they raised a yearning, fanatic cry—"Oh-o-oh! if we only could—"

"Yes!"

"Yes!"

"And then I'd—"

"O-o-oh!"

8

The Swede, tightly gripping his valise, tacked across the face of the storm as if he carried sails. He was following a line of little naked, gasping trees, which he knew must mark the way of the road. His face, fresh from the pounding of Johnnie's fists, felt more pleasure than pain in the wind and the driving snow. A number of square shapes loomed upon him finally, and he knew them as the houses of the main body of the town. He found a street and made travel along it, leaning heavily upon the wind whenever, at a corner, a terrific blast caught him.

He might have been in a deserted village. We picture the world as thick with conquering and elate humanity, but here, with the bugles of the tempest pealing, it was hard to imagine a peopled earth. One viewed the existence of man then as a marvel, and conceded a glamour of wonder to these lice which were caused to cling to a whirling, fire-smote, ice-locked, disease-stricken, space-lost bulb. The conceit of man was explained by this storm to be the very engine of life. One was a coxcomb not to die in it. However, the Swede found a saloon.

In front of it an indomitable red light was burning, and the snow-flakes were made blood color as they flew through the circumscribed territory of the lamp's shining. The Swede pushed open the door of the saloon and entered. A sanded expanse was before him, and at the end of it four men sat about a table drinking. Down one side of the room extended a radiant bar, and its guardian was leaning upon his elbows listening to the talk of the men at the table. The Swede dropped his valise upon the floor, and, smiling fraternally upon the barkeeper, said, "Gimme some whiskey, will you?" The man placed a bottle, a whiskey-glass, and a glass of ice-thick water upon the bar. The Swede poured himself an abnormal portion of whiskey and drank it in three gulps. "Pretty bad night," remarked the bartender, indifferently. He was making the pretension of blindness which is usually a distinction of his class; but it could have been seen that he was furtively studying the half-erased blood-stains on the face of the Swede. "Bad night," he said again.

"Oh, it's good enough for me," replied the Swede, hardily, as he poured himself some more whiskey. The barkeeper took his coin and maneuvered it through its reception by the highly nickelled cash-machine. A bell rang; a card labelled "20 cts." had appeared.

"No," continued the Swede, "this isn't too bad weather. It's good enough for me."

"So?" murmured the barkeeper, languidly.

The copious drams made the Swede's eyes swim, and he breathed a trifle heavier. "Yes, I like this weather. I like it. It suits me." It was apparently his design to impart a deep significance to these words.

"So?" murmured the bartender again. He turned to gaze dreamily at the scroll-like birds and bird-like scrolls which had been drawn with soap upon the mirrors back of the bar.

"Well, I guess I'll take another drink," said the Swede, presently. "Have something?"

"No, thanks; I'm not drinkin'," answered the bartender. Afterwards he asked, "How did you hurt your face?"

The Swede immediately began to boast loudly. "Why, in a fight. I thumped the soul out of a man down here at Scully's hotel."

The interest of the four men at the table was at last aroused.

"Who was it?" said one.

"Johnnie Scully," blustered the Swede. "Son of the man what runs it. He will be pretty near dead for some weeks, I can tell you. I made a nice thing of him, I did. He couldn't get up. They carried him in the house. Have a drink?"

Instantly the men in some subtle way incased themselves in reserve. "No, thanks," said one. The group was of curious formation. Two were prominent local business men; one was the district-attorney; and one was a professional gambler of the kind known as "square." But a scrutiny of the group would not have enabled an observer to pick the gambler from the men of more reputable pursuits. He was, in fact, a man so delicate in manner, when among people of fair class, and so judicious in his choice of victims, that in the strictly masculine part of the town's life he had come to be explicitly trusted and admired. People called him a thoroughbred. The fear and contempt with which his craft was regarded was undoubtedly the reason that his quiet dignity shone conspicuous above the quiet dignity of men who might be merely hatters, billiard markers, or grocery-clerks. Beyond an occasional unwary traveller, who came by rail, this gambler was supposed to prey solely upon reckless and senile farmers, who, when flush with good crops, drove into town in all the pride and confidence of an absolutely invulnerable stupidity. Hearing at times in circuitous fashion of the despoilment of such a farmer, the important men of Romper invariably laughed in contempt of the victim, and, if they thought of the wolf at all, it was with a kind of pride at the knowledge that he would never dare think of attacking their wisdom and courage. Besides, it was popular that this gambler had a real wife and two real children in a neat cottage in a suburb, where he led an exemplary home life; and when any one even suggested a discrepancy in his character, the crowd immediately vociferated descriptions of this virtuous family circle. Then men who led exemplary home lives, and men who did not lead exemplary home lives, all subsided in a bunch, remarking that there was nothing more to be said.

However, when a restriction was placed upon him—as, for instance, when a strong clique of members of the new Pollywog Club refused to permit him, even as a spectator, to appear in the rooms of the organization—the candor and gentleness with which he accepted the judgment disarmed many of his foes and made his friends more desperately partisan. He invariably distinguished between himself and a respectable Romper man so quickly and frankly that his manner actually appeared to be a continual broadcast compliment.

And one must not forget to declare the fundamental fact of his entire position in Romper. It is irrefutable that in all affairs outside of his business, in all matters that occur eternally and commonly between man and man, this thieving card-player was so generous, so just, so moral, that, in a contest, he could have put to flight the consciences of nine-tenths of the citizens of Romper.

And so it happened that he was seated in this saloon with the two prominent local merchants and the district-attorney.

The Swede continued to drink raw whiskey, meanwhile babbling at the barkeeper and trying to induce him to indulge in potations. "Come on. Have a drink. Come on. What—no? Well, have a little one, then. By gawd, I've whipped a man to-night, and I want to celebrate. I whipped him good, too. Gentlemen," the Swede cried to the men at the table, "have a drink?"

"Ssh!" said the barkeeper.

The group at the table, although furtively attentive, had been pretending to be deep in talk, but now a man lifted his eyes towards the Swede and said, shortly, "Thanks. We don't want any more."

At this reply the Swede ruffled out his chest like a rooster. "Well," he exploded, "it seems I can't get anybody to drink with me in this town. Seems so, don't it? Well!"

"Ssh!" said the barkeeper.

"Say," snarled the Swede, "don't you try to shut me up. I won't have it. I'm a gentleman, and I want people to drink with me. And I want 'em to drink with me now. Now—do you understand?" He rapped the bar with his knuckles.

Years of experience had calloused the bartender. He merely grew sulky. "I hear you," he answered.

"Well," cried the Swede, "listen hard then. See those men over there? Well, they're going to drink with me, and don't you forget it. Now you watch."

"Hi!" yelled the barkeeper, "this won't do!"

"Why won't it?" demanded the Swede. He stalked over to the table, and by chance laid his hand upon the shoulder of the gambler. "How about this?" he asked, wrathfully. "I asked you to drink with me."

The gambler simply twisted his head and spoke over his shoulder. "My friend, I don't know you."

"Oh, hell!" answered the Swede, "come and have a drink."

"Now, my boy," advised the gambler, kindly, "take your hand off my shoulder and go 'way and mind your own business." He was a little, slim man, and it seemed strange to hear him use this tone of heroic patronage to the burly Swede. The other men at the table said nothing.

"What! You won't drink with me, you little dude? I'll make you then! I'll make you!" The Swede had grasped the gambler frenziedly at the throat, and was dragging him from his chair. The other men sprang up. The barkeeper dashed around the corner of his bar. There was a great tumult, and then was seen a long blade in the hand of the gambler. It shot forward, and a human body, this citadel of virtue, wisdom, power, was pierced as easily as if it had been a melon. The Swede fell with a cry of supreme astonishment.

The prominent merchants and the district attorney must have at once tumbled out of the place backward. The bartender found himself hanging limply to the arm of a chair and gazing into the eyes of a murderer.

"Henry," said the latter, as he wiped his knife on one of the towels that hung beneath the bar-rail, "you tell 'em where to find me. I'll be home, waiting for 'em." Then he vanished. A moment afterwards the barkeeper was in the street dinning through the storm for help, and, moreover, companionship.

The corpse of the Swede, alone in the saloon, had its eyes fixed upon a dreadful legend that dwelt atop of the cash-machine: "This registers the amount of your purchase."

9

Months later, the cowboy was frying pork over the stove of a little ranch near the Dakota line, when there was a quick thud of hoofs outside, and presently the Easterner entered with the letters and the papers.

"Well," said the Easterner at once, "the chap that killed the Swede has got three years. Wasn't much, was it?"

"He has? Three years?" The cowboy poised his pan of pork, while he ruminated upon the news. "Three years. That ain't much."

"No. It was a light sentence," replied the Easterner as he unbuckled his spurs. "Seems there was a good deal of sympathy for him in Romper."

"If the bartender had been any good," observed the cowboy, thoughtfully, "he would have gone in and cracked that there Dutchman on the head with a bottle in the beginnin' of it and stopped all this here murderin'."

"Yes, a thousand things might have happened," said the Easterner, tartly.

The cowboy returned his pan of pork to the fire, but his philosophy continued. "It's funny, ain't it? If he hadn't said Johnnie was cheatin' he'd be alive this minute. He was an awful fool. Game played for fun, too. Not for money. I believe he was crazy."

"I feel sorry for that gambler," said the Easterner.

"Oh, so do I," said the cowboy. "He don't deserve none of it for killin' who he did."

"The Swede might not have been killed if everything had been square."

"Might not have been killed?" exclaimed the cowboy. "Everythin' square? Why, when he said that Johnnie was cheatin' and acted like such a jackass? And then in the saloon he fairly walked up to git hurt?" With these arguments the cowboy browbeat the Easterner and reduced him to rage.

"You're a fool!" cried the Easterner, viciously. "You're a bigger jackass than the Swede by a million majority. Now let me tell you one thing. Let me tell you something. Listen! Johnnie was cheating!"

"'Johnnie,'" said the cowboy, blankly. There was a minute of silence, and then he said, robustly, "Why, no. The game was only for fun."

"Fun or not," said the Easterner, "Johnnie was cheating. I saw him. I know it. I saw him. And I refused to stand up and be a man. I let the Swede fight it out alone. And you—you were simply puffing around the place and wanting to fight. And then old Scully himself! We are all in it! This poor gambler isn't even a noun. He is kind of an adverb. Every sin is the result of a collaboration. We, five of us, have collaborated in the murder of this Swede. Usually there are from a dozen to forty women really involved in every murder, but in this case it seems to be only five men—you, I, Johnnie, old Scully, and that fool of an unfortunate gambler came merely as a culmination, the apex of a human movement, and gets all the punishment."

The cowboy, injured and rebellious, cried out blindly into this fog of mysterious theory: "Well, I didn't do anythin', did I?"

COLLEGE WRITING 1: REFLECTION WITHIN THE TEXT

Try to prevent what happens at the end of "The Blue Hotel" by choosing and changing the behavior of one of the characters in the story. What would the character say to the Swede to change the ending? Where and when would they say it?

COLLEGE WRITING 2: RESEARCH OUTSIDE THE TEXT

Imagine a time and place. What would it be like to live in that place at that time? Don't do any research yet! Write your thoughts down.

Now research the place at that time. Compare what you imagined with what you found in your research. How were you right and how were you wrong? List the differences.

Use your list to write a story. In the story you will travel to that time and place. With your fictional traveling self not having done any research, what mistakes would you make? What misadventures would you have?

IDEAS AND VALUES: CONNECT THE TEXT

» In London's "To Build A Fire" the main character is always referred to as "the man," or simply "he." In Gilman's "The Yellow Wallpaper" the narrator never directly gives us her name, while her husband refers to her only as: "blessed little goose," "Darling," "his darling," and "little girl." In Crane's "The Blue Hotel" there are the characters of the Easterner, the Cowboy, the Swede, and the Gambler, but also Pat and Johnnie Scully. What is the nature of anonymity? What do the anonymous characters in these stories have in common? Between these texts, does anonymity seem to be a good thing? Are the anonymous characters the most powerful, or fortunate characters in their respective stories? Ultimately why are some characters named and others not?

» What meaning is there in a color? Why are stop signs red? What is the color of sadness? Why do we wrap little boys in blue and girls in pink? Why do brides wear white on their wedding day? What is the significance of the title colors in their respective stories: "The Yellow Wallpaper," by Gilman, "Porcelain and Pink," by Fitzgerald, and "The Blue Hotel," by Crane? Could different colors have been used without changing these stories?

» What is a stereotype? Do you consider the " Cowboy," the "Easterner" or the "Swede" in Crane's "The Blue Hotel" stereotypes? How about the children in Swift's "A Modest Proposal"? Lastly, what use of stereotypes has Du Bois's in "Of Our Spiritual Strivings" found necessary to make his points? How do the stereotypes help the reader to better understand the characters or topics discussed in these writings? Do we need stereotypes to help aid in our understanding of ourselves and others?

» How is the truth manipulated in Crane's "The Blue Hotel," Fitzgerald's "Porcelain and Pink," and Twain's "The Stolen White Elephant"? How does the reader know what is true in each story? What is the truth in each story? Who relies on the truth in each story? Who relies on the perversion of truth? What are the stakes? What is truth? Why do humans have a concept of truth—if our surroundings are self evident? Should one always strive to be truthful?

The Machine Stops

by E. M. Forester

12,247 WORDS. 1 HOUR, 8 MINUTES.
READING LEVEL: GRADE 9.3

1: THE AIR-SHIP

Imagine, if you can, a small room, hexagonal in shape, like the cell of a bee. It is lighted neither by window nor by lamp, yet it is filled with a soft radiance. There are no apertures for ventilation, yet the air is fresh. There are no musical instruments, and yet, at the moment that my meditation opens, this room is throbbing with melodious sounds. An armchair is in the centre, by its side a reading-desk — that is all the furniture. And in the armchair there sits a swaddled lump of flesh — a woman, about five feet high, with a face as white as a fungus. It is to her that the little room belongs.

An electric bell rang.

The woman touched a switch and the music was silent.

"I suppose I must see who it is", she thought, and set her chair in motion. The chair, like the music, was worked by machinery and it rolled her to the other side of the room where the bell still rang importunately.

"Who is it?" she called. Her voice was irritable, for she had been interrupted often since the music began. She knew several thousand people, in certain directions human intercourse had advanced enormously.

But when she listened into the receiver, her white face wrinkled into smiles, and she said: "Very well. Let us talk, I will isolate myself. I do not expect anything important will happen for the next five minutes — for I can give you fully five minutes, Kuno. Then I must deliver my lecture on 'Music during the Australian Period'."

She touched the isolation knob, so that no one else could speak to her. Then she touched the lighting apparatus, and the little room was plunged into darkness.

"Be quick!" she called, her irritation returning. "Be quick, Kuno; here I am in the dark wasting my time."

But it was fully fifteen seconds before the round plate that she held in her hands began to glow. A faint blue light shot across it, darkening to purple, and presently she could see the image of her son, who lived on the other side of the earth, and he could see her.

"Kuno, how slow you are."

He smiled gravely.

"I really believe you enjoy dawdling."

"I have called you before, mother, but you were always busy or isolated. I have something particular to say."

"What is it, dearest boy? Be quick. Why could you not send it by pneumatic post?"

"Because I prefer saying such a thing. I want —"

"Well?"

"I want you to come and see me."

Vashti watched his face in the blue plate.

"But I can see you!" she exclaimed. "What more do you want?"

"I want to see you not through the Machine," said Kuno. "I want to speak to you not through the wearisome Machine."

"Oh, hush!" said his mother, vaguely shocked. "You mustn't say anything against the Machine."

"Why not?"

"One mustn't."

"You talk as if a god had made the Machine," cried the other. "I believe that you pray to it when you are unhappy. Men made it, do not forget that. Great men, but men. The Machine is much, but it is not everything. I see something like you in this plate, but I do not see you. I hear something like you through this telephone, but I do not hear you. That is why I want you to come. Pay me a visit, so that we can meet face to face, and talk about the hopes that are in my mind."

She replied that she could scarcely spare the time for a visit.

"The air-ship barely takes two days to fly between me and you."

"I dislike air-ships."

"Why?"

"I dislike seeing the horrible brown earth, and the sea, and the stars when it is dark. I get no ideas in an air-ship."

"I do not get them anywhere else."

"What kind of ideas can the air give you?"

He paused for an instant.

"Do you not know four big stars that form an oblong, and three stars close together in the middle of the oblong, and hanging from these stars, three other stars?"

"No, I do not. I dislike the stars. But did they give you an idea? How interesting; tell me."

"I had an idea that they were like a man."

"I do not understand."

"The four big stars are the man's shoulders and his knees. The three stars in the middle are like the belts that men wore once, and the three stars hanging are like a sword."

"A sword?"

"Men carried swords about with them, to kill animals and other men."

"It does not strike me as a very good idea, but it is certainly original. When did it come to you first?"

"In the air-ship —" He broke off, and she fancied that he looked sad. She could not be sure, for the Machine did not transmit nuances of expression. It only gave a general idea of people — an idea that was good enough for all practical purposes, Vashti thought. The imponderable bloom, declared by a discredited philosophy to be the actual essence of intercourse, was rightly ignored by the Machine, just as the imponderable bloom of the grape was ignored by the manufacturers of artificial fruit. Something "good enough" had long since been accepted by our race.

"The truth is," he continued, "that I want to see these stars again. They are curious stars. I want to see them not from the air-ship, but from the surface of the earth, as our ancestors did, thousands of years ago. I want to visit the surface of the earth."

She was shocked again.

"Mother, you must come, if only to explain to me what is the harm of visiting the surface of the earth."

"No harm," she replied, controlling herself. "But no advantage. The surface of the earth is only dust and mud, no advantage. The surface of the earth is only dust and mud, no life remains on it, and you would need a respirator, or the cold of the outer air would kill you. One dies immediately in the outer air."

"I know; of course I shall take all precautions."

"And besides —"

"Well?"

She considered, and chose her words with care. Her son had a queer temper, and she wished to dissuade him from the expedition.

"It is contrary to the spirit of the age," she asserted.

"Do you mean by that, contrary to the Machine?"

"In a sense, but —"

His image is the blue plate faded.

"Kuno!"

He had isolated himself.

For a moment Vashti felt lonely.

Then she generated the light, and the sight of her room, flooded with radiance and studded with electric buttons, revived her. There were buttons and switches everywhere — buttons to call for food for music, for clothing. There was the hot-bath button, by pressure of which a basin of (imitation) marble rose out of the floor, filled to the brim with a warm deodorized liquid. There was the cold-bath button. There was the button that produced literature. And there were of course the buttons by which she communicated with her friends. The room, though it contained nothing, was in touch with all that she cared for in the world.

Vashti's next move was to turn off the isolation switch, and all the accumulations of the last three minutes burst upon her. The room was filled with the noise of bells, and speaking-tubes. What was the new food like? Could she recommend it? Has she had any ideas lately? Might one tell her one's own ideas? Would she make an engagement to visit the public nurseries at an early date? — say this day month.

To most of these questions she replied with irritation — a growing quality in that accelerated age. She said that the new food was horrible. That she could not visit the public nurseries through press of engagements. That she had no ideas of her own but had just been told one-that four stars and three in the middle were like a man: she doubted there was much in it. Then she switched off her correspondents, for it was time to deliver her lecture on Australian music.

The clumsy system of public gatherings had been long since abandoned; neither Vashti nor her audience stirred from their rooms. Seated in her armchair she spoke, while they in their armchairs heard her, fairly well, and saw her, fairly well. She opened with a humorous account of music in the pre-Mongolian epoch, and went on to describe the great outburst of song that followed the Chinese conquest. Remote and primæval as were the methods of I-San-So and the Brisbane school, she yet felt (she said) that study of them might repay the musicians of today: they had freshness; they had, above all, ideas.

Her lecture, which lasted ten minutes, was well received, and at its conclusion she and many of her audience listened to a lecture on the sea; there were ideas to be got from the sea; the speaker had donned a respirator and visited it lately. Then she fed, talked to many friends, had a bath, talked again, and summoned her bed.

The bed was not to her liking. It was too large, and she had a feeling for a small bed. Complaint was useless, for beds were of the same dimension all over the world, and to have had an alternative size would have involved vast alterations in the Machine. Vashti isolated herself-it was necessary, for neither day nor night existed under the ground-and reviewed all that had happened since she had summoned the bed last. Ideas? Scarcely any. Events — was Kuno's invitation an event?

By her side, on the little reading-desk, was a survival from the ages of litter — one book. This was the Book of the Machine. In it were instructions against every possible contingency. If she was hot or cold or dyspeptic or at a loss for a word, she went to the book, and it told her which button to press. The Central Committee published it. In accordance with a growing habit, it was richly bound. Sitting up in the bed, she took it reverently in her hands. She glanced round the glowing room as if some one might be watching her. Then, half ashamed, half joyful, she murmured

"O Machine! O Machine!" and raised the volume to her lips. Thrice she kissed it, thrice inclined her head, thrice she felt the delirium of acquiescence. Her ritual performed, she turned to page 1367, which gave the times of the departure of the air-ships from the island in the southern hemisphere, under whose soil she lived, to the island in the northern hemisphere, whereunder lived her son.

She thought, "I have not the time."

She made the room dark and slept; she awoke and made the room light; she ate and exchanged ideas with her friends, and listened to music and attended lectures; she make the room dark and slept. Above her, beneath her, and around her, the Machine hummed eternally; she did not notice the noise, for she had been born with it in her ears. The earth, carrying her, hummed as it sped through silence, turning her now to the invisible sun, now to the invisible stars. She awoke and made the room light.

"Kuno!"

"I will not talk to you," he answered, "until you come."

"Have you been on the surface of the earth since we spoke last?"

His image faded.

Again she consulted the book. She became very nervous and lay back in her chair palpitating. Think of her as without teeth or hair. Presently she directed the chair to the wall, and pressed an unfamiliar button. The wall swung apart slowly. Through the opening she saw a tunnel that curved slightly, so that its goal was not visible. Should she go to see her son, here was the beginning of the journey.

Of course she knew all about the communication-system. There was nothing mysterious in it. She would summon a car and it would fly with her down the tunnel until it reached the lift that communicated with the air-ship station: the system had been in use for many, many years, long before the universal establishment of the Machine. And of course she had studied the civilization that had immediately preceded her own — the civilization that had mistaken the functions of the system, and had used it for bringing people to things, instead of for bringing things to people. Those funny old days, when men went for change of air instead of changing the air in their rooms! And yet — she was frightened of the tunnel: she had not seen it since her last child was born. It curved — but not quite as she remembered; it was brilliant — but not quite as brilliant as a lecturer had suggested. Vashti was seized with the terrors of direct experience. She shrank back into the room, and the wall closed up again.

"Kuno," she said, "I cannot come to see you. I am not well."

Immediately an enormous apparatus fell on to her out of the ceiling, a thermometer was automatically laid upon her heart. She lay powerless. Cool pads soothed her forehead. Kuno had telegraphed to her doctor. So the human passions still blundered up and down in the Machine. Vashti drank the projected into her mouth, and the machinery retired into the ceiling.

The voice of Kuno was sheard asking how she felt.

"Better." Then with irritation: "But why do you not come to me instead?"

"Because I cannot leave this place."

"Why?"

"Because, any moment, something tremendous many happen."

"Have you been on the surface of the earth yet?"

"Not yet."

"Then what is it?"

"I will not tell you through the Machine."

She resumed her life.

But she thought of Kuno as a baby, his birth, his removal to the public nurseries, her own visit to him there, his visits to her — visits which stopped when the Machine had assigned him a room on the other side of the earth. "Parents, duties of," said the book of the Machine, "cease at the moment of birth. P.422327483." True, but there was something special about Kuno — indeed there had been something special about all her children — and, after all, she must brave the journey if he desired it. And "something tremendous might happen." What did that mean? The nonsense of a youthful man, no doubt, but she must go. Again she pressed the unfamiliar button, again the wall swung back, and she saw the tunnel that curves out of sight. Clasping the Book, she rose, tottered on to the platform, and summoned the car. Her room closed behind her: the journey to the northern hemisphere had begun.

Of course it was perfectly easy. The car approached and in it she found arm-chairs exactly like her own. When she signalled, it stopped, and she tottered into the lift. One other passenger was in the lift, the first fellow creature she had seen face to face for months. Few travelled in these days, for, thanks to the advance of science, the earth was exactly alike all over. Rapid intercourse, from which the previous civilization had hoped so much, had ended by defeating itself. What was the good of going to Pekin when it was just like Shrewsbury? Why return to Shrewsbury when it would all be like Pekin? Men seldom moved their bodies; all unrest was concentrated in the soul.

The air-ship service was a relic from the former age. It was kept up, because it was easier to keep it up than to stop it or to diminish it, but it now far exceeded the wants of the population. Vessel after vessel would rise from the vomitories of Rye or of Christchurch (I use the antique names), would sail into the crowded sky, and would draw up at the wharves of the south — empty. So nicely adjusted was the system, so independent of meteorology, that the sky, whether calm or cloudy, resembled a vast kaleidoscope whereon the same patterns periodically recurred. The ship on which Vashti sailed started now at sunset, now at dawn. But always, as it passed above Rheims, it would neighbour the ship that served between Helsingfors and the Brazils, and, every third time it surmounted the Alps, the fleet of Palermo would cross its track behind. Night and day, wind and storm, tide and earthquake, impeded man no longer. He had harnessed Leviathan. All the old literature, with its praise of Nature, and its fear of Nature, rang false as the prattle of a child. Yet as Vashti saw the vast flank of the ship, stained with exposure to the outer air, her horror of direct experience returned. It was not quite like the air-ship in the cinematophote.

For one thing it smelt — not strongly or unpleasantly, but it did smell, and with her eyes shut she should have known that a new thing was close to her. Then she had to walk to it from the lift, had to submit to glances from the other passengers. The man in front dropped his Book — no great matter, but it disquieted them all. In the rooms, if the Book was dropped, the floor raised it mechanically, but the gangway to the air-ship was not so prepared, and the sacred volume lay motionless. They stopped — the thing was unforeseen — and the man, instead of picking up his property, felt the muscles of his arm to see how they had failed him. Then some one actually said with direct utterance: "We shall be late" — and they trooped on board, Vashti treading on the pages as she did so. Inside, her anxiety increased. The arrangements were old-fashioned and rough. There was even a female attendant, to whom she would have to announce her wants during the voyage. Of course a revolving platform ran the length of the boat, but she was expected to walk from it to her cabin. Some cabins were better than others, and she did not get the best. She thought the attendant had been unfair, and spasms of rage shook her. The glass valves had closed, she could not go back. She saw, at the end of the vestibule, the lift in which she had ascended going quietly up and down, empty. Beneath those corridors of shining tiles were rooms, tier below tier, reaching far into the earth, and in each room there sat a human being, eating, or sleeping, or producing ideas. And buried deep in the hive was her own room. Vashti was afraid.

"O Machine!" she murmured, and caressed her Book, and was comforted. Then the sides of the vestibule seemed to melt together, as do the passages that we see in dreams, the lift vanished, the Book that had been dropped slid to the left and vanished, polished tiles rushed by like a stream of water, there was a slight jar, and the air-ship, issuing from its tunnel, soared above the waters of a tropical ocean.

It was night. For a moment she saw the coast of Sumatra edged by the phosphorescence of waves, and crowned by lighthouses, still sending forth their disregarded beams. These also vanished, and only the stars distracted her. They were not motionless, but swayed to and fro above her head, thronging out of one skylight into another, as if the universe and not the air-ship was careening. And, as often happens on clear nights, they seemed now to be in perspective, now on a plane; now piled tier beyond tier into the infinite heavens, now concealing infinity, a roof limiting for ever the visions of men. In either case they seemed intolerable. "Are we to travel in the dark?" called the passengers angrily, and the attendant, who had been careless, generated the light, and pulled down the blinds of pliable metal. When the air-ships had been built, the desire to look direct at things still lingered in the world. Hence the extraordinary number of skylights and windows, and the proportionate discomfort to those who were civilized and refined. Even in Vashti's cabin one star peeped through a flaw in the blind, and after a few hours' uneasy slumber, she was disturbed by an unfamiliar glow, which was the dawn.

Quick as the ship had sped westwards, the earth had rolled eastwards quicker still, and had dragged back Vashti and her companions towards the sun. Science could prolong the night, but only for a little, and those high hopes of neutralizing the earth's diurnal revolution had passed, together with hopes that were possibly higher. To "keep pace with the sun," or even to outstrip it, had been the aim of the civilization preceding this. Racing aeroplanes had been built for the purpose, capable of enormous speed, and steered by the greatest intellects of the epoch. Round the globe they went, round and round, westward, westward, round and round, amidst humanity's applause. In vain. The globe went eastward quicker still, horrible accidents occurred, and the Committee of the Machine, at the time rising into prominence, declared the pursuit illegal, unmechanical, and punishable by Homelessness. Of Homelessness more will be said later.

Doubtless the Committee was right. Yet the attempt to "defeat the sun" aroused the last common interest that our race experienced about the heavenly bodies, or indeed about anything. It was the last time that men were compacted by thinking of a power outside the world. The sun had conquered, yet it was the end of his spiritual dominion. Dawn, midday, twilight, the zodiacal path, touched neither men's lives not their hearts, and science retreated into the ground, to concentrate herself upon problems that she was certain of solving.

So when Vashti found her cabin invaded by a rosy finger of light, she was annoyed, and tried to adjust the blind. But the blind flew up altogether, and she saw through the skylight small pink clouds, swaying against a background of blue, and as the sun crept higher, its radiance entered direct, brimming down the wall, like a golden sea. It rose and fell with the air-ship's motion, just as waves rise and fall, but it advanced steadily, as a tide advances. Unless she was careful, it would strike her face. A spasm of horror shook her and she rang for the attendant. The attendant too was horrified, but she could do nothing; it was not her place to mend the blind. She could only suggest that the lady should change her cabin, which she accordingly prepared to do.

People were almost exactly alike all over the world, but the attendant of the air-ship, perhaps owing to her exceptional duties, had grown a little out of the common. She had often to address passengers with direct speech, and this had given her a certain roughness and originality of manner. When Vashti swerved away from the sunbeams with a cry, she behaved barbarically — she put out her hand to steady her.

"How dare you!" exclaimed the passenger. "You forget yourself!"

The woman was confused, and apologized for not having let her fall. People never touched one another. The custom had become obsolete, owing to the Machine.

"Where are we now?" asked Vashti haughtily.

"We are over Asia," said the attendant, anxious to be polite.

"Asia?"

"You must excuse my common way of speaking. I have got into the habit of calling places over which I pass by their unmechanical names."

"Oh, I remember Asia. The Mongols came from it."

"Beneath us, in the open air, stood a city that was once called Simla."

"Have you ever heard of the Mongols and of the Brisbane school?"

"No."

"Brisbane also stood in the open air."

"Those mountains to the right — let me show you them." She pushed back a metal blind. The main chain of the Himalayas was revealed. "They were once called the Roof of the World, those mountains."

"What a foolish name!"

"You must remember that, before the dawn of civilization, they seemed to be an impenetrable wall that touched the stars. It was supposed that no one but the gods could exist above their summits. How we have advanced, thanks to the Machine!"

"How we have advanced, thanks to the Machine!" said Vashti.

"How we have advanced, thanks to the Machine!" echoed the passenger who had dropped his Book the night before, and who was standing in the passage.

"And that white stuff in the cracks? — what is it?"

"I have forgotten its name."

"Cover the window, please. These mountains give me no ideas." The northern aspect of the Himalayas was in deep shadow: on the Indian slope the sun had just prevailed. The forests had been destroyed during the literature epoch for the purpose of making newspaper-pulp, but the snows were awakening to their morning glory, and clouds still hung on the breasts of Kinchinjunga. In the plain were seen the ruins of cities, with diminished rivers creeping by their walls, and by the sides of these were sometimes the signs of vomitories, marking the cities of to-day. Over the whole prospect air-ships rushed, crossing the inter-crossing with incredible aplomb, and rising nonchalantly when they desired to escape the perturbations of the lower atmosphere and to traverse the Roof of the World.

"We have indeed advanced, thanks to the Machine," repeated the attendant, and hid the Himalayas behind a metal blind. The day dragged wearily forward. The passengers sat each in his cabin, avoiding one another with an almost physical repulsion and longing to be once more under the surface of the earth. There were eight or ten of them, mostly young males, sent out from the public nurseries to inhabit the rooms of those who had died in various parts of the earth. The man who had dropped his Book was on the homeward journey. He had been sent to Sumatra for the purpose of propagating the race. Vashti alone was travelling by her private will. At midday she took a second glance at the earth. The air-ship was crossing another range of mountains, but she could see little, owing to clouds. Masses of black rock hovered below her, and merged indistinctly into grey. Their shapes were fantastic; one of them resembled a prostrate man.

"No ideas here," murmured Vashti, and hid the Caucasus behind a metal blind. In the evening she looked again. They were crossing a golden sea, in which lay many small islands and one peninsula. She repeated, "No ideas here," and hid Greece behind a metal blind.

2: THE MENDING APPARATUS

By a vestibule, by a lift, by a tubular railway, by a platform, by a sliding door — by reversing all the steps of her departure did Vashti arrive at her son's room, which exactly resembled her own. She might well declare that the visit was superfluous. The buttons, the knobs, the reading-desk with the Book, the temperature, the atmosphere, the illumination — all were exactly the same. And if Kuno himself, flesh of her flesh, stood close beside her at last, what profit was there in that? She was too well-bred to shake him by the hand. Averting her eyes, she spoke as follows:

"Here I am. I have had the most terrible journey and greatly retarded the development of my soul. It is not worth it, Kuno, it is not worth it. My time is too precious. The sunlight almost touched me, and I have met with the rudest people. I can only stop a few minutes. Say what you want to say, and then I must return."

"I have been threatened with Homelessness," said Kuno. She looked at him now.

"I have been threatened with Homelessness, and I could not tell you such a thing through the Machine." Homelessness means death. The victim is exposed to the air, which kills him.

"I have been outside since I spoke to you last. The tremendous thing has happened, and they have discovered me."

"But why shouldn't you go outside?" she exclaimed, "It is perfectly legal, perfectly mechanical, to visit the surface of the earth. I have lately been to a lecture on the sea; there is no objection to that; one simply summons a respirator and gets an Egression-permit. It is not the kind of thing that spiritually minded people do, and I begged you not to do it, but there is no legal objection to it."

"I did not get an Egression-permit."

"Then how did you get out?"

"I found out a way of my own."

The phrase conveyed no meaning to her, and he had to repeat it.

"A way of your own?" she whispered. "But that would be wrong."

"Why?"

The question shocked her beyond measure.

"You are beginning to worship the Machine," he said coldly. "You think it irreligious of me to have found out a way of my own. It was just what the Committee thought, when they threatened me with Homelessness."

At this she grew angry. "I worship nothing!" she cried. "I am most advanced. I don't think you irreligious, for there is no such thing as religion left. All the fear and the superstition that existed once have been destroyed by the Machine. I only meant that to find out a way of your own was— Besides, there is no new way out."

"So it is always supposed."

"Except through the vomitories, for which one must have an Egression-permit, it is impossible to get out. The Book says so."

"Well, the Book's wrong, for I have been out on my feet."

For Kuno was possessed of a certain physical strength. By these days it was a demerit to be muscular. Each infant was examined at birth, and all who promised undue strength were destroyed. Humanitarians may protest, but it would have been no true kindness to let an athlete live; he would never have been happy in that state of life to which the Machine had called him; he would have yearned for trees to climb, rivers to bathe in, meadows and hills against which he might measure his body. Man must be adapted to his surroundings, must he not? In the dawn of the world our weakly must be exposed on Mount Taygetus, in its twilight our strong will suffer euthanasia, that the Machine may progress, that the Machine may progress, that the Machine may progress eternally.

"You know that we have lost the sense of space. We say 'space is annihilated,' but we have annihilated not space, but the sense thereof. We have lost a part of ourselves. I determined to recover it, and I began by walking up and down the platform of the railway outside my room. Up and down, until I was tired, and so did recapture the meaning of 'Near' and 'Far.' 'Near' is a place to which I can get quickly on my feet, not a place to which the train or the air-ship will take me quickly. 'Far' is a place to which I cannot get quickly on my feet; the vomitory is 'far,' though I could be there in thirty-eight seconds by summoning the train. Man is the measure. That was my first lesson. Man's feet are the measure for distance, his hands are the measure for ownership, his body is the measure for all that is lovable and desirable and strong. Then I went further: it was then that I called to you for the first time, and you would not come.

"This city, as you know, is built deep beneath the surface of the earth, with only the vomitories protruding. Having paced the platform outside my own room, I took the lift to the next platform and paced that also, and so with each in turn, until I came to the topmost, above which begins the earth. All the platforms were exactly alike, and all that I gained by visiting them was to develop my sense of space and my muscles. I think I should have been content with this — it is not a little thing — but as I walked and brooded, it occurred to me that our cities had been built in the days when men still breathed the outer air, and that there had been ventilation shafts for the workmen. I could think of nothing but these ventilation shafts. Had they been destroyed by all the food-tubes and medicine-tubes and music-tubes that the Machine has evolved lately? Or did traces of them remain? One thing was certain. If I came upon them anywhere, it would be in the railway-tunnels of the topmost story. Everywhere else, all space was accounted for.

"I am telling my story quickly, but don't think that I was not a coward or that your answers never depressed me. It is not the proper thing, it is not mechanical, it is not decent to walk along a railway-tunnel. I did not fear that I might tread upon a live rail and be killed. I feared something far more intangible — doing what was not contemplated by the Machine. Then I said to myself, 'Man is the measure,' and I went, and after many visits I found an opening.

"The tunnels, of course, were lighted. Everything is light, artificial light; darkness is the exception. So when I saw a black gap in the tiles, I knew that it was an exception, and rejoiced. I put in my arm — I could put in no more at first — and waved it round and round in ecstasy. I loosened another tile, and put in my head, and shouted into the darkness: 'I am coming, I shall do it yet,' and my voice reverberated down endless passages. I seemed to hear the spirits of those dead workmen who had returned each evening to the starlight and to their wives, and all the generations who had lived in the open air called back to me, 'You will do it yet, you are coming.'"

He paused, and, absurd as he was, his last words moved her. For Kuno had lately asked to be a father, and his request had been refused by the Committee. His was not a type that the Machine desired to hand on.

"Then a train passed. It brushed by me, but I thrust my head and arms into the hole. I had done enough for one day, so I crawled back to the platform, went down in the lift, and summoned my bed. Ah what dreams! And again I called you, and again you refused."

She shook her head and said: "Don't. Don't talk of these terrible things. You make me miserable. You are throwing civilization away."

"But I had got back the sense of space and a man cannot rest then. I determined to get in at the hole and climb the shaft. And so I exercised my arms. Day after day I went through ridiculous movements, until my flesh ached, and I could hang by my hands and hold the pillow of my bed outstretched for many minutes. Then I summoned a respirator, and started.

"It was easy at first. The mortar had somehow rotted, and I soon pushed some more tiles in, and clambered after them into the darkness, and the spirits of the dead comforted me. I don't know what I mean by that. I just say what I felt. I felt, for the first time, that a protest had been lodged against corruption, and that even as the dead were comforting me, so I was comforting the unborn. I felt that humanity existed, and that it existed without clothes. How can I possibly explain this? It was naked, humanity seemed naked, and all these tubes and buttons and machineries neither came into the world with us, nor will they follow us out, nor do they matter supremely while we are here. Had I been strong, I would have torn off every garment I had, and gone out into the outer air unswaddled. But this is not for me, nor perhaps for my generation. I climbed with my respirator and my hygienic clothes and my dietetic tabloids! Better thus than not at all.

"There was a ladder, made of some primæval metal. The light from the railway fell upon its lowest rungs, and I saw that it led straight upwards out of the rubble at the bottom of the shaft. Perhaps our ancestors ran up and down it a dozen times daily, in their building. As I climbed, the rough edges cut through my gloves so that my hands bled. The light helped me for a little, and then came darkness and, worse still, silence which pierced my ears like a sword. The Machine hums! Did you know that? Its hum penetrates our blood, and may even guide our thoughts. Who knows! I was getting beyond its power. Then I thought: 'This silence means that I am doing wrong.' But I heard voices in the silence, and again they strengthened me." He laughed. "I had need of them. The next moment I cracked my head against something."

She sighed.

"I had reached one of those pneumatic stoppers that defend us from the outer air. You may have noticed them on the air-ship. Pitch dark, my feet on the rungs of an invisible ladder, my hands cut; I cannot explain how I lived through this part, but the voices still comforted me, and I felt for fastenings. The stopper, I suppose, was about eight feet across. I passed my hand over it as far as I could reach. It was perfectly smooth. I felt it almost to the centre. Not quite to the centre, for my arm was too short. Then the voice said: 'Jump. It is worth it. There may be a handle in the centre, and you may catch hold of it and so come to us your own way. And if there is no handle, so that you may fall and are dashed to pieces — it is still worth it: you will still come to us your own way.' So I jumped. There was a handle, and —"

He paused. Tears gathered in his mother's eyes. She knew that he was fated. If he did not die to-day he would die to-morrow. There was not room for such a person in the world. And with her pity disgust mingled. She was ashamed at having borne such a son, she who had always been so respectable and so full of ideas. Was he really the little boy to whom she had taught the use of his stops and buttons, and to whom she had given his first lessons in the Book? The very hair that disfigured his lip showed that he was reverting to some savage type. On atavism the Machine can have no mercy.

"There was a handle, and I did catch it. I hung tranced over the darkness and heard the hum of these workings as the last whisper in a dying dream. All the things I had cared about and all the people I had spoken to through tubes appeared infinitely little. Meanwhile the handle revolved. My weight had set something in motion and I span slowly, and then— "I cannot describe it. I was lying with my face to the sunshine. Blood poured from my nose and ears and I heard a tremendous roaring. The stopper, with me clinging to it, had simply been blown out of the earth, and the air that we make down here was escaping through the vent into the air above. It burst up like a fountain. I crawled back to it — for the upper air hurts — and, as it were, I took great sips from the edge. My respirator had flown goodness knows where, my clothes were torn. I just lay with my lips close to the hole, and I sipped until the bleeding stopped. You can imagine nothing so curious. This hollow in the grass — I will speak of it in a minute, — the sun shining into it, not brilliantly but through marbled clouds, — the peace, the nonchalance, the sense of space, and, brushing my cheek, the roaring fountain of our artificial air! Soon I spied my respirator, bobbing up and down in the current high above my head, and higher still were many air-ships. But no one ever looks out of air-ships, and in any case they could not have picked me up. There I was, stranded. The sun shone a little way down the shaft, and revealed the topmost rung of the ladder, but it was hopeless trying to reach it. I should either have been tossed up again by the escape, or else have fallen in, and died. I could only lie on the grass, sipping and sipping, and from time to time glancing around me.

"I knew that I was in Wessex, for I had taken care to go to a lecture on the subject before starting. Wessex lies above the room in which we are talking now. It was once an important state. Its kings held all the southern coast from the Andredswald to Cornwall, while the Wansdyke protected them on the north, running over the high ground. The lecturer was only concerned with the rise of Wessex, so I do not know how long it remained an international power, nor would the knowledge have assisted me. To tell the truth I could do nothing but laugh, during this part. There was I, with a pneumatic stopper by my side and a respirator bobbing over my head, imprisoned, all three of us, in a grass-grown hollow that was edged with fern."

Then he grew grave again.

"Lucky for me that it was a hollow. For the air began to fall back into it and to fill it as water fills a bowl. I could crawl about. Presently I stood. I breathed a mixture, in which the air that hurts predominated whenever I tried to climb the sides. This was not so bad. I had not lost my tabloids and remained ridiculously cheerful, and as for the Machine, I forgot about it altogether. My one aim now was to get to the top, where the ferns were, and to view whatever objects lay beyond.

"I rushed the slope. The new air was still too bitter for me and I came rolling back, after a momentary vision of something grey. The sun grew very feeble, and I remembered that he was in Scorpio — I had been to a lecture on that too. If the sun is in Scorpio, and you are in Wessex, it means that you must be as quick as you can, or it will get too dark. (This is the first bit of useful information I have ever got from a lecture, and I expect it will be the last.) It made me try frantically to breathe the new air, and to advance as far as I dared out of my pond. The hollow filled so slowly. At times I thought that the fountain played with less vigour. My respirator seemed to dance nearer the earth; the roar was decreasing."

He broke off.

"I don't think this is interesting you. The rest will interest you even less. There are no ideas in it, and I wish that I had not troubled you to come. We are too different, mother."

She told him to continue.

"It was evening before I climbed the bank. The sun had very nearly slipped out of the sky by this time, and I could not get a good view. You, who have just crossed the Roof of the World, will not want to hear an account of the little hills that I saw — low colourless hills. But to me they were living and the turf that covered them was a skin, under which their muscles rippled, and I felt that those hills had called with incalculable force to men in the past, and that men had loved them. Now they sleep — perhaps for ever. They commune with humanity in dreams. Happy the man, happy the woman, who awakes the hills of Wessex. For though they sleep, they will never die."

His voice rose passionately.

"Cannot you see, cannot all you lecturers see, that it is we that are dying, and that down here the only thing that really lives is the Machine? We created the Machine, to do our will, but we cannot make it do our will now. It has robbed us of the sense of space and of the sense of touch, it has blurred every human relation and narrowed down love to a carnal act, it has paralysed our bodies and our wills, and now it compels us to worship it. The Machine develops — but not on our lines. The Machine proceeds — but not to our goal.

We only exist as the blood corpuscles that course through its arteries, and if it could work without us, it would let us die. Oh, I have no remedy — or, at least, only one — to tell men again and again that I have seen the hills of Wessex as Ælfrid saw them when he overthrew the Danes.

"So the sun set. I forgot to mention that a belt of mist lay between my hill and other hills, and that it was the colour of pearl."

He broke off for the second time.

"Go on," said his mother wearily.

He shook his head.

"Go on. Nothing that you say can distress me now. I am hardened."

"I had meant to tell you the rest, but I cannot: I know that I cannot: good-bye."

Vashti stood irresolute. All her nerves were tingling with his blasphemies. But she was also inquisitive. "This is unfair," she complained. "You have called me across the world to hear your story, and hear it I will. Tell me — as briefly as possible, for this is a disastrous waste of time — tell me how you returned to civilization."

"Oh — that!" he said, starting. "You would like to hear about civilization. Certainly. Had I got to where my respirator fell down?"

"No — but I understand everything now. You put on your respirator, and managed to walk along the surface of the earth to a vomitory, and there your conduct was reported to the Central Committee."

"By no means."

He passed his hand over his forehead, as if dispelling some strong impression. Then, resuming his narrative, he warmed to it again.

"My respirator fell about sunset. I had mentioned that the fountain seemed feebler, had I not?"

"Yes."

"About sunset, it let the respirator fall. As I said, I had entirely forgotten about the

Machine, and I paid no great attention at the time, being occupied with other things. I had my pool of air, into which I could dip when the outer keenness became intolerable, and which would possibly remain for days, provided that no wind sprang up to disperse it. Not until it was too late did I realize what the stoppage of the escape implied. You see — the gap in the tunnel had been mended; the Mending Apparatus; the Mending Apparatus, was after me.

"One other warning I had, but I neglected it. The sky at night was clearer than it had been in the day, and the moon, which was about half the sky behind the sun, shone into the dell at moments quite brightly. I was in my usual place — on the boundary between the two atmospheres

— when I thought I saw something dark move across the bottom of the dell, and vanish into the shaft. In my folly, I ran down. I bent over and listened, and I thought I heard a faint scraping noise in the depths.

"At this — but it was too late — I took alarm. I determined to put on my respirator and to walk right out of the dell. But my respirator had gone. I knew exactly where it had fallen — between the stopper and the aperture — and I could even feel the mark that it had made in the turf. It had one, and I realized that something evil was at work, and I had better escape to the other air, and, if I must die, die running towards the cloud that had been the colour of a pearl. I never started. Out of the shaft — it is too horrible. A worm, a long white worm, had crawled out of the shaft and was gliding over the moonlit grass.

"I screamed. I did everything that I should not have done, I stamped upon the creature instead of flying from it, and it at once curled round the ankle. Then we fought. The worm let me run all over the dell, but edged up my leg as I ran. 'Help!' I cried. (That part is too awful. It belongs to the part that you will never know.) 'Help!' I cried. (Why cannot we suffer in silence?) 'Help!' I cried. Then my feet were wound together, I fell, I was dragged away from the dear ferns and the living hills, and past the great metal stopper (I can tell you this part), and I thought it might save me again if I caught hold of the handle. It also was enwrapped, it also. Oh, the whole dell was full of the things. They were searching it in all directions, they were denuding it, and the white snouts of others peeped out of the hole, ready if needed. Everything that could be moved they brought — brushwood, bundles of fern, everything, and down we all went intertwined into hell. The last things that I saw, ere the stopper closed after us, were certain stars, and I felt that a man of my sort lived in the sky. For I did fight, I fought till the very end, and it was only my head hitting against the ladder that quieted me. I woke up in this room. The worms had vanished. I was surrounded by artificial air, artificial light, artificial peace, and my friends were calling to me down speaking-tubes to know whether I had come across any new ideas lately."

Here his story ended. Discussion of it was impossible, and Vashti turned to go.

"It will end in Homelessness," she said quietly.

"I wish it would," retorted Kuno.

"The Machine has been most merciful."

"I prefer the mercy of God."

"By that superstitious phrase, do you mean that you could live in the outer air?"

"Yes."

"Have you ever seen, round the vomitories, the bones of those who were extruded after the Great Rebellion?"

"Yes."

"They were left where they perished for our edification. A few crawled away, but they perished, too — who can doubt it? And so with the Homeless of our own day. The surface of the earth supports life no longer."

"Indeed."

"Ferns and a little grass may survive, but all higher forms have perished. Has any air-ship detected them?"

"No."

"Has any lecturer dealt with them?"

"No."

"Then why this obstinacy?"

"Because I have seen them," he exploded.

"Seen what?"

"Because I have seen her in the twilight — because she came to my help when I called— because she, too, was entangled by the worms, and, luckier than I, was killed by one of them piercing her throat."

He was mad. Vashti departed, nor, in the troubles that followed, did she ever see his face again.

3: THE HOMELESS

During the years that followed Kuno's escapade, two important developments took place in the Machine. On the surface they were revolutionary, but in either case men's minds had been prepared beforehand, and they did but express tendencies that were latent already. The first of these was the abolition of respirators. Advanced thinkers, like Vashti, had always held it foolish to visit the surface of the earth. Air-ships might be necessary, but what was the good of going out for mere curiosity and crawling along for a mile or two in a terrestrial motor? The habit was vulgar and perhaps faintly improper: it was unproductive of ideas, and had no connection with the habits that really mattered. So respirators were abolished, and with them, of course, the terrestrial motors, and except for a few lecturers, who complained that they were debarred access to their subject-matter, the development was accepted quietly. Those who still wanted to know what the earth was like had after all only to listen to some gramophone, or to look into some cinematophote. And even the lecturers acquiesced when they found that a lecture on the sea was none the less stimulating when compiled out of other lectures that had already been delivered on the same subject. "Beware of first-hand ideas!" exclaimed one of the most advanced of them. "First-hand ideas do not really exist. They are but the physical impressions produced by love and fear, and on this gross foundation who could erect a philosophy? Let your ideas be second-hand, and if possible tenth-hand, for then they will be far removed from that disturbing element — direct observation. Do not learn anything about this subject of mine — the French Revolution. Learn instead what I think that Enicharmon thought Urizen thought Gutch thought Ho-Yung thought Chi-Bo-Sing thought Lafcadio Hearn thought Carlyle thought Mirabeau said about the French Revolution.

Through the medium of these ten great minds, the blood that was shed at Paris and the windows that were broken at Versailles will be clarified to an idea which you may employ most profitably in your daily lives. But be sure that the intermediates are many and varied, for in history one authority exists to counteract another. Urizen must counteract the scepticism of Ho-Yung and Enicharmon, I must myself counteract the impetuosity of Gutch. You who listen to me are in a better position to judge about the French Revolution than I am. Your descendants will be even in a better position than you, for they will learn what you think I think, and yet another intermediate will be added to the chain. And in time" — his voice rose — "there will come a generation that had got beyond facts, beyond impressions, a generation absolutely colourless, a generation 'seraphically free From taint of personality,' which will see the French Revolution not as it happened, nor as they would like it to have happened, but as it would have happened, had it taken place in the days of the Machine." Tremendous applause greeted this lecture, which did but voice a feeling already latent in the minds of men — a feeling that terrestrial facts must be ignored, and that the abolition of respirators was a positive gain. It was even suggested that air-ships should be abolished too. This was not done, because air-ships had somehow worked themselves into the Machine's system. But year by year they were used less, and mentioned less by thoughtful men. The second great development was the re-establishment of religion. This, too, had been voiced in the celebrated lecture. No one could mistake the reverent tone in which the peroration had concluded, and it awakened a responsive echo in the heart of each. Those who had long worshipped silently, now began to talk. They described the strange feeling of peace that came over them when they handled the Book of the Machine, the pleasure that it was to repeat certain numerals out of it, however little meaning those numerals conveyed to the outward ear, the ecstasy of touching a button, however unimportant, or of ringing an electric bell, however superfluously.

"The Machine," they exclaimed, "feeds us and clothes us and houses us; through it we speak to one another, through it we see one another, in it we have our being. The Machine is the friend of ideas and the enemy of superstition: the Machine is omnipotent, eternal; blessed is the Machine." And before long this allocution was printed on the first page of the Book, and in subsequent editions the ritual swelled into a complicated system of praise and prayer. The word "religion" was sedulously avoided, and in theory the Machine was still the creation and the implement of man. But in practice all, save a few retrogrades, worshipped it as divine. Nor was it worshipped in unity. One believer would be chiefly impressed by the blue optic plates, through which he saw other believers; another by the mending apparatus, which sinful Kuno had compared to worms; another by the lifts, another by the Book. And each would pray to this or to that, and ask it to intercede for him with the Machine as a whole. Persecution — that also was present. It did not break out, for reasons that will be set forward shortly. But it was latent, and all who did not accept the minimum known as "undenominational Mechanism" lived in danger of Homelessness, which means death, as we know.

To attribute these two great developments to the Central Committee, is to take a very narrow view of civilization. The Central Committee announced the developments, it is true, but they were no more the cause of them than were the kings of the imperialistic period the cause of war. Rather did they yield to some invincible pressure, which came no one knew whither, and which, when gratified, was succeeded by some new pressure equally invincible. To such a state of affairs it is convenient to give the name of progress. No one confessed the Machine was out of hand. Year by year it was served with increased efficiency and decreased intelligence. The better a man knew his own duties upon it, the less he understood the duties of his neighbour, and in all the world there was not one who understood the monster as a whole. Those master brains had perished. They had left full directions, it is true, and their successors had each of them mastered a portion of those directions. But Humanity, in its desire for comfort, had over-reached itself. It had exploited the riches of nature too far. Quietly and complacently, it was sinking into decadence, and progress had come to mean the progress of the Machine.

As for Vashti, her life went peacefully forward until the final disaster. She made her room dark and slept; she awoke and made the room light. She lectured and attended lectures. She exchanged ideas with her innumerable friends and believed she was growing more spiritual. At times a friend was granted Euthanasia, and left his or her room for the homelessness that is beyond all human conception. Vashti did not much mind. After an unsuccessful lecture, she would sometimes ask for Euthanasia herself. But the death-rate was not permitted to exceed the birth-rate, and the Machine had hitherto refused it to her. The troubles began quietly, long before she was conscious of them.

One day she was astonished at receiving a message from her son. They never communicated, having nothing in common, and she had only heard indirectly that he was still alive, and had been transferred from the northern hemisphere, where he had behaved so mischievously, to the southern — indeed, to a room not far from her own. "Does he want me to visit him?" she thought. "Never again, never. And I have not the time."

No, it was madness of another kind.

He refused to visualize his face upon the blue plate, and speaking out of the darkness with solemnity said:

"The Machine stops."

"What do you say?"

"The Machine is stopping, I know it, I know the signs."

She burst into a peal of laughter. He heard her and was angry, and they spoke no more.

"Can you imagine anything more absurd?" she cried to a friend. "A man who was my son believes that the Machine is stopping. It would be impious if it was not mad."

"The Machine is stopping?" her friend replied. "What does that mean? The phrase conveys nothing to me."

"Nor to me."

"He does not refer, I suppose, to the trouble there has been lately with the music?"

"Oh no, of course not. Let us talk about music."

"Have you complained to the authorities?"

"Yes, and they say it wants mending, and referred me to the Committee of the Mending Apparatus. I complained of those curious gasping sighs that disfigure the symphonies of the Brisbane school. They sound like some one in pain. The Committee of the Mending Apparatus say that it shall be remedied shortly."

Obscurely worried, she resumed her life. For one thing, the defect in the music irritated her. For another thing, she could not forget Kuno's speech. If he had known that the music was out of repair — he could not know it, for he detested music — if he had known that it was wrong, "the Machine stops" was exactly the venomous sort of remark he would have made. Of course he had made it at a venture, but the coincidence annoyed her, and she spoke with some petulance to the Committee of the Mending Apparatus.

They replied, as before, that the defect would be set right shortly.

"Shortly! At once!" she retorted. "Why should I be worried by imperfect music? Things are always put right at once. If you do not mend it at once, I shall complain to the Central Committee."

"No personal complaints are received by the Central Committee," the Committee of the Mending Apparatus replied.

"Through whom am I to make my complaint, then?"

"Through us."

"I complain then."

"Your complaint shall be forwarded in its turn."

"Have others complained?"

This question was unmechanical, and the Committee of the Mending Apparatus refused to answer it.

"It is too bad!" she exclaimed to another of her friends. "There never was such an unfortunate woman as myself. I can never be sure of my music now. It gets worse and worse each time I summon it."

"I too have my troubles," the friend replied. "Sometimes my ideas are interrupted by a slight jarring noise."

"What is it?"

330

"I do not know whether it is inside my head, or inside the wall."

"Complain, in either case."

"I have complained, and my complaint will be forwarded in its turn to the Central Committee."

Time passed, and they resented the defects no longer. The defects had not been remedied, but the human tissues in that latter day had become so <u>subservient</u>, that they readily adapted themselves to every caprice of the Machine. The sigh at the crises of the Brisbane symphony no longer irritated Vashti; she accepted it as part of the melody. The jarring noise, whether in the head or in the wall, was no longer resented by her friend. And so with the mouldy artificial fruit, so with the bath water that began to stink, so with the defective rhymes that the poetry machine had taken to emit. All were bitterly complained of at first, and then acquiesced in and forgotten. Things went from bad to worse unchallenged.

It was otherwise with the failure of the sleeping apparatus. That was a more serious stoppage. There came a day when over the whole world — in Sumatra, in Wessex, in the innumerable cities of Courland and Brazil — the beds, when summoned by their tired owners, failed to appear. It may seem a ludicrous matter, but from it we may date the collapse of humanity. The Committee responsible for the failure was assailed by complainants, whom it referred, as usual, to the Committee of the Mending Apparatus, who in its turn assured them that their complaints would be forwarded to the Central Committee. But the discontent grew, for mankind was not yet sufficiently adaptable to do without sleeping.

"Some one is meddling with the Machine—" they began.

"Some one is trying to make himself king, to reintroduce the personal element."

"Punish that man with Homelessness."

"To the rescue! Avenge the Machine! Avenge the Machine!"

"War! Kill the man!"

But the Committee of the Mending Apparatus now came forward, and allayed the panic with well-chosen words. It confessed that the Mending Apparatus was itself in need of repair.

The effect of this frank confession was admirable.

"Of course," said a famous lecturer — he of the French Revolution, who gilded each new decay with splendour — "of course we shall not press our complaints now. The Mending Apparatus has treated us so well in the past that we all sympathize with it, and will wait patiently for its recovery. In its own good time it will resume its duties. Meanwhile let us do without our beds, our tabloids, our other little wants. Such, I feel sure, would be the wish of the Machine."

Thousands of miles away his audience applauded. The Machine still linked them. Under the seas, beneath the roots of the mountains, ran the wires through which they saw and heard, the enormous eyes and ears that were their heritage, and the hum of many workings clothed their thoughts in one garment of subserviency. Only the old and the sick remained ungrateful, for it was rumoured that Euthanasia, too, was out of order, and that pain had reappeared among men.

It became difficult to read. A blight entered the atmosphere and dulled its luminosity. At times Vashti could scarcely see across her room. The air, too, was foul. Loud were the complaints, impotent the remedies, heroic the tone of the lecturer as he cried: "Courage! courage! What matter so long as the Machine goes on? To it the darkness and the light are one." And though things improved again after a time, the old brilliancy was never recaptured, and humanity never recovered from its entrance into twilight. There was an hysterical talk of "measures," of "provisional dictatorship," and the inhabitants of Sumatra were asked to familiarize themselves with the workings of the central power station, the said power station being situated in France. But for the most part panic reigned, and men spent their strength praying to their Books, tangible proofs of the Machine's omnipotence. There were gradations of terror — at times came rumours of hope — the Mending Apparatus was almost mended — the enemies of the Machine had been got under — new "nerve-centres" were evolving which would do the work even more magnificently than before. But there came a day when, without the slightest warning, without any previous hint of feebleness, the entire communication-system broke down, all over the world, and the world, as they understood it, ended.

Vashti was lecturing at the time and her earlier remarks had been punctuated with applause. As she proceeded the audience became silent, and at the conclusion there was no sound. Somewhat displeased, she called to a friend who was a specialist in sympathy. No sound: doubtless the friend was sleeping. And so with the next friend whom she tried to summon, and so with the next, until she remembered Kuno's cryptic remark, "The Machine stops".

The phrase still conveyed nothing. If Eternity was stopping it would of course be set going shortly. For example, there was still a little light and air — the atmosphere had improved a few hours previously. There was still the Book, and while there was the Book there was security.

Then she broke down, for with the cessation of activity came an unexpected terror — silence.

She had never known silence, and the coming of it nearly killed her — it did kill many thousands of people outright. Ever since her birth she had been surrounded by the steady hum. It was to the ear what artificial air was to the lungs, and agonizing pains shot across her head. And scarcely knowing what she did, she stumbled forward and pressed the unfamiliar button, the one that opened the door of her cell.

Now the door of the cell worked on a simple hinge of its own. It was not connected with the central power station, dying far away in France. It opened, rousing immoderate hopes in Vashti, for she thought that the Machine had been mended. It opened, and she saw the dim tunnel that curved far away towards freedom. One look, and then she shrank back.

For the tunnel was full of people — she was almost the last in that city to have taken alarm. People at any time repelled her, and these were nightmares from her worst dreams. People were crawling about, people were screaming, whimpering, gasping for breath, touching each other, vanishing in the dark, and ever and anon being pushed off the platform on to the live rail. Some were fighting round the electric bells, trying to summon trains which could not be summoned. Others were yelling for Euthanasia or for respirators, or blaspheming the Machine. Others stood at the doors of their cells fearing, like herself, either to stop in them or to leave them. And behind all the uproar was silence — the silence which is the voice of the earth and of the generations who have gone.

No — it was worse than solitude. She closed the door again and sat down to wait for the end. The disintegration went on, accompanied by horrible cracks and rumbling. The valves that restrained the Medical Apparatus must have weakened, for it ruptured and hung hideously from the ceiling. The floor heaved and fell and flung her from the chair. A tube oozed towards her serpent fashion. And at last the final horror approached

— light began to ebb, and she knew that civilization's long day was closing.

She whirled around, praying to be saved from this, at any rate, kissing the Book, pressing button after button. The uproar outside was increasing, and even penetrated the wall. Slowly the brilliancy of her cell was dimmed, the reflections faded from the metal switches. Now she could not see the reading-stand, now not the Book, though she held it in her hand. Light followed the flight of sound, air was following light, and the original void returned to the cavern from which it has so long been excluded. Vashti continued to whirl, like the devotees of an earlier religion, screaming, praying, striking at the buttons with bleeding hands.

It was thus that she opened her prison and escaped — escaped in the spirit: at least so it seems to me, ere my meditation closes. That she escapes in the body — I cannot perceive that. She struck, by chance, the switch that released the door, and the rush of foul air on her skin, the loud throbbing whispers in her ears, told her that she was facing the tunnel again, and that tremendous platform on which she had seen men fighting. They were not fighting now. Only the whispers remained, and the little whimpering groans. They were dying by hundreds out in the dark.

She burst into tears.

Tears answered her.

They wept for humanity, those two, not for themselves. They could not bear that this should be the end. Ere silence was completed their hearts were opened, and they knew what had been important on the earth. Man, the flower of all flesh, the noblest of all creatures visible, man who had once made god in his image, and had mirrored his strength on the constellations, beautiful naked man was dying, strangled in the garments that he had woven. Century after century had he toiled, and here was his reward. Truly the garment had seemed heavenly at first, shot with colours of culture, sewn with the threads of selfdenial. And heavenly it had been so long as it was a garment and no more, man could shed it at will and live by the essence that is his soul, and the essence, equally divine, that is his body. The sin against the body — it was for that they wept in chief; the centuries of wrong against the muscles and the nerves, and those five portals by which we can alone apprehend — glozing it over with talk of evolution, until the body was white pap, the home of ideas as colour-less, last sloshy stirrings of a spirit that had grasped the stars.

334

"Where are you?" she sobbed.

His voice in the darkness said, "Here."

"Is there any hope, Kuno?"

"None for us."

"Where are you?"

She crawled over the bodies of the dead. His blood spurted over her hands.

"Quicker," he gasped, "I am dying — but we touch, we talk, not through the Machine."

He kissed her.

"We have come back to our own. We die, but we have recaptured life, as it was in Wessex, when Ælfrid overthrew the Danes. We know what they know outside, they who dwelt in the cloud that is the colour of a pearl."

"But Kuno, is it true? Are there still men on the surface of the earth? Is this — this tunnel, this poisoned darkness — really not the end?"

He replied:

"I have seen them, spoken to them, loved them. They are hiding in the mist and the ferns until our civilization stops. To-day they are the Homeless — to-morrow—"

"Oh, to-morrow — some fool will start the Machine again, to-morrow."

"Never," said Kuno, "never. Humanity has learnt its lesson."

As he spoke, the whole city was broken like a honeycomb. An air-ship had sailed in through the vomitory into a ruined wharf. It crashed downwards, exploding as it went, rending gallery after gallery with its wings of steel. For a moment they saw the nations of the dead, and, before they joined them, scraps of the untainted sky.

COLLEGE WRITING 1: REFLECTION WITHIN THE TEXT

The world in E.M. Forester's tale "The Machine Stops," may seem like a bad episode of Star Trek, but is there something familiar about the idea of "vicarious experience," what with today's Internet and related technologies—Google, Youtube, Amazon, Netflix, and Facebook? What can't we do from the comfort of our own home? We even have "Alexa" (or "smart speakers") to keep us company in lieu of human contact. Reflect on your own life, and consider what it would look like if you rejected "the machine" of today—and sought to "visit the surface," to live life more "directly."

COLLEGE WRITING 2: RESEARCH OUTSIDE THE TEXT

Research the world before the Internet; how did people do research? How did people communicate? How did people know which items were the best ones to buy, without user reviews? How did people find the best places to eat? How did people read the news?

What would happen if the Internet "stopped" tomorrow—how would the world change? How would you change? Would things return to the way they were—or are we forever changed as a species?

And consider this question—has this machine truly improved our lives, or merely changed them?

IDEAS AND VALUES: CONNECT THE TEXT

» In Twain's "The War Prayer" he writes that "The country was up in arms, the war was on, in every breast burned the holy fire of patriotism," when a stranger mounts the stage, declares himself the messenger of God, and explains what the people's "War Prayer" truly means for the enemy. In "Occurrence at Owl Creek Bridge," Peyton Farquhar seems to be the "enemy," the one that doesn't belong—and finally in "The Machine Stops," E.M. Forester writes about a different kind of belonging—not to a nation, but to a way of life; to a machine not unlike today's Internet. These are three different views of belonging; what does it mean to belong? What is it for? What is the "other side" of belonging? In order for one to belong, must there be others who do not belong? What effect does it have, and why do humans do it? Is belonging ultimately a good, or a bad thing?

» In Chopin's "Story of an Hour" Louise Mallard's marriage seems to have ended abruptly with a sudden "railroad accident," and we find her in her room, celebrating her newfound freedom, while in "The Yellow Wallpaper," the narrator's husband uses his role as patriarch and physician to prescribe his wife's country home into a prison. Lastly, in E.M. Forester's "The Machine Stops," Kuno's mother, Vashti becomes increasingly alarmed at her son's rejection of their underground culture, as he derides her unquestioning fealty to the machine as mere worship—and eventually he reveals to her his will to live on the surface. In these three texts there is a force that holds captive one or more person; consider these forces individually, and explore how they operate, their functions, how they came into being, and what good or evil they do. What is the essence of captivity? Why does it exist? Is it pure cruelty—or is there something else?

» In H.G. Wells's "The Star" a mathematician predicts that a celestial body that has collided with Neptune will approach Earth and all manner of nature will wreak havoc on mankind, while in Jack London's "To Build a Fire," the man fails to appreciate the dangers of his surroundings, and finally in "The Machine Stops" a whole society has shut themselves away from "the surface," choosing rather to experience life as indirectly as possible. In these stories we have three visions of man's relationship to nature; what unites them? What makes them different? Is nature a force to be conquered, bent to man's will? Is nature a god to be feared, or even worshipped? Is mankind something set apart from nature—or are we nature as well?

» Humankind has invented the Internet, the telephone, the motor vehicle, air travel, the atomic bomb... Look at Oscar Wilde's "Impressions of America," and his focus on "practical education" and the beauty of American engineering—and then move to "The Gun," when an alien ship approaches Earth but cannot reach it because of Earth's engineering, and then "The Machine Stops," a world in which "the machine" is all that matters—not human progress—but the progress of "the machine." And finally "Earth's Holocaust," in which the people of the world decide to burn everything—all ideas—all progress, all technology. What roll does technological progress play, and what roll should technology play in the progress of mankind? How would you define progress?

APPENDICES

Glossary of Difficult Vocabulary

A

Aggregate—collected into one body.

Allocution—A formal address or exhortation by a general to his soldiers; hence in R.C. Ch. A public address by the Pope to his clergy, or to the Church generally; gen. The action of addressing or exhorting; hortatory or authoritative address.

Anon—in the distance; over there; somewhere (out there).

Aperture—small hole, as in an eye, or camera lense, in which light is let through to expose an image onto film.

Aplomb—'The perpendicular'; perpendicularity; Assurance, confidence, self-possession, coolness; Self-possessed, confident.

Apostle—One sent on an errand, a messenger; the twelve witnesses whom Jesus Christ sent forth to preach his Gospel to the world; also the subsequently-commissioned Barnabas (Acts xiii. 2, xiv. 14), and Paul, the 'Apostle of the Gentiles.'

B

Bacchanal—Of or pertaining to Bacchus or his worship; indulging in drunken revelry; riotous drunken, roystering.

Bawble; bauble— A showy trinket or ornament such as would please a child, a piece of finery of little worth, a pretty trifle, a gewgaw.

Bespoken—custom ordered, or arranged ahead of time.

Bid adieu—say goodbye; bid farewell (a kind of French-ism—from the English bid and the French adieu).

Blockaded—blocked, blocked-off. A blockade stops movement from one place to another.

Bosom—chest.

C

Cadmus—Pertaining to Cadmus, the legendary founder of Thebes in Bœotia, and introducer of the alphabet into Greece. Cadmean victory 'a victory involving one's own ruin' (Liddell and Scott); usually associated with Thebes or the Thebans.

Catharsis—Purgation of the excrements of the body; esp. evacuation of the bowels; the purification of the emotions by vicarious experience, esp. through the drama.

Circuitous—Of the nature of a circuit, roundabout, indirect.

Circumscribed—Having clearly defined limits; Limited, confined, restricted; Of a figure: Described about another.

Citadel—The fortress commanding a city, which it serves both to protect and to keep in subjection.

Commingled—Mingled together, blended (co + mingle).

Commodiously; Commodious—In a commodious manner: †a.a advantageously, profitably (obs.); b.b conveniently, now esp. in respect to ready access and roominess.

Constant—"a constant husband" or a "contant lover," generally means to be faithful, or to never cheat on one's wife or lover.

Contrivance—The action of contriving or ingeniously endeavouring the accomplishment of anything; the bringing to pass by planning, scheming, or stratagem; manœuvring, plotting; deceitful practice.

Corpuscle—A minute body or particle of matter. Sometimes identified with atom or with molecule.

Credulous—Over-ready to believe; apt to believe on weak or insufficient grounds.

Czar—formerly the usual spelling of tsar; The title of the autocrat or emperor of Russia; historically, borne also by Serbian rulers of the 14th c., as the Tsar Stephen Dushan; A person having great authority or absolute power; a tyrant, 'boss'.

D

Damme—Shortened form of damn me! used as a profane imprecation; the oath itself, or an utterance.

Deference—showing your obedience, or your cooperation, or your willingness to take orders.

Desirous—having or showing desire.

Diatetic—In Greek and mediæval music: The interval of a fourth; a medicine composed of four ingredients; A harmony of the four Gospels.

Dictum—A saying or utterance.

Disquiet; Disquieted—To deprive of quietness, peace, or rest, bodily or mental; to trouble, disturb, alarm; to make uneasy or restless; The reverse of quiet; unquiet, restless, uneasy, disturbed.

E

Eloquent; Eloquently—Possessing or exercising the power of fluent, forcible, and appropriate expression.

Embrasure—something that holds, or "embraces" something else; a brace.

Encircled—made a circle around.

Encompass—to circle or girdle round. To surround on all sides. Similar to Encircle.

Erect—standing up.

Etiquette—formal rules of behavior.

Expedience—haste, speed, dispatch; That which requires speed; an enterprise, expedition.

Expostulate—To ask for, demand, claim.

F

Fain—to fake, or pretend

Furgot—forgot.

Feeble—weak.

Fervid—Burning, glowing, hot; intensely impassioned.

Flotsam—Such part of the wreckage of a ship or its cargo as is found floating on the surface of the sea. Usually associated with jetsam.

G

Gait—the way in which one walks or runs.

Gibbet—Originally synonymous with gallows n., but in later use signifying an upright post with projecting arm from which the bodies of criminals were hung in chains or irons after execution.

Gloze; Glozing; Gloss—A comment, or marginal note; an exposition.

Grotesque—horrible, ugly, monster-like.

Guinea—The European name of a portion of the West Coast of Africa, extending from Sierra Leone to Benin; An English gold coin, not coined since 1813, first struck in 1663 with the nominal value of 20s., but from 1717 until its disappearance circulating as legal tender at the rate of 21s

Guise—Manner, method, way; fashion, style

H

Halters—A rope, cord, or strap with a noose or head-stall, by which horses or cattle are led or fastened up.

Hottentot—One of the two sub-races of the Khoisanid race (the other being the Sanids or Bushmen), characterized by short stature, yellow-brown skin colour, and tightly curled hair. They are of mixed Bushman-Hamite descent with some Bantu admixture, and are now found principally in South-West Africa. Also, a member of this race.

Howbeit—how + be + it; however it may be; regardless; anyway.

Hitherto—until now; until then.

I

Importunity—The condition of being unseasonable or inopportune; unseasonableness; an unsuitable time.

Incomparable—not comparable; something for which there is no comparison; something or someone that has no equal.

Incur—to accumulate (debt), or sustain (an injury).

Ineffable—That cannot be expressed or described in language; too great for words; transcending expression; unspeakable, unutterable, inexpressible.

Inexorable—Incapable of being persuaded or moved by entreaty; that cannot be prevailed upon to yield to request, esp. in the way of mercy or indulgence; not to be moved from one's purpose or determination; relentless, rigidly severe. a.a Of persons, their actions or attributes.

Inquire—to ask, or ask about.

Insignia—Badges or distinguishing marks of office or honour; emblems of a nation, person, etc.

Intercede— To come between, in time, space, or action; to intervene.

J

Jetsam—the throwing of goods overboard.

L

Laplander—an inhabitant of Lapland.

Lapland—The region which forms the most northerly portion of the Scandinavian peninsula, now divided politically between Finland, Norway, Sweden, and the Soviet Union.

Letterpress—The text of a piece of printing, distinguished from illustrations, etc; Material printed from a relief surface, distinguished from lithographic or intaglio printing.

M

Manifestations—the way something occurs or appears—"manifestations of respect" could mean a salute, or the reading of last rites, or a last meal, or last words.

Maxim—a self-evident proposition assumed as a premiss in mathematical or dialectical reasoning; a proposition (esp. in aphoristic or sententious form) ostensibly expressing some general truth of science or of experience.

Meagre—thin, bony, emaciated, malnourished, or small amount, as in "meagre rations."

Meridian—mid-day, or noon. The "meridian of Wakefield's life" would essentially mean the middle of Wakefield's life; middle-age; around 35 to 45 years old, or so.

Milliner—one who comes from Milan; also a vendor of fancy wares and apparel.

Moise—To thrive; to increase, improve, mend.

Moulded—shaped, or changed the shape of. To mould is to pour something into a mould, or a container used to shape liquids that will eventually cool and turn solid, like molten steel, or stone, or plastic, or glass. To mould one's mind is to shape one's mind.

Multitudinous—many, multitudes, from multiple.

N

Nonchalant; Nonchalantly—Lacking in warmth of feeling; lacking in enthusiasm or interest; indifferent.

O

Obliquity—slight, indirect; here Wakefield is taking shallow steps, his gait or the way in which he walks, is oblique, or in other words, not a ninety degree angle—shuffling around, dragging his feet.

Odious—Deserving of hatred, hateful; causing or exciting hatred or repugnance, disagreeable, offensive, repulsive; exciting odium.

Officious—Doing or ready to do kind offices; eager to serve or please; attentive, obliging, kind; Unduly forward in proffering services or taking business upon oneself; doing, or prone to do, more than is asked or required; interfering with what is not one's concern; pragmatical, meddlesome.

Opulence—Wealth, riches, affluence; abundance of resources or power.

Oscillate; Oscillation—swinging like a pendulum, or the act thereof.

P

Parable—A comparison, a similitude; any saying or narration in which something is expressed in terms of something else; an allegory, an apologue. Also vaguely extended (chiefly after Heb. or other oriental words so rendered) to any kind of enigmatical, mystical, or dark saying, and to proverbs, maxims, or ancient saws, capable of application to cases as they occur.

Parabolic—like a parable or parabola.

Parabola—One of the conic sections; the plane curve formed by the intersection of a cone with a plane parallel to a side of the cone; also definable as the locus of a point whose distance from a given point (the focus) is equal to its distance from a given straight line (the directrix).

Pecuniary—Consisting of money; exacted in money.

Perfunctory; Perfunctorily—In a perfunctory manner; as a necessary duty to be got rid of; as a matter of mere form or routine.

Peroration—The concluding part of an oration, speech, or written discourse, in which the speaker or writer sums up and commends to his audience with force or earnestness the matter which he has placed before them; hence, any rhetorical conclusion to a speech.

Phosphates—A salt, ester or other organic derivative of a phosphoric acid; esp. in Biochem., any of these derivatives of sugars, nucleosides, etc., which occur widely in living organisms. Also, a radical or group derived from a phosphoric acid.

Phosphoric—Pertaining to or of the nature of a phosphorus.

Piazza—A public square or market-place: originally, and still usually, one in an Italian town; but in 16th to 18th c. often applied more widely to any open space surrounded by buildings, as the parade ground in a fort or the like.

Piller—a robber, despoiler, plunderer; a thief.

Planking—planks of wood; a kind of bridge.

Portend; Portents—to tell the future; that which portends or foretells something momentous about to happen, esp. of a calamitous nature; an omen, significant sign or token.

Portmanteau—basically a dufflebag, or a bag for carrying clothing and other things for a long journey.

Precipitate—Moisture condensed from the state of vapour by cooling, and deposited in drops, as rain, dew, etc; to follow.

Preposterous—Having or placing last that which should be first; inverted in position or order; contrary to the order of nature, or to reason or common sense; monstrous; irrational; perverse, foolish, nonsensical; in later use, utterly absurd.

Procure—To obtain by care or effort; to gain, win, get possession of, acquire. (Now the leading sense.) In early use, to gain the help of, to win over (a person) to one's side.

Promulgate—To make known by public declaration; to publish; esp. to disseminate (some creed or belief), or to proclaim (some law, decree, or tidings).

Protruded—stuck out (of something else).

Q

Querulous—Complaining, given to complaining, full of complaints, peevish.

Quixotic—Of persons: Resembling Don Quixote; hence, striving with lofty enthusiasm for visionary ideals.

R

Rapport—relationship; connexion, correspondence, conformity. Also, harmonious accord, co-ordination.

Refract; Refractive—Of substances: To break the course of (light or other waves) and turn (it or them) out of the direct line; esp. to deflect at a certain angle at the point of passage from one medium into another of different density.

Relinquish—To withdraw from, desert, abandon; abandon in fleeing.

Resolved to—decided to, made up his mind, determined to (do something).

Retardation—The action of retarding, delaying, or making slower in respect of action or movement, or later in happening; an instance of this.

Retrograde—Of the planets: Apparently moving in a direction contrary to the order of the signs, or from east to west.

Retrospect—literally to "to look backward," or figuratively to think of or consider something in the past, or something that happened.

S

Scarcely—barely.

Secessionist—One who favours secession; one who joins in a secession—in this case one in favor of the attempt of the Southern United States States to withdraw from the Union.

Seduous; Seduously—Of persons or agents: Diligent, active, constant in application to the matter in hand; assiduous, persistent.

Sentinal—a guard or soldier, guarding something.

Sequestered—Separated; cut off from congenial surroundings.

Singularity—a kind of independence, or free will, or separate existence apart from something else, or other things. Wakefield, having lost the "perception of singularity," is similar to being "spellbound," in that he has lost himself somehow.

Spellbound—fascinated; interested; obsessed, to be "bound" by a "spell".

Sodden—Boiled; cooked or prepared by boiling; Of persons, their features, etc.: Having the appearance of, or resembling, that which has been soaked or steeped in water; rendered dull, stupid, or expressionless, esp. owing to drunkenness or indulgence in intoxicants; pale and flaccid.

Stuccato—from stucco (a fine plaster, esp. one composed of gypsum and pulverized marble, used for covering walls, ceilings, and floors, and for making cornices, mouldings, and other decorations)—stuccato usually refers to a sort of percussive sound.

Stupify, Stupefaction—the act of making or being stupid, numb, or insensitive.

Subordinates—people lower in rank, underlings, employees.

Superfluous—too much, unnecessary amount.

T

Tarry—spend time, procrastinate, waste time.

Tertiary— Of, in, or belonging to the third order, rank, degree, class, or category; third.

Thither—there.

Throng—crowds of people.

Tithes—The tenth part of the annual produce of agriculture, etc., being a due or payment (orig. in kind) for the support of the priesthood, religious establishments, etc.; spec. applied to that ordained by the Mosaic law, and to that introduced in conformity therewith in England and other Christian lands. (The latter sense appears first in quots.) Also, in recent use, in certain religious denominations: a tenth part of an individual's income which is pledged to the church.

To-morrow—tomorrow.

Tumult; Tumultuous; Tumuluously—In a tumultuous manner; with tumult or commotion; with confusion and uproar; riotously.

Tramp—homeless, poor, or uncouth or uncivil person, a castout.

Twopence—A sum of money equal to two pennies.

U

Undenominational—Not belonging to any particular religious denomination.

Unerring—Making no error or mistake; not going or leading astray in judgement or opinion.

Unprecedented—it means there is no precedent for the thing that is unprecedent. A precedent is like an example of something having happened before—if it is unprecedented, it is unique or strange or new—it's never happened before and therefor it is implied that anyone involved has no experience with such a thing.

Unpremeditated—unplanned.

V

Vagary—vague things; Wakefield's uncertain life.

Veranda—An open portico or light roofed gallery extending along the front (and occas. other sides) of a dwelling or other building, freq. having a front of lattice-work, and erected chiefly as a protection or shelter from the sun or rain.

Versailles—The name of a hunting lodge to the south-west of Paris built by Louis XIII and enlarged into a palace by Louis XIV in the 17th century. Also used to denote the Treaty of Versailles: The site of the peace conference held there at the conclusion of the 1914–18 war which gave its name to the treaty signed there in 1919.

Vertical—standing straight up; pointing upwards.

Vex—To trouble, afflict, or harass (a person, etc.) by aggression, encroachment, or other interference with peace and quiet.

Vindicate—to exercise in revenge; to avenge.

Vintners—One who deals in or sells wine; a wine-merchant.

W

Wane—decline, in reference to the moon, which waxes and wanes, that is, appears and disappears from sight.

Well to do—well off; wealthy.

Whither—where.

Z

Zenithward—towards the point of the sky directly overhead; the highest point of the celestial sphere as viewed from any particular place; the upper pole of the horizon

» 1729: Jonathan Swift publishes "A Modest Proposal".

» AMERICAN WESTWARD EXPANSION

» 1803: The United States more than doubles in size when it buys out France's territorial claims in North America via the Louisiana Purchase. This begins the U.S.'s westward expansion to the Pacific referred to as its Manifest Destiny which involves annexing and conquering land from Mexico, Britain, and Native Americans.

» 1804: Nathaniel Hawthorne born on July 4, in Salem, MA. First steam locomotive begins operation.

» 1812–1815: War of 1812 between the United States and Britain; ends in a draw, except that Native Americans lose power.

» 1818: Mary Shelley publishes *Frankenstein*.

» 1820: Discovery of Antarctica. Liberia founded by the American Colonization Society for freed American slaves.

» 1825: First isolation of aluminium.

» 1829: First electric motor built. Sir Robert Peel founds the Metropolitan Police Service, the first modern police force.

» 1833: Slavery Abolition Act bans slavery throughout the British Empire.

» 1835: Nathaniel Hawthorne publishes "Wakefield". Mark Twain (Samuel Clemens) born in Hannibal, Missouri.

» Victorian Era

» 1837: Queen Victoria's reign is considered the apex of the British Empire and is referred to as the Victorian era. Charles Dickens publishes *Oliver Twist*. Telegraphy patented.

» 1838: By this time, 46,000 Native Americans have been forcibly relocated in the Trail of Tears.

» 1841: The word "dinosaur" is coined by Richard Owen.

» 1843: The first wagon train sets out from Missouri.

» 1844: First publicly funded telegraph line in the world—between Baltimore and Washington—sends demonstration message on 24 May, ushering in the age of the telegraph. This message read "What hath God wrought?" (Bible, Numbers 23:23)

» 1847: Ignaz Semmelweis proposes hand washing as a way to stop the spread of diseases.

» 1848: The Communist Manifesto published. Seneca Falls Convention is the first women's rights convention in the United States and leads to the battle for women's suffrage.

» 1849: Roman Republic's constitutional law becomes the first to abolish capital punishment. The safety pin and the gas mask are invented. Earliest recorded air raid, as Austria launches from land and from the ship SMS Vulcano some 200 Incendiary balloons against Venice.

» 1850: The first National Women's Rights Convention.

» 1852: Frederick Douglass delivers his speech "The Meaning of July Fourth for the Negro" in Rochester, New York.

» 1854: Oscar Wilde Born: October 16, 1854, Westland Row, Dublin, Republic of Ireland

» 1855: Bessemer process enables steel to be mass-produced. Cocaine is isolated by Friedrich Gaedcke.

» 1856: Neanderthal man first identified, age still unknown.

» 1857: Sir Joseph Whitworth designs the first long-range sniper rifle.

» 1858: Charles Chesnutt is born in Cleveland Ohio. Invention of the phonautograph, the first true device for recording sound. Construction of Big Ben is completed.

» 1859: Charles Darwin publishes On the Origin of Species.

» 1860: Charlotte Perkins Gilman born in Hartford, CT.

» American Civil War

» 1861: American Civil War between the Union and seceding Confederacy.

» 1863: United States President Abraham Lincoln issues the

Emancipation Proclamation. Lincoln issued a preliminary on September 22, 1862, warning that in all states still in rebellion (Confederacy) on January 1, 1863, he would declare their slaves "then, thenceforward, and forever free." The Thirteenth Amendment to the Constitution, ratified in 1865, officially abolished slavery in the entire country.

» AMERICAN RECONSTRUCTION

» 1865: Robert E. Lee surrenders the Army of Northern Virginia (26,765 troops) to Ulysses S. Grant at Appomattox Courthouse, Virginia, effectively ending the American Civil War. Reconstruction in the United States; Slavery is banned in the United States by the Thirteenth Amendment to the United States Constitution. Gregor Mendel formulates his laws of inheritance.

» 1866: Successful transatlantic telegraph cable follows an earlier attempt in 1858.

» 1866–1869: After the Meiji Restoration, Japan embarks on a program of rapid modernization.

» 1867: The United States purchases Alaska from Russia. Alfred Nobel invents dynamite.

» 1868: The Fourteenth Amendment to the United States Constitution is approved, granting "equal protection under the law" to all US Citizens.

» 1868: Cro-Magnon man first identified.

» 1869: First Transcontinental Railroad completed in United States on 10 May.

» 1869: The first national suffrage organizations were established in 1869 when two competing organizations were formed, one led by Susan B. Anthony and Elizabeth Cady Stanton and the other by Lucy Stone.

» 1871: The feudal system is dismantled in Japan.

» 1872: Susan B. Anthony succeeds in voting in 1872 is arrested for that act and found guilty in a widely publicized trial that gave the Suffrage Movement fresh momentum.

» 1873: Maxwell's A Treatise on Electricity and Magnetism

published. The samurai class is abolished in Japan. Blue jeans and barbed wire are invented.

»   1875: Supreme Court rules against voting rights for women. Suffragists began the decades-long campaign for an amendment to the U.S. Constitution that would enfranchise women.

» THE GILDED AGE

»   1876: Beginning of the Gilded Age: the massive expansion in population, territory, industry and wealth in the United States.

»   1877: End of Reconstruction in the United States. Great Railroad Strike in the United States may have been the world's first nationwide labour strike. Crazy Horse surrenders and is later killed. Asaph Hall discovers the moons of Mars. Thomas Edison invents the phonograph.

»   1879: Thomas Edison tests his first light bulb.

»   1881: Gunfight at the O.K. Corral. Sitting Bull surrenders. First electrical power plant and grid in Godalming, Britain. President James A. Garfield is assassinated.

»   1882: Oscar Wilde publishes "Impressions of America".

»   1884: Sir Hiram Maxim invents the first self-powered Machine gun.

»   1885: Singer begins production of the 'Vibrating Shuttle'. which would become the most popular model of sewing machine.

»   1886: Construction of the Statue of Liberty; Coca-Cola is developed.

»   1887: Sir Arthur Conan Doyle publishes his first Sherlock Holmes story, *A Study in Scarlet*.

»   1889: Vincent van Gogh paints *Starry Night*. Aspirin patented.

»   1890: The Wounded Knee Massacre in South Dakota was the last battle in the American Indian Wars. This event represents the end of the American Old West. Charles Chesnutt publishes "The Sheriff's Children". First use of the electric chair as a method of execution. Ambrose Bierce publishes "An Occurrence at Owl Creek Bridge".

»   1890: After years of rivalry, the first national suffrage organizations

354

established in 1869 merged as the National American Woman Suffrage Association (NAWSA) with Susan B. Anthony as its leading force.

» 1892: Fingerprinting is officially adopted for the first time. John Froelich develops and constructs the first gasoline/petrol-powered tractor. Charlotte Perkins Gilman publishes "The Yellow Wallpaper".

» 1893: US forces overthrow the government of Hawaii.

» 1894: First gramophone record. Karl Elsener invents the Swiss Army knife. Kate Chopin publishes "The Story of an Hour".

» 1895: Trial of Oscar Wilde and premiere of his play *The Importance of Being Earnest.*

» 1897: H.G. Wells publishes "The Star".

» 1898: The United States gains control of Cuba, Puerto Rico, and the Philippines after the Spanish–American War.

» 1902: Jack London publishes: "To Build a Fire".

» 1903: W.E.B. De Buis publishes "Of Our Spiritual Strivings". First controlled heavier-than-air flight of the Wright Brothers. The teddy bear is invented.

» 1905: Mark Twain publishes "The War Prayer".

» 1909: E.M. Forester publishes "The Machine Stops".

» 1911: Eugene B. Ely lands on the deck of the USS Pennsylvania stationed in San Francisco harbor, marking the first time an aircraft lands on a ship.

» 1913: Niels Bohr formulates the first cohesive model of the atomic nucleus, and in the process paves the way to quantum mechanics.

» 1914: End of The Gilded Age in the United States.

» World War I

» 1914: Gavrilo Princip assassinates Archduke Franz Ferdinand of Austria in Sarajevo, triggering the start of World War I.

» 1915: Akutagawa publishes "Rashōmon".

» 1916: Alice Paul forms the National Woman's Party (NWP), a militant group focused on the passage of a national suffrage amendment. Over 200 NWP supporters, the Silent Sentinels, are arrested in 1917 while picketing the White House, some of whom go on hunger strike and endure forced feeding after being sent to prison.

» 1917: Russian Revolution ends the Russian Empire; beginning of Russian Civil War.

» 1918: The Hundred Days Offensive sends Germany into defeat. Armistice of 11 November 1918 ends World War I.

» 1919: Treaty of Versailles redraws European borders. German Revolution ends with the collapse of the German Empire and the establishment of the Weimar Republic. First experimental evidence for the General theory of relativity obtained by Arthur Eddington.

» PROHIBITION AND THE ROARING TWENTIES

» 1920: After a hard-fought series of votes in the U.S. Congress and in state legislatures, the Nineteenth Amendment becomes part of the U.S. Constitution on August 26, 1920. It states, "The right of citizens of the United States to vote shall not be denied or abridged by the United States or by any State on account of sex."

» 1920: Prohibition in the United States enforced.

» 1921: Adolf Hitler becomes Führer of the Nazi Party as hyperinflation in the Weimar Republic begins.

» 1921: Russia invades Georgia and incorporates it into the Soviet Union. End of Russian Civil War, Polish-Soviet War and Ukrainian–Soviet War.

» 1922: F. Scott Fitzgerald publishes "Porcelain and Pink".

» 1922: March on Rome brings Benito Mussolini to power in Italy.

» 1923: The Walt Disney Company is founded.

» 1924: Death of Vladimir Lenin triggers power struggle between Leon Trotsky and Joseph Stalin.

» 1924: Virginia Woolf publishes "The New Dress".

» 1925: Benito Mussolini gains dictatorial powers in Italy. Adolf Hitler publishes "Mein Kampf".

» 1927: The Jazz Singer, the first "talkie", is released.

» 1927: Joseph Stalin becomes leader of the Soviet Union. Chinese

Civil War begins.

» 1928: Discovery of penicillin by Alexander Fleming. Hassan al-Banna founds the Muslim Brotherhood. Philip K. Dick born in Chicago, Illinois.

» THE GREAT DEPRESSION

» 1929: Wall Street crash of 1929 and the beginning of the Great Depression. Leon Trotsky is exiled First people sent to the gulag in the Soviet Union as Stalin assumes effective control. Pope Pius XI signs the Lateran Treaty with Italian leader Benito Mussolini. Vatican City is recognised as a sovereign state. Saint Valentine's Day Massacre. The first Academy Awards are presented.

» 1930: Aided by the Great Depression, the Nazi Party increases its share of the vote from 2.6% to 18.3%. First FIFA World Cup hosted.

» 1931: Construction of the Empire State Building. "The Star-Spangled Banner" is adopted as the United States's national anthem. The Second Spanish Republic is declared. The Chinese Soviet Republic is proclaimed by Mao Zedong.

» 1932: Franklin D. Roosevelt is elected President of the United States. The Nazi party becomes the largest single party in the German parliament. BBC World Service starts broadcasting. The Neutron is discovered.

» THE NEW DEAL

» 1933: Adolf Hitler becomes Chancellor of Germany. New Deal begins in America. Japan and Germany announce they are going to leave the League of Nations. Prohibition in the United States is abolished.

» WORLD WAR II AND THE HOLOCAUST

» 1945: July 16, first nuclear test takes plac in New Mexico. August 6, uranium-based bomb Little boy detonated above Hiroshima, Japan. August 9, the plutonium based Fatman was detonated above Nagasaki, Japan.

» 1952: Philip K. Dick publishes "The Gun".

Ideas and Values: Connect the Text

1. Anonymity

» To Build A Fire

» The Yellow Wallpaper

» The Blue Hotel

In London's "To Build A Fire" the main character is always referred to as "the man," or simply "he." In Gilman's "The Yellow Wallpaper" the narrator never directly gives us her name, while her husband refers to her only as: "blessed little goose," "Darling," "his darling," and "little girl." In Crane's "The Blue Hotel" there are the characters of the Easterner, the Cowboy, the Swede, and the Gambler, but also Pat and Johnnie Scully.

What is the nature of anonymity? What do the anonymous characters in these stories have in common? Between these texts, does anonymity seem to be a good thing? Are the anonymous characters the most powerful, or fortunate characters in their respective stories? Ultimately why are some characters named and others not?

2. Color

» The Yellow Wallpaper

» Porcelain and Pink

» The Blue Hotel

What meaning is there in a color? Why are stop signs red? What is the color of sadness? Why do we wrap little boys in blue and girls in pink? Why do brides wear white on their wedding day?

What is the significance of the title colors in their respective stories: "The Yellow Wallpaper," by Gilman, "Porcelain and Pink," by Fitzgerald, and "The Blue Hotel," by Crane? Could different colors have been used without changing these stories?

3. Survival

- » Rashōmon
- » Occurrence at Owl Creek Bridge
- » To Build A Fire

In Jack London's "To Build A Fire" the main character is faced with the necessity of building a fire to ensure his survival. Yet his need for fire is determined by earlier choices he made. In Ambrose Bierce's "Occurrence at Owl Creek Bridge" Peyton Farquhar is fighting to escape his situation in order to survive—but again, his earlier choices are what led to his hanging. In Ryunosuke Akutagawa's "Rashōmon" Rashōmon must make a choice that will determine his ability to survive after he is let go a servant due only to the economic situation of his master. His conversation with the wig-maker leads him to his decision.

How do each of these characters survive? What specific elements affects each of their ability to survive? What choices do the characters face that affect their ability to survive? What sacrifices are worth making in order to survive? Why are the characters willing and able, or not, to make these choices?

4. Outcasts

- » "Wakefield"
- » "The New Dress"
- » "The Sheriff's Children"

How do the outcasts in Hawthorne's "Wakefield," Woolf's "The New Dress," and Chesnutt's "The Sheriff's Children" differ? How are they the same? Why are the characters outcasts? Who casts them out? How does society view each of the outcasts in these stories? What kind of society would cast these people out?

5. Absurdity

- » The Stolen White Elephant
- » Porcelain and Pink

» A Modest Proposal

Absurdity is the quality of being illogical, unreasonable, or just plain ridiculous. But absurdity often has a logic of its own—and in real life, as in literature, people end up in situations, and doing things, both noble and tragic, that can be characterized as absurd. How can this be? In Twain's "The Stolen White Elephant," the caretaker of a priceless White Elephant is led on a wild goose chase, and seems to have been swindled of all his savings by a fantastic detective agency. In "Porcelain and Pink," the main character finds herself in the nude among her date that afternoon, and matter-of-factly, renounces the norms of her society, and in Swift's essay "A Modest Proposal," the author offers a solution to a looming problem in Ireland of hungry and illiterate children—to eat them. Each of these texts touches upon aspects of the absurd. How are they the same? How are they different? What is the quality of their absurdity—that is— what makes them absurd? And are they truly—or can you find a hint of reason in any of them?

6. Identity

» Rashōmon

» The New Dress

» Of Our Spiritual Strivings

In Akutagawa's short story "Rashōmon" the ex-servant of a samurai struggles with whether or not to become a thief, and in Virginia Woolf's "The New Dress," Mabel is absolutely consumed with the question of her appearance in her new dress, and the judgments of those who surround her, and in W.E.B. Du Bois's "Of Our Spiritual Strivings" he writes, "It dawned upon me with a certain suddenness that I was different from the others; or like, mayhap, in heart and life and longing, but shut out from their world by a vast veil."

In these three texts there are three extremely different accounts of a struggle for identity—of that question of sameness and of quality of a person. What can be said for all of them? What makes them different? What can be made of this struggle for identity—why is it important—is it?

7. Belonging

» The War Prayer

» Occurrence at Owl Creek Bridge

» The Machine Stops

In Twain's "The War Prayer" he writes that "The country was up in arms, the war was on, in every breast burned the holy fire of patriotism," when a stranger mounts the stage, declares himself the messenger of God, and explains what the people's "War Prayer" truly means for the enemy. In "Occurrence at Owl Creek Bridge," Peyton Farquhar seems to be the "enemy," the one that doesn't belong—and finally in "The Machine Stops," E.M. Forester writes about a different kind of belonging—not to a nation, but to a way of life; to a machine not unlike today's Internet. These are three different views of belonging; what does it mean to belong? What is it for? What is the "other side" of belonging? In order for one to belong, must there be others who do not belong? What effect does it have, and why do humans do it? Is belonging ultimately a good, or a bad thing?

8. Glory

» The War Prayer

» Occurrence at Owl Creek Bridge

» The Stolen White Elephant

How does the thought of glory motivate the characters in Mark Twain's "The War Prayer," Ambrose Bierce's "Occurrence at Owl Creek Bridge," and Twain's "The Stolen White Elephant"? Does glory motivate people to do good? Is one man's glory another man's glory as well? What is glory, after all?

9. Independence

» One Day More

» Wakefield

» The Machine Stops

What is independence in Conrad's "One Day More", Hawthorne's "Wakefield", and Forester's "The Machine Stops"? What are the consequences of independence, for not only the individual but for society? Can a balance be struck between independence and the needs of a community?

10. Captivity

» The Yellow Wallpaper

» The Story of an Hour

» The Machine Stops

In Chopin's "Story of an Hour" Louise Mallard's marriage seems to have ended abruptly with a sudden "railroad accident," and we find her in her room, celebrating her newfound freedom, while in "The Yellow Wallpaper," the narrator's husband uses his role as patriarch and physician to prescribe his wife's country home into a prison. Lastly, in E.M. Forester's "The Machine Stops," Kuno's mother, Vashti becomes increasingly alarmed at her son's rejection of their underground culture, as he derides her unquestioning fealty to the machine as mere worship—and eventually he reveals to her his will to live on the surface.

In these three texts there is a force that holds captive one or more person; consider these forces individually, and explore how they operate, their functions, how they came into being, and what good or evil they do. What is the essence of captivity? Why does it exist? Is it pure cruelty—or is there something else?

11. Being a Problem

» A Modest Proposal

» The Sheriff's Children

» Of Our Spiritual Strivings

Swift's "A Modest Proposal" Chesnutt's "The Sheriff's Children" and W.E.B. Du Bois's "Of Our Spiritual Strivings," explore the concepts of compassion and empathy—the ability to imagine what it's like to be another person, or the unwillingness to do so. How do the problems in each of the texts compare? What happens when an individual, or group of people, are classified as a "problems"? How should society deal with societal problems? How does it deal with the problems in these three texts? What is the nature of people as problem—is it even fair to think of a person as a problem? What does it do to a person to call them a problem?

12. Conformity

» The Sheriff's Children

» The Stolen White Elephant

» The War Prayer

In Chesnutt's "The Sheriff's Children," Twain's "The Stolen White Elephant," and Twain's "The War Prayer" there exists forms of conformity and nonconformity. What is conformity—is it one's actions, one's thoughts, more, less? And how is it determined what conforming is and what isn't? Why does one conform in the first place? Why would one choose to not conform? Look at the challenges faced by the nonconformists in these stories: are the nonconformists successful? What challenges do they face?

13. Perspective

» Impressions of America

» Of Our Spiritual Strivings

» The Yellow Wallpaper

Oscar Wilde writes in "Impressions of America" about the strange differences both good and bad between England and its former colony, the United States; W.E.B. Du Bois writes in "Of Our Spiritual Strivings" that "the words I longed for, and all their dazzling opportunities, were theirs, not mine," and in Gilman's "Yellow Wallpaper", the main character, having found herself on the "wrong side," of matrimony, country living, and her husband's medical opinion, gives us her unique perspective as well.

What does perspective mean—how is it formed? What makes a perspective unique? What makes a perspective important, or worthwhile to understand? How does one get the perspective of another—or is it even possible to see through the eyes of another?

14. Culture

- » The Gun
- » Earth's Holocaust
- » Impressions of America

In Philip K. Dick's "The Gun" culture is the one treasure that "the dragon guards," but in Nathanial Hawthorne's "Earth's Holocaust," culture is merely fuel for the fire, while in Wilde's "Impressions of America" culture is neither here nor there, but a category of different perspectives, perhaps a tool to be used one way or another, in practicality or fashion—as he doesn't enter into geography ("latitude or longitude"), economics ("the value of its dry goods"), or politics.

But what is culture? What is its value—ultimately? Is it a way of life? A relic of the past? Does it hold us back, or does it tell us who we are? What relationship should we strike towards culture itself—? And what care should we take to understand its origins, if any at all?

15. Stereotypes

- » The Blue Hotel
- » Of Our Spiritual Strivings
- » A Modest Proposal

What is a stereotype? Do you consider the " Cowboy," the "Easterner" or the "Swede" in Crane's "The Blue Hotel" stereotypes? How about the children in Swift's "A Modest Proposal"? Lastly, what use of stereotypes has Du Bois's in "Of Our Spiritual Strivings" found necessary to make his points? How do the stereotypes help the reader to better understand the characters or topics discussed in these writings? Do we need stereotypes to help aid in our understanding of ourselves and others?

16. Justice

- » The Sheriff's Children
- » Rashōmon
- » Occurrence at Owl Creek Bridge

In Chesnutt's "The Sheriff's Children" the townspeople want to lynch Tom in order to achieve justice for the death of Captain Walker. In Akutagawa's "Rashōmon" the wig-maker weighs her own survival against justice for the dead. In Bierce's "Occurrence at Owl Creek Bridge" Peyton Farquhar is facing justice for attempting to sabotage the enemy's supply line.

What forms of justice occur in each of the stories and how do they differ? Who has determined the laws in each story and how do the punishments, or lack of punishment, fit the crime? What, ultimately is justice? Is justice itself always just?

17. Nature

- » The Star
- » To Build a Fire
- » The Machine Stops

In H.G. Wells's "The Star" a mathematician predicts that a celestial body that has collided with Neptune will approach Earth and all manner of nature will wreak havoc on mankind, while in Jack London's "To Build a Fire," the man fails to appreciate the dangers of his surroundings, and finally in "The Machine Stops" a whole society has shut themselves away from "the surface," choosing rather to experience life as indirectly as possible. In these stories we have three visions of man's relationship to nature; what unites them? What makes them different? Is nature a force to be conquered, bent to man's will? Is nature a god to be feared, or even worshipped? Is mankind something set apart from nature—or are we nature as well?

18. Truth

- » The Blue Hotel
- » Porcelain and Pink
- » "The Stolen White Elephant"

How is the truth manipulated in Crane's "The Blue Hotel," Fitzgerald's "Porcelain and Pink," and Twain's "The Stolen White Elephant"? How does the reader know what is true in each story? What is the truth in each story? Who relies on the truth in each story? Who relies on the perversion of truth? What are the stakes? What is truth? Why do humans have a concept of truth—if our surroundings are self evident? Should one always strive to be truthful?

19. Technology

- » Impressions of America
- » The Gun
- » The Machine Stops

Humankind has invented the Internet, the telephone, the motor vehicle, air travel, the atomic bomb… Look at Oscar Wilde's "Impressions of America," and his focus on "practical education" and the beauty of American engineering—and then move to "The Gun," when an alien ship approaches Earth but cannot reach it because of Earth's engineering, and then "The Machine Stops," a world in which "the machine" is all that matters—not human progress—but the progress of "the machine." And finally "Earth's Holocaust," in which the people of the world decide to burn everything—all ideas—all progress, all technology. What roll does technological progress play, and what roll should technology play in the progress of mankind? How would you define progress?

20. Mental Illness

- » The Yellow Wallpaper
- » The Dress
- » One Day More

In Gilman's "The Yellow Wallpaper" the main character believes she can see a woman living in the walls, and in Woolf's "The Dress" a young woman obsesses over her appearance, and lastly in Conrad's "One Day More", Captain Hagbeard is said to be crazy, as he always believes that his son will return "tomorrow," even after his son has returned today! But what is the nature of what we call "mental illness?" Is it an illness, like the common cold—do we "catch it" from the air? Or does it form some other way? Is there an environmental aspect to mental illnesses, or are we merely born destined to be sane or…ill?

College Writing 1: Reflect Within the Text

READING LEVEL: GRADE 6.7

The Story of an Hour

Conduct two interviews with Brently Mallard. Interview him before the story takes place—investigate what his life is like and how he feels about it. Interview him again after the events of the story—what is his perspective on everything that occurred?

Wakefield

Think about Wakefield's wife's response to him leaving. How did she feel when he was first missing and how did her feelings change as time passed? What state of mind is she in at the moment of his arrival? How would she deal with all of her emotions from the past 20 years?

From the wife's perspective add an additional scene at the end of "Wakefield", after he returns.

The Gun

Imagine you are an inhabitant of Franklin Apartments. Describe the final days of your civilization. What did you put in the vault, and why? Include at least one personal item.

The Yellow Wallpaper

You've been diagnosed with melancholia. Who in your life would you be forced to turn to for advice? Why would you be expected to trust this person?

Imagine that this person asks you to stay in your room, and speak to no one for a week. They take away your phone, computer, TV. You have no music to listen to or books to read.

Your room has a bed, a table and chair, and no other objects. Describe what the room looks like. What color is it? What does that color mean? What would you do to pass the time? Write a story similar to "The Yellow Wallpaper" of going mad in isolation.

The Sheriff's Children

Chesnutt's "The Sheriff's Children" is as much about race, slavery, and corruption as it is about belonging; look at the title of the story—it is not "The Sheriff's Son," or "The Sheriff's Child," but "The Sheriff's Children". Why? Why did Chesnutt choose to give the Sheriff a daughter, and to include her in the title? What does she have to do with the sheriff's son?

Consider—what would have happened if the son had not allowed himself to die in that prison cell. Imagine if he had been acquitted and saved as was the sheriff's plan. Imagine the best possible outcome—that they make amends and the sheriff offers to take his son back into his home. Then what?

To Build A Fire

Remember or imagine a difficult situation you've been in—like the man in Jack London's "To Build a Fire". Imagine not heeding the advice given you and instead doing what you think is best. How does the situation turn out? What advice are you given and why do you not listen to it? What choices do you make and why do you make them?

Would you change anything if you had the opportunity to go back in time?

The Earth's Holocaust

Imagine—that you are about to have a bonfire of your own, and you burn everything that is burned in Hawthorne's "Earth's Holocaust". And after you have emptied your life of every thing that was burned in the story, save the floors and the walls, and enough clothes to cover you, ask yourself: who are you? Are you free? Are you different?

List everything that goes to the fire. What defined you? What entertained you? What tools and toys and necessities did you destroy? Consider what they meant to you—or why you held on to these things in the first place. If you hesitate to get rid of anything, even in your imagination, why?

One Day More

Look at the blind Josiah Carvil's dependence upon his daughter Bessie Carvil; look at Bessie Carvil's dependence on Captain Hagberd for escape from her father, and look at what Harry Hagberd wants from Bessie Carvil.

In all of these cases each character is both dependent yet wishes for independence at the same time. That is, they need something from someone, yet wish that they didn't.

Compare your dependence to one of the relationships in "One Day More". Perhaps it's a parent, lover, or friend. Ask yourself—is it possible to be completely free of this dependence? Is it possible to manage one's level of dependence, on people in general, or individuals specifically?

An Occurrence at Owl Creek Bridge

Imagine joining something to gain recognition. Imagine that you don't totally believe in the cause. How do you feel participating in something that you do not truly believe in? What happens? What becomes of you—and your relationships. Do you regret it? Write a story, like Farquhar's delusion of escape, in which you somehow get out of the consequences of joining.

The War Prayer

Report on the events of "The War Prayer" from two different news stations—one liberal, and the other conservative.

Rashōmon

Put yourself in the position of the samurai's servant—now homeless, in the rain, and hungry. How would you treat the old wigmaker? What would you do to survive? And why? What is your philosophy regarding what is and is not okay to do to survive?

Impressions of America

Write your own Impressions—of a place of your own choosing. That is, choose two places, one that you feel comfortable with and that you know very well, and another that you don't feel comfortable in, one that you don't know very well. Now, enter the place in that you don't know well, and report on it in the style of Oscar Wilde's "Impressions of America."

Of Our Spiritual Strivings

Consider W.E.B Du Bois's spiritual striving as your own. Put yourself in his shoes—write as if you are the problem in your society: what do you do? What do you tell yourself? How do you design your life—your self image—your relationships, to survive? How do you get along in a society that regards your very existence as "a problem"?

Porcelain and Pink

Fitzgerald's "Porcelain and Pink" is ultimately a story about being ones self and a woman in the 1920's. There were a number of expectations about being a woman in the 1920s—and a number of those expectations being thrown out with the bathwater. How have expectations changed since your parent's generation? Write a one scene play in which you do something that your parents would not do when they were your age. Make it backfire on you in the same way it does in "Porcelain and Pink".

A Modest Proposal

Identify a problem that is personal but also political. It could be a problem of yours, or a problem for your school, your parents, your employer, or a friend.

In the style of Jonathan Swift, write a tongue in cheek "modest proposal" to fix this ill. Swift's proposal is satire—that means he doesn't really believe we should go about eating starving children. He is satirizing the callousness of certain members of his society and their political views, by taking them to the extreme.

The New Dress

Insert yourself into the party, and knowing the anxiety that Mabel feels about her new dress—say something to her. While you're at it, write a letter to Mrs. Barnet, explaining exactly the situation with Mabel, and what Mrs. Barnet could do differently—if anything—for her young friend Mabel.

The Star

You are the mathematician from the story. What do you do? Do you tell anyone? Do you tell everyone? What do you and your family and loved ones do? Do you merely go about your life, and hope for the best? Do you go feverish with anticipation and try to fix the problem? Do you embark on a crime spree and hope that all possibility of your punishment will be destroyed? Tell the story.

The Stolen White Elephant

Have you ever asked someone to help you—and found that the help was worse than the original problem? Have you ever lost something and discovered that it was under your nose the entire time! It seems like Twain's "A Stolen White Elephant," is in part about common sense and the absurdity of ready-made solutions; compose your own "White Elephant," but this time with the trappings and circumstances of your life.

The Blue Hotel

Try to prevent what happens at the end of "The Blue Hotel" by choosing and changing the behavior of one of the characters in the story. What would the character say to the Swede to change the ending? Where and when would they say it?

The Machine Stops

The world in E.M. Forester's tale "The Machine Stops," may seem like a bad episode of Star Trek, but is there something familiar about the idea of "vicarious experience," what with today's Internet and related technologies—Google, Youtube, Amazon, Netflix, and Facebook? What can't we do from the comfort of our own home? We even have "Alexa" (or "smart speakers") to keep us company in lieu of human contact. Reflect on your own life, and consider what it would look like if you rejected "the machine" of today—and sought to "visit the surface," to live life more "directly."

College Writing 2: Research Outside the Text

READING LEVEL: GRADE: 9.5

The Story of an Hour

Research the institution of marriage in the 1890s. What options did women have during this time? Is it reasonable to assume that other women of the time would feel and react the way that Louise Mallard does, and why?

Wakefield

Research a factual account of a person who intentionally disappeared from their own life. Why did the person leave? Did they return? How did the people they left behind react? Compare the text you found to Wakefield. How are Wakefield and the person from your research the same? How do they differ? How does Hawthorne's telling of Wakefield's story compare to the text you found? Does one help you understand the other? Why, or why not?

Bonus: Find a news story about someone that you find strange. In the style of Hawthorne's "Wakefield" explore what happened from that persons's point of view. Write a story that ends where the news story begins.

The Gun

Research the most credible threat to humanity. What is it? Is it external, or internal? Given this threat what is the best method to preserving the world's various cultural artifacts?

The Yellow Wallpaper

Research medical views of women in the 1890s. What is the scientific rationale, at that time, for the treatments John prescribes for the narrator? Were his views held by the majority of people at the time? What were some of the other opinions of the time? Using what you've learned from your research, write a piece from John's perspective that explains and defends his medical treatment of the narrator.

The Sheriff's Children

Research belonging—why do humans do it? Why do humans form groups, and socialize? Why do groups cast certain members out—even if they've done nothing wrong, committed no crimes, and contribute to the survival of the group? What is the significance between identity and group membership in human social relations?

To Build A Fire

Research extreme cold weather survival techniques. Beyond the advice given to the man in "To Build a Fire", what else could the man have done to survive his trip? Use only materials and knowledge that would have been available in 1908. Write a How-to-Guide for surviving the trip. Include a list of supplies. You may also include advice from the story.

Earth's Holocaust

Consider the character of "the bookworm," as he is described in the text: "one of those men who are born to gnaw dead thoughts. His clothes, you see, are covered with the dust of libraries. He has no inward fountain of ideas." Consider the human drive to preserve—and taken at its extreme—to hoard. Why do humans behave in this manner? Why do we collect things in the first place? Things seem to give humans a feeling of comfort. But why? Research this phenomenon.

One Day More

Research the notion of "codependence." What is it? How does it manifest in "One Day More"? What is the difference between codependence and dependence? How does it inform your understanding of "One Day More"? Consider the occupations and conditions of the characters in your assessment, and how that affects their relationships.

An Occurrence at Owl Creek Bridge

In Bierce's "Occurrence at Owl Creek Bridge," Peyton Farquhar attempts to sabotage a Union Army supply line. Like Payton, people choose to fight for their countries in times of war, even though there is a risk of dying. What could possibly convince someone to gamble with their life? Or is that not how soldiers see it? Do all soldiers fully believe that they could die?

Research how recruits are convinced to risk their lives. Does the way in which we talk about war, and the causes being fought for, affect the soldier's expectations?

The War Prayer

Research the relationship between war and religion; look at the history. Look specifically at the Abrahamic religion referenced in "The War Prayer," namely Christianity, Judaism, or Islam—choose one. How compatible is the practice of war with the teachings of this religion? Is it truly a problem, as Twain implies in "The War Prayer"?

Rashōmon

Look at the history of the "gates" like the Rashōmon. Now consider the meaning of the gates in the context of the events of the story—look at the general economic and cultural conditions and beliefs of Osaka at the time of the story's publication—1915. Research the Rashōmon—what significance does it hold to the events of the text? What were they for? What did they mean to their society?

Impressions of America

Research America in the 1880s. Choose an aspect of Wilde's impressions and explain it—that is—perhaps the fashions of the time, or the noise, or the education. Write about the development of that thing until that point in time, and explain the difference from what Wilde was used to in England.

Of Our Spiritual Strivings

Research life for black Americans 40 years after emancipation, but 60 years before the Civil Rights Movement. What's changed? What's the same? Has institutional racism been solved? Has equality been achieved? How does life for black Americans at the turn of the 20th century compare to the turn of the 21st century?

Porcelain and Pink

Research "the roaring twenties." How did it come by that name? What were women "up to" at that time? What were the important political issues of the time concerning women? Bring what you find back to "Porcelain in Pink," and consider whether this changes how you view the behavior of the main character.

A Modest Proposal

Research Ireland in 1729. Look at the situation to which Jonathan Swift was referring. Research the policies and prevalent attitudes towards the Irish in England at the time, and consider why Swift thought it necessary to write such a scathing and satirical essay.

The New Dress

Research the role of women leading up to the 1920s. How had it evolved and why had it evolved to that point? What were the economic and social pressures that affected women in America at that time? Using your research explain Mabel's behavior and perspective.

The Star

Research a cataclysmic event. It could be something in the future—like the super-volcano under Yellowstone, or perhaps the fault off the West Coast of the United States, or man made climate change—or perhaps if you are so inclined the coming Rapture. Research the "preparation" that certain people are making for this event. You could also research previous events—wildfires, earthquakes, mudslides and tidal waves, droughts, floods and the like—and tell us what happened, what preparation had been made for these potential events, and how effective the preparation was, or will be.

The Stolen White Elephant

Research Siam in the 1880s. Where is it—what do we call it today? Is Twain's story based in truth? Or is completely made up—right down to the King of Siam love for his white elephant? What was the state of police detectives, and private detectives, at the time Twain wrote this? Had detective fiction become popular at this point in American literature? Was his work meant to make fun of other popular authors at the time? If so, which ones (and why)?

The Blue Hotel

Imagine a time and place. What would it be like to live in that place at that time? Don't do any research yet! Write your thoughts down.

Now research the place at that time. Compare what you imagined with what you found in your research. How were you right and how were you wrong? List the differences.

Use your list to write a story. In the story you will travel to that time and place. With your fictional traveling self not having done any research, what mistakes would you make? What misadventures would you have?

The Machine Stops

Research the world before the Internet; how did people do research? How did people communicate? How did people know which items were the best ones to buy, without user reviews? How did people find the best places to eat? How did people read the news?

What would happen if the Internet "stopped" tomorrow—how would the world change? How would you change? Would things return to the way they were—or are we forever changed as a species?

And consider this question—has this machine truly improved our lives, or merely changed them?

Reading Grade Level

This anthology uses the SMOG (Simple Measure of Gobbledygook) system to assign a grade-level of readability to each text. These "Reading Level: Grades" refer directly to the reading ability of an idea primary or secondary school "Reading Level: Grade" using a mathematical algorythm. This algorithm approximates the relative Reading Level: Grade of a given reading.

The SMOG grade yields a 0.985 correlation with a standard error of 1.5159 grades with the grades of readers who had 100% comprehension of test materials.

» PRIMARY SCHOOL LEVEL

- » 6—Conrad, Joseph. "One Day More".
- » 6.9—Dick, Philip K.. "The Gun".
- » 7.6—Fitzgerald, F. Scott. "Porcelain and Pink".
- » 8.3—Gilman, Charlotte Perkins. "The Yellow Wallpaper".
- » 8.4—Akutagawa, Ryunosuke. "Rashōmon".

» SECONDARY SCHOOL LEVEL

- » 8.5—Crane, Stephen. "The Blue Hotel".
- » 8.8—London, Jack. "To Build a Fire".
- » 9—Chopin, Kate. "Story of an Hour".
- » 9.3—Forester, E.M. "The Machine Stops".
- » 10.2—Twain, Mark. "The Stolen White Elephant".
- » 10.2—Chesnutt, Charles. "The Sheriff's Children".
- » 10.3—Bierce, Ambrose. "Occurrence at Owl Creek Bridge".
- » 11.1—Wells, H.G.. "The Star".
- » 11.1—Twain, Mark. "The War Prayer".
- » 11.2—Woolf, Virginia. "The New Dress".
- » 11.3—Wilde, Oscar. "Impressions of America".

» Post-Secondary Level

- » 12—Hawthorne, Nathaniel. "Wakefield".
- » 12.2—W.E.B. Du Bois. "Of Our Spiritual Strivings".
- » 12.9—Hawthorn, Nathaniel. "Earth's Holocaust".
- » 16—Swift, Jonathan. "A Modest Proposal".

86538962R00212

Made in the USA
Middletown, DE
30 August 2018